Morphodynamic Evolution and Sustainable Development of Coastal Systems

Morphodynamic Evolution and Sustainable Development of Coastal Systems

Editors

Pushpa Dissanayake
Jennifer Brown
Marissa Yates

MDPI • Basel • Beijing • Wuhan • Barcelona • Belgrade • Manchester • Tokyo • Cluj • Tianjin

Editors
Pushpa Dissanayake
Kiel University
Germany

Jennifer Brown
National Oceanographic Centre
UK

Marissa Yates
University of Paris-Est and Cerema
France

Editorial Office
MDPI
St. Alban-Anlage 66
4052 Basel, Switzerland

This is a reprint of articles from the Special Issue published online in the open access journal *Journal of Marine Science and Engineering* (ISSN 2077-1312) (available at: https://www.mdpi.com/journal/jmse/special_issues/morphodynamic_coas_sys).

For citation purposes, cite each article independently as indicated on the article page online and as indicated below:

LastName, A.A.; LastName, B.B.; LastName, C.C. Article Title. *Journal Name* **Year**, *Volume Number*, Page Range.

ISBN 978-3-0365-4907-1 (Hbk)
ISBN 978-3-0365-4908-8 (PDF)

Cover image courtesy of Pushpa Dissanayake
Westerland, North Sea coast of Sylt, Germany

© 2022 by the authors. Articles in this book are Open Access and distributed under the Creative Commons Attribution (CC BY) license, which allows users to download, copy and build upon published articles, as long as the author and publisher are properly credited, which ensures maximum dissemination and a wider impact of our publications.

The book as a whole is distributed by MDPI under the terms and conditions of the Creative Commons license CC BY-NC-ND.

Contents

About the Editors . . . . **vii**

Pushpa Dissanayake, Jennifer Brown and Marissa Yates
Morphodynamic Evolution and Sustainable Development of Coastal Systems
Reprinted from: *J. Mar. Sci. Eng.* **2022**, *10*, 647, doi:10.3390/jmse10050647 . . . . **1**

Tanita Averes, Jacobus L. A. Hofstede, Arfst Hinrichsen, Hans-Christian Reimers and Christian Winter
Cliff Retreat Contribution to the Littoral Sediment Budget along the Baltic Sea Coastline of Schleswig-Holstein, Germany
Reprinted from: *J. Mar. Sci. Eng.* **2021**, *9*, 870, doi:10.3390/jmse9080870 . . . . **5**

Uwe Dornbusch
Destabilisation and Accelerated Roll-Back of a Mixed Sediment Barrier in Response to a Managed Breach
Reprinted from: *J. Mar. Sci. Eng.* **2021**, *9*, 374, doi:10.3390/jmse9040374 . . . . **29**

Ben R. Evans, Iris Möller and Tom Spencer
Topological and Morphological Controls on Morphodynamics of Salt Marsh Interiors
Reprinted from: *J. Mar. Sci. Eng.* **2021**, *9*, 311, doi:10.3390/jmse9030311 . . . . **59**

Anh T. K. Do, Nicolas Huybrechts and Philippe Sergent
Sand Net Device to Control the Meanders of a Coastal River: The Case of the Authie Estuary (France)
Reprinted from: *J. Mar. Sci. Eng.* **2021**, *9*, 1325, doi:10.3390/jmse9121325 . . . . **81**

Christiane Eichmanns and Holger Schüttrumpf
Influence of Sand Trapping Fences on Dune Toe Growth and Its Relation with Potential Aeolian Sediment Transport
Reprinted from: *J. Mar. Sci. Eng.* **2021**, *9*, 850, doi:10.3390/jmse9080850 . . . . **95**

Pushpa Dissanayake, Marissa L. Yates, Serge Suanez, France Floc'h and Knut Krämer
Climate Change Impacts on Coastal Wave Dynamics at Vougot Beach, France
Reprinted from: *J. Mar. Sci. Eng.* **2021**, *9*, 1009, doi:10.3390/jmse9091009 . . . . **125**

Jannek Gundlach, Anna Zorndt, Bram C. van Prooijen and Zheng Bing Wang
Two-Channel System Dynamics of the Outer Weser Estuary—A Modeling Study
Reprinted from: *J. Mar. Sci. Eng.* **2021**, *9*, 448, doi:10.3390/jmse9040448 . . . . **151**

Cyprien Bosserelle, Shari L. Gallop, Ivan D. Haigh and Charitha B. Pattiaratchi
The Influence of Reef Topography on Storm-Driven Sand Flux
Reprinted from: *J. Mar. Sci. Eng.* **2021**, *9*, 272, doi:10.3390/jmse9030272 . . . . **173**

Constantin Schweiger and Holger Schuettrumpf
Considering the Effect of Land-Based Biomass on Dune Erosion Volumes in Large-Scale Numerical Modeling
Reprinted from: *J. Mar. Sci. Eng.* **2021**, *9*, 843, doi:10.3390/jmse9080843 . . . . **193**

Pushpa Dissanayake and Jennifer Brown
Modelling the Effect of 'Roller Dynamics' on Storm Erosion: Sylt, North Sea
Reprinted from: *J. Mar. Sci. Eng.* **2022**, *10*, 305, doi:10.3390/jmse10030305 . . . . **215**

i

About the Editors

Pushpa Dissanayake

Pushpa Dissanayake (Ph.D.): Researcher since 2018 at Kiel University (CAU, Germany), and before at University of Konstanz (Germany), Swansea University (UK) and Coastal Research Station (NLWKN, Germany). His research experience is related to understanding of physical processes in coastal and inland water systems by numerical modelling and statistical analyses, and field data collection. He has participated in several national and international research projects (e.g. SEA-EU) and has been a visiting researcher at renowned research institutes: NOC (Liverpool, UK), IOW (Warnemünde, Germany), IUEM (University of Brest, France). He is author of more than 50 scientific papers in peer-reviewed international journals and conference proceedings. He has acted as a reviewer for more than 15 journals and is a Topical Advisory Board member of Journal of Marine Science and Engineering, and Review Editor in Frontiers in Marine Science.

Jennifer Brown

Jennifer Brown (Ph.D.): Researcher at the National Oceanography Centre (NOC, UK) since 2007. She is a coastal oceanographer interested in model development and application to coastal and estuarine problems. Her research focus is on coupled wave-circulation simulation to understand the dynamics influencing flood and erosion risk to coastal communities and infrastructure. Through the use of observational data to force, validate and develop physical models, she aims to provide decision support for coastal hazard management and reduce the uncertainty associated with storm impacts in changing coastal environments. She received the 2019 Mersey Maritime Industry award for Positive Impact and her research was highly commended in 2018 at the International Dredging and Port Construction awards. She has over 55 peer-reviewed publications, of which more than 20 are first author, and has acted as a reviewer for 30 journals.

Marissa Yates

Marissa Yates (Ph.D.): Researcher for the Cerema since 2011, working in the Saint-Venant Hydraulics Laboratory (Chatou, France). Her research is focused on two closely related themes, wave hydrodynamics and coastal morphological evolution, with the common objective of improving the understanding of and capacity to model numerically coastal morphological evolution and wave propagation for a wide range of applications, including evaluating coastal risks, estimating marine energy potential, designing and managing coastal structures, etc. She was a visiting researcher at the University of Cambridge, and has participated in and led several national and international research projects (e.g. Sakura program, Interreg Europe, SEA-EU). She is author of more than 30 scientific papers in peer-reviewed international journals and conference proceedings, has acted as a reviewer for more than 20 journals.

Editorial

Morphodynamic Evolution and Sustainable Development of Coastal Systems

Pushpa Dissanayake [1,*], Jennifer Brown [2] and Marissa Yates [3]

1. Coastal Geology and Sedimentology, Institute of Geosciences, Kiel University, 24118 Kiel, Germany
2. Marine Physics and Ocean Climate, National Oceanographic Centre, Southampton SO14 3ZH, UK; jebro@noc.ac.uk
3. Saint-Venant Hydraulics Laboratory, University of Paris-Est and Cerema, 78400 Chatou, France; marissa.yates@cerema.fr
* Correspondence: pushpa.dissanayake@ifg.uni-kiel.de

Coastal systems are highly dynamic morphological environments due to erosion and sedimentation at different spatio-temporal scales as a result of natural forcing [1–3] and human interventions [4,5]. These morphodynamics are expected to increase in the future due to sea level rise and climate change [6], as well as other anthropogenic effects. Understanding the forcing factors, natural morphological evolution, and response to potential future forcing scenarios will help coastal policy makers to develop suitable adaptation strategies and to assure the sustainable use of coastal systems, enhancing the socio-economic and environmental benefits.

In this Special Issue, 10 articles are published that can be categorized into 3 main groups:

- Analyses of field data for morphodynamic evolution [1–3];
- Sustainable development for coastal protection [4,5];
- Numerical modelling of hydro-morphodynamic processes [6–10];

These topics are discussed below in the context of the articles.

- Analyses of Field Data for Morphodynamic Evolution

Averes et al. [1] analysed the contribution of cliff retreat to the littoral sediment budget along the Baltic Sea coastline of Schleswig-Holstein (Germany). This analysis used field data of cliff retreat and the geological and sedimentological characteristics of cohesive cliffs in the study area from scientific publications and unpublished work such as project data and reports and PhD and student theses. The littoral sediment budget (Equations (1)–(4) [1]) was assessed based on volumetric material erosion from cliffs, the degree of decompaction of the highly compacted glacial material was due to mobilization, and the loss of carbonate and fine fractions was due to reworking and transport. In areas without observations, it was assumed that cliffs are entirely composed of glacial till with a homogeneous sediment composition. The analysis found that ongoing cliff erosion contributed a sediment (0.063–64 mm) volume of about $39–161 \times 10^3$ m^3 annually to the littoral sediment budget as a result of an annual average cliff retreat rate of 0.24 m (range: 0.10–0.73 m). The authors suggest that including the sediment supply from the hard bottom seafloor erosion (abrasion) is an important sediment source for littoral transport, though it was not considered in this analysis.

The barrier beach roll-back at Medmerry (southern England), after ceasing management, was investigated by Dornbisch [2]. The study used 40 topographical surveys collected over 7 years (2013–2020) along a 1.5 km long micro-tidal shingle barrier stretch. The field data were analysed using several parameters (Section 3), including Barrier Inertia (BI). A high BI indicates stability, while instability by overtopping and overwash are represented by low values. These two morphological states are bounded by wave steepness. The estimated historical (1876–1896) retreat was equivalent to 1.5 m/y, while the predicted retreat for the 50-year design life was 0.4–0.7 m/y. This analysis showed that the barrier

Citation: Dissanayake, P.; Brown, J.; Yates, M. Morphodynamic Evolution and Sustainable Development of Coastal Systems. *J. Mar. Sci. Eng.* **2022**, *10*, 647. https://doi.org/10.3390/jmse10050647

Received: 5 May 2022
Accepted: 5 May 2022
Published: 10 May 2022

Publisher's Note: MDPI stays neutral with regard to jurisdictional claims in published maps and institutional affiliations.

Copyright: © 2022 by the authors. Licensee MDPI, Basel, Switzerland. This article is an open access article distributed under the terms and conditions of the Creative Commons Attribution (CC BY) license (https://creativecommons.org/licenses/by/4.0/).

roll-back is influenced by the creation of an artificial tidal breach, the elevation of the underlaying marsh and clay sediments, storm occurrence, and the presence of groynes. The estimated roll-back averaged over the analysis period exceeded 16 m/y, which is an order of magnitude higher than the historic shoreline retreat. The BI can be used to describe the observed morphological response of a micro-tidal barrier as long as the foreshore geometry is similar to the state when the BI is developed.

Evans et al. [3] investigated the multi-decadal morphodynamic evolution of the salt marsh in the East Anglia region, UK. The approach is based on a time series of Landsat satellite images from 1984 to present. These images, which have a 25 cm resolution, were analysed using 30 m × 30 m pixels to estimate the morphodynamics of vegetated surfaces, creeks, pools and pans within the salt marsh area. The areal unvegetated–vegetated marsh ratio was calculated to indicate the marsh's vulnerability. From Google Earth Engine, the normalised difference vegetation index, which indicates chlorophyll and thus vegetation, was estimated to reflect the percentage change of vegetation cover of each pixel. The analysed results were then represented by matrices of topographical and morphological changes separately. Marsh degradation at pixel-scales indicated loss of vegetation. The overall probability of marsh degradation was 0.144 for the entire dataset (~1985–2016). These results suggest that marsh areas that already have some form of fragmentations and are located far from the nearest creek and towards headlands of estuaries and inlets are the most likely to exhibit degradation.

- Sustainable Development for Coastal Protection

The performance of a new soft coastal defence, the Sand Net Device (SND), against erosion along the northern shoreline of the Authie estuary (Normandy, France) was investigated by Do et al. [4]. The SND is implemented using several nets assembled in an inverted V-shape creating a porous structure designed to trap sediment. This hydraulic structure for coastal protection is under consideration for a patent. The objective of the SND is to decrease the flow velocity and therefore enhance sedimentation. The effectiveness of the SND was investigated using 2DH/3D numerical experiments with the TELEMAC-MASCARET modelling suite. The presence of the SND was implemented at the model bed by applying an additional drag force over the enclosed area (Section 3.3 [4]). The model was forced using the predicted astronomical tide only. The simulations spanned a 45-day period starting on 15 February 2019. The measured bathymetries indicated sedimentation near the shoreline after deployment of the SND. The simulated morphodynamics qualitatively showed no sedimentation with zero drag coefficient and an increase in sedimentation towards the shoreline as the drag coefficient increases. Numerical experiments indicated that the influence of the SND extends about 500 m in the upstream and downstream directions.

Eichmanns and Shüttrumpt [5] investigated the effectiveness of sand trapping fences on coastal dune evolution at two East Frisian islands: Norderney and Langeoog (southern North Sea coast, Germany). This analysis was based on digital elevation models, which were developed using drone images (Norderney: 24 August 2020 to 9 March 2021, Langeoog: 20 May 2020 to 12 March 2021). The dune volume was estimated by analysing images in ArcGIS, and the aeolian transport was calculated using the Bagnold model (Section 4 [5]). The porosities of the sand trapping fences were determined by processing photographs using the MATLAB tool, Colour Thresholder Application. Dune toe growth and its relation to the aeolian transport were derived for boundary conditions and the characteristics of the sand trapping fences. The results showed that the dune toe growth is significant immediately after the construction of a sand trapping fence, and the effectiveness decreases over time. Protruding height and porosity of the branches are less important in sand trapping when fences are in place for a long time. The lower porosity of the sand trapping fences promotes dune toe growth at the fence location, while a higher porosity results in deposition further downwind. The dune toe growth influenced by sand trapping fences is a product of potential transport and sand trapping.

- Numerical Modelling for Hydro-Morphodynamic Processes

Climate change impacts on coastal-scale wave dynamics were investigated by Dissanayake et al. [6] applying the Delft3D modelling suite at Vougot Beach, France. Simulations were carried out using a measured historical wave time series, which was then projected into the future. Three globally averaged sea level rise scenarios for 2100 (SLR_{min} = 0.53 m; SLR_{avg} = 0.74 m and SLR_{max} = 0.98 m) and combined SLR and wave climate scenarios for A1B, A2, and B1 emissions paths of the IPCC were considered. Future waves following the B1 scenario indicated an increase in storm occurrence. Future scenarios showed larger relative changes at the beach than in the nearshore area. Increases in both the wave energy and bed shear stress relative to the historical values are higher in the combined scenarios (wave energy: +95%, bed shear stress: +190%) than the SLR only scenarios (+50% and +35%, respectively). This investigation emphasized that combined SLR and future wave climate scenarios need to be used to evaluate future changes in local hydrodynamics and their impacts.

Gundlach et al. [7] investigated the long-term development of two channels in the Outer Weser estuary (North Sea coast, Germany) using a schematised flat bathymetry in Delft3D. The long-term morphodynamic evolution was simulated considering the influence of the tidal range, Coriolis effect, Kelvin waves, and river discharge. All simulations predicted reaching morphodynamic equilibria over a period of 4000 years with different two-channel shapes. The two-channel system was developed as a result of the tidal forcing interacting with the basin geometry. The dominance of each channel depends on the tidal influence for the west channel and the river discharge influence for the east channel when the Coriolis force is included. The period of the simulated pattern of alternation between the 1- and 2-channel system was about 10 times larger than the observations (between 20 and 120 years). The alternation pattern and the period were dominated by the tide rather than the river discharge. Kelvin waves influenced the generation of a dominant eastern channel, while the Coriolis force resulted in an enhanced western channel because the incoming tides approached the east side of the Outer Weser based on the northwestern origin of the Kelvin wave inertia. These results qualitatively agree with the nautical charts with respect to the extent and migration area of individual channels, though the exact locations and dimensions vary.

Beach morphodynamics in a geologically controlled area from calcarenite limestone reefs were investigated by Bosserelle et al. [8]. Numerical experiments during a winter storm event were carried out using a modified version of the XBeach model at Yanchep beach in Southwest Australia. The modification of the model formulation included considering different values for the bottom dissipation parameter (see f_w in Equation (1) [8]) and the bed friction parameter (see c_f in Equation (2) [8]) for sandy and reef outcrops. Simulated currents showed that the model was twice as sensitive to roughness than wave braking parameters, and three-times more sensitive to the roughness than to the roller dissipation viscosity factor (see Table 4 [8]). The morphodynamic response of the beach varied considerably along the shore due to sharp variations in the reef topography. Strong current jets (>1 m/s) enhanced the beach's erosion at the boundary of the reef and influenced the morphological response of the beach hundreds of meters away from the reef.

Applying a novel root model in XBeach, Schweiger and Schuettrumpt [9] investigated the effect of belowground biomass on dune erosion volumes. The root model allows two modes: a constant mode with a unique rooting depth and a dynamic mode with spatial varying rooting depth. The Manning roughness coefficient in vegetated areas varied following Equation (3) [9] in order to account for spatial and temporal variability of the bed friction. The root model was validated for a large-scale experiment by upscaling a small-scale model setup (flume experiment). Control experiments without vegetation resulted in overestimated erosion around the waterline, even though the parameters of the morphodynamic processes were adjusted. Applying the root model to the upscaled below ground biomass cases reduced the prediction of dune erosion. These results were further improved at the dune front by applying spatially varying rooting depths. However, the overall effect of the root model differed due to different hydrodynamic conditions. Separate investigations are suggested to analyse the effects of above and below ground biomass on the wave-induced dune erosion and the individual contribution of different plant characteristics.

The effect of roller dynamics on storm erosion was investigated by Dissanayake and Brown [10] using XBeach and Delft3D. Simulations were carried out based on the North Sea coast of the Sylt island. Wave predictions in Delft3D agreed better with the measured data than the predictions with XBeach. Both models predicted the highest sensitivity to the roller parameter *beta*. The simulated storm erosion and accretion patterns along the coast were similar in both models, albeit with different magnitudes. Delft3D cannot produce comparable storm erosion to XBeach when the roller dynamics and avalanching are considered. Delft3D was less sensitive to roller dynamics compared to XBeach. In the nearshore area, including roller dynamics increased storm erosion up to 31% in Delft3D and decreased erosion up to 58% in XBeach, while the erosion in the dune area increased up to 13% in Delft3D and up to 97% in XBeach. The choice of model had more impact on the hydrodynamic and morphological predictions than the option to include or omit roller dynamics. These results indicate that both models produce increased storm erosion in the dune area with roller dynamics.

These articles present novel approaches in estimating coastal morphodynamics and related processes, enhancing the general understanding of these complex systems and the applications of soft engineering measures for coastal protection. The different proposed approaches could be applied to similar systems aiming to develop sustainable coastal management strategies.

Author Contributions: Conceptualization and writing—original draft preparation, P.D.; writing—review and editing, P.D., J.B. and M.Y. All authors have read and agreed to the published version of the manuscript.

Acknowledgments: All contributing authors are greatly acknowledged for their efforts.

Conflicts of Interest: The authors declare no conflict of interest.

References

1. Averes, T.; Hofstede, J.L.A.; Hinrichsen, A.; Reimers, H.C.; Winter, C. Cliff Retreat Contribution to the Littoral Sediment Budget along the Baltic Sea Coastline of Schleswig-Holstein, Germany. *J. Mar. Sci. Eng.* **2021**, *9*, 870. [CrossRef]
2. Dornbusch, U. Destabilisation and Accelerated Roll-Back of a Mixed Sediment Barrier in Response to a Managed Breach. *J. Mar. Sci. Eng.* **2021**, *9*, 374. [CrossRef]
3. Evans, B.R.; Möller, I.; Spencer, T. Topological and Morphological Controls on Morphodynamics of Salt Marsh Interiors. *J. Mar. Sci. Eng.* **2021**, *9*, 311. [CrossRef]
4. Do, A.T.K.; Huybrechts, N.; Sergent, P. Sand Net Device to Control the Meanders of a Coastal River: The Case of the Authie Estuary (France). *J. Mar. Sci. Eng.* **2021**, *9*, 1325. [CrossRef]
5. Eichmanns, C.; Schüttrumpf, H. Influence of Sand Trapping Fences on Dune Toe Growth and Its Relation with Potential Aeolian Sediment Transport. *J. Mar. Sci. Eng.* **2021**, *9*, 850. [CrossRef]
6. Dissanayake, P.; Yates, M.L.; Suanez, S.; Floc'h, F.; Krämer, K. Climate Change Impacts on Coastal Wave Dynamics at Vougot Beach, France. *J. Mar. Sci. Eng.* **2021**, *9*, 1009. [CrossRef]
7. Gundlach, J.; Zorndt, A.; van Prooijen, B.C.; Wang, Z.B. Two-Channel System Dynamics of the Outer Weser Estuary-A Modeling Study. *J. Mar. Sci. Eng.* **2021**, *9*, 448. [CrossRef]
8. Bosserelle, C.; Gallop, S.L.; Haigh, I.D.; Pattiaratchi, C.B. The Influence of Reef Topography on Storm-Driven Sand Flux. *J. Mar. Sci. Eng.* **2021**, *9*, 272. [CrossRef]
9. Schweiger, C.; Schuettrumpf, H. Considering the Effect of Land-Based Biomass on Dune Erosion Volumes in Large-Scale Numerical Modeling. *J. Mar. Sci. Eng.* **2021**, *9*, 843. [CrossRef]
10. Dissanayake, P.; Brown, J. Modelling the Effect of 'Roller Dynamics' on Storm Erosion: Sylt, North Sea. *J. Mar. Sci. Eng.* **2022**, *10*, 305. [CrossRef]

Article

Cliff Retreat Contribution to the Littoral Sediment Budget along the Baltic Sea Coastline of Schleswig-Holstein, Germany

Tanita Averes [1,*], Jacobus L. A. Hofstede [2], Arfst Hinrichsen [3], Hans-Christian Reimers [4] and Christian Winter [1]

1. Institute of Geosciences, Coastal Geology and Sedimentology, Kiel University, 24118 Kiel, Germany; christian.winter@ifg.uni-kiel.de
2. Schleswig-Holstein Ministry of Energy Transition, Agriculture, Environment, Nature and Digitization (MELUND), 24105 Kiel, Germany; jacobus.hofstede@melund.landsh.de
3. Schleswig-Holstein State Office for Coastal Protection, National Park and Marine Protection (LKN-SH), 25813 Husum, Germany; arfst.hinrichsen@lkn.landsh.de
4. State Agency for Agriculture, Environment and Rural Areas (LLUR), 24220 Flintbek, Germany; hans-christian.reimers@llur.landsh.de
* Correspondence: tanita.averes@ifg.uni-kiel.de

Citation: Averes, T.; Hofstede, J.L.A.; Hinrichsen, A.; Reimers, H.-C.; Winter, C. Cliff Retreat Contribution to the Littoral Sediment Budget along the Baltic Sea Coastline of Schleswig-Holstein, Germany. *J. Mar. Sci. Eng.* **2021**, *9*, 870. https://doi.org/10.3390/jmse9080870

Academic Editor: Alfredo L. Aretxabaleta

Received: 14 July 2021
Accepted: 9 August 2021
Published: 12 August 2021

Publisher's Note: MDPI stays neutral with regard to jurisdictional claims in published maps and institutional affiliations.

Copyright: © 2021 by the authors. Licensee MDPI, Basel, Switzerland. This article is an open access article distributed under the terms and conditions of the Creative Commons Attribution (CC BY) license (https://creativecommons.org/licenses/by/4.0/).

Abstract: Mobile coastal sediments, such as sand and gravel, build up and protect wave-dominated coastlines. In sediment-starved coastal environments, knowledge about the natural sources and transport pathways of those sediments is of utmost importance for the understanding and management of coastlines. Along the Baltic Sea coast of Schleswig-Holstein (Germany), the retreat of active cliffs—made of cohesive Pleistocene deposits—supplies a wide size range of sediments to the coastal system. The material is reworked and sorted by hydrodynamic forcing: the less mobile stones and boulders remain close to the source area; the finest sediments, mostly clay and silt, are transported offshore into areas of low energy; and the fractions of sand and fine gravels mostly remain in the nearshore zone, where they make up the littoral sediment budget. They contribute to the morphodynamic development of sandy coastlines and nearshore bar systems. Exemplarily for this coastal stretch and based on an extensive review of local studies we quantify the volume of the potential littoral sediment budget from cliff retreat. At an average retreat rate of 0.24 m yr^{-1} (<0.1–0.73 m yr^{-1}), the assessment indicates a weighted average sediment volume of 1.5 m^3 yr^{-1} m^{-1} (<0.1–9.5 m^3 yr^{-1} m^{-1}) per meter active cliff. For the whole area, this results in an absolute sediment budget $V_{s,total}$ of 39,000–161,000 m^3 yr^{-1}. The accuracy of the results is limited by system understanding and data quality and coverage. The study discusses uncertainties in the calculation of littoral sediment budgets from cliff retreat and provides the first area-wide budget assessment along the sediment-starved Baltic Sea coastline of Schleswig-Holstein.

Keywords: cliff retreat; littoral sediment; sediment budget; coastal protection; sediment-starved environment; Baltic Sea

1. Introduction

Sands and gravels are valuable resources in coastal zones. These mobile sediments characterize and stabilize sandy coastlines in wave-dominated environments and determine the littoral material transport [1–3]. In the context of global warming, and the associated sea-level rise and extreme weather events (precipitation, storms), the hydrodynamic pressure on the coasts increases [4–6]. This leads to enhanced erosion capacity along exposed coastlines. In areas with a limited supply of coast-stabilizing material, sediment deficits occur and the vulnerability of the coastlines increases [5].

The availability of coast-stabilizing sediments in the littoral environment depends on the natural sources, such as rivers, coastal cliffs, and seafloor sediments [3,7,8]. In this study, we focus on the sediment contribution from cohesive cliffs—soft-rock deposits with a high content of clay and silt [9,10].

The retreat of those cliffs is a natural process [2,11]. It is controlled by hydrodynamic impact—wind-induced waves and resulting currents, short-term water level fluctuations, long-term sea-level rise [2,11,12]; the resisting nature of the cliff material—its geological structure, geomechanical properties, lithological, and sedimentological composition [13,14]; and the beach and nearshore morphology [15,16]. The cliff retreat does not occur continuously but episodic or irregular [17,18]. Under the impact of marine forces, e.g., during storm surges, material is removed from the lower cliff face. This leads to steepening of the slope and, simultaneously, decreases the cliff stability, until mass movement occurs. The mobilized material creates a cliff dump or talus in front of the cliff toe [11,19].

During mobilization of the consolidated cliff material the bulk density decreases, which results in an increase in volume [13,20]. Subsequently, the volume of the exposed bulk material is reduced again as it is subject to reworking, sorting, and transport processes [3,21]. Atmospheric and marine influence initiate chemical and physical weathering as well as transport and sorting of the sediments [21,22]. Hereby, the carbonate contained is mostly removed [22,23].

The remaining siliciclastic sediment is sorted into different grain size fractions according to their behavior under hydrodynamic impact [3]: less mobile stones and boulders remain near the source area or relocate within short distances [3,24,25]. The finest sediments—mostly clay and silt—are transported in suspension and deposited in sheltered areas or deeper waters [26–28]. The fractions of sand and fine gravels feed the long- and cross-shore sediment transport in the littoral zone. With a temporary decrease in transport capacity, it comes to accumulation in potential sink areas, such as lowland beaches, sand spits, or nearshore bars. This may contribute to the preservation or even to a seaward shift of the current shoreline [1,29,30]. The volume of those mobile and potentially coast-stabilizing sands and gravels is hereafter referred to as the 'littoral sediment budget'.

A quantitative assessment of the littoral sediment budget is of vital importance for the coastal management, e.g., the planning and installation of coastal stabilization measures. This applies in particular in a sediment-starved system, where shoreline erosion determines the natural dynamics. As an example of a sediment-starved shoreline, in this study, we estimate the annual littoral sediment budget provided by the cliff retreat along the German Baltic Sea coastline of Schleswig-Holstein (S-H). Despite the known lack of sandy resources for shoreline preservation, comprehensive budgeting has not yet been performed for this area.

Based on an extensive literature review, we determine the amount of decalcified sand and gravels, eroded from the cliff sites, with a grain size range of 0.063–64 mm. We further point out the uncertainties of this literature-based budget assessment due to data gaps, inaccurate measurements and methods, and the complexity of the system.

2. Regional Setting

The wave-dominated and micro-tidal Baltic Sea coast of the German federal state of Schleswig-Holstein has a reference length of 399 km (mainland: 328 km; Fehmarn Island: 71 km, excluding the Schlei inlet) [5]. The coastline is overall exposed to the NE, while the regional exposition of individual sections varies in all directions.

The geomorphology results from the deposition of glacial and interstadial sediments during the Pleistocene [31,32]. With the Holocene sea-level rise—the Littorina Transgression starting ~8400 BP in this area—the Pleistocene deposits were increasingly affected by marine forces [26,33]. The initiated processes of erosion, material transport, and accumulation led to the formation of the present-day appearance of alternating cohesive cliffs and coastal lowlands [26,34]. The active cliffs—potentially within reach of marine hydrodynamic forces—make up about 85 km (~20%) of the current coastline [35], of which ~57 km have been investigated by Ziegler and Heyen [36] regarding cliff retreat and material erosion (Figure 1a). During the last century, the cliffs experienced an average annual retreat of ~0.2 m yr^{-1} [8,36]. The resulting qualitative and quantitative sediment supply to the littoral system depends on the local character of those cliffs.

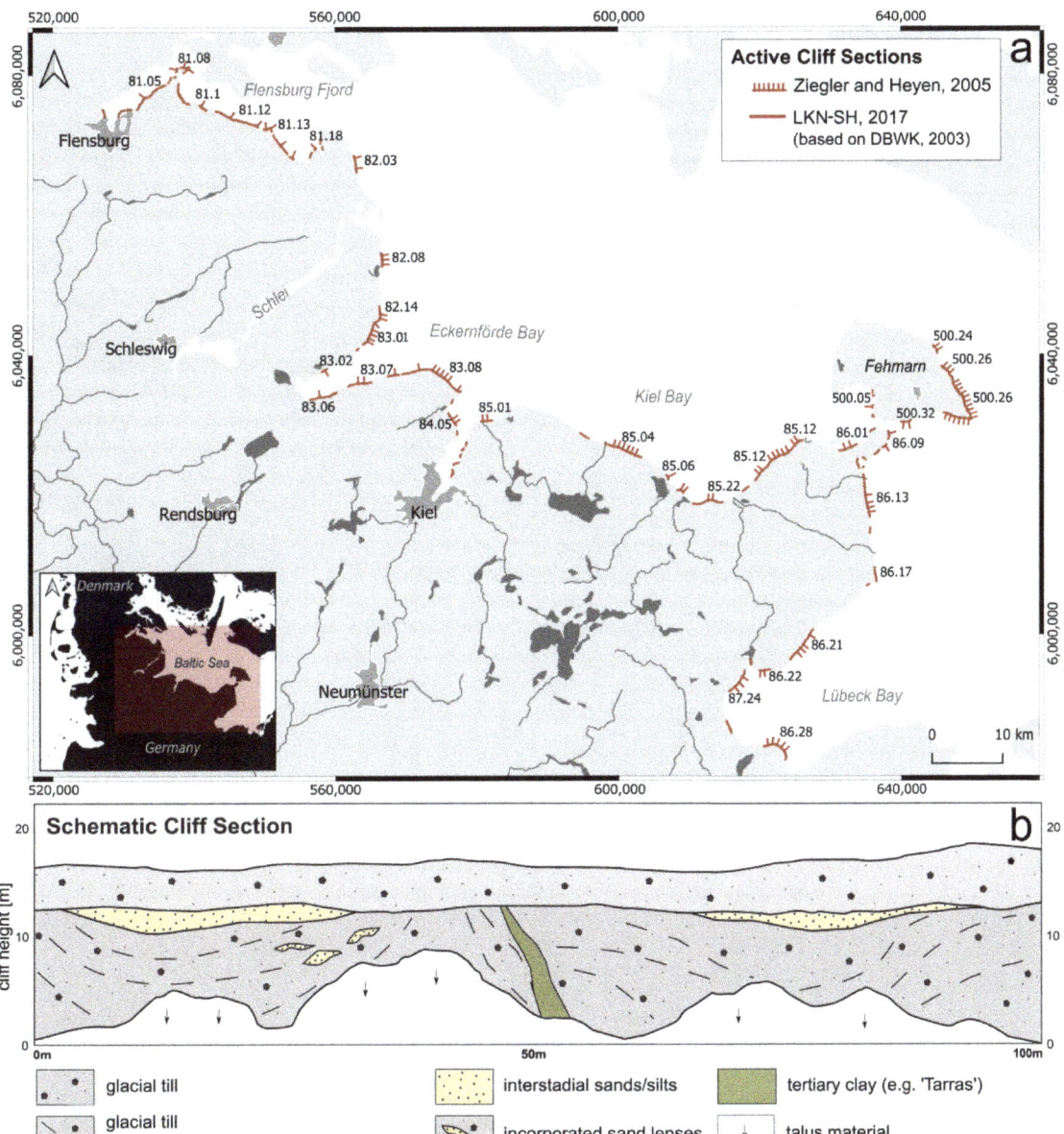

Figure 1. (**a**) Baltic Sea coastline of S-H, Germany, with active cliff sections defined by Ziegler and Heyen [36] and LKN-SH [35] based on the digital map of federal waterways (DBWK 2003) [37]. Labels refer to the numbers of the coastal subsections where the cliffs are located (mainland: 81.01–86.32; Fehmarn Island: 500.01–500.32) [35]. (**b**) Schematic overview of a typical Pleistocene cliff deposit in the study area.

The cohesive cliffs along the Baltic Sea coastline have a highly variable geological and sedimentological character (Figure 1b) [26,38], which results from the nature of the material sources, the transport and the depositional conditions [39–41], and glaciotectonic influences during the latest Ice Ages (Weichselian, Saalian) [20,42]. The majority of the cliffs were formed in Weichselian morainic deposits, referred to as glacial till or boulder clay. In most areas, the glacial till can be distinguished into at least two geological complexes, which result from successive ice advances [31,43,44]. The till mainly appears in grey to brownish, massive, and compact layers [41]. With its clay- and silt-rich matrix and incorporated sand, pebbles, and boulders, it covers a very wide grain-size spectrum [13,45]. The proportions of the different sediment fractions can vary greatly within the individual layers of glacial till [45–47]. The till deposits are calcareous [23]. The carbonate is heterogeneously distributed within the matrix and stems from Cretaceous material, which was incorporated during glacial transport as fine particles, larger chunks (<20 cm diameter), or extended bands [23,48].

Between and within the glacial till complexes, glaciolimnic silts, glaciofluvial sands, and gravels are present in the geological cliff succession [26,34,38]. Their deposition is associated with temporary recessions and subsequent advances of the glaciers [26,39]. Thereby, the material was overlain by another moraine deposit and partially incorporated [39,45]. While on most cliffs along the studied coastline the interstadial sediments only make up a minor part of the outcrops, there are a few exceptions: the cliffs of Dahmeshöved (86.17) and Schilksee (84.05), for example, are almost exclusively built of interstadial sands and gravels [8]. The cliff of western Holnis (81.08) consists mainly of glaciolimnic deposits [49].

Except for the uppermost glacial till complex, assigned to the latest ice advance, all underlying deposits were affected by glaciotectonic forces. Due to the repeated impact of overriding ice masses, the Pleistocene material is mostly overconsolidated and exhibits high dry bulk densities and high geotechnical cohesion [13,45]. The deposits also experienced tilting, folding, and thrusting in many areas [23,50]. At some cliff locations, e.g., at Stohl (83.03), Heiligenhafen (85.12), and along Fehmarn, this resulted in outcrops of older material, such as tertiary clay—so-called Tarras—and clay deposits from the Eem interglacial [42,47,51].

Due to the irregular distribution of sedimentological and lithological components and the glaciotectonic imprint, the cliff deposits show high variability in their physical properties (e.g., dry bulk density, internal shear strength, and water absorption capacity) and, thus, react locally differently to hydrodynamic forces and environmental impacts [13,14].

3. Data and Methods
3.1. Origin and Use of Data

The data basis of this work is a compilation of accessible literature concerning cliff retreat and the geological and sedimentological properties of the cohesive cliffs in the study area. This includes scientific publications as well as unpublished work (project data and reports, as well as Ph.D. and student theses).

For the assessment of the cliff retreat, we focused on three investigations that observed the spatial change of the upper cliff edge during different periods (Table A1). Kannenberg [8] provides the earliest data on this topic based on a comparison of comprehensive geodetic and cadastral surveys (1:2000) from around 1878 and 1950 (exact dates not available). A study by Ziegler and Heyen [36] compared two compilations of coastal surveys performed by the former *Landesamt für Wasserhaushalt und Küsten* (LW) at the scale of 1:2000 (1st survey ~1949–1968, 2nd survey ~1974–1987, supplementary measurements 1999–2002). A third unpublished analysis presents a comparison between the geodetic measurements from ~1878 (*Preußische Landesaufnahme*; 1:25,000) and aerial photographs from 2016 (DOP20).

For the sediment budgeting, we use the data base of Ziegler and Heyen [36], who provide volume values on the annual material loss at individual cliff sections based on their retreat analyses (Table A2). Further, we included quantitative information about the grain size distribution, the carbonate content, and the thickness of the geological layers, if available (Table A2). The data were derived from local studies. For the majority of cliffs, no adequate local data were available on this concern.

3.2. Sediment Budget Assessment

In the context of this study, the littoral sediment budget is calculated considering (a) the volumetric material erosion at the cliffs given by [36]; (b) the degree of decompaction of the highly compacted glacial material due to mobilization; and (c) the loss of carbonate and the fine siliciclastic sediment fractions (<0.063 mm) during reworking and transport processes. Due to the high heterogeneity of the coastline and the limited data coverage in the study area, this approach should be understood as an approximation or best guess of the littoral sediment budget.

The amount of eroded material at a cliff site per year is referred to as the erosional volume V_e (m^3 yr^{-1}):

$$V_e = L\,H\,r \quad (1)$$

where L (m) is the length of the active cliff sections with a minimum height of 2 m and a minimum length of 50 m (status ~1974); H (m) is the estimated average height between the lower and upper cliff edge; and r (m y^{-1}) is the annual retreat rate. The latter was determined as the spatial change of the upper cliff edge for time intervals between 1949 and 2002—measured in one meter steps and averaged over the local cliff length [36].

The sum of V_e of all individual cliff sites represents the total amount of eroded material $V_{e,total}$ in the study area per year.

The specific erosional volume v_e describes the eroded material per meter active cliff:

$$v_e = \frac{V_e}{L} \quad (2)$$

The degree of deconsolidation of the cohesive material during erosion has an impact on the resulting material volume. We calculate the specific bulk volume vb (m^3 yr^{-1} m^{-1}):

$$v_b = v_e\,h \quad \{1.5 < h < 2\} \quad (3)$$

where h is the bulk factor proposed by Seifert [20] for the prevailing cliff material.

For a simplified result presentation, an average bulk factor h1.75 is applied. For further calculations based on the bulk volume, the whole range of h (1.5;2) is considered.

The specific sediment budget vs (m^3 yr^{-1} m^{-1}) is quantified by including the geological-lithological and sedimentological information of the source material in the calculation.

$$v_s = v_b\,(1-c)\,n \quad (4)$$

where c is the fraction of carbonate and n is the fraction of siliciclastic material with a grain size range of 0.063–64 mm.

Due to the high variability in geological structures, lithological and sedimentological properties, and the limited observational data in the study area, no generally valid average values can be determined for the variables c and n. Hence, they are based on assumptions. At cliff sections where local information regarding the prevalence and thickness of the geological layers, grain size distribution, and carbonate content was available, it was included in the calculation of vs. For the areas without the corresponding information, the following assumptions were made to approximate vs in the best possible way:

1. The cliff sections are composed entirely of glacial till with a homogenous sediment composition;
2. The quantities of c and n, given in local studies, set the value range of c and n for all cliffs in the study area.

The sum of all values of vs multiplied by the respective cliff lengths represents the final estimate of the total littoral sediment budget $V_{s,total}$ supplied to the nearshore system from all observed cliff sites along the Baltic Sea coast of S-H.

4. Results

4.1. Cliff Retreat

The retreat of active cliffs has been the subject of several studies along the S-H coastline. These studies report estimates for the annual rates of retreat for individual cliff sections (Figure 2). The results refer to different periods. They are also based on data sets that have different levels of accuracy and were obtained by different methodologies.

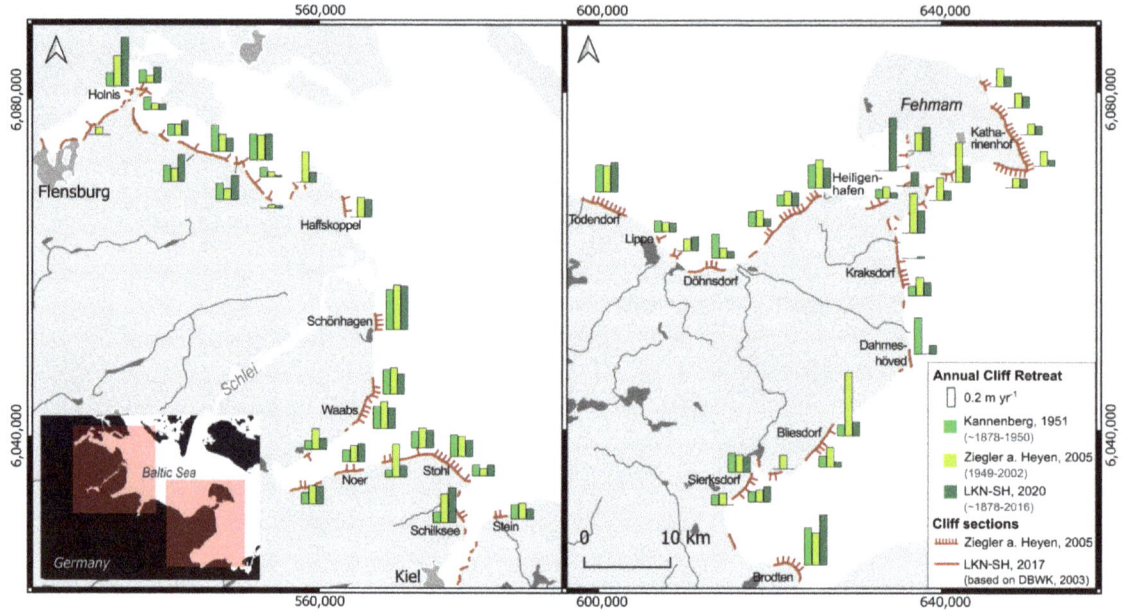

Figure 2. Annual cliff retreat (m yr^{-1}) based on study results of Kannenberg [8], Ziegler and Heyen [36], and unpublished data from LKN-SH [52]. Detailed values in Table A1.

The investigations of Kannenberg [8] present the annual rates of cliff retreat of <0.1–0.46 m yr^{-1} and an overall weighted average of ~0.22 m yr^{-1} for the observed ~73-years interval. In the study of Ziegler and Heyen [36], a weighted average retreat of 0.24 m yr^{-1} was estimated ranging from <0.1 to 0.73 m yr^{-1} at the individual cliffs for an average interval of 26 years (max. 44 years) between the surveys compared. The comparison of the cliff status between ~1878 and 2016 shows the long-term retreat of ~138 years along the entire coastline. Here, the weighted average rate of cliff retreat is ~0.19 m yr^{-1}, ranging from <0.1 to 0.64 m yr^{-1} [52].

The rates of retreat differ between the different studies and locations (Figure 2, Table A1). While the annual retreat in the areas like Schönhagen (0.46–0.51 m yr^{-1}), Stohl (0.19–0.24 m yr^{-1}), and Heiligenhafen (0.23–0.33 m yr^{-1}) shows similar values in all three studies, greater differences occur in areas such as Schilksee and Bliesdorf (north). Here, the provided values for coastal retreat vary from 0.13 to 0.41 m yr^{-1} and from 0.13 to 0.73 m yr^{-1}, respectively. However, the overall average cliff retreat for the Baltic Sea coast appears similar in all observations, with a range of 0.19–0.24 m yr^{-1} (Table 1).

Table 1. Length L (m) and yearly retreat rates r (m yr^{-1}) for the selected cliff sections and compiled for all active S-H cliffs (all local values shown in Table A1).

Location	Kannenberg, 1951 (~1878–1950)		Ziegler & Heyen, 2005 (~1949–2002)		LKN-SH (~1878–2016)	
	L (m)	r (m yr^{-1})	L (m)	r (m yr^{-1})	L (m)	r (m yr^{-1})
82.09 Schönhagen	1600	0.46	1880	0.51	1570	0.50
83.08 Stohl	3000	0.25	3640	0.24	3880	0.19
84.05 Schilksee	1000	0.13	1140	0.34	1139	0.41
85.12 Heiligenhafen	1500	0.27	1560	0.33	2220	0.23
86.21 Bliesdorf (north)	No data	0.13	460	0.73	1270	0.16
All Cliffs S-H	47,400	0.22	57,000	0.24	85,000	0.19

4.2. Erosional and Bulk Volume

The volume of sediments eroding during the process of cliff retreat was determined for 50 cliff sections, in total spanning ~57 km [36]. The results provide values for the specific volume v_e—the annual material loss at the outcrop per meter—and the resulting specific bulk volume $v_{b,1.75}$ (Figure 3; Table A2). In the studied area, the minimum value of v_e is 0.3 m^3 yr^{-1} m^{-1} (85.06 Lippe), and the maximum value is 7.4 m^3 yr^{-1} m^{-1} (86.21 Bliesdorf (north)). A weighted average for the whole area—considering the local cliff lengths—amounts to about ~2 m^3 yr^{-1} m^{-1}. The absolute erosional volume from all the observed cliff sites $V_{e,total}$ amounts to ~135,000 m^3 yr^{-1}. The corresponding weighted average (min/max) of $v_{b,1.75}$ is ~3.5 m^3 yr^{-1} m^{-1} (0.5/12.9 m^3 yr^{-1} m^{-1}) and the absolute volume of $V_{b,total}$ is ~237,000 m^3 yr^{-1}.

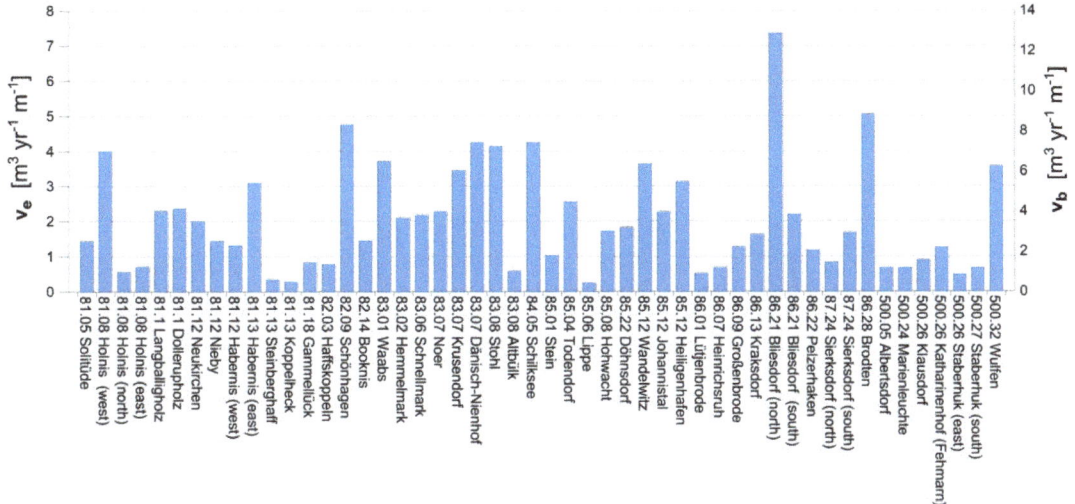

Figure 3. Specific eroded volumes v_e (**left** axis) and specific bulk volumes v_b (bulk factor h1.75) (**right** axis) of the observed 50 cliff sites, based on [36].

4.3. Sediment Budget

To calculate the littoral sediment budget vs per meter active cliff, site-specific values for the carbonate content c and the grain size fraction n (0.063–64 mm) were applied if available in the reviewed literature: For 37 (~51 km) of the 50 locations (~57 km), a local carbonate value c is given, only for eight cliff sections (~15 km) local values of n could be determined (Table A2). For these eight locations, a specific local sediment budget vs was calculated (Equation (4)).

The values of vs range from a minimum of 0.2 m³ yr⁻¹ m⁻¹ (86.09 Großenbrode) to a maximum of 5.5 m³ yr⁻¹ m⁻¹ (86.28 Brodten) within the eight shown cliff sites (Figure 4). The values amount to 12–109% of the initially eroded volume v_e and 7–62% of the bulk volume vb at the individual locations.

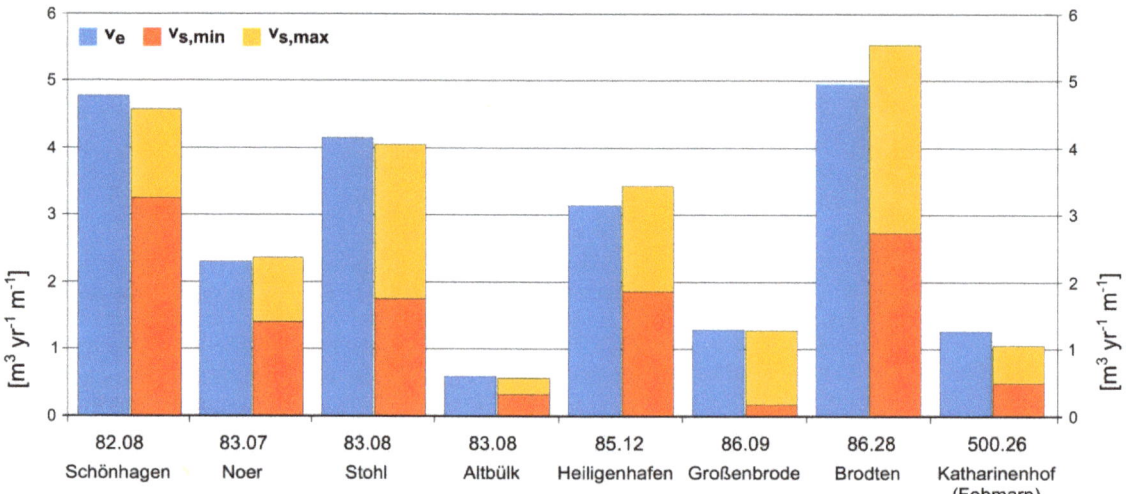

Figure 4. Specific erosional volume v_e (blue) based on cliff retreat [36] and the calculated sediment budget range, $v_{s,min}$ (orange) to $v_{s,max}$ (yellow), for the eight well-studied cliff locations. For specific values see Table A2.

Minimum and maximum estimates for the variables c and n were derived from local studies to describe the properties of the cliff-building material in the entire area (Table 2). They are in a range of 2.7–27% for the carbonate content c and of 11–70% for the sediment fraction n (0.063–64 mm). No data are available on the amount of material >64 mm (cobbles, boulders), which therefore must be neglected.

Table 2. Minima and maxima portions of c and n (0.063–64 mm) in the cliff-building glacial till derived from local studies *. The sediment is classified according to Wentworth [53].

	Glacial till Components	Estimated Value Range (%)
c	Carbonate	2.7–27
n	Sand (0.063–2 mm)	11–61
	Granules, Pebbles (2–64 mm)	0–9
	Cobbles, boulders (>64 mm)	No data

* [8,23,31,39–41,43,46,47,54–58].

The derived estimates of c and n (Table 2) were applied to determine the littoral sediment budget for the remaining 42 locations (~42 km) with insufficient local information (Figure 5). Compiling all results, we obtain a range of <0.1–9.5 m³ yr⁻¹ m⁻¹ for vs with a weighted average of 1.5 m³ yr⁻¹ m⁻¹. This implies an absolute range of 39,000–161,000 m³ yr⁻¹ for the littoral sediment budget $V_{s,total}$ of the whole S-H coastline. It corresponds to 29–119% of the absolute erosional volume $V_{e,total}$ and 19–60% of the bulk volume $V_{b,total}$ of the area.

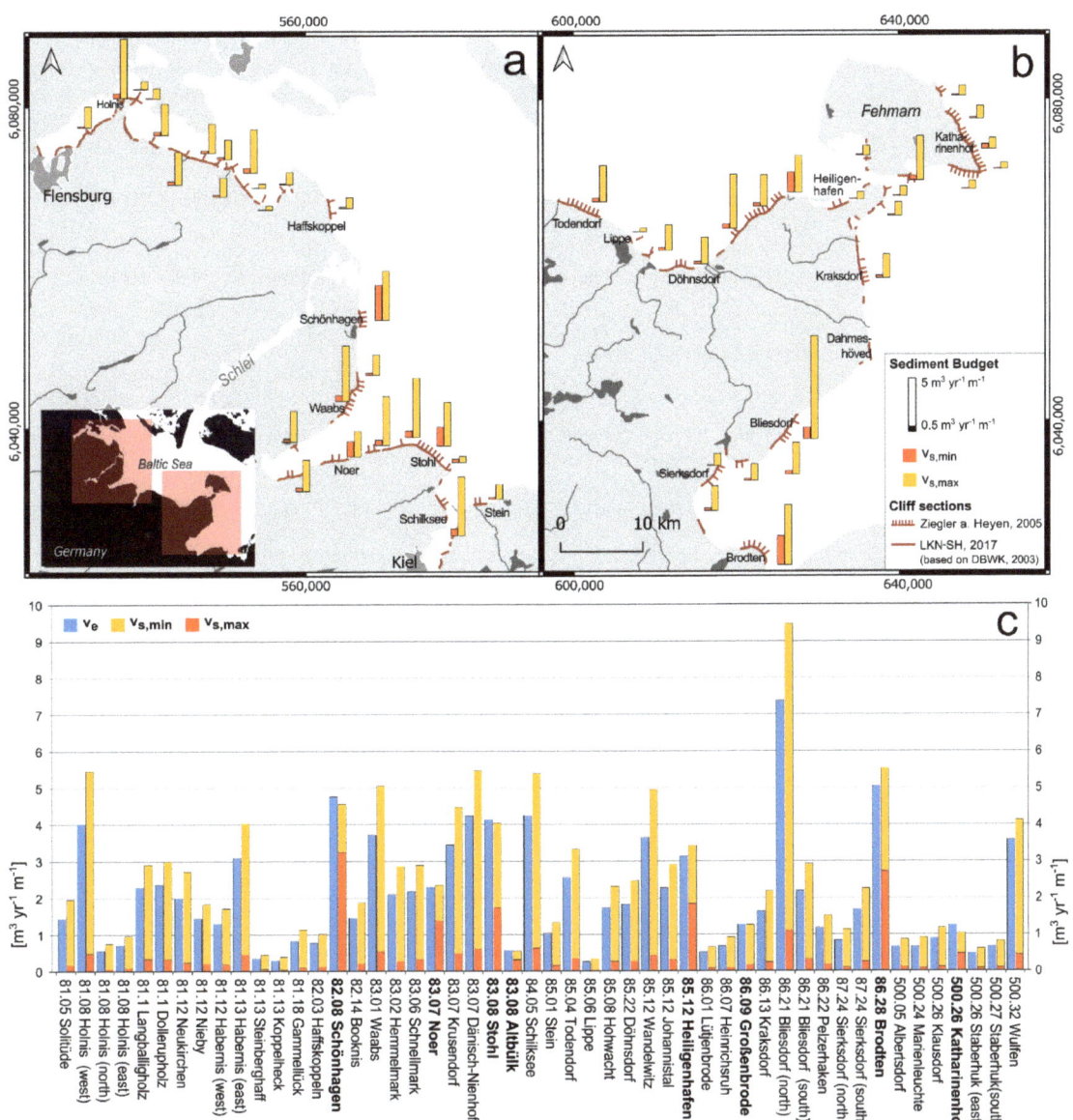

Figure 5. (**a**,**b**) Maps showing the calculated littoral sediment budget, $v_{s,min}$ (orange) to $v_{s,max}$ (yellow), for the local cliff sections; (**c**) comparison of the specific values of the erosional volume v_e (blue) [36] and the littoral sediment budget $v_{s,min}$ (orange) to $v_{s,max}$ (yellow). Bold labels represent results based on available local data (Figure 4); all other results are based on derived estimates (Table 2).

5. Discussion

5.1. Data Availability

The present study builds on existing data from the literature. The results reflect the availability, characteristics, and quality of the data basis. The compilation of regional and local studies shows that the status of geoscientific research along the coastline is very diverse. Some areas have been the subject of extensive fundamental research due to, e.g., their geological specifications, their representative value for the regional coast, and/or their high political interest. These areas show good data coverage, e.g., Schönhagen (82.09), Heiligenhafen (85.12), and Brodten (86.28). In contrast, many other cliff sections, especially subsections in Flensburg Inner and Outer Fjord, in Lübeck Bay, and on Fehmarn Island, have barely been studied yet. Here, the literature does not contribute profitable information for our approach.

Thus, for the assessment of the littoral sediment budget (Equation (4)), we used the available data of well-studied locations to derive the minimum and maximum estimates for the input parameters of the entire area (Table 2). This takes into account the potential heterogeneity of the material but leads to the wide value range of the resulting budget volume. Intensifying the in situ operations at the poorly studied cliffs regarding local geology and sedimentology could decrease the factor of uncertainty of the input data and narrow down the resulting budget interval.

5.2. Reliability of Data and Methods

A high variety of interacting factors and processes influence the character and amount of the littoral sediment budget in the study area (Figure 6) [9,59].

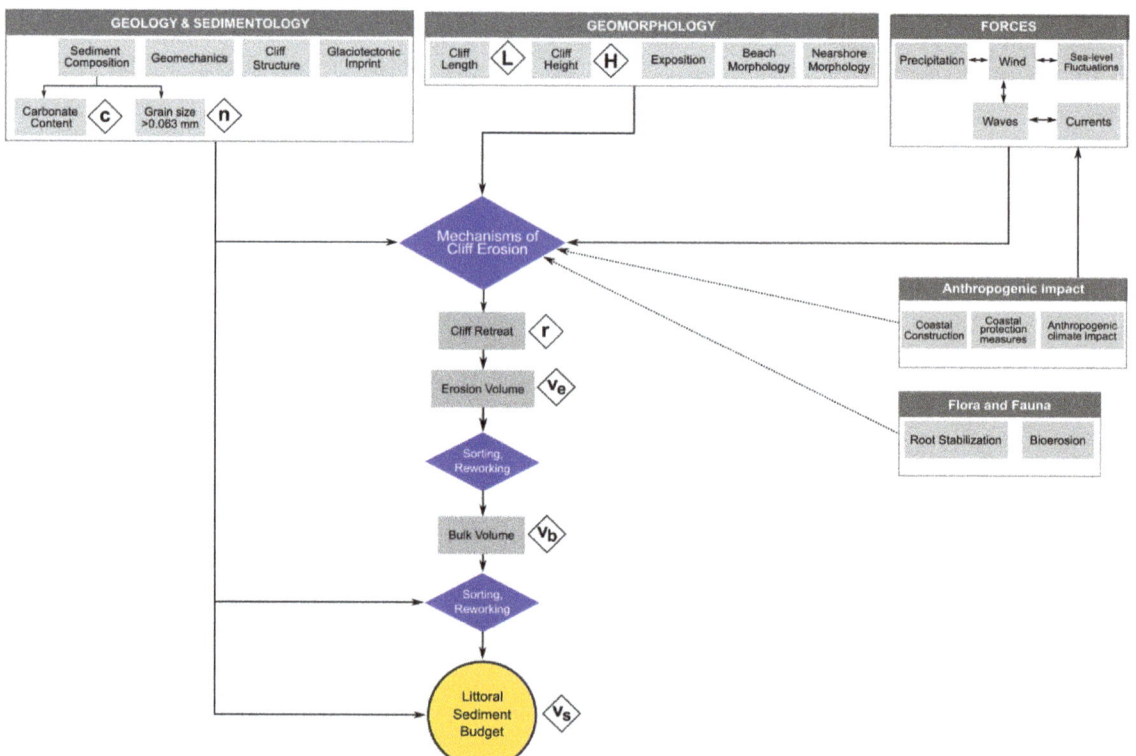

Figure 6. Factors and variables generating and/or affecting the littoral sediment budget from cliff erosion in a wave-dominated environment.

Many of the involved factors, such as the cliff and beach morphology or the hydrodynamic forcing, do not specifically occur in the applied Equations ((1)–(4)). However, they are credited with an effect on the littoral sediment budget and are indirectly included in the calculation. So does the variable v_e by definition (Equations (1) and (2)) include the rate of retreat r, which itself is controlled by, i.a., the sedimentological cliff properties, the nearshore morphology, and the intensity of the hydrodynamic forces [12,36,60].

With ongoing observations and an evolving understanding of the system complexity, even more factors may need consideration, such as the influence of vegetation on the cliff stability and the anthropogenic activity [11,59,61]. While the introduction of new parameters can improve the study's reliability, at the same time it increases the complexity of the calculation and, thus, may enhance the number of measurement inaccuracies. This indicates an enhanced demand for scientific research on the effect of all considered factors and mutual dependencies in the system.

The following factors occur directly in this study's methodology (Equations (1)–(4)) as specific variables: the rate of cliff retreat r, the eroded volume ve, the bulk factor h, the carbonate content c, and the grain size fraction n (0.063–64 mm). The nature and conditions of these input data account for uncertainties of different kinds and dimensions in the results. Their cause and significance for the final sediment budget assessment as well as proposals to reduce these uncertainties are discussed in the following paragraphs.

5.2.1. Rate of Cliff Retreat r

The various results on cliff retreat presented in this study refer to different data bases (Figure 2; Table A1). These data bases may inherit positional inaccuracies due to their methods of measurement or interpretation. Visual evaluation of the *Preußische Landesaufnahme* (~1878) revealed potential spatial inaccuracies up to ±25 m in reference to the DBWK [62]. For the resulting annual rate of retreat, this would apply an uncertainty of ±0.18 m yr^{-1} considering an average retreat of 0.19 m yr^{-1} for a period of ~138 years [52]. The long period can partly compensate for the high spatial inaccuracies. Still, the uncertainty is almost as high as the actual retreat rate and, hence, of little informative value. Spatial evaluations of the compiled surveys used by Ziegler and Heyen [36] indicate relatively small inaccuracies of ±0.15 m, which propose a small error of about ±0.005 m yr^{-1} with respect to the average retreat of 0.24 m yr^{-1} for an average period of ~26 years. Despite the smaller uncertainty, we cannot verify the higher reliability of the data in reference to the DBWK.

In general, the comparability between the different study results is limited by the varying observed time intervals and the mechanisms of cliff erosion, as single erosion events highly affect the short-term and local retreat velocity [11,17]. We assume that the different rates of retreat (Figure 2) do not necessarily represent a change in the retreat behavior over time but instead represent the discrepancies within the data bases. For a reliable approximation of r, a compromise must be worked out between the long measuring periods and data accuracy.

5.2.2. Volume Erosion ve

The budget assessment in this study is based on the erosional volumes V_e determined from L, H, and r [36] (Equation (1)). Other studies [8,52] that show deviating values for the input parameters L and r (Figure 2; Table 1) would produce differing values of Ve. While the deviations of r are explained above (5.2.1), further deviations can be triggered by the following:

(a) The definitions of the active cliff sections, on which the retreat analyses are based, are not equal. Ziegler and Heyen [36] included the cliff sections with a minimum height of 2 m and a minimum length of 50 m in their investigations referring to a coastal survey from ~1974 by the former *Landesamt für Wasserhaushalt und Küsten* (LW). More recent analyses from LKN-SH use the cliff definition by the *Schleswig-Holstein state ordinance on legally protected biotopes*, which states a minimum of 1.2 m in height and 25 m in length [63]. Additionally, the status of activity, based on DBWK (2003) [35,37], has not been applied in the study of [36]. The comparison proposes an underestimation of the active cliff length L applied in this study [36].

(b) The retreat analysis of [36] is based on the cliff status from ~1974. The status of the cliffs—active or inactive—could have changed with time, e.g., due to a natural intensification or a decrease in the local hydrodynamic impact or the installation of coastal protection measures [25,26].

For a major improvement of the accuracy and validity of this study's results, we suggest a recalculation of V_e based on an updated and reviewed definition of the active cliff length and the best possible approximation of the retreat rate r considering the current data [52] and future measurements.

5.2.3. Bulk Volume vb

During cliff erosion, when the material breaks or slumps down, the structure is loosened, the density decreases, and hence the material volume increases. The extent of this volume expansion depends on the material properties and the degree of consolidation in its initial state—here represented by the bulk factor h [13,20] (Equation (3)). For the cohesive cliff sediments in the area, a bulk factor h of 1.5–2 was proposed [20]. We assume that neither the vertical nor the horizontal heterogeneity of the material properties at the cliffs are sufficiently represented by the variable h. However, due to a lack of local information regarding the dry bulk density and the grain size distribution, this is the best available approximation for h in the studied area.

Certainly, local investigations of the cliff's geomechanical properties and bulk experiments could help to define an individual bulk factor h for each cliff section, which would more accurately represent the material properties and may decrease the uncertainties contained in the variable h.

5.2.4. Carbonate Content c

Due to the atmospheric and marine influence on the outcrop, the carbonate content of the exposed cliff material can be strongly reduced over time. Along the cliff face, rainwater and surface runoff intrude into cracks and fissures and initiate chemical weathering [22,23]. With the start of a marine hydrodynamic impact, physical erosion, sorting, and transport processes are initiated. The fine carbonate particles are removed within suspension, such as the fine siliciclastic particles. Hence, we assume a full removal of the contained carbonate c for the assessment of the littoral sediment volume (Equation (4)). From local analyses of the cliff matrix, values between 2.7% (83.01 Waabs) and 27% (500.26 Klausdorf, Fehmarn) were identified for c. However, according to Glückert [23], in most cliff samples, the carbonate content is in a narrower range of 6–17%, whereas local accumulations contain up to 60% carbonate (e.g., chalk marl at Brodten (86.28)) [23,40]. This heterogeneity makes it difficult to apply representative values for c to the budget calculations.

The influence of precipitation on the carbonate-rich cliff material can also lead to cementing of siliciclastic sediment grains due to alternating reprecipitation and drying [22]. This may lead to a shift of the grain size modus towards larger particles and, thus, potentially to an overestimation of the littoral sediment budget. It remains unclear if and how fast the cemented carbonate particles are removed from the sediment under the prevalent environmental conditions and hence if the carbonate still plays a role in the initiated phases of sediment transport and deposition.

To narrow down the uncertainties of factor c in the budget calculation, dedicated quantitative sediment analyses are necessary at the cliff sites that (a) provide the amount of carbonate at local sites that have not yet been investigated and (b) demonstrate the evolution of carbonate removal during the process of sediment mobilization from the cliff source towards the nearshore areas.

5.2.5. Sediment Fraction n

In this study, the sediment fraction n (0.063–64 mm) represents the proportion of siliciclastic particles that enters the marine environment and contributes to the littoral sediment transport and coastal accumulation. However, parts of the sand fraction with grain sizes <0.2 mm can be transported further offshore by strong current and wave action and, thus, be removed from the littoral system [27,64,65]. Thereby, the lower grain size limit of the sediment that remains in the nearshore area is not temporally and spatially consistent. It rather depends on the interplay between the hydrodynamic forcing and local morphology, and the general availability of sediments [21,65,66]. For a differentiated analysis of the sandy sediment according to their mobility behavior, we require further knowledge of the local dynamics and detailed quantitative information about sedimentary sub-fractions, which is not provided by most local studies in S-H.

In this approach, we considered the whole sand fraction as part of the littoral sediment budget vs, which may lead to an overestimation of the budget volume by the varying amount of the fine-grained particles (0.063–0.2 mm). At the same time, there is the risk of an underestimation of the budget volume by the coarser sediment fraction: Besides the sandy sediments, larger stones and boulders are mobilized from the Pleistocene cliff deposits and contribute to the beach and nearshore sediment [11,24]. Due to issues of sample representativity and difficulties in the analyses of the coarse grain size fractions [67], the literature lacks quantitative data of those fractions. The number of granules and pebbles (2–64 mm) could only be included in the budget calculation in very few cases, e.g., from studies of [8,47,54,57]. For grain sizes >64 mm (cobbles, boulders), no quantitative data were available. Although stones and boulders have been proven to be partly mobile in the nearshore system [11,24], they are underrepresented in this study's budget estimation.

For the actual budget calculation, only from eight (~15 km) of the observed 50 (~57 km) cliff locations detailed grain size information is available (Figure 4). For all other locations, we applied the minimum and maximum estimates shown in Table 2 and assumed that the cliffs are built exclusively of glacial till with homogeneous geological properties. This is a strong simplification of the prevailing situation. Sediment samples of different locations show that the grain size distribution of the cliff-building material is highly variable on a small spatial scale due to their geological genesis [39,56]. Thus, all local budget calculations, based on available local data or derived estimates, hold a certain degree of uncertainty and cannot fully represent the highly heterogenous cliff geology.

To decrease this degree of uncertainty, we need to expand the geological and sedimentological investigations of the local cliff areas. It is crucial to access the uncategorized grain size data for differentiated analyses of the sediment availability and mobility. Moreover, investigations on coarse-grained material have to be enhanced, e.g., by using digital image analyses.

5.3. Comparison and Evaluation of the Littoral Sediment Budget

This study is the first assessment of the material contribution from cliff retreat to the littoral sediment budget for the entire Baltic Sea coastline of S-H. To evaluate the result, we may compare it to areas with similar regional conditions and consider other potential material sources.

5.3.1. National and International Comparison

Eastward of our study area extends the German Baltic Sea coastline of Mecklenburg-Vorpommern (M-V). Similar to S-H, the coastal appearance is characterized by alternating cliffs and lowlands and is constantly modified by marine forces and dynamic processes [68]. We expect a larger material erosion v_e from the cliffs of M-V compared to S-H due to the prevailing circumstances:

1. The length of the currently active, unprotected cliffs in M-V is ~125 km—about 40 km longer than in S-H (~85 km; Schlei excluded) [68,69].
2. The proposed average annual cliff retreat in M-V is ~0.34 m yr^{-1} [70]—slightly higher than in S-H (~0.19–0.24 m yr^{-1}).
3. The M-V cliffs are higher on average. Some of them reach up to ~120 m high, e.g., the Jasmund cliff on Rügen Island.

The average proposed v_e for the whole M-V coast is ~7 m³ yr⁻¹ m⁻¹. The highest material input of 30 m³ yr⁻¹ m⁻¹ is observed at the cliffs of Sellin (Rügen Island) and Streckelsberg (Usedom Island) [71]. Looking even further eastward to the adjoining coastline of western Poland, case studies report a volume erosion v_e >5.5 m³ yr⁻¹ m⁻¹ for the cliff sections of Wolin Island (Pomeranian Bay) [72,73].

For comparison, the average v_e in S-H is only 2 m³ yr⁻¹ m⁻¹, with a maximum of 7.4 m³ yr⁻¹ m⁻¹ (Bliesdorf (north)). Only from 1% of the active cliffs v_e > 5.5 m³ yr⁻¹ m⁻¹ is expected (Table A2). Thus, a relatively low amount of sediments is provided from the S-H cliffs compared to the adjacent areas.

However, for a valid comparison, the cliffs have to be distinguished according to their geological and sedimentological properties. Besides the cohesive cliff deposits, made up mainly of glacial till, glaciofluvial, and glaciolimnic sediments, Cretaceous hard-rock cliffs are present in the eastern part of M-V (Jasmund, Rügen Island), which vary in their retreat behavior under hydrodynamic impact. They deliver mostly calcareous material that does not contribute to the littoral sediment budget. Others of the M-V and Polish Baltic Sea cliffs are mainly build-up of interstadial basin sediments, mostly glaciolimic silts and fine sands [71]. These sediments also play a minor role in the littoral sediment budget.

It becomes apparent that not only in S-H but also in the adjacent coastal areas the sediment supply by cliffs is limited and thus most of the beaches and nearshore bar systems constantly suffer from a deficit in coast-stabilizing sediment. For the protection of the current coastline, beach nourishment is crucial. In M-V, sand has been procured from offshore deposits since 1968 [71]. S-H lacks such deposits. Hence, sand nourishment is a significantly less frequent coastal protection measure in S-H. It is mostly performed for economic reasons with imported resources and high financial expenses [74].

The erosion of cohesive shorelines also occurs in other areas of the mid- to high latitudes, e.g., in parts of the English and Irish coast [18,29] as well as in North America and Canada [75,76].

At the lower Great Lakes, for example, about 40% of the shoreline is characterized by 2–30 m-high cliffs. They consist of glacial, glaciofluvial, and glaciolimnic sediments and are bordered by narrow beaches. Retreat rates are comparatively high: they exceed 0.5 m yr⁻¹ in most areas and locally reach values > 1.5 m yr⁻¹ [77]. Similar to the S-H coastline, high temporal and spatial variation occurs. Due to comparable characteristics regarding morphology, geology, and retreat, we expect similar mechanisms of erosion, sorting, and transport with the impact of hydrodynamic forces to the S-H Baltic Sea coastline. Case studies at individual lake sections provide further information about the availability of sediments from cliff retreat. Here, per meter cliff, an input of sand and gravel (vs) of 1.6–8.2 m³ yr⁻¹ m⁻¹ was calculated [78], which presents a comparable value range to the littoral sediment budget in S-H of <0.1–9.5 m³ yr⁻¹ m⁻¹. We assume that the Great Lakes represent a potential comparison area to S-H to perform further research on the complex system interplay and evaluate the role of the littoral sediment budget supplied by cohesive cliff deposits.

5.3.2. Comparison of Sediment Sources: Seafloor Abrasion

To assess the role of the active cliffs as a sediment source for the coastal zones, we consult other potential source areas. Besides the cohesive cliff deposits, other suppliers of littoral sediments are rivers and submarine abrasion platforms [3,79]. In the study area, the river discharge can be neglected as a material source [27], whereas the abrasion platforms are highly relevant [80]. Here, the Pleistocene hard substrate, glacial till, of the seafloor is eroded mostly due to wave action [11,39,79]. The mobilized material accounts for a considerable amount of sediment that enters the coastal system [7,11]. Case studies propose that the abrasion platforms in front of active cliffs may supply more than 80% of the absolute local material input [27,80] and, thus, may constitute an even more valuable sediment source than the terrestrial cliffs [81]. However, for a reliable quantitative assessment of the sediment provided from seafloor abrasion, more research is required regarding, e.g., the geomechanical properties, the mineralogical and sedimentological composition of the hard substrate, as well as the influence of biological activity, e.g., boring organisms [80,82,83]. Additionally, the local intensity and the seaward delimitation of the abrasive activity have to be determined. As they vary with, e.g., changing wave heights and water levels, this is difficult to implement [11,84]. Thus, the quantification of the littoral sediment supplied from the seafloor remains speculative due to limited knowledge and measuring techniques.

Besides the role as a highly relevant sediment source, the seafloor abrasion promotes the ongoing cliff recession [79]. It influences the nearshore morphology and, hence, the intensity of the hydrodynamic impact of the cliff [11,79,80]. This emphasizes again the need for research in the offshore areas.

6. Conclusions

In this study, we have compiled data from available literature and performed analyses regarding the active cliff sections of the sediment-starved German Baltic Sea coast of the state of Schleswig-Holstein, Germany. Based on the dynamic and static properties of these cliffs and their contribution to the littoral sediment availability—compiled in Tables A1 and A2—we draw the following conclusions:

1. The active cliffs present a major sediment source for the sediment-starved Baltic Sea coast of S-H. Due to ongoing cliff erosion, about 39,000–161,000 m^3 yr^{-1} of sediments (0.063–64 mm) are annually supplied to the nearshore system. This is essential for the coastal transport and the stabilization of adjacent sandy shorelines. As such, the active cliffs deliver an important ecosystem service for coastal protection.
2. Due to the complex interplay of cliff properties, forces, and processes, and the limited data availability, uncertainties remain with respect to the exact volumes of the littoral sediment budget. Although those cannot be quantified on the given data basis, we assume that the determined volume interval gives a fair indication of the dimension of the sediment budget.
3. For a comprehensive evaluation of the littoral sediment budget along the S-H coastline, the study has to be expanded offshore. Here, the erosion of the hard-bottom seafloor accounts for a considerable amount of sediment and, thus, adds another relevant sediment source to the system. The volumes of supplied material from abrasion platforms have not yet been reliably quantified.

The findings of this study indicate that further research is required to decrease uncertainties and improve the accuracy and reliability of the final result—the littoral sediment budget. Investigations shall aim towards an improved local knowledge of the heterogenous cliff properties and an enhanced understanding of the interplay of forces that control the local cliff retreat. Additionally, we aim to improve the data basis for investigations of cohesive cliff morphodynamics. However, the review of available studies and the implementation of older data remains inevitable to provide a well-founded assessment for the long-term development along the Baltic Sea coast of S-H and to derive future prospects.

Author Contributions: Conceptualization, T.A. and C.W.; formal analysis, T.A.; funding acquisition, J.L.A.H.; investigation, T.A.; methodology, T.A.; project administration, J.L.A.H., A.H., H.-C.R. and C.W.; resources, T.A., A.H., H.-C.R. and C.W.; supervision, C.W.; visualization, T.A.; writing—original draft, T.A.; writing—review and editing, T.A., J.L.A.H., A.H., H.-C.R. and C.W. All authors have read and agreed to the published version of the manuscript.

Funding: This research resulted from the project Sediment Budget Baltic Sea, a research cooperation between the Kiel University and the Schleswig-Holstein Ministry of Energy Transition, Agriculture, Environment, Nature and Digitization (MELUND), the Schleswig-Holstein State Office for Coastal Protection, National Park and Marine Protection (LKN-SH), and the State Agency for Agriculture, Environment and Rural Areas—Schleswig-Holstein (LLUR). The project was funded by the Schleswig-Holstein Ministry of Energy Transition, Agriculture, Environment, Nature and Digitization (MELUND). We acknowledge financial support by Land Schleswig-Holstein within the funding programme Open Access Publikationsfonds.

Institutional Review Board Statement: Not applicable.

Informed Consent Statement: Not applicable.

Acknowledgments: We would like to greatly thank Klaus Schwarzer for sharing his broad expertise in the field of local geology, cliff retreat, and sediment dynamics in the studied area. We also want to acknowledge his initiation and heading of the project 'Sediment Budget Baltic Sea' and his constructive contribution during the project work and manuscript preparation. We also want to thank Kay Krienke (LLUR) for his participation in discussions regarding cliff geology. We thank the anonymous reviewers for their suggestions to improve the manuscript. Finally, we wish to thank Giuliana A. Diaz Mendoza, Gianna Persichini, Gitta A. von Rönn, and Joscha Loose for lively discussions and helpful and solution-oriented support in many aspects.

Conflicts of Interest: The authors declare no conflict of interest.

Appendix A

Table A1. Compilation of Cliff Retreat along the Baltic Sea coast of S-H, Germany, based on data from [8,36,52].

Section No.	Location	Kannenberg, 1951 (~1878–1950)		Ziegler and Heyen, 2005 (1949–2002)			LKN-SH (~1878–2016)	
		r (m yr^{-1})	L (m)	r (m yr^{-1})	r_{max} (m yr^{-1})	L (m)	r (m yr^{-1})	L (m)
81.05	Solitüde			0.09	0.12	110	-	105
81.08	Holnis (west)	Holnis	0.15	0.35	0.49	240	0.56	478
81.08	Holnis (north)			0.09	0.12	240	0.18	237
81.08	Holnis (east)		800	0.08	0.16	280	0.07	276
81.1	Langballiholz	Lanballigholz	-	800	0.32	0.41	330	0.23	335
81.1	Dollerupholz	Dollerupholz	0.13	2300	0.13	0.2	610	0.17	610
81.12	Neukirchen	Neukirchen	0.19	1000	0.15	0.21	310	0.31	311
81.12	Nieby			0.13	0.18	470	0.28	470
81.12	Habernis (west)	Habernis	0.30	800	0.2	0.26	340	0.15	338
81.13	Habernis (east)			0.29	0.93	590	0.30	591
81.13	Steinberghaff	Steinberghaff	0.11	1200	0.06	0.09	870	0.02	747
81.13	Koppelheck		-	-	0.04	0.08	190	0.03	345
81.18	Gammellück	Geltinger Bucht	-	1800	0.35	0.48	280	0.11	178
82.03	Haffskoppel	Düttebüll	-	1000	0.23	0.18	840	0.20	1396
82.08	Schönhagen	Schönhagen	0.46	1600	0.51	0.96	1880	0.50	1571
82.14	Booknis	Boknis	0.29	1600	0.3	0.44	2010	0.24	2637
83.01	Waabs	Waabs	0.25	2200	0.31	0.6	2140	0.24	2902
83.02	Hemmelmark	Hemmelmark	0.10	400	0.24	0.38	640	0.13	754
83.06	Schnellmark	Altenhof	0.13	1000	0.21	0.48	900	0.20	1553
83.07	Noer	Nör	0.14	1500	0.19	0.26	1340	0.21	1334
83.07	Krusendorf	Surendorf	0.08	800	0.38	0.53	750	0.13	1555
83.07	Dänisch-Nienhof	Dän. Nienhof	0.19	1300	0.23	0.38	440	0.20	1096
83.08	Stohl	Stohl	0.25	3000	0.24	0.68	3640	0.19	3884
83.08	Altbülk	Alt-Bülk	0.13	300	0.09	0.15	310	0.13	796
84.05	Schilksee	Schilksee	0.13	1000	0.34	0.56	1140	0.41	1139
85.01	Stein	Stein	0.17	1200	0.19	0.39	1290	0.12	1510
85.04	Todendorf	Satjendorf	0.31	3000	0.3	0.86	4120	0.34	5493

Table A1. Cont.

Section No.	Location	Kannenberg, 1951 (~1878–1950)		Ziegler and Heyen, 2005 (1949–2002)			LKN-SH (~1878–2016)	
		r (m yr^{-1})	L (m)	r (m yr^{-1})	r$_{max}$ (m yr^{-1})	L (m)	r (m yr^{-1})	L (m)
85.06	Lippe	Lippe	0.13	200	0.11	0.15	180	0.10	680
85.08	Hohwacht	Hohwacht	-	300	0.14	0.2	430	0.16	536
85.22	Döhnsdorf	Weißenhaus	0.28	1200	0.12	0.26	1530	0.08	2196
85.12	Wandelwitz	Putlos	0.17	2000	0.19	0.36	1080	0.09	3180
85.12	Johannistal	Johannistal	0.13	1500	0.17	0.46	3080	0.15	3428
85.12	Heiligenhafen	Heiligenhafen	0.27	1500	0.33	1.16	1560	0.23	2215
86.01	Lütjenbrode	Lütjenbrode	0.10	2000	0.13	0.19	1370	0.06	2655
86.05	Fehmarnsund							0.16	863
86.07	Heinrichsruh				0.26	0.49	550	0.11	1148
86.09	Großenbrode	Großenbrode		1000	0.46	0.69	710	0.26	721
86.13	Ölendorf							0.02	758
86.13	Kraksdorf	Siggen	0.11	3800	0.21	0.34	2980	0.15	4943
86.15	Rosenfelde							0.00	705
86.17	Dahmeshöved	Dahmeshöved	0.42	1600				0.10	2071
86.21	Bliesdorf (north)	Bliesdorf	0.13	3000	0.73	0.96	460	0.16	1267
86.21	Bliesdorf (south)				0.23	0.62	1470	0.06	2237
86.22	Pelzerhaken	Pelzerhaken		1000	0.16	0.23	590	0.00	1054
86.24	Sierksdorf (north)	Wintershagen	0.22	300	0.2	0.39	230	0.18	272
86.24	Sierksdorf (med)	Sierksdorf	0.12	1300	0.14	0.26	910	0.18	1445
86.24	Sierksdorf (south)				0.14	0.36	630	0.00	627
86.28	Brodten	Brodten	0.43	4000	0.37	1.18	3420	0.58	4213
500.03	Strukkamphuk							0.61	499
500.05	Albertsdorf				0.21	0.4	90	0.27	359
500.24	Marienleuchte				0.21	0.52	450	0.12	1253
500.26	Klausdorf				0.17	0.43	2360	0.13	2223
500.26	Katharinenhof				0.13	0.34	2480	0.10	6383
500.26	Staberhof (east)				0.11	0.34	860		
500.27	Staberhdorf (south)				0.17	0.53	2400	0.07	3938
500.32	Wulfen				0.46	0.65	1020	0.19	986
Total			0.22	47,400	0.24	1.18	57,140	0.19	85,493

Table A2. Database of the littoral sediment budget assessment. Values of V_e are based on [36] *. Geological/sedimentological information was provided by the listed literature **. Calculations of $v_{s,min}$ and $v_{s,max}$ for sections with missing data for n, c were based on min/max estimates derived from local data (Table 2).

Section No.	Location	V_e (m³ yr⁻¹) *	v_e (m³ yr⁻¹ m⁻¹)	$v_{s,min}$ (m³ yr⁻¹ m⁻¹)	$v_{s,max}$ (m³ yr⁻¹ m⁻¹)	nmin (%)	nmax (%)	cmin (%)	cmax (%)	Literature **
81.05	Solitüde	158	1.44	0.17	1.96					
81.08	Holnis (west)	963	4.01	0.48	5.47					
81.08	Holnis (north)	134	0.56	0.07	0.76					
81.08	Holnis (east)	199	0.71	0.09	0.97					
81.1	Langballigholz	759	2.30	0.34	2.91			0.10	0.10	[23]
81.1	Dolleruppholz	1442	2.36	0.33	2.99			0.10	0.17	[23]
81.12	Neukirchen	620	2.00	0.24	2.72					
81.12	Nieby	678	1.44	0.21	1.84			0.09	0.10	[23]
81.12	Habernis (west)	447	1.31	0.19	1.71			0.07	0.10	[23]
81.13	Habernis (east)	1825	3.09	0.46	4.03			0.07	0.10	[23]
81.13	Steinberghaff	303	0.35	0.05	0.45			0.09	0.12	[23,85]
81.13	Koppelheck	55	0.29	0.03	0.39					[85]
81.18	Gammellück	234	0.84	0.10	1.14					
82.03	Haffskoppel	658	0.78	0.12	1.02			0.07	0.07	[23]
82.08	Schönhagen	8960	4.77	3.24	4.57	0.50	0.50	0.04	0.09	[11,23,28,54,86]
82.14	Booknis	2933	1.46	0.21	1.88			0.08	0.12	[23]
83.01	Waabs	7963	3.72	0.55	5.07			0.03	0.11	[23]
83.02	Hemmelmark	1343	2.10	0.27	2.86			0.03	0.23	[23,40]
83.06	Schnellmark	1964	2.18	0.32	2.89	0.50	0.50	0.06	0.10	[23,87]
83.07	Noer	3072	2.29	0.32	2.35			0.06	0.09	
			2.29	1.07	1.91	0.43	0.56	0.06	0.09	[23,31,41]
			2.29	1.39	4.26					
83.07	Krusendorf	2583	3.44	0.49	4.47			0.07	0.14	[23,31,40]

Table A2. Cont.

Section No.	Location	V_e (m³ yr⁻¹) *	v_e (m³ yr⁻¹ m⁻¹)	$v_{s,min}$ (m³ yr⁻¹ m⁻¹)	$v_{s,max}$ (m³ yr⁻¹ m⁻¹)	nmin (%)	nmax (%)	cmin (%)	cmax (%)	Literature **
83.07	Dänisch-Nienhof	1871	4.25	0.61	5.48			0.08	0.13	[23,31]
83.08	Stohl	15,076	4.14	0.21	1.40	0.13	0.57	0.04	0.17	[23,26,31,41,55,56,88,89]
			4.14	1.53	2.65	0.43	0.48	0.04	0.17	
			4.14	1.74	4.04					
83.08	Altbülk	181	0.58	0.31	0.56	0.49	0.49			[41]
84.05	Schilksee	4849	4.25	0.64	5.40			0.09	0.09	[23,31]
85.01	Stein	1341	1.04	0.15	1.34			0.08	0.10	[23,42]
85.04	Todendorf	10,568	2.57	0.35	3.33			0.07	0.18	[23,90]
85.06	Lippe	46	0.26	0.03	0.35					[90]
85.08	Hohwacht	745	1.73	0.26	2.31			0.05	0.10	[23,42,90]
85.22	Döhnsdorf	2797	1.83	0.27	2.47			0.04	0.09	[23,42]
85.12	Wandelwitz	3935	3.64	0.44	4.96			0.08	0.14	[23]
85.12	Johannistal	6992	2.27	0.32	2.92					
85.12	Heiligenhafen	4885	3.13	1.85	3.42	0.47	0.58	0.06	0.16	[23,40,43,57]
86.01	Lütjenbrode	713	0.52	0.08	0.66			0.09	0.09	[23]
86.07	Heinrichsruh	378	0.69	0.08	0.94					
86.09	Großenbrode	906	1.28	0.15	1.24	0.11	0.50			[47]
86.13	Kraksdorf	4874	1.64	0.25	2.20			0.04	0.09	
86.21	Bliesdorf (north)	3391	7.37	1.11	9.47			0.08	0.09	[23]
86.21	Bliesdorf (south)	3235	2.20	0.33	2.92			0.05	0.10	[23]
86.22	Pelzerhaken	697	1.18	0.18	1.51			0.09	0.09	[23]
86.24	Sierksdorf (north)	954	0.84	0.10	1.14			0.04	0.06	
86.24	Sierksdorf (south)	1061	1.68	0.26	2.25					[23]
86.28	Brodten	17,279	5.05	2.72	5.53	0.40	0.60	0.09	0.10	[8,23,39,46,58]
500.05	Albertsdorf	61	0.68	0.10	0.87			0.08	0.08	[23]

Table A2. Cont.

Section No.	Location	V_e (m³ yr⁻¹) *	v_e (m³ yr⁻¹ m⁻¹)	$v_{s,min}$ (m³ yr⁻¹ m⁻¹)	$v_{s,max}$ (m³ yr⁻¹ m⁻¹)	nmin (%)	nmax (%)	cmin (%)	cmax (%)	Literature **
500.24	Marienleuchte	303	0.67	0.08	0.92			0.06	0.27	[23]
500.26	Klausdorf	2137	0.91	0.11	1.19			0.13	0.23	[23,47]
500.26	Katharinenhof (Fehmarn)	3115	1.26	0.48	1.04	0.34	0.48			
500.26	Staberhuk (east)	417	0.48	0.07	0.62			0.09	0.12	[23]
500.27	Staberhuk (south)	1618	0.67	0.09	0.82			0.13	0.16	[23]
500.32	Wulfen	3647	3.58	0.45	4.12			0.18	0.24	[23,40]

References

1. Schwarzer, K. *Sedimentdynamik in Sandriffsystemen Einer Tidefreien Küste Unter Berücksichtigung Von Rippströmen*; Dissertation, Geologisch-Paläontologisches Institut und Museum der Universität Kiel: Kiel, Germany, 1989.
2. Hupfer, P.; Harff, J.; Sterr, H.; Stigge, H.J. Die Wasserstände an Der Ostsee. Entwicklung-Sturmfluten-Klimawandel. *Küste* **2003**, *66*, 331.
3. Davidson-Arnott, R.G.D. *Introduction to Coastal Processes & Geomorphology*; Cambridge University Press: Cambridge, UK, 2010; ISBN 9780521874458.
4. Hamann, M.; Klug, H. Sturmflutgefährdete Gebiete und potentielle Werteverluste an den Küsten Schleswig-Holsteins. Planungs-grundlagen für künftige Küstenschutzstrategien. *Schr. Nat. Ver. Schlesw Holst* **1997**, *67*, 17–28.
5. Ministerium für Energiewende, Landwirtschaft, Umwelt und ländliche Räume des Landes Schleswig-Holstein (MELUR). Generalplan Küstenschutz des Landes Schleswig-Holstein. Fortschreibung 2012. Available online: https://www.schleswig-holstein.de/DE/Fachinhalte/K/kuestenschutz/Downloads/Generalplan.pdf%3F__blob%3DpublicationFile%26v%3D1 (accessed on 12 January 2021).
6. Oppenheimer, M.; Glavovic, B.C.; Hinkel, J.; van de Wal, R.; Magnan, A.K.; Abd-Elgawad, A.; Cai, R.; Cifuentes-Jara, M.; DeConto, R.M.; Ghosh, T.; et al. Sea Level Rise and Implications for Low-Lying Islands, Coasts and Communities. In *IPCC Special Report on the Ocean and Cryosphere in a Changing Climate*; Pörtner, H.-O., Roberts, D.C., Masson-Delmotte, V., Zhai, P., Tignor, M., Poloczanska, E., Mintenbeck, K., Alegría, A., Nicolai, M., Okem, A., Petzold, J., Rama, B., Weyer, N.M., Eds.; 2019; in press; p. 126.
7. Healy, T.; Wefer, G. The Efficacy of Submarine Abrasion vs Cliff Retreat as a Supplier of Marine Sediment in the Kieler Bucht, Western Baltic. *Meyniana* **1980**, *32*, 89–96.
8. Kannenberg, E.-G. Die Steilufer der Schleswig-Holsteinischen Ostseeküste. Probleme der marinen und klimatischen Abtragung. *Schr. Geogr. Inst. Univ. Kiel* **1951**, *14*, 101.
9. Amin, S.M.N.; Davidson-Arnott, R.G.D. A Statistical Analysis of the Controls on Shoreline Erosion Rates, Lake Ontario. *J. Coast. Res.* **1997**, *13*, 1093–1101.
10. Philpott, K.L. Comparison of cohesive coasts and beach coasts. In *Proceedings, Coastal Engineering in Canada*; Kamphuis, J.W., Ed.; USA Army Corps of Engineers. Coastal Engineering Manual. Engineer Manual 1110-2-1100; Army Corps of Engineers: Washington, DC, USA, 1984; pp. 227–244.
11. Schrottke, K. *Rückgangsdynamik Schleswig-Holsteinischer Steilküsten Unter Besonderer Betrachtung Submariner Abrasion und Restsedimentmobilität*. Dissertation; Kiel University: Kiel, Germany, 2001.
12. Terefenko, P.; Paprotny, D.; Giza, A.; Morales-Nápoles, O.; Kubicki, A.; Walczakiewicz, S. Monitoring Cliff Erosion with LiDAR Surveys and Bayesian Network-Based Data Analysis. *Remote Sens.* **2019**, *11*, 843. [CrossRef]
13. Richter, H.-C. Einfluß Der Material-Und Verbandseigenschaften Sowie Des Unterirdischen Wassers Auf Die Geschiebemergel-steilufer Der Ostküste. *Mitt. Forsch. Schiffahrt Wasser Grundbau Schr. Wasser Grundbau* **1989**, *54*, 92–103.
14. Sunamura, T. *Geomorphology of Rocky Coasts*; John Wiley & Son: Chichester, NY, USA, 1992; Volume 3.
15. Walker, H.J. Bluff erosion at Barrow and Wainwright, Artic Alaska. In *Z. Geomorph. N. F., 81*; Gebrüder Borntraeger: Stuttgart, Germany, 1991; pp. 53–61.
16. Davidson-Arnott, R.G.D.; Ollerhead, J. Nearshore Erosion on a Cohesive Shoreline. *Mar. Geol.* **1995**, *122*, 349–365. [CrossRef]
17. Sterr, H. Der Abbruch von Steilküsten in der südwestlichen Kieler Bucht-unter spezieller Berücksichtigung des Januarsturmes 1987. *Küste* **1989**, *50*, 45–54.
18. Dong, P.; Guzzetti, F. Frequency-Size Statistics of Coastal Soft-Cliff Erosion. *J. Waterw. Port Coast. Ocean Eng.* **2005**, *131*, 37–42. [CrossRef]
19. Hampton, M.A.; Griggs, G.B. *Formation, Evolution, and Stability of Coastal Cliffs—Status and Trends*; U. S. Geological Survey (USGS) Professional Paper 1963. Available online: https://books.google.com.hk/books?hl=zh-CN&lr=&id=F8Ze3v9JrVkC&oi=fnd&pg=PR3&dq=Formation,+Evolution,+and+Stability+of+Coastal+Cliffs%E2%80%94Status+and+Trends%3B&ots=rRWErYrfM0&sig=fPk96NsD8F8w0IiJLATXDF4HBy4&redir_esc=y#v=onepage&q=Formation%2C%20Evolution%2C%20and%20Stability%20of%20Coastal%20Cliffs%E2%80%94Status%20and%20Trends%3B&f=false (accessed on 11 August 2021).
20. Seifert, G. *Bestandsaufnahme Der Steilufer An Den Küsten Fehmarns Und Wagriens Mit Dem Versuch, Den Verbleib Des Abbruchmaterials Nachzuweisen. Report (Unpublished)*; WSA: Kiel, Germany, 1953.
21. Seifert, G. Die Steilufer als Materiallieferanten der Sandwanderung. *Meyniana* **1955**, *4*, 78–83.
22. Nichols, G. *Sedimentology and Stratigraphy*, 2nd ed.; Wiley-Blackwell: Chichester, UK, 2009; ISBN 9788578110796.
23. Glückert, G. Über den Kalkgehalt des Geschiebemergels der schleswig-holsteinischen Ostsee-Steilküste. *Meyniana* **1974**, *25*, 15–19.
24. Von Rönn, G.A.; Krämer, K.; Franz, M.; Schwarzer, K.; Reimers, H.-C.; Winter, C. Dynamics of Stone Habitats in Coastal Waters of the Southwestern Baltic Sea (Hohwacht Bay). *Geosciences* **2021**, *11*, 171. [CrossRef]
25. Petersen, M. Abbruch und Schutz der Steilufer an der Ostseeküste (Samland bis Schleswig-Holstein). *Küste* **1952**, *1*, 100–152.
26. Niedermeyer, R.O.; Lampe, R.; Janke, W.; Schwarzer, K.; Duphorn, K.; Kliewe, H.; Werner, F. *Die deutsche Ostseeküste; Sammlung Geologischer Führer, Gebr*; Borntraeger: Stuttgart, Germany, 2011; Volume 105.
27. Seibold, E. Geological Investigation of Nearshore Sand-Transport—Examples of Methods and Problems from the Baltic and North Sea. *Prog. Oceanogr.* **1963**, *1*, 3–70. [CrossRef]

28. Jannsen, J. Sedimentdynamik am Strand vor dem Schönhagener Kliff (Schleswig-Holstein). Diploma Thesis, Kiel University, Kiel, Germany, 1997.
29. Brooks, S.M.; Spencer, T. Temporal and Spatial Variations in Recession Rates and Sediment Release from Soft Rock Cliffs, Suffolk Coast, UK. *Geomorphology* **2010**, *124*, 26–41. [CrossRef]
30. Masselink, G.; Hughes, M.G. *Introduction to Coastal Processes and Geomorphology*; Edward Arnold: London, UK, 2003.
31. Prange, W. Gefügekundliche Untersuchungen der weichselzeitlichen Ablagerungen an den Steilufern des Dänischen Wohlds, Schleswig-Holstein. *Meyniana* **1987**, *39*, 85–110.
32. Dreimanis, A.; Lundqvist, J. What should be called till? *Striae* **1984**, *20*, 5–10.
33. Fleming, K.; Johnston, P.; Zwartz, D.; Yokoyama, Y.; Lambeck, K.; Chappell, J. Refining the Eustatic Sea-Level Curve since the Last Glacial Maximum Using Far- and Intermediate-Field Sites. *Earth Planet. Sci. Lett.* **1998**, *163*, 327–342. [CrossRef]
34. Schwarzer, K.; Reimers, H.-C.; Störtenbecker, M.; Von Waldow, K.-R. Das Küstenholozän in der westlichen Hohwachter Bucht. *Meyniana* **1993**, *45*, 131–144.
35. Landesbetrieb Für Küstenschutz, Nationalpark Und Meeresschutz Des Landes Schleswig-Holstein (LKN-SH). Fachplan Küstenschutz Ostseeküste. Grundlagen. Available online: https://www.schleswig-holstein.de/DE/Fachinhalte/K/kuestenschutz_fachplaene/Ostseekueste/2_Grundlagen/2_0_grundlagen.html#doc25f3538c-ce42-4123-93fd-3e4d85986168bodyText13 (accessed on 23 September 2020).
36. Ziegler, B.; Heyen, A. Rückgang der Steilufer an der schleswig-holsteinischen westlichen Ostseeküste. *Meyniana* **2005**, *57*, 61–92.
37. Bundesministerium für Verkehr, Bau und Stadtentwicklung (BMVBS). *Digitale Bundeswasserstraßenkarte 1:2000 (DBWK 2)*; Bundesministerium für Verkehr, Bau und Stadtentwicklung (BMVBS): Berlin, Germany, 2003.
38. Gripp, K. *Erdgeschichte von Schleswig-Holstein*; Karl-Wachholtz-Verlag: Neumünster, Germany, 1964.
39. Dücker, A. Die Ursachen des Kliffrückgangs am Brodtener Ufer bei Travemünde. In *Beiträge zur Landeskunde von Schleswig-Holstein*; Schott, C., Ed.; Ferdinand Hirt: Kiel, Germany, 1953; pp. 38–53.
40. Kabel, C. Geschiebestratigraphische Untersuchungen im Pleistozän Schleswig-Holstein und angrenzender Gebiete. Ph.D. Dissertation, Kiel University, Kiel, Germany, 1982.
41. Livingstone, S.J.; Piotrowski, J.A.; Bateman, M.D.; Ely, J.C.; Clark, C.D. Discriminating between Subglacial and Proglacial Lake Sediments: An Example from Dänischer Wohld Peninsula, Northern Germany. *Quat. Sci. Rev.* **2015**, *112*, 86–108. [CrossRef]
42. Prange, W. Geologie der Steilufer zwischen Kieler Förde und Hohwachter Bucht. *Schr. Nat. Ver. Schlesw Holst* **1991**, *61*, 1–18.
43. Stephan, H.-J. Exkursionsführer Heiligenhafener "Hohes Ufer". *Geschiebesammler* **1985**, *18*, 83–99.
44. Stephan, H.-J. Der jungbaltische Gletschervorstoß in Norddeutschland. *Schr. Nat. Ver. Schlesw Holst* **1994**, *64*, 1–15.
45. Ehlers, J. *Das Eiszeitalter*; Springer: Berlin, Heidelberg, Germany, 2020.
46. Groschopf, P. Physikalische Bedingungen des Kliffrückganges an der Kieler und Lübecker Bucht. *Kiel. Meeresforsch* **1936**, *1*, 335–342.
47. Pour-Nagshsband, G.R. Tonmineralbestand und Baugrundeigenschaften der Tarras-Tone, Beckentone und des Geschiebemergels in Teilgebieten Schleswig-Holsteins. *Meyniana* **1978**, *30*, 55–60.
48. Picard, K. Der Einfluß der Tektonik auf das pleistozäne Geschehen in Schleswig-Holstein. *Schr. Nat. Ver. Schlesw Holst* **1964**, *35*, 99–113.
49. Köster, R. Die Küsten Der Flensburger Förde. Ein Beispiel Für Morphologie Und Entwicklung Einer Bucht. *Schr. Nat. Ver. Schlesw Holst* **1958**, *29*, 5–18.
50. Stephan, H.-J. Zur Entstehung der eiszeitlichen Landschaft Schleswig-Holsteins. *Schr. Nat. Ver. Schlesw Holst* **2003**, *68*, 101–118.
51. Kubisch, M.; Schönfeld, J. Eine neue "Cyprinen-Ton"-Scholle bei Stohl (Schleswig-Holstein): Mikrofauna und Grobfraktionsanalyse von Sedimenten der Eem-zeitlichen Ostsee. *Meyniana* **1985**, *37*, 89–95.
52. Landesbetrieb für Küstenschutz, Nationalpark und Meeresschutz des Landes Schleswig-Holstein (LKN-SH). *Änderungsraten Obere Abbruchkante 1878-2016. Table (Unpublish)*; Landesbetrieb für Küstenschutz, Nationalpark und Meeresschutz des Landes Schleswig-Holstein (LKN-SH): Husum, Germany, 2019.
53. Wentworth, C.K. A Scale of Grade and Class Terms for Clastic Sediments. *J. Geol.* **1922**, *30*, 377–392. [CrossRef]
54. Weinhold, H. *Untersuchungen am Ostsee-Steilufer bei Schönhagen. Landabtrag—Geologie und Ursachen. Ing. geol. Bericht (unpublished)*; Geologisches Landesamt Schleswig-Holstein: Kiel, Germany, 1989.
55. Wenghöfer, S. Die weichselzeitliche Entwicklung des Dänischen Wohlds im Bereich Stohl/Marienfelde. Quartärgeologische Kartierung und Kliffaufnahme. Diploma Thesis, Kiel University, Kiel, Germany, 1991.
56. Piotrowski, J.A. Till Facies and Depositional Environments of the Upper Sedimentary Complex from the Stohler Cliff, Schleswig-Holstein, North Germany. *Z. Geomorph. N. F. Supp.* **1992**, *84*, 37–54.
57. Schlieker, M. Glazialgeologie des "Hohen Ufers" bei Heiligenhafen und des angrenzenden Gebietes. Diploma Thesis, Kiel University, Kiel, Germany, 1997, (1st part) (unpublished).
58. Dücker, A. Über die physikalischen Eigenschaften der das Brodtener Ufer aufbauenden Bodenarten und ihre Bedeutung für den Steiluferrückgang und Errichtung eines Uferschutzwerkes. *Küste* **1952**, *2*, 21–33.
59. Sunamura, T. Processes of sea cliff and platform erosion. In *Handbook of Coastal Processes and Erosion*; Komar, P.D., Ed.; CRC Press: Boca Raton, FL, USA, 1983; pp. 233–265.
60. Bray, M.J.; Hooke, J.M. Prediction of Soft-Cliff Retreat with Accelerating Sea-Level Rise. *J. Coast. Res.* **1997**, *13*, 453–467.

61. Hünicke, B.; Zorito, E.; von Storch, H. The Challenge of Baltic Sea-level Change. In *Coastline Changes of the Baltic Sea from South to East. Past and Future Projection*; Harff, J., Furmańczyk, K., von Storch, H., Eds.; Springer International Publishing: Berlin, Germany, 2017; Volume 19, pp. 37–54, ISBN 9783319842660.
62. Köntje, L. Vorstrand-und Uferveränderungen an der Schleswig-Holsteinischen Ostseeküste über Zwei Dekaden (1980–2000). Master's Thesis, Kiel University, Kiel, Germany, 2015.
63. Ministerium für Landwirtschaft, Umwelt und Ländliche Räume des Landes Schleswig-Holstein (MLUR-SH). Landesverordnung über Gesetzlich Geschützte Biotope (Biotopverordnung). Available online: https://www.gesetze-rechtsprechung.sh.juris.de/jportal/?quelle=jlink&query=BiotopV+SH&psml=bsshoprod.psml&max=true (accessed on 5 July 2021).
64. Flemming, B.; Wefer, G. Tauchbeobachtungen an Wellenrippeln und Abrasionserscheinungen in der Westlichen Ostsee südöstlich Bokniseck. *Meyniana* **1973**, *23*, 9–18.
65. Köster, R.; Schwarzer, K. *Geologische Untersuchungen zur Sandvorspülung vor der Probstei/Ostsee*; Geologisch-Paläontologisches Institut und Museum der Universität Kiel: Kiel, Germany, 1988; p. 113.
66. Amt für Land-und Wasserwirtschaft Kiel; Leichtweiss-Institut für Wasserbau der TU Braunschweig; Geologisch-Paläontologisches Institut der Univ. Kiel. In *KFKI-Forschungsvorhaben "Vorstranddynamik Einer Tidefreien KÜSTE", Förderkennzeichen: MTK 0494*; Uni Kiel: Kiel, Germany, 1997; p. 232.
67. Simmer, K. *Grundbau 1: Bodenmechanik Und Erdstatische Berechnungen*, 19th ed.; Benedictus Gotthelf Teubner: Stuttgart, Germany, 2012.
68. Ministerium Für Landwirtschaft, Umwelt Und Verbraucherschutz Mecklenburg-Vorpommern. Regelwerk Küstenschutz Mecklenburg-Vorpommern. Available online: http://www.stalu-mv.de/mm/Themen/K%C3%BCstenschutz/Regelwerk-K%C3%BCstenschutz-Mecklenburg%E2%80%93Vorpommern/ (accessed on 2 March 2021).
69. Ministerium für Energiewende, Landwirtschaft, Umwelt und Ländliche Räume des Landes Schleswig-Holstein Fachplan Küstenschutz Ostseeküste: Zahlen Daten Fakten. Available online: https://www.schleswig-holstein.de/DE/Landesregierung/V/Presse/PI/PDF/2014/Fachplan_Kuestenschutz.pdf?__blob=publicationFile&v=2 (accessed on 23 November 2020).
70. Schnick, H.H. Zur Morphogenese der Steilufer Ost-Jasmund (Insel Rügen)—eine landschaftsgeschichtliche Betrachtung. *Z. Geol. Wiss. Berl.* **2006**, *34*, 73–97.
71. Ministerium für Bau, Landesentwicklung und Umwelt Mecklenburg-Vorpommern. Generalplan Küsten-und Hochwasserschutz Mecklenburg-Vorpommern. Available online: http://www.stalu-mv.de/mm/Themen/K%C3%BCstenschutz/Generalplan-K%C3%BCsten%E2%80%93-und-Hochwasserschutz-Mecklenburg%E2%80%93Vorpommern-1993/ (accessed on 10 March 2021).
72. Kolander, R.; Morche, D.; Bimböse, M. Quantification of Moraine Cliff Coast Erosion on Wolin Island (Baltic Sea, Northwest Poland). *Baltica* **2013**, *26*, 37–44. [CrossRef]
73. Dudzińska-Nowak, J.; Wężyk, P. Volumetric Changes of a Soft Cliff Coast 2008-2012 Based on DTM from Airborne Laser Scanning (Wolin Island, Southern Baltic). *J. Coast. Res.* **2014**, *SI 70*, 59–64. [CrossRef]
74. Landesbetrieb für Küstenschutz, Nationalpark und Meeresschutz des Landes Schleswig-Holstein (LKN-SH). Fachplan Küstenschutz Ostseeküste. Bisheriger Küstenschutz. Available online: https://www.schleswig-holstein.de/DE/Fachinhalte/K/kuestenschutz_fachplaene/Ostseekueste/3_BishKuestenschutz/3_0_bisherig.html (accessed on 11 August 2021).
75. Jibson, R.W.; Staude, J.M. Bluff Recession Rates along the Lake Michigan Shoreline in Illinois. *Bull. Assoc. Eng. Geol.* **1992**, *29*, 103–117. [CrossRef]
76. Amin, S.M.N.; Davidson-Arnott, R.G.D. Toe Erosion of Glacial till Bluffs: Lake Erie South Shore. *Can. J. Earth Sci.* **1995**, *32*, 829–837. [CrossRef]
77. Davidson-Arnott, R.G.D.; Amin, S.M.N. An Approach to the Problem of Coastal Erosion in Quaternary Sediments. *Appl. Geogr.* **1985**, *5*, 99–116. [CrossRef]
78. Meadows, G.A.; Mackey, S.D.; Goforth, R.R.; Mickelson, D.M.; Edil, T.B.; Fuller, J.; Guy, D.E.; Meadows, L.A.; Brown, E.; Carman, S.M.; et al. Cumulative Habitat Impacts of Nearshore Engineering. *J. Gt. Lakes Res.* **2005**, *31*, 90–112. [CrossRef]
79. Gurwell, B. Grundsätzliche Anmerkungen zur langfristigen Abrasionswirkung und ihrer Quantifizierung. *Mitt Forsch. Schifffahrt Wasser Grundbau Berl* **1989**, *54*, 22–39.
80. Wefer, G.; Flemming, B.; Kiel, T. Submarine Abrasion des Geschiebemergels vor Bokniseck (Westl. Ostsee). *Meyniana* **1976**, *28*, 87–94.
81. Schrottke, K.; Schwarzer, K.; Fröhle, P. Mobility and Transport Directions of Residual Sediments on Abrasion Platforms in Front of Active Cliffs (Southwestern Baltic Sea). *J. Coast. Res.* **2006**, *SI 39*, 459–464.
82. Kasten, S. Der Erosive Einfluss von Sedimentbedeckung, Morphologie und Bioturbation auf Verschiedene Abrasionsplattformen in der Kieler und Lübecker Bucht. Diploma Thesis, Kiel University, Kiel, Germany, 2012, (unpublished).
83. Schwarzer, K.; Bohling, B.; Heinrich, C. Submarine Hard-Bottom Substrates in the Western Baltic Sea—Human Impact versus Natural Development. *J. Coast. Res.* **2014**, *SI 70*, 145–150. [CrossRef]
84. Dette, H.H.; Manzenrieder, H. *Modelluntersuchungen Zur Optimierung Von Deichprofilen Und Buhnensystemen Vor Der Probstei*; Leichtweiss-Institut für Wasserbau Der Technischen Universität Braunschweig: Braunschweig, Germany, 1979.
85. Exon, N.F. An Extensive Offshore Sand Bar Field in the Western Baltic Sea. *Mar. Geol.* **1975**, *18*, 197–212. [CrossRef]
86. Walther, M.; Grossmann, M. Das Schönhagener "Head"-Kliff an der Ostseeküste Schwansens (Schleswig-Holstein). *Geogr. Oekologica* **1991**, *4*, 1–83.

87. Prange, W. Glazialgeologische Aufschlußuntersuchung im weichselzeitlichen Vereisungsgebiet zwischen Schleswig und Kiel. *Meyniana* **1990**, *42*, 65–92.
88. Piotrowski, J. *Dynamik Und Subglaziale Paläohydrogeologie Der Weichselzeitlichen Eiskappe in Zentral-Schleswig-Holstein*; Geologisch-Paläontologisches Institut der Universität Kiel: Kiel, Germany, 1996; p. 188.
89. Piotrowski, J.A.; Döring, U.; Harder, A.; Qadirie, R.; Wenghöfer, S. "Deforming Bed Conditions on the Dänischer Wohld Peninsula, Northern Germany": Comments. *Boreas* **1997**, *26*, 73–77. [CrossRef]
90. Ernst, T. Die Hohwachter Bucht: Morphologsiche Entwicklung Einer Küstenlandschaft. *Schr. Nat. Ver. Für Schlesw Holst* **1974**, *44*, 47–96.

Article

Destabilisation and Accelerated Roll-Back of a Mixed Sediment Barrier in Response to a Managed Breach

Uwe Dornbusch

Environment Agency, Worthing BN11 1LD, UK; uwe.dornbusch@environment-agency.gov.uk

Abstract: Sea level rise increases the pressure on many coastlines to retreat landwards which will lead to coastlines previously held in position through management, being allowed to retreat where this is no longer affordable or sustainable. Barrier beaches have historically rolled back in response to different hydrodynamic events and sea level rise, but very little is known as to how quickly and how far roll-back is going to occur once management has ceased. Data from more than 40 topographical surveys collected over 7 years along the 1.5 km long, almost swash-aligned shingle barrier at Medmerry (southern England) are used together with hydrodynamic data in a wide-ranging assessment of barrier roll-back. This study shows that roll-back is progressing through time along the barrier in downdrift direction in response to a gradual reduction in cross-sectional area through longshore transport. The Barrier Inertia concept provides a practical means to assess stability/instability for events experienced, but also a tool to assess the short- to medium term risk to the coast downdrift of the immediate study area where flood risk still needs to be managed. Roll-back is influenced particularly by the creation of an artificial tidal breach and removal of its sediment, the elevation of the underlying marsh and clay sediments, the number and severity of storms experienced and the presence of legacy groynes; roll-back has exceeded modelled predictions and expert judgement by an order of magnitude.

Keywords: shingle beach; coastal catch-up; longshore transport; marsh cliff erosion; overwash; overtopping; barrier stability; back barrier marsh; Barrier Inertia

Citation: Dornbusch, U. Destabilisation and Accelerated Roll-Back of a Mixed Sediment Barrier in Response to a Managed Breach. *J. Mar. Sci. Eng.* **2021**, *9*, 374. https://doi.org/10.3390/jmse9040374

Academic Editors: Francesca De Serio and Pushpa Dissanayake

Received: 11 February 2021
Accepted: 26 March 2021
Published: 1 April 2021

Publisher's Note: MDPI stays neutral with regard to jurisdictional claims in published maps and institutional affiliations.

Copyright: © 2021 by the author. Licensee MDPI, Basel, Switzerland. This article is an open access article distributed under the terms and conditions of the Creative Commons Attribution (CC BY) license (https://creativecommons.org/licenses/by/4.0/).

1. Introduction

Unmanaged coastal barrier islands and beaches transgress with relative sea level rise where the back-barrier topography allows for this to occur. For gravel dominated barriers it is suggested that this may also occur in the absence of sea level rise [1]. For the mixed sand and gravel beaches of the south coast of England sea level rise associated roll-back is documented for example for the mid Holocene [2] and more widely for the last centuries through ground penetrating radar [3] or based on historical mapping [4–7].

Managed coastal barriers on the other hand are generally kept in position through active (beach recharge and recycling), passive (using structures such as groynes) or a combination of both types of sediment management. For many such managed shorelines, the pressure for morphological change has increased over the period of management, which in the southeast of England started in the early 18th century [8], due to historic sea level rise of between at least 0.2 and 0.3 m (broad extrapolation from [9]).

At several sites, this management becomes unsustainable into the future, raising the question as to what might happen if sediment management ceases and natural processes can return unchecked to these frontages. In the 1980s and 90s, a number of publications were dedicated to the natural ontogeny and in particular roll-back of coarse clastic barrier beaches focussing on barriers in Ireland [10–12] and Canada [13–15] followed from 2000 by publications on barriers like Hurst Spit [16], Porlock [17,18], Cley [19–21] and Sillon de Talbert [22–24], where previous management including sediment movement had ceased or hard structures been removed, or where new management was going to be introduced [16].

Overwashing and roll-back are also documented in other parts of the world although the conditions in terms of tidal range, grain size, nearshore bathymetry, underlying geology or degree of beach management are often significantly different from the study site and other locations in the United Kingdom. Roll-back associated with a sudden rise in sea level due to tectonic sinking has been observed on macro-tidal beaches in Alaska [25] and is suggested for a fine gravel beach in the micro-tidal environment of Hawke Bay, New Zealand [26]. Intense roll-back over the past decades due to storms and increasing sediment deficit is evidenced for the micro-tidal barrier fronting the Torreblanca Cabanes marsh in the Gulf of Valencia (Spain) [27]. At the same time, modelling of beach response to storms has become more advanced but is often restricted to short periods of observations on a small number of profiles (e.g., at the fine gravel barrier of Loe Bar, in southwest England [28], at Newgale in West Wales [29] or at Hurst Spit [30]) and appears to be poorer for macro-tidal coarse clastic barriers where roll-back has occurred (e.g., [31]). Recently the cross-shore response from Xbeach-G has been coupled with longshore transport for the micro-tidal fine gravel beach at Playa Granada in southern Spain [32].

A focus of most of the earlier studies was the process by which barriers roll back and more explicitly the conditions under which this happened. Overwashing is essential for the initiation of roll-back and has been investigated in flume experiments (e.g., [33]) and numerical models (e.g., [34]). This had been recognised much earlier and fed into the concept of barrier inertia (BI), which was first proposed in 1995 [15] and quantified for beaches similar to Medmerry (MMR) in 2000 [16]. The Medmerry barrier was covered under this aspect in a dedicated study [35,36] which nevertheless was hampered by the classification of events into overtopping or overwashing events through third party observations and the limited availability of topographic surveys and measured hydrodynamic data. Following laboratory experiments, the boundary conditions for barrier overwashing were simplified in 2008 [37] and in 2013 the original parametrisation was compared with the developing Xbeach-G model [38]. This comparison found that additional information in relation to the depth of the gravel beach toe and the beach slope might improve the BI model. In retrospect, it is striking that the dynamic component of BI, namely the hydrodynamic conditions (wave parameters and water level) appears to have been treated independent of its duration (see also [35] though it is acknowledged that the beach itself changes during a storm). This might be applicable to laboratory conditions where tides are rarely included, micro-tidal coasts or particular barriers like Hurst Spit [30], for which the BI model was developed, which have small tidal ranges (at Hurst the mean spring tide range is 2 m). However, using the maximum hydrodynamic conditions as the variable to test against the barrier geometry may be less applicable to locations with a larger tidal range where conditions an hour or two before the peak of the tide are likely to be more important as it takes some time for a barrier to move from overtopping to overwashing to crest lowering and roll-back in just one tide; for example, it is unlikely for crest lowering to keep pace with the falling tide as the distance over which the crest needs to be lowered and the sediment to be transported to the back increases while the energy to do this work decreases [17].

Studies have also usually focused on individual profiles or uniform laboratory set-ups [39] rather than how and why roll-back may change or progress along a beach and what role legacy structures like groynes might play.

A critical aspect for future coastal management is not just the processes or conditions that lead to roll-back, but the speed and potential (temporary) endpoint following the release from unnatural constraints termed coastal catch-up. This process has been recognised for some time in relation to coastal (cliff) erosion where it is said to constitute "a rapid (probably non-linear) catch-up process, i.e., the cliff reassuming its position had defences not existed by initially eroding at a rate much faster than the natural rate" [40]. The same should apply to barrier roll-back, in particular if the previously managed high barrier crest is over-washed soon after a change in management and thus makes successive overwashing more likely due to the reduced crest height [41].

Finally, a limitation of many previous studies has been the lack of high frequency spatio-temporal topographic data covering several storm events, thus often focussing on a very small number of events (often just one) for one site or profile (e.g., [31,38,42]) or having difficulty in attributing processes to individual driving conditions [36].

Recently, sites with higher spatio-temporal survey resolution have become available [21,43] and the present study is an extension of this early work at Medmerry. As such the paper addresses the following questions:

1. What is the profile response to changing hydrodynamic conditions and exposure of underlying geology?
2. How is profile response changing along the coast?
3. How are points 1 and 2 linked to the alongshore transport of beach material?
4. Is Barrier Inertia still a useful concept at high temporal resolution of events and how useful is it as a predictive tool?

Following an introduction to the study site (Section 2) and a description of the data and methodology in Section 3, the paper starts out by documenting beach volume changes of the MMR site and along the downdrift frontage to create a sediment budget (Section 4.1). This provides a framework for assessment of individual cross-shore profile response through time (Section 4.2) and alongshore progression of barrier roll-back (Section 4.3). The role of hydrodynamic conditions in profile ontogeny (Section 4.4) is explored first in broader terms before it is applied to the Barrier Inertia concept (Section 4.5). The wider impact of the findings and potential future research are given in Section 5 with the conclusion in Section 6.

2. Site

Medmerry is located on the mainland east of the Isle of Wight near the centre of the English south coast (Figure 1). It forms a 1.5 km long section of the 12 km long shingle) barrier/fringing beach between Selsey Bill and the East Head sand spit. 'Shingle' is used in this paper as the local description of a gravel and pebble dominated mixed sediment (up to ~30% of sediment < 2 mm) upper beach that terminates with a distinct break of slope (or toe) in the intertidal fronted by a sub-horizontal intertidal sand covered platform at that extends into the sub-tidal Historically, the back barrier marsh was connected with Pagham Harbour, leaving Selsey as a slightly raised island of Quaternary raised beach deposits. Erosion of this previously more extensive island contributed to the barrier beaches either side of Selsey Bill sealing off the low lying channel and promoting sedimentation. As a consequence, the marsh area behind the shingle barrier ranges in elevation from ~1.5 to 3 mOD (Figure 2). The increasing management requirements due to regular overtopping and overwashing (details in [35]) to maintain the shingle barrier at Medmerry led to a large open-coast Managed Realignment project creating 183 ha intertidal habitats within a site of 400 ha contained between two rock arms at the beach and connected by a clay embankment following the landscape contours. Details about the Medmerry Managed Realignment (MMR) project are given in Maplesden [44]. In August 2013, a cut was made through the shingle barrier and the underlying marsh sediment to establish a tidal breach channel with no further management of the shingle beach except for the removal of redundant and life-expired timber groynes and some limited sediment movement on the west beach in 2014. The design of the cut dimensions was primarily concerned with the breach stability and the avoidance of closure under varying longshore transport rates and morphological evolution inside the site [45].

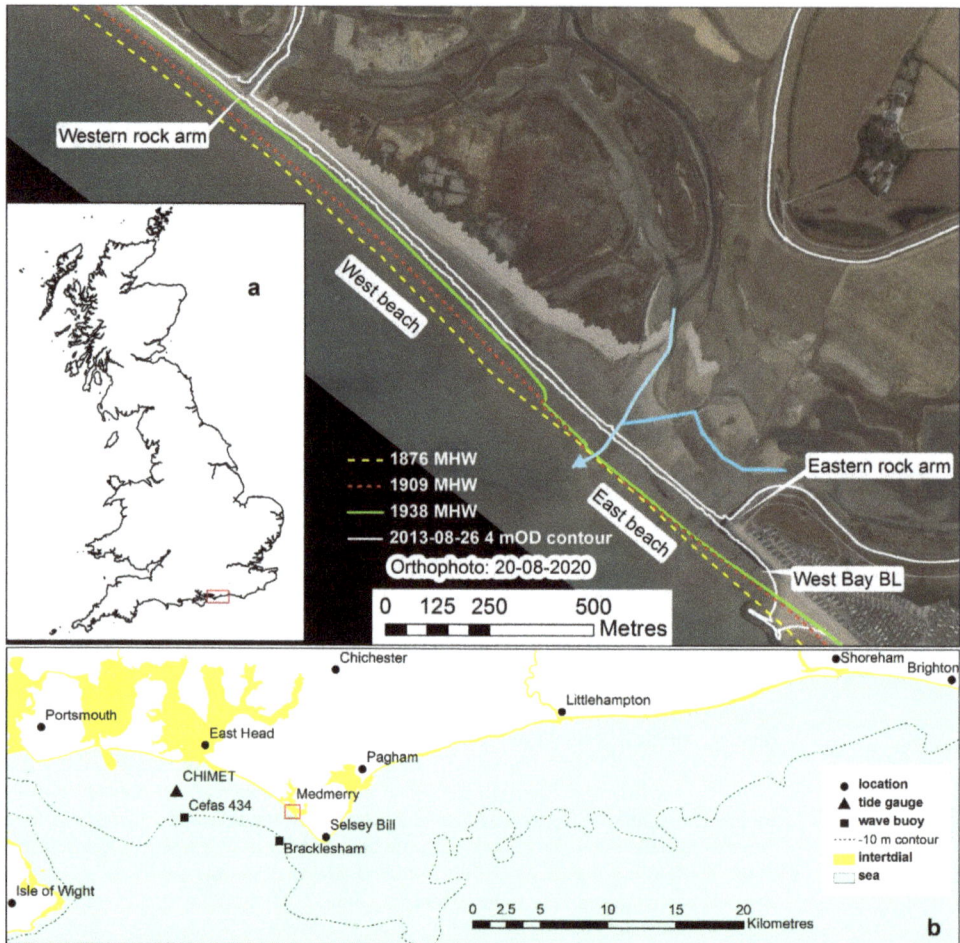

Figure 1. Overview of the study location in southern UK (**a**) and within a regional setting (**b**). Main map shows the 4 mOD contour prior to breach, marking the front and rear of the shingle barrier and the inside of the earth bund as the landward edge of the Managed Realignment site. Additionally, shown are historic Mean High Water (MHW) lines digitised from Ordnance Survey maps and the light blue line tracing the dug breach and drainage channels. The background aerial photo was flown on 20 August 2020 at low tide highlighting the displacement of the light coloured shingle barrier and some of the locations mentioned in the text.

Updrift (southeast) of the MMR site, a private (Bunn Leisure) scheme was completed in 2012 to protect a large caravan site [46]. This scheme provides a shingle beach fixed between two nearshore detached breakwaters. As a consequence, no sediment from east of the western Bunn Leisure breakwater is entering the study site, however, the bay west of this western breakwater and east of the eastern MMR rock arm (visible towards the southern boundary in Figure 1) was designed as an equilibrium bay that was anticipated to lose part of its beach recharge over time.

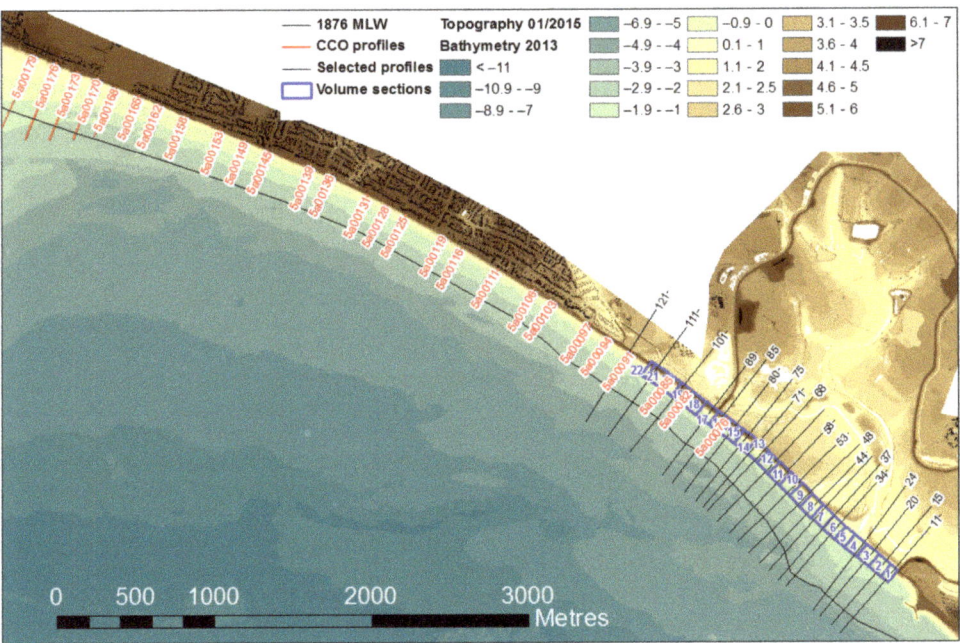

Figure 2. Overview of the frontage including swath bathymetry collected in the summer of 2013, LIDAR survey from 24 January 2015. Black profile lines were selected from the 20 m profile lines extracted from DEMs focussing on the MMR frontage between the rock arms and red profile lines are based on dedicated profile surveys and extracted from DEMs covering an overlapping area west of the western rock arm and further west.

Downdrift (northwest) of the MMR site, the shingle barrier continues for 1 km in the same shape and with the same hinterland elevation as inside the MMR site (Figure 2). From there, the hinterland rises a few metres above Highest Astronomical Tide and as a consequence is lined for the next 4 km with coastal properties and a timber groyne field to contain the shingle beach. Over the remaining 3 km from Profile 5a00179 (Figure 2) to East Head, sand from the Chichester Harbour ebb delta dominates the beach and widening foreshore towards the harbour entrance.

Mean spring tide range is 4.5 m at Selsey Bill, decreasing to 4 m at the entrance to Chichester Harbour placing the Mean High Water Springs contour at ~2.2 to 2.25 mOD. The 1 in 1 year significant wave height at the Bracklesham directional wave rider is 3.74 m (2008–2019) with annual maximum Hs over the last 11 years ranging between 3.28 and 4.47 m; the dominant wave direction is between 195° and 225° [47] against a pre-breach shoreline orthogonal between the MMR rock arms of 225°. Therefore, the beach is almost swash-aligned [48], especially considering wave refraction over the shallow sub-horizontal intertidal and subtidal topography. Apart from wind waves generated in the English Channel, the frontage is influenced by Atlantic swell and waves with bi-modal frequency distribution [49]. Longshore transport has been calculated and estimated in several studies ranging from measurements from maps to tracer studies of up to several tens of thousands of cubic metres per year. A review in 2004 [50] of various values from the grey literature settles on "A present day mean actual drift volume of between 2800 and 7000 m^3 per year" which is broadly in line with the 2000 m^{3}y^{-1} suggested by Cope in 2005 [36] for the 'net drift of shingle' towards the northwest, However, both sources fail to clarify to which part of this frontage the values apply, but the lower values support the notion of the barrier being almost swash-aligned.

2.1. Historic Changes and Design Predictions

It is thought that the barrier developed in the 6th to 7th century linking the Island of Selsey with higher ground at Bracklesham to the NW. The barrier has been subject to storms and roll-back for centuries and over the last decades, overwashing has been reported on several occasions, for example in 1910, and evidence of bulldozers pushing overwashed material back to the crest in 1950 was observed [51]. "*Analysis of Tithe maps and Ordnance Survey maps has shown that mean rate of recession of the High Water Mark between 1672 and 1932 has varied from 1.0 to 1.4 m per annum*" [52]. Some historic water lines from Ordnance Survey maps are shown in Figure 1, however, a more detailed account of their movement and any defence structures can be found in [43]. Between 1876 and 1896, MHW moved landwards by approximately 30 m which is equivalent to 1.5 my^{-1}. In the following decades, different structures were installed at different times but essentially those areas still free to retreat did so at a rate of 1.4 my^{-1}. Since at least 1950 [51], the entire frontage has been stabilised by groynes, reprofiling and recharges with no further retreat which could equate to a 'retreat need' of ~100 m based on past rates and ~70 years of forced stability.

A range of modelling was carried out for the design of the MMR scheme, and while mainly concerned with the stability of the inlet morphological change of the barrier was also looked at. This can be summarised by the statement that "the beaches appear to remain resilient to storm impacts" [45] and the design length of the rock armour along the rock arms to accommodate 'erosion' of 0.4 to 0.7 my^{-1} over the 50 year design life [53]. With most of the modelling concerned about the breach area, the following scenario was envisaged: "Sediment from the [upstream private scheme] recharge will continue to move (slowly) along the coast in a westerly direction to reach the [. . .] breach site where it is likely that the material will contribute to the formation of an ebb delta and to the sediment accumulations along the eastern shore of the breach site. The ebb delta is likely to slowly grow to a size large enough to allow longshore transport sediment to effectively bypass the inlet opening and accumulate downdrift thus offsetting any erosion that may have occurred as a result of a small reduction of sediment supply immediately after the breach" [45].

3. Data and Methodology

The MMR project included a 5-year monitoring project that carried out frequent topographic surface surveys of the shingle barrier. Initially, these were focused around the breach area but with increasing spread of coastal change the survey area was extended to cover the entire 1.5 km between the rock arms. The frontage to the northwest was only surveyed as parts of the Regional Coastal Monitoring programme [54] with far fewer surveys consisting mainly of surveys along dedicated beach profiles twice a year but also a small number of LIDAR flights.

For the MMR site a total number of 13 LIDAR surveys cover the entire site and 32 ground based topographic surveys of increasing extent are available, covering August 2013 to October 2020. The ground based surveys were carried out at different intervals, often associated with storms or observational reports of coastal change. Topographic surveys were carried out using a Leica C10 terrestrial laser scanner and Global Navigation Satellite System (GNSS) equipment. The static set-up of the scanner was not ideal as the survey area grew along the beach and in the cross-shore direction with view shadows at the back slope of the shingle ridge requiring manual post-survey editing of the data (see below). Vegetation filtering behind the initial shingle barrier was of varying quality. In contrast, the LIDAR surveys provide very reliable data of the bare surface, however, both survey methods to not penetrate to the bottom of water-filled depressions and drainage ditches that started to change early on in the monitoring period when they also became influenced by sedimentation from the beach rolling back into them. Aerial photography was captured annually between 2013 and 2018 and most recently during the summer of 2010 providing additional data for interpreting the change observed in the topographic data.

3.1. Volume Analysis

To distinguish between loss of beach material and historic marsh clay inside the MMR site, it was necessary to reconstruct the historic marsh surface on which the beach was resting in 2013 (see Figure 3 inset). This work was carried out in ArcMap 9.3. Photographic evidence and DEM survey data from the eroding beach suggest that the seaward cliff of the marsh surface was located approximately under the front of the crest prior to breach. The data also show that elevation of that cliff is well represented by the marsh elevation behind the beach (see for example Figure 4 in [43]). In addition, the clay surface seaward of the cliff (or the toe of the marsh cliff) can be inferred to have been about 30 m seawards at a level of −0.7 mOD which equates to a slope of between 1:7.5 and 1:11. From there, the clay surface continues seaward at a slope of 1:50 to 1:60 for ~55 m to cover the spatial extent of interest for this study. From these contours, a 3D model of the underlying clay was created and combined with the LIDAR surveys landward of the shingle beach surveyed pre-breach and the first terrestrial laser scan survey post-breach to account for channels and the dugout portion of the breach area. In the area east of the breach, later LIDAR surveys of the back barrier area were also used to capture the changing location and topography of the drainage network just prior to roll-over. The volume change analysis was carried out by subtracting the marsh surface only from the LIDAR surveys due to their more extensive coverage and better capture of the landward portions of the rolled-back beach.

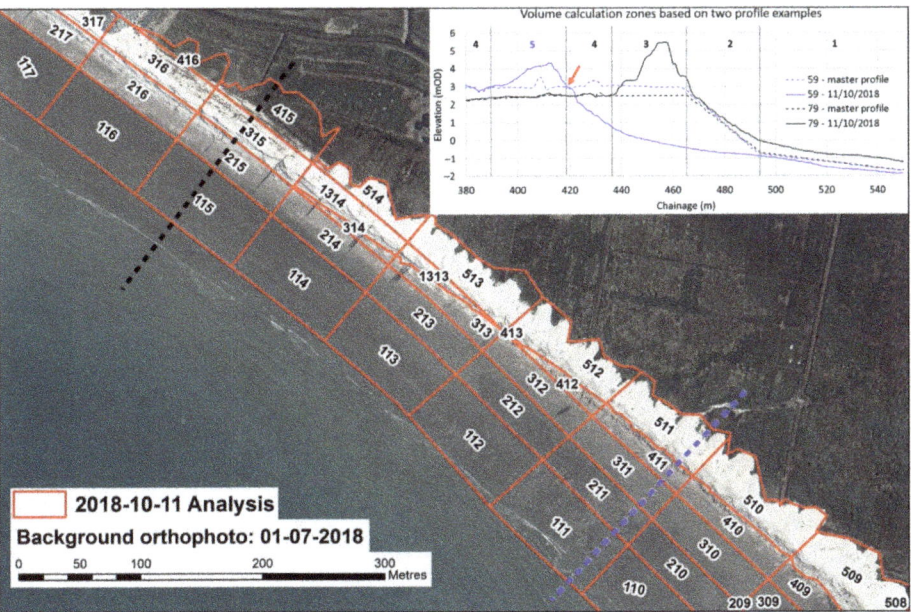

Figure 3. Aerial orthophoto flown on 11 October 2018 showing the western end of the MMR frontage (the western rock arm can be seen in the northwest corner. The red grid shows the 100 m wide alongshore segments (last 2 digits of the number code starting from the eastern rock arm) and the up to five cross-shore segments (first digit). The black and blue lines are the profile positions for profile 59 and 79 shown in the inset for the marsh surface master profile (dotted lines) and the LIDAR survey flown at the same time. Red arrows in the profile plot and on the aerial photo point to the same short length of marsh surface exposed seaward of the shingle beach ridge.

For the downdrift frontage outside the MMR site, only the first ~4.5 km are included (Figure 2), because further downdrift sand takes over as the main beach material so that any volume changes are not representative of the shingle fraction. Far fewer surveys are available for this frontage and not all of them are full DEM surveys but many are simple profile surveys. Therefore, these profiles surveys and profiles extracted from DEMs (red profile codes in Figure 2) were used to assess volume changes by multiplying the changes in Cross Sectional Area (CSA) with the distance between the profiles using the profile analysis tool SANDS [55]. 26 profiles have been used with the distance between profiles varying between 127 m and 315 m with an average distance of 191 m. Inevitably, the derived volumes depend heavily on the accuracy and representativeness of the profile for a length of beach of more than 100 m length. For example, the presence of beach cusps can introduce local variations that may not be representative of the wider beach. In addition, surveys along this stretch have been carried out at different dates for different subsections so that these have been collated into summer and winter surveys which again can introduce variations in the calculated volumes unrelated to actual volume changes; for example, part of the volume in a downdrift subsection surveyed before the updrift subsection could have move into updrift section by the time its survey was carried out.

3.2. Profile Lines, Contour Line Retreat and Cross Sectional Area (CSA)

Profile lines at 20 m alongshore distance where created through all surveys covered by the black profile lines in Figure 2. Profile lines were created by first generating a smoothed line from the 4 mOD contour of the pre-breach survey. Profile lines were then created at right angles to this smoothed line every 20 m extending 500 m land- and seawards. From the profile lines, the position and height of the highest point of the beach ridge was determined as well as the position of various contour lines reflecting the beach and the clay geology. For selected profiles shown in Figure 2 (due to the large manual editing requirements) a master profile of the underlying clay geology was constructed and merged with the pre-breach LIDAR survey using SANDS [55]. Each survey for this profile was then manually edited to remove the topography landwards of the rear shingle toe, and the subtraction of the surveyed profile from the master profile is the CSA of the beach ridge on top of the clay geology (see Figure 3 inset).

3.3. Hydrodynamic Condition and Wave Run-Up

Roll-back of beach barriers is determined by overwashing and overwashing is dependent on the crest height in relation to wave run-up [56] which is a combination of wave parameters, water level and beach properties like grain size, permeability and morphology (e.g., [31,57,58]). Wave data is available for the entire study period at 30 min intervals from the coastal monitoring wave buoy at Bracklesham 2.2 km seawards of the southern end of the MMR site with a bathymetry level of ~−14.7 mOD (Figure 1b). Water level data is taken from the CHIMET station [59] at the entrance to Chichester Harbour ~7.5 km away from the site. Missing records (January to May 2014) have been substituted by using the predicted astronomical tide for the CHIMET station plus the surge component from the tide gauge at Littlehampton 28 km east of CHIMET. Given the magnitude of the wave component during this period difference between this substituted data and measured are likely to be negligent for the analysis in this paper. From the joint 30 min interval time series of waves and water levels, data for the 3 h either side of high tide have been extracted and used in empirical run-up elevation calculations for shingle beaches [60,61].

For the analysis of changes in wave direction pre-and post-breach to put calculated rates of longshore transport in perspective with values from the literature the wave buoy data, which started in August 2008, was supplemented with wave hindcast data available from Cefas [62] for point 434 (Figure 1b).

3.4. Barrier Inertia (BI)

According to [63] $BI = R_C B_A / H_S^3$ where R_C is the distance between the maximum crest level and the still water level, B_A is the cross sectional barrier area above the still water level and H_S the significant wave height taken from the wave buoy. To explore the model of BI, its value was calculated at 30 min intervals from the buoy and tide gauges detailed in 0. Both barrier parameters (R_C and B_A) are based on the survey preceding the hydrodynamic conditions (which might be days or months earlier) with B_A being interpolated from the CSA at 2 mOD and 3.2 mOD based on the still water level. This results in BI values for every 30 min rather than just one for every high tide. Higher BI values indicate stability and lower values indicate overtopping and overwashing. The boundary between theses morphological responses is given in the following equations when BI is plotted against the wave steepness H_S/L_M where $L_M = gT_m^2/2\pi$ and T_m is taken from the wave buoy data (T_z). Two boundaries from the literature have been used (Equation (1), Bradbury (2000) [16] and Equation (2), Obhrai et al. (2008) [37]):

$$\frac{R_C B_A}{H_S^3} < 0.0006 \left(\frac{H_S}{L_M}\right)^{-2.5375} \quad (1)$$

$$\frac{R_C B_A}{H_S^3} < -153.1 \frac{H_S}{L_M} + 10.9 \quad (2)$$

4. Results

4.1. Wider Beach Volume and Sediment Budget

To distinguish between changes to the shingle barrier, the underlying marsh surface, and the intertidal platform, the volume analysis was split into 100 m long sections along the beach and into up to five sections across the beach as illustrated in Figure 3. In the example, the black profile in the inset represents a portion of the shingle barrier (profile 79) that has not yet overwashed by the survey date of 11 October 2018 and the beach profile overlays the master profile marsh surface. Zone 4 is the unchanged marsh surface landward of the shingle barrier; zone 3 is the shingle barrier up to the crest of the underlying marsh surface and represents the bulk of shingle volume in the cross section prior to roll-back; zone 2 is the slope of the marsh surface down to its toe and is overlain by a comparatively thin shingle beach (initially up to ~2 m); zone 1 is the shallow sloping clay platform covered by sand. Once the beach is rolling back (blue line for profile 59), zone 5 delimits the shingle barrier sitting on top of the marsh surface and the then seaward zones represent the areas of erosion of the marsh surface and underlying clay. The blue profile represents this situation showing, at the position of the red arrow in the profile and on the map, where marsh surface (zone 4) crops out for a few metres in front of the shingle barrier. This situation appears to be similar to the barrier 'overstepping' mentioned in Forbes et al. [13], however, the height of the cliff does not preclude sediment to move onto the marsh surface and continue to be part of the rolling-back barrier. While the retreating marsh cliff/seaward slope may be covered with sediment, this was generally found to very thin with clay cropping out on the slope and has been ignored for the volume calculations.

The volume development of these zones is shown in Figure 4. In this figure, the 'shingle ridge' volume is composed of the volumes for zones 5 and the positive volumes of zones 3 and 2 where appropriate. In the example shown in Figure 3 the shingle barrier volume in area x15 includes segment 215 and 315 while in the rolled-backed area x11 it is only in segment 511. In the transition areas x12 to x14 segment, 3xx is split manually along contour lines associated with the elevation of the marsh surface in that area.

The first two surveys shown in Figure 4 (individual surveys are highlighted as dots on the 'shingle ridge' line) capture the pre-breach volumes. The sharp drop from the second to the third survey in autumn 2013 is due to the removal of the shingle ridge (7200 m^3) and underlying marsh and clay (7000 m^3) to create the breach over a length of 150 m. The shingle removed was deposited west of the western rock arm (~1200 m^3) and east of the private scheme (~6000 m^3) and thus outside of any future relevance for this study. The clay and silt was used onsite.

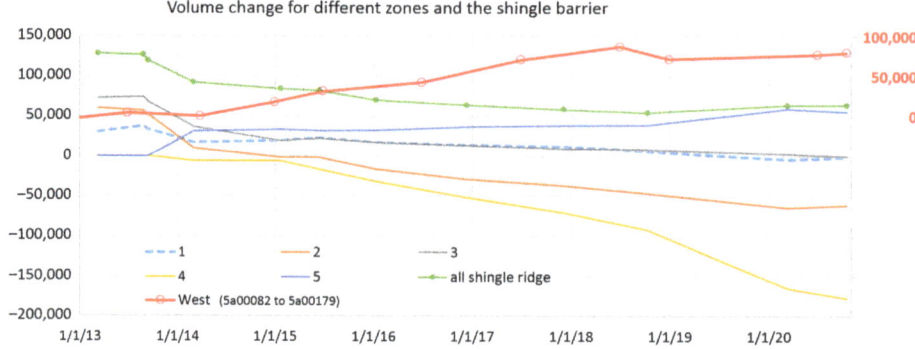

Figure 4. Change in beach volume over time for different beach zones in MMR (left hand y-axis). For location of beach segments in the cross-shore direction see Figure 3. Right hand y-axis for the change in volume west of MMR compared to the summer 2013 volume.

The shallow intertidal foreshore (zone 1) has changed very little over the last 7 years in contrast to any of the other zones. This confirms for a much larger area and longer time scale the initial findings in [43] that elevation changes at the low water line are small in absolute terms and in relation to other contour lines. Zones 2, 3 and 4, representing the marsh sediment and clay, have lost a total of 445,000 m^3. The rate of loss has been steady, though sector 4 shows a significantly larger dip over the winter 2019/20. The rolled-back shingle ridge zone (zone 5) shows a gradual increase following the initial larger increase over the winter 2013/14 when the entire east beach had rolled back and shingle recurves on both sides along the channel had formed. However, taking all sediment in the mobile shingle beach into account, it has lost 55,000 m^3 following the breach in August 2013.

Neither roll-back nor the exposure of underlying geology has occurred on the downdrift frontage west of MMR, so here the entire volume change relates to the mobile shingle sediment. Taking the summer 2013 volume as the baseline for this frontage, Figure 4 also includes the volume development for the frontage west of MMR on the secondary y-axis showing a total increase of 80,000 m^3 over the last 7 years. Figure 5 shows the volumes in a stacked chart suggesting that the total volume of the combined frontages has remained stable or increased slightly, i.e., as the original barrier beach inside MMR (red line) loses material to the downdrift frontage (black line) or into the increasing rolled-back barrier (green line), the total volume is largely maintained. However, the MMR frontage has lost 55,000 m^3 in comparison to the 80,000 m^3 gain of the downdrift frontage.

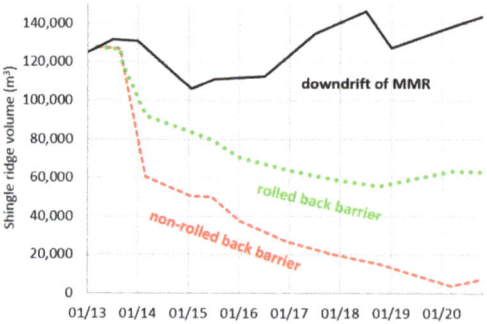

Figure 5. Stacked beach volume over time. Volumes for the non-rolled-back and rolled-back barrier (segments 3xx and 5xx in Figure 3) plus the shingle barrier volume west of MMR. Volumes are stacked so that the black solid line represents the total volume for MMR and the frontage to the west.

From a total volume budget perspective, the 'missing' 25,000 m³ can be accounted for by the loss from the western bay of the private Bunn Leisure scheme (see 'West Bay BL' in Figure 1). Over the winter 2013/14 (between the surveys on 26 August 2013 and 30 March 2014), the beach placed in 2012 in an equilibrium bay shape associated with average wave conditions lost 19,500 m³ due to more southerly waves and the readjustment of the bay shape. While this nearly balances out the sediment budget over the 7 year period, this substantial pulse of sediment cannot be detected in Figure 4 or Figure 5.

A major point of uncertainty of the volume calculations are the assumptions of seaward extent and slope of the marsh sediments under the barrier as these have not been surveyed on first exposure. Given the MMR frontage is 1.5 km long, a volume of 20,000 m³ equates to 13.3 m³m^{-1}. With the marsh cliff 2 m to 3.5 m high, the volume of 20,000 m³ can reflect a difference of the marsh cliff position of between 6.7 m and 3.8 m which is quite possible. Therefore, if the marsh cliff had been further seaward than its assumed position, some of the 20,000 m³ could have substituted the eroded clay. The other uncertainty concerns the infill of the breach and dug tidal channels landwards. As these areas contain water during laser scan surveys, changes in the depth of the channel cannot be recorded and the inlet and central channel areas have been masked out from the analysis based on this uncertainty. That sediment temporarily 'disappeared' into channels can be seen in aerial photos and the survey data on the east beach (Figure 6). This material, at least in part, appears to emerge again as can be seen in Figure 1 landwards of the drainage channel and is suggested in Figure 5 by the slight increase in the MMR barrier volume.

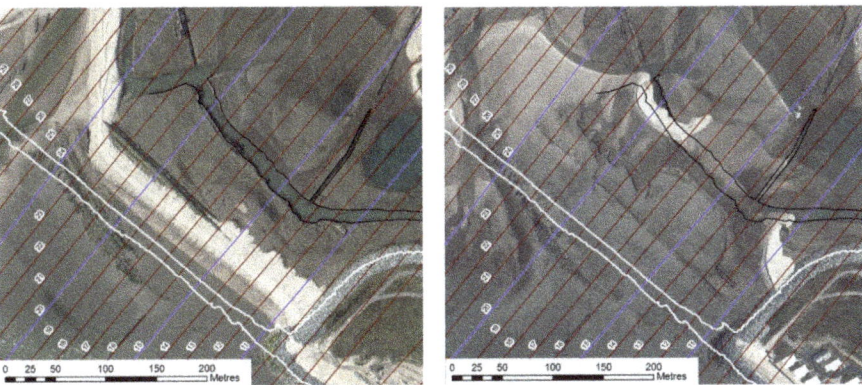

Figure 6. Position of the east beach barrier on 26 August 2013 (white lines are the 4 mOD contour at the front and the back) overlain over low tide orthophotos from June 2015 (**left**) and July 2018 (**right**) showing infilling of the main outfall channel (black lines) from the eastern leaf of the MMR site. Additionally, shown are the numbered profile lines.

Figure 7a breaks down the volume change for the frontage west of MMR into the spatio-temporal components. As volumes between profiles vary due to the distance between them, Figure 7a shows the volume change as a percentage of the summer 2013 volume. It shows relative stability at the eastern end (profiles 82–111)—though the three most easterly profiles have seen some small gain—and only in the last year profiles 82 and 85 have started to experience a loss. On the other hand, between profiles 111 and 165 the increase seen prior to breach continued more pronounced from 2013 both increasing the volume of individual profiles but also spreading the increase to more profiles, particularly downdrift where between 165 and 179 an initial loss persisted for several years but where all profiles are now at least slightly above the 2013 volumes. Figure 7b shows total volume changes between individual LIDAR surveys for the MMR frontage. The removal of shingle from the breach can be seen in the survey on 12 September 2013 for segment 5. At the end of the severe winter 2013/14, losses have been high from segments 6 to 8 with some of these losses most likely responsible for the gain in segment 5 by drawing sediment into the recurve along the eastern side of the outflow channel. Following this initial change, the most important pattern is shown on the west beach where major temporary sediment loss progresses westwards with time followed by volume stability, that is, once the beach has rolled back onto the marsh surface the volume remains largely stable.

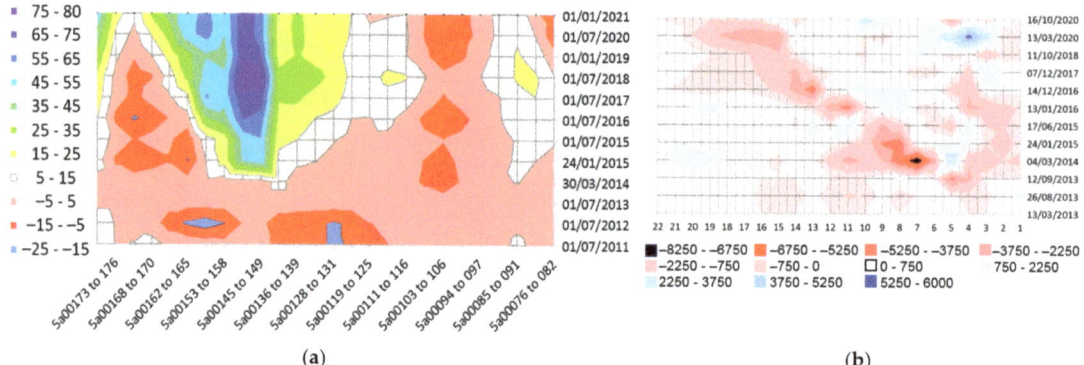

Figure 7. (a) Volume change at each profile downdrift of MMR as a percentage in comparison to the 2011 volume. (b) Beach volume change in m³ between surveys for the MMR frontage.

Compared with previous estimates of longshore transport, the loss of 55,000 m³ from the MMR frontage would equate to an average of ~7800 m³y^{-1} passing the western rock arm in a northwesterly direction; adding the loss from the Bunn Leisure scheme or using the gain on the frontage west of the MMR scheme would result in ~11,400 m³y^{-1}. This is higher than rates suggested from studies in the early 2000s and primarily due to the particularly stormy winter 2013/14 [64] resulting in a loss of 27,000 m³ (Figure 5) or nearly half the loss over the entire 7 years. Taking the remaining loss since that winter, the average rate drops to a more comparable rate of ~5600 m³y^{-1} which nevertheless is still double the rate suggested more recently [36]. It is likely that this relates to the fact that the entire post-breach period was experiencing a higher percentage of higher waves than during either the 5 years pre-breach based on the wave buoy (see also [65]), or compared to the 20 years prior to 2000, on which the literature value is based, based on the hindcast wave data (Figure 8). In addition, groynes were largely still functional prior to 2010 on the MMR site which led to a lower rate of longshore transport than the essentially open, ungroyned beach following the breach.

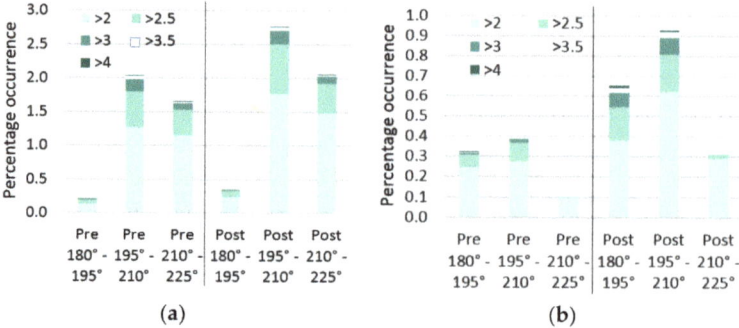

Figure 8. Percentage occurrence of wave height for different directional sectors: (a) Bracklesham wave buoy, where 'Pre' data relates to the period August 2008 to July 2013 and 'Post' covers August 2013 to July 2020, (b) Cefas hindcast point 434 where 'Pre' data relates to the period January 1980 to December 1999 and 'Post' covers August 2013 to December 2019.

4.2. Profile Response

Section 4.1 (see also inset in Figure 3) has highlighted that the primary process occurs in the cross-shore direction with the beach ridge rolling back over the back barrier marsh. Figure 9 shows profile 71 as an example (some additional examples can be found in [43]). The profile change can be described in modification and expansion of the five 'response categories' in [16]:

- 'overtopping and crest raising' illustrated between 26 August 2013 and 10 January 2014, which also moved the maximum crest elevation seaward,
- 'barrier face erosion and accretion' illustrated between 10 January 2014 and 13 January 2016,
- 'overwashing with small scale crest retreat' illustrated between 13 January 2016 and 09 August 2016, and between 11 January 2017 and 17 March 2017,
- 'large scale overwashing with crest destruction and overwash fan' illustrated between 12 October 2017 and 07 December 2017, which in this case did not move the highest crest point, though it changed from being at the back of the crest to the front,
- 'crest build-up with crest advance' between 07 December 2017 and 11 October 2018 and
- 'large scale overwashing with full roll-back' between 15 October 2019 and 13 March 2020.

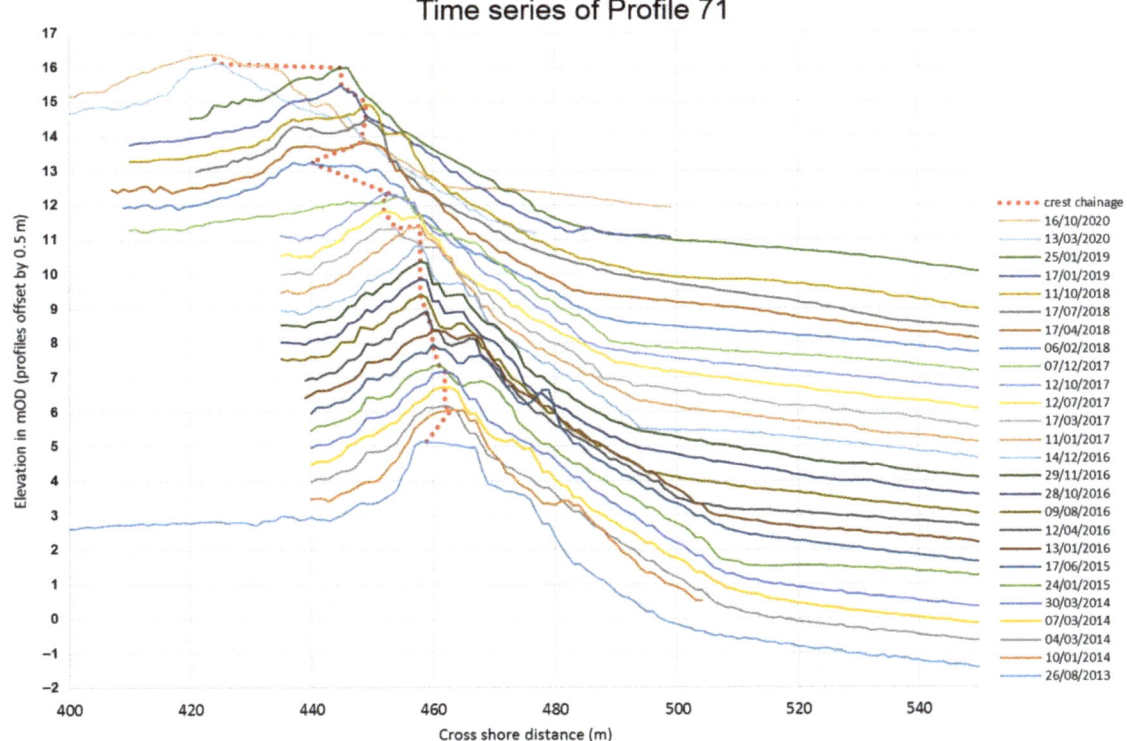

Figure 9. Cross-shore profile example for profile 71 showing profiles offset vertically by 0.5 m for better identification of each profile. As an example the calculated maximum crest position and elevation for each profile is also shown by the red dotted line.

The only response not shown by this profile is one of crest lowering due to cut back of a landward sloping crest because the starting crests were either generally horizontal or sloping seawards like profile 71. However, an example of this response (though some overtopping and sediment deposition on the rear slope did occur) can be seen in Figure 10.

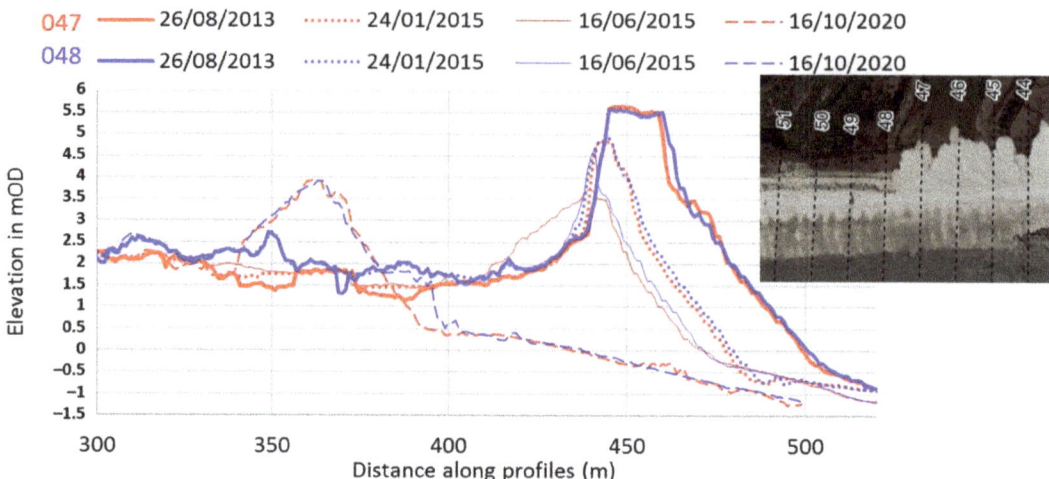

Figure 10. Comparison of 2 profiles 20 m apart showing synchronous and asynchronous behaviour together with the plan-shape change (inset) at this temporary processes boundary. Inset shows the beach (rotated by 45° from north) on 18 June 2015 showing both profiles and their neighbours. Additionally, note the beach cusps with a wave length of ~8 m.

However, it is important to bear in mind that the surveys are not pre- and post-event surveys and are often several months apart so that they were shaped by multiple events and processes. Along the entire frontage these 'evolutionary steps' or response categories happened in different locations at different times. Figure 10 shows an example of the neighbouring profiles 47 and 48 which are just 20 m apart. Both profiles started out almost identical and underwent almost identical changes over 17 months of barrier face erosion, with mild overwashing and crest lowering. However, the storm on 20 February 2015 removed only more of the beach face leaving a very narrow ridge standing in profile 48 while at profile 47, it resulted in a major overwash event that reduced the crest height by up to 1.2 m and created a 28 m long overwash fan. As the inset in Figure 10 shows, an almost continuous overwash fan extends from profile 47 eastwards, while none is visible at profile 48 and westwards. However, this asynchroneity was only short-lived and for example the latest survey in October 2020 shows the two profiles to be as similar as two profiles 20 m apart might be expected to be. For example, 48 shows some of the original marsh surface on the beach side while 47 does not, yet the beach ridge is almost identical.

On a previously managed frontage like Medmerry legacy structures provide spatial focus for overwashing and crest lowering. It is well known that groynes can increase wave height towards the upper beach either through simply funnelling oblique waves along its updrift face or through more complicated process interactions [66] leading to outflanking pressure. In the case of Medmerry, the timber groynes carry on through the barrier and re-appear on the back slope. This is captured in the ground photos in Figure 11. In addition, shoreline perturbations introduced by groynes may incite resonance along the beach and create beach cusps (see profile 49 in Figure 10 inset which runs across a groyne located in a cusp embayment) that have been found to act as initial pathways for overwashing [11]. However, even without these legacy structures beach cusps form readily along the frontage due to the frequency of bimodal-frequency or swell wave conditions [49].

Figure 11. (**Left**) Photo along groyne between profiles 53 and 54 taken on 18 February 2014 showing overwashing guided by the groyne; (**Right**) Photo looking west along the access path behind the barrier with overwash fan along profile 42 behind the groyne. Arrows point to the landward termination of the groynes. Photo taken following the February 2014 storms.

While most profile responses described can happen under stable CSA within a profile as a function of more extreme hydrodynamic conditions in a flume [56,67], the profile analysis suggests that for the roll-back observed and the corresponding hydrodynamic conditions, reduction in CSA was a pre-requisite and is covered in more detail in Section 4.4.

4.3. Alongshore Progression of Roll-Back

To assess the roll-back progression along the frontage as suggested in Figures 1 and 10 a number of indicators have been explored including the maximum height and position of the crest (illustrated in Figure 9 and shown in Figure 12), the position of a range of seaward contours (illustrated for the 3 mOD contour in Figure 13 and the 1 mOD contour in Figure 14), the width of the crest at certain contours and the CSA of the shingle beach component (Figure 15c). The vegetation line recently explored along the Cley barrier [21] was not deemed suitable as it would have reduced the temporal resolution to annual and the extent of overwash fans (that determine the vegetation line) could not be extracted with any certainty from the survey data.

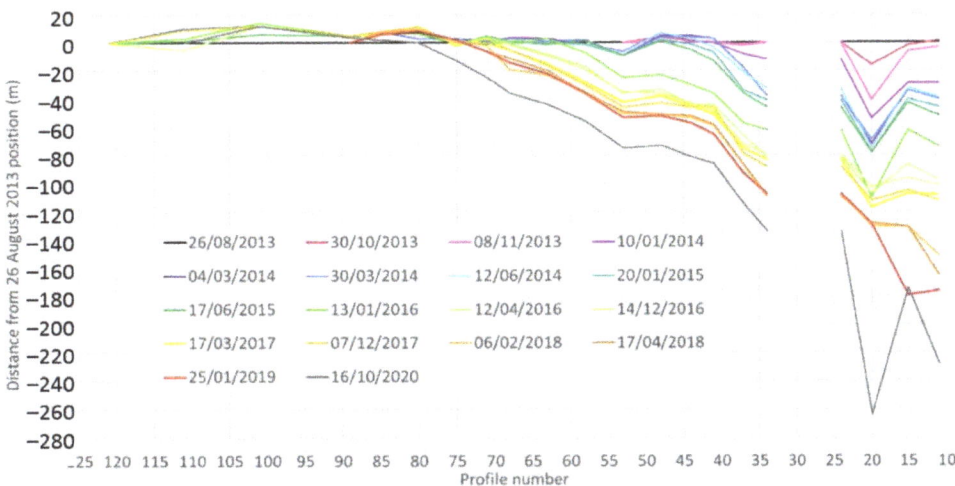

Figure 12. Position of the maximum crest elevation in relation to the starting position on 26 August 2013 for selected surveys and selected profiles from east (right hand side) to west (left hand side). For profile locations see Figure 2.

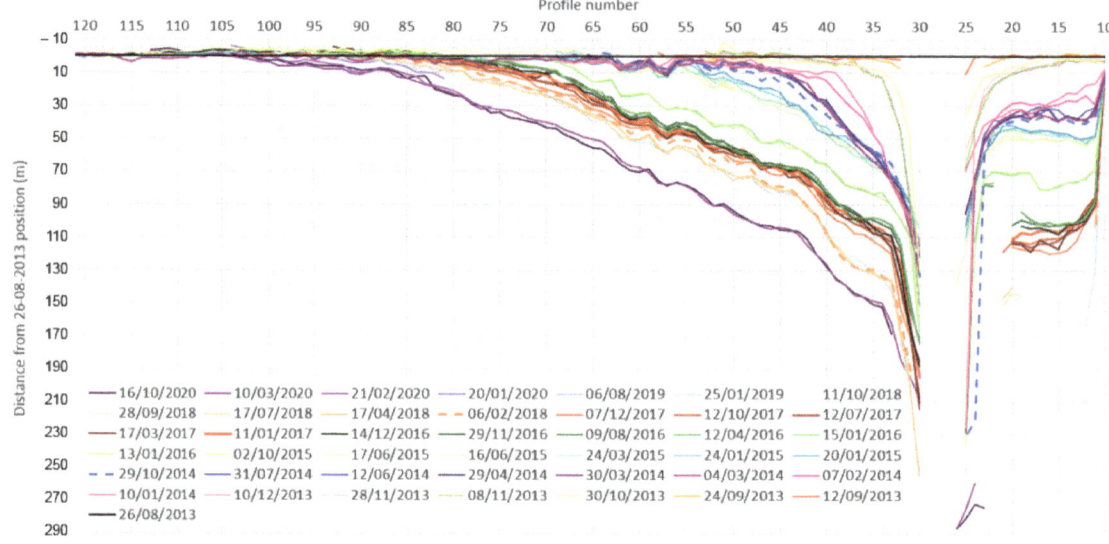

Figure 13. Position of the 3 mOD contour on the seaward side of the shingle barrier for all surveys at all profiles 20 m apart.

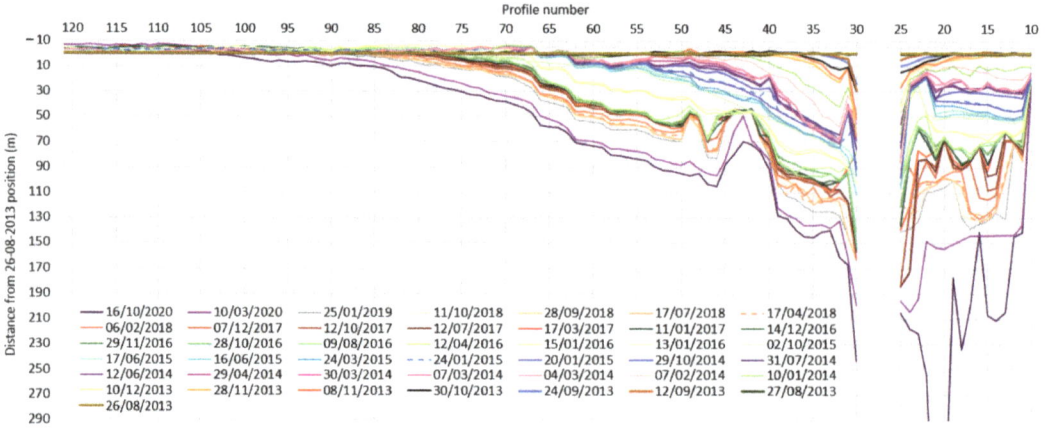

Figure 14. Position of the 1 mOD contour on the seaward side of the shingle barrier representing the position of the lower beach and the marsh cliff where it is exposed for all surveys at all profiles 20 m apart.

Figure 12 shows the alongshore change of the position of the maximum crest elevation for selected surveys and profiles. As already indicated in Figure 9, the position of the maximum crest elevation may not capture cross-shore development due to the possibility of the maximum crest elevation remaining in the same position while the crest has lowered and overwashing has occurred. However, the general development suggests that the east beach rolled back faster than the eastern end of the west beach, that there are periods of rapid change, more gradual change or no change which appear to happen simultaneously on both sides of the breach and that roll-back is progressing westwards, though some western areas have experienced seaward advance of the crest prior to cut-back and roll-back.

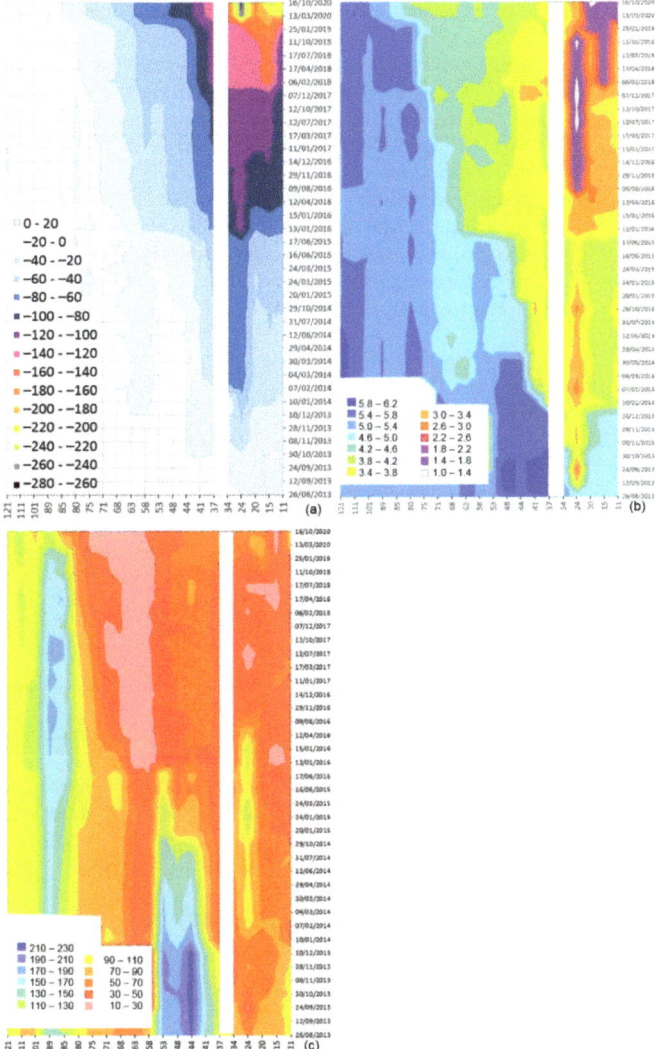

Figure 15. Distance of the maximum crest height position in relation to that on 26 August 2013 (**a**), maximum crest elevation (**b**) and CSA (**c**) for all surveys and selected profiles. The white area between profiles 24 and 34 represents the breach and channel area splitting the graphs into the shorter east beach and the longer west beach. The western rock arm is located between profiles 80 and 85. Note that the time axis does not have equal intervals and that the legend in panels (**b**,**c**) covers profiles which were not surveyed on these dates.

Overall, the reduced data shows a very similar development to that shown in Figure 13 for the 3 mOD contour based on all profiles (20 m spacing) and almost all surveys (only three surveys with almost identical results have been removed). The 3 mOD contour was chosen because it is higher than the marsh surface behind so is not capturing the marsh cliff when exposed and it is low enough to capture shingle accumulations that do not stand high above the marsh surface. However, it does not capture the disintegration of the east beach following the winter 2017/18 very well (see also Figure 1). At the most eastern profile (profile 11), retreat is lagging behind compared with those profiles towards the centre of the east beach because of wave energy dissipation along the side of the western rock arm (e.g., [68]). Contact between beach and the eastern rock arm was eventually lost after January 2019 as can also be seen in Figure 1. Landward movement has been most rapid and started immediately following the breach either side of the breach channel reaching more than 100 m inland within a year after the breach and now extends more than 200 m inland along the recurves from the east and west beach. This led initially to a sharp change in orientation which over time, especially visible on the west beach, changed to a much more gradual change in alignment with an almost straight alignment from the western point at which roll-back is starting to occur to within ~80 m of the channel (see also Figure 1). Within this nearly straight line are a number of 'steps' with the most pronounced around profiles 42 and 43, where the back barrier marsh surface remains in its most seaward position (Figures 14 and 16).

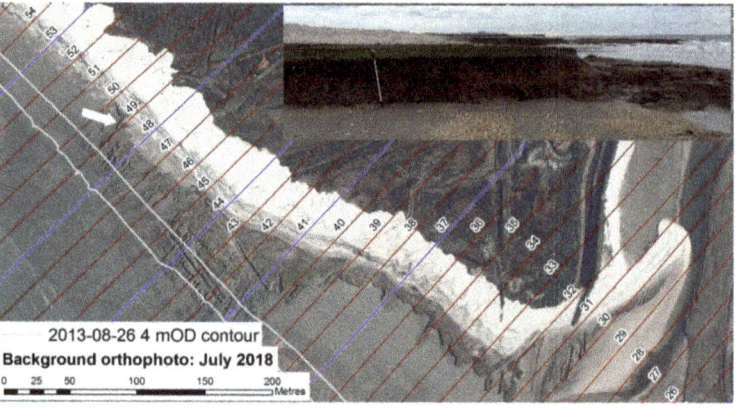

Figure 16. View of the eastern end of the west beach highlighting areas where the back barrier marsh surface crops out extensively. Inset shows a view eastwards towards profile 49 (white arrow on map) showing a 1 m high cliff, taken on 12 October 2020. The white lines show the front and back of the crest pre-breach as in Figure 1 for reference.

While Figure 16 provides an illustration of the area of marsh surface cropping out in front of the barrier, Figure 14 shows the positional change through time using the 1 mOD contour that best represents the cliff of the marsh surface when exposed on the seaward side of the barrier in direct comparison with the position of the 3 mOD contour in Figure 13. The east beach initially retreated parallel up to 2016 following which an embayment formed at profile 14 and then widened westwards to profile 17 until the beginning of 2018. In the winter 2018/19, the retreating bay captured the main outflow channel for the eastern area of the MMR site with associated further rapid erosion of the marsh surface. At the eastern end of west beach, first signs of the more resistant marsh surface cropping out can be seen at profile 40 in March 2014. This small area of resistance has disappeared by spring 2015, starts developing again in the winter 2015/16 between profiles 39 to 51 and in the following focusses on profiles 40 to 45.

Figure 15 shows heat maps for the spatio-temporal ontogeny of the position and height of the maximum crest elevation and the CSA for selected profiles. The position of the maximum crest height shows a very similar pattern to the position of contour lines except that the original crest was an engineered sub-horizontal feature. This resulted in the maximum elevation being anywhere between the front and rear of this feature. This could lead to a change from the rear to the front through small-scale overtopping and deposition on the front edge or a change from the front to the rear through only small-scale erosion of the front edge. However, once overwashing and roll-back had started, the maximum height of the crest reflects better the behaviour of the barrier. The maximum elevation of the barrier

(Figure 15b) shows for each profile times of stability or gradual change and abrupt drops associated with major overwashing events. On the east beach, these started immediately after the breach, progressing eastwards with a drop of >1 m in the winter 2013/14 all along the east beach. From winter 2017/18, the crest has largely disappeared from the east beach. On the west beach, the abrupt drop in maximum crest elevation progresses westwards through time. Once dropped, levels are generally lower from approximately east of profile 53 which coincides with the frontage where the marsh surface crops out in front of the barrier. This would suggest that while the outcrop is not reducing the impact of waves during severe events to reduce crest height and roll back of the barrier, it reduces the ability of waves during smaller events to build the crest up again due to the discontinuity of sediment (as suggested in the case of barrier overstepping [13]) or impact on wave breaking and shoaling. Finally, CSA values in August 2013 were different along the frontage due to the different level of the underlying marsh surface (see Figure 2) and different crest levels (Figure 15b). This difference has been largely maintained as CSA reduced over time to levels of 10 to 30 m^2 for the profiles with low starting CSAs and 50 to 70 m^2 for profiles with higher starting CSAs. Similar to previous figures, Figure 15c shows the change progressing from the breach westwards on the west beach and from the breach eastwards on the east beach during the first year. As roll-back conserves shingle barrier CSA, changes observed must relate to the longshore loss of sediment described in Section 4.1.

4.4. Overwashing Conditions

To assess the hydrodynamic conditions that drive the cross-shore response, run-up has been calculated for all conditions. Conditions that created a run-up to higher than 4 mOD have been plotted in Figure 17 for selected profiles together with the water level, Tz and Tp, CSA, crest elevation and position of the 3 mOD contour. It is clear from the Tp plot that almost all run-up events had a swell component which has been demonstrated to create higher overwash volumes [30]. When comparing crest elevations with run-up elevations one needs to bear in mind that the run-up calculations used are based on the assumptions of a typical beach in Southeast England, that is, similar to the barrier at the time of breach. Roll-back of the barrier creates longer and shallower slopes (see Figure 10) which introduces more shoaling related energy loss [69] that reduces run-up at the rolled back position compared to the pre-breach position. The comparison between run-up and crest elevation is therefore more appropriate for the conditions when the barrier was close to its pre-breach location than at later stages in the roll-back process. Figure 17 shows the similarities and differences between profile ontogeny within the MMR site.

Profile 15 in the centre of east beach changed almost immediately following the breach in autumn 2013 by decreasing the CSA and retreating the beach face in particular during the first November storms. Run-up during the storm in January 2014 exceeded the maximum crest height and together with a narrowed crest, led to crest lowering of about 1 m and roll-back of the crest by 20 metres. Further storms in early 2014 rolled the crest further back but maintained crest elevation and CSA. The winter 2014/15 had a number of storms that primarily reduced CSA, rolled back the beach and gradually lowered the crest. With CSA reduced from the breach condition of ~80 m^2 to ~40 m^2, the storms in the winter 2015/16 drove the beach another 50 m landwards lowering the maximum crest level to 3 mOD. Winter 2015/16 only saw a few events that still rolled the barrier back but otherwise had little impact. The storm in January 2017 lowered the crest to below 2 mOD and thus below the storm still water level. Essentially, the CSA of <30 m^2 reflects the infilling with shingle of the drainage channel that ran behind the east beach and thus does not reflect a surface projecting shingle ridge. No new ridge has reformed along this profile line in the past 3 years though Figure 1 shows shingle 'regrouping' landwards of the drainage channel.

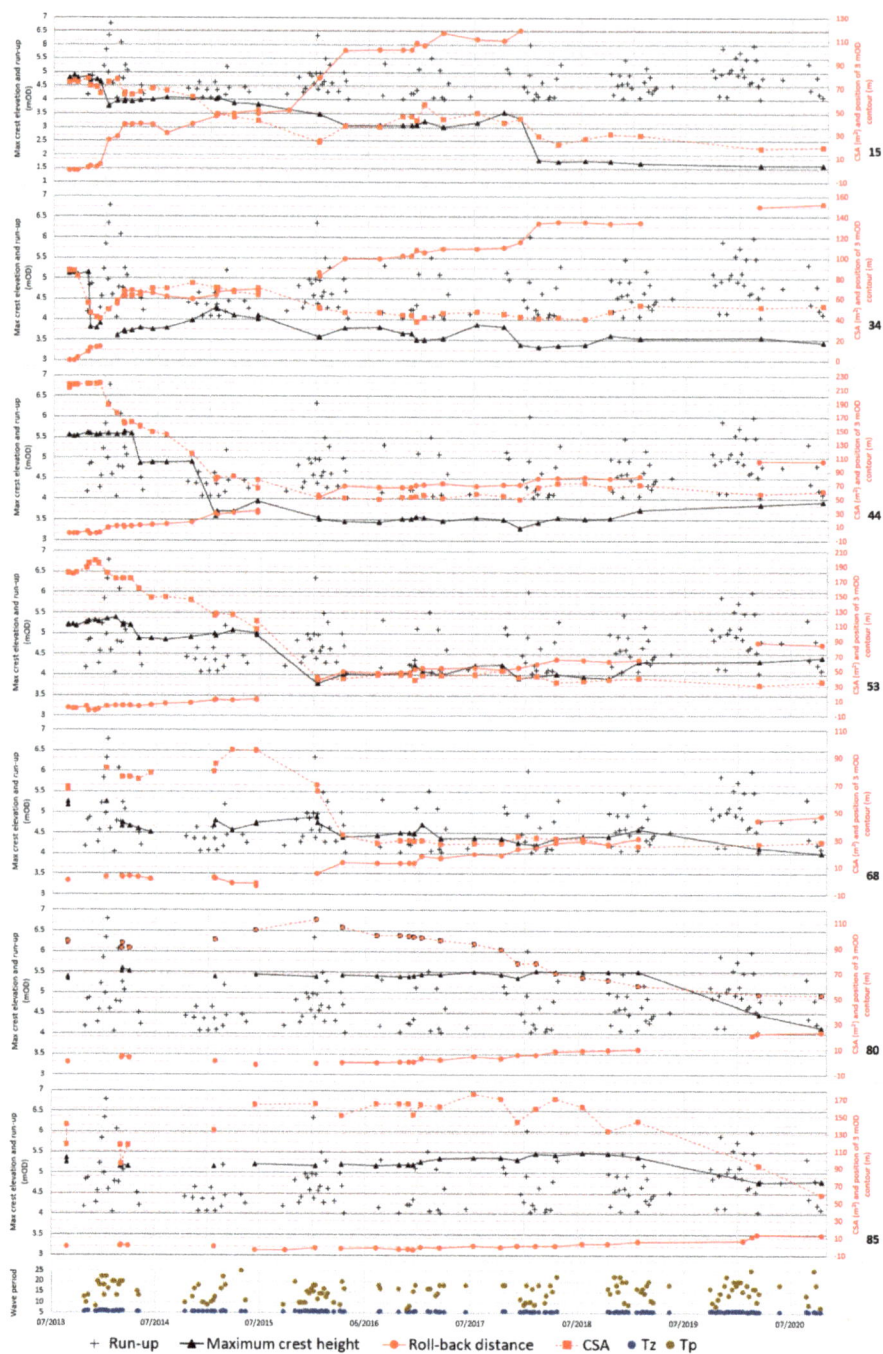

Figure 17. Time series of wave run-up (markers are the maximum value per calendar week), maximum height of crest (both on the left *y*-axis), CSA and position of the seaward 3 mOD contour in relation to the pre-breach position where positive values indicate erosion (both on the right *y*-axis). The bottom panel shows Tz and Tp coincident with wave run-up value. Black numbers on the right hand side are the profile numbers.

Profile 34 lies almost opposite profile 15 on the west beach. It is the easternmost profile that is not affected by the recurve into the MMR site channel and thus allows for an investigation into shore parallel roll-back. Figure 15b shows a decrease in CSA and retreat of the beach face immediately following the breach and prior to the first November storm which, despite having run-up levels lower than the crest level and not having caused any change in profile 15, lowered the crest by >1 m, rolled back the beach by ~10 m and reduced the CSA by 20 m². This loss of CSA has most likely been the result of sediment having been driven into the breach prior to the storm rather than being lost alongshore towards the west. It shows that the reduction in CSA through longshore transport can weaken the barrier to the point of roll-back even without the hydrodynamic conditions leading to overwashing. With run-up in January 2014 exceeding the lowered crest and smaller barrier, the beach rolled back another ~40 m, but while roll-back continued in the spring, CSA and crest levels increased again. In fact, winter 2014/15 saw the crest level rising to above 4 mOD. As at profile 15, the winter 2015/16 saw a further ~50 m of roll back as well as a reduction in crest height and CSA. CSA has remained quite stable since then at around 50 m² with fluctuations of the crest height between 3.3 and 3.9 mOD, but a continued storm related roll back of the barrier.

Profile 44 represents the frontage at the western border of the marsh surface cropping out in front of the beach ridge. CSA started to decrease later than in the profiles to the east during the January 2014 storm through loss from the front of the beach indicated by the retreat of the 3 mOD contour, while crest elevation remained unchanged. The first drop in crest height (~0.8 m) occurred in March 2014 with no comparable change in CSA or change in contour line position and no overwashing event. Profile data and ground photos show that this was a last-ditch management intervention that flattened and slightly widened the crest to infill some overwash throats from the February 2014 storms that had overwashed and rolled back the barrier to the east. Further loss of CSA over spring and summer 2014 narrowed the barrier through erosion from the front leading to overwashing up to January 2015 with associated roll-back of ~15 m and crest lowering of ~1.4 m. Crest level, CSA and contour position deteriorated further up to and during the winter 2015/16 but since then CSA has remained around 50–60 m², increasing to over 70 m² in summer 2018. Similarly, crest elevations have been fluctuating between 3.3 and 3.6 mOD, rising to above 3.9 mOD in 2020. At the same time, the contour position has seen periods of stability (e.g., summer 2016 to December 2017) punctuated by storm related roll-back (e.g., December 2017 and winter 2019/20).

Following a brief increase in CSA in the autumn of 2013, CSA for profile 53 dropped steadily until autumn 2015/16. This was accompanied by a steady retreat of the contour line of up to ~10 m, but an initial slight increase of the crest elevation followed by a slight dip and general stability. The roll-back of ~30 m, drop in crest by ~1 m and reduction in CSA by ~70 m² occurred in the early winter of 2015/16. Following this, crest levels have been maintained around 4 mOD, i.e., ~0.5 m higher than for profile 44, CSA has been steady at about 40 to 50 m² in 2016 and 2017 and at about 30 to 40 m² following further roll-back during winter 2017/18 and 2019/20.

The development for profile 68 is very similar to that for profile 53 except that the peak in CSA came in spring 2015 (accompanied by a seaward move of the 3 mOD contour), that the roll-back occurs over the entire winter 2015/16, and that the reduction in crest elevation is very small over most of the study period at around 4.5 mOD, dropping to below 4 mOD only at the last survey linked to the storms in 2019 and 2020. This drop is associated with further roll-back but the CSA remained unchanged.

Profiles 80 and 85 are at the western end of west beach and have been the latest to be impacted by roll-back. Both show an increase in CSA in 2015 which started to drop at profile 80 in 2016, while at profile 85 this was delayed till 2018. Retreat of the contour line position reached 10 m in winter 2018/19 for profile 80 and in winter 2019/20 for profile 85. Crest lowering for both happened in the winter 2019/20 though at profile 85 this has only led to a lowering to 4.77 mOD and the crest is still within the cross-section of the barrier in its pre-breach configuration, i.e., roll-back has not yet happened.

4.5. Barrier Inertia (BI)

The BI concept (Section 3.4) can be used retrospectively to assess (a) what the beach and environmental conditions were during known overwashing events, (b) periods of likely overwashing to investigate beach profiles for morphological signs of this having occurred and (c) as a predictive tool to assess the likelihood of overwashing for sections of beach that have not been overwashed yet [35]. For the Medmerry datasets, there are no dedicated pre-and post-storm surveys that bracket a single event. Therefore, the period covered by surveys that show crest lowering (Figure 17) have been identified and BI values calculated for all 30-min conditions within that time window and with a still water level > 2 mOD. These have been plotted for a selection of events and profiles in Figure 18 together with BI thresholds (1) and (2). For profile 15, the values have been linked by lines to illustrate more clearly the sequence over a tidal cycle and the number of values during different tidal cycles. For example, the event on 04 January 2014 covered 2.5 h and started with a BI value of 1.04 on the still rising tide but as water level rose a bit more, wave height fell away leading to higher BI values; the same applies to 02 January 2014. On the other hand, the line and points for 03 January 2014 represent the combination of the morning and lunch time high tides with low BI values over 2.5 h each; the same applies to the 01 January 2014 with low BI values over 1.5 h each. The most BI values for one tide are shown for profile 34 on 03 November 2013 and an example for only one value during a tidal cycle can be found for profile 75 on 31 December 2017.

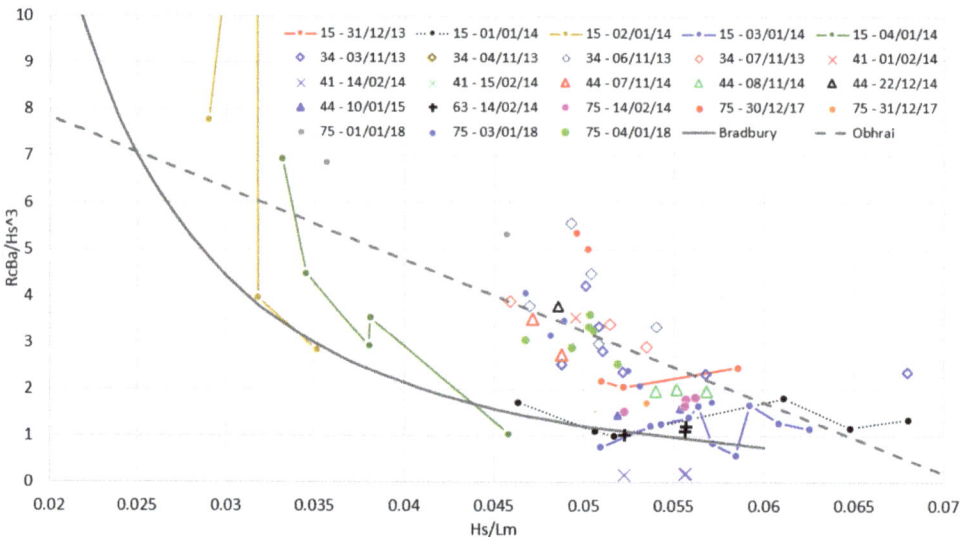

Figure 18. 30-min BI values plotted against Hs/Lm for selected profiles (the two figures preceding the hyphen in the legend) and dates together with published threshold curves (1) and (2).

Whether only one event (and then which) created the crest lowering (1.1 m) and roll-back (20 m) observed for example for Profile 15 between 10 December 2013 and 10 January 2014 cannot be resolved from the data because of the feedback created by loss of CSA and crest lowering during an event at high tide and the resultant changed geometry of the beach for the following high tides. However, the event on 31-12-2013 is quite short, covering 1.5 h, and thus is highly unlikely to have achieved the observed change on its own, but it is likely to have narrowed the crest and removed CSA from the profile. The two high tides on 01 January 2014 would then have had a larger effect that would have been further exploited by the longer waves on 02 January 2014.

For profile 41 on the other hand, crest lowering from 4.29 to 3.48 mOD and roll-back of the 3 mOD contour by 13 m (with lowering by 1.3 m but no roll-back prior to this between 10 January and 07 February 2014), and for profile 63 crest lowering from 5.39 to 4.37 mOD with no roll-back occurred between 07 February and 04 March 2014 with only one tide (14 February 2014) with low BI values. For profile 41, there was a 'preparatory' high tide with just one value on 01 February 2014 just above the threshold which is the only candidate for the 1.3 m crest lowering mentioned above that reduced B_A from 16 to 5.4 m^2, and then followed on 14 February 2014 by very low BI values over 1.5 h. For profile 63, the starting B_A area was 29 m^2 which would explain the higher BI values and more limited profile response.

The benefit of the BI approach to identify overwashing that is not obvious from the topographic data can be shown using profile 75 as an example (Figure 18). It is located at the western end of the MMR frontage which does not show any change in crest elevation or position before December 2017 although CSA has been decreasing prior to that Figure 15. However, running the BI calculation for the entire period has identified four BI values on 14 February 2014 that are comparable, though slightly higher than for profile 63. On closer inspection of the annual aerial photography, the crest around profile 75 (and most of the western section of the MMR) shows subtle changes on the backslope (Figure 19) mainly in terms of vegetation loss and some new sediment landward of the access track suggesting a few individual waves overwashing during the event resulting in some sediment transport but no detectable morphological change. The B_A area for the event was 46 m^2 so that for the event on 14 February 2014 three difference profile responses could have occurred depending on the BI value.

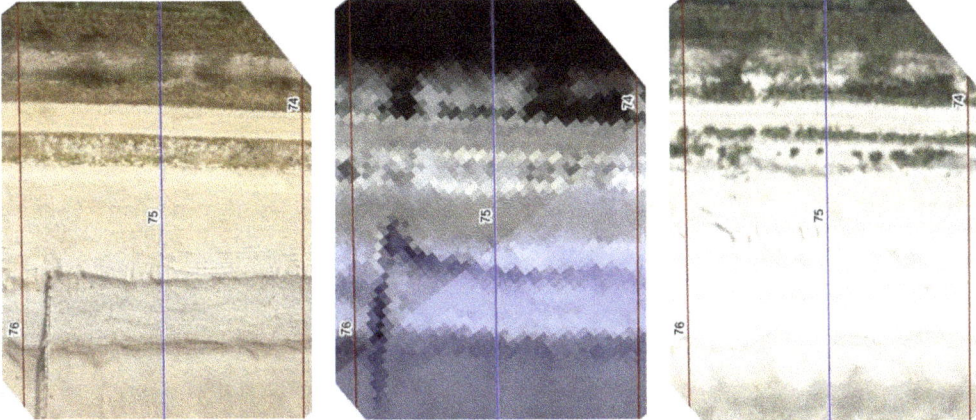

Figure 19. Orthophotos showing profiles 74 to 76 (40 m distance) for summer 2013 (**left**), a CASI image for 14 July 2014 (**middle**) and another orthophoto for June 2015 (**right**). Photos rotated from true north by 42°.

Most of the data suggests that the straight Obhrai threshold seems to fit the data better than the Bradbury curve, i.e., that there are plenty of events with BI values that can account for the observed overwashing and crest lowering below the Obhrai threshold, whereas only a very small number make it to and below the Bradbury line. The exceptions appear to be events and profile responses on 14 February 2014 illustrated by profiles 41, 63 and 75. However, this event was dominated by swell waves leading to the widespread overwashing of Hurst Spit during the same event [6] yet the wave spectra do not explicitly form part of the threshold equations. The Obhrai line is based on laboratory flume experiments with two wave steepnesses, namely 0.06, close to most of the data for Medmerry, and 0.01

reflecting swell waves. It is therefore not surprising that conditions calculated with steep waves but composed of less steep waves fall below the Obhrai threshold although the profile response at least for profile 75 should have plotted above it.

Finally, the BI concept can be applied to assess when the frontage west of MMR is likely to experience overwashing and roll-back. Figure 20 summarises the point in time when roll-back occurred at each profile west of the breach. The definition used for the start of roll-back is subjective and based on profile behaviour but is generally taken to be when the crest of the rolled back beach is landwards of the rear slope of the beach as surveyed on 26 August 2013. An example is given in Figure 10 where the barrier at the survey on 24 January 2015 has not rolled-back at either of the two profiles, while profile 47 has rolled back by the survey on 16 June 2015. In Figure 20 the date is given for each profile survey prior to roll-back and post roll-back, i.e., providing a bracketing time range because the exact date cannot be ascertained with certainty. As an alternative measure, the date of the survey for when the seaward 3 mOD contour was more than 15 m landwards from the start position on 26 August 2013 is also given, representing a significant amount of thinning and loss of CSA. Again, the example profiles in Figure 10 show the different in position of the 3 mOD contour on 24 January 2015 compared to 26 August 2013 to be 17 m for profile 48 and 19 m for profile 47. It is clear that different definitions of roll-back initiation provide different date as shown in this example and in Figure 20. To link the initial roll-back events to the state of the beach at that time, the cross-sectional area of the barrier above 2.3 mOD is shown for the same pre- and post-survey date but also for the survey preceding the pre roll-back survey (CSA pre+1 R-B). For the frontage west of the western rock arm, the two 'pre' lines simply refer to the last two available surveys as roll-back has not happened. Finally, the CSA above the same level at the start (26 August 2013) is also shown in black. The level of 2.3 mOD for the CSA calculation was chosen because it is the average water level for the events shown in Figure 18.

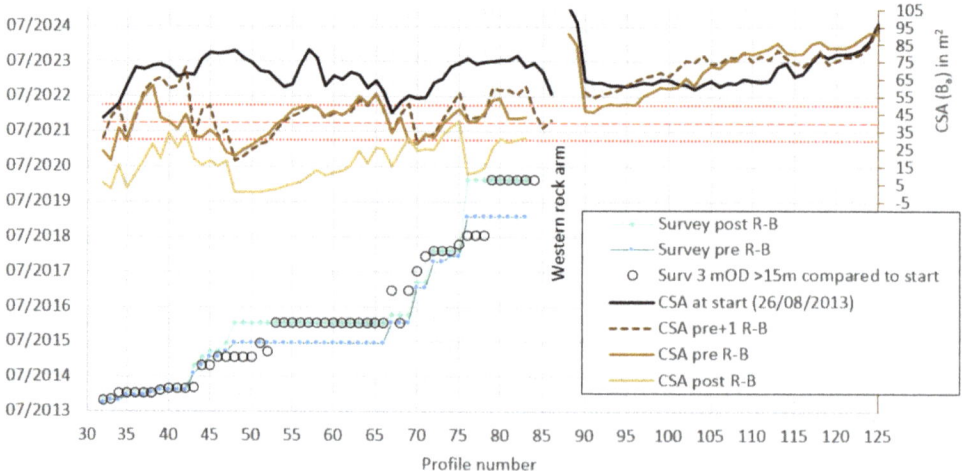

Figure 20. Summary diagram showing for the frontage east of the western rock arm the time of surveys between which the first roll-back has occurred at each profile together with CSA of the Barrier Area above 2.3 mOD for the same surveys. Broken horizontal line is the average 'CSA pre R-B' of 40 m² with the two dotted lines representing the standard deviation. For the area west of the rock arm, the two brown lines are the CSA for the last two surveys. See text for more details.

Figure 20 shows that barrier roll-back from the starting position on 26 August 2013 has sometimes progressed westwards gradually (up to summer 2015 and between spring 2016 and winter 2019) and sometimes in large steps (early winter 2015 and winter 2019/20) when several profiles rolled-back during the same storm event (bearing in mind that the entire barrier was overtopped by at least a few waves during the storm on 14 February 2014). It also shows that in all cases the barrier had become smaller in terms of the CSA prior to the event compared to the starting point on 26 August 2013; in some cases this CSA loss occurred during the preceding survey interval. The difference between pre- and post-roll-back CSAs shows large variations but there is a significant correlation ($\rho = 0.39$, $p < 0.005$) between the two which is even more pronounced for the roll-back of profiles 48 to 66 ($\rho = 0.8$, $p < 0.0001$). The average pre-roll back CSA was 40 m^2 ($\sigma = 10$ m^2) and it is evident that there is a stretch 100 m long west of the western rock arm (profile 87) that has already (by October 2020) fallen to within the band of CSA that is likely to result in overwashing and roll-back under storm events similar to those experienced several times in the last 7 years. This has come about due to continued longshore transport that has led to beach loss over the last two surveys and which will be exacerbated in the near future when the rock arm, which has so far terminated within the beach, emerges from the beach and will increasingly act as a groyne with associated downdrift consequences.

To address the flood risk posed by overwashing west of the western rock arm which is also impacted by legacy structures, planks have been removed from the groynes in that area and shingle has been placed behind these groynes along short stretches that have the most vulnerable cross-shore profile (Figure 21), pre-empting the natural process illustrated in Figure 11). West of profile 100 the overwashing risk is very low in particular as the beach has grown since 2013, however, the future loss of CSA needs to be monitored.

Figure 21. Management intervention in 2021 showing before (top on 12 October 2020) and after (bottom on 29 January 2021) groyne plank removal and increasing the CSA behind the groyne at the back of the beach. Pole in the top photo is 3 m long.

5. Discussion

Speed and magnitude of the coastal ontogeny over the 7 years since the breach is incompatible with any modelling or 'expert knowledge' prior to the breach and bears no relationship to the development envisaged, as quoted in Section 2.1. This assumed an average rate of up to 0.7 my^{-1} for design purposes or up to 1.5 my^{-1} based on historic data. After 7.16 years (August 2013 to October 2020), mean annual roll-back based of the position of the 3 mOD contour ranges from 27 to 28 my^{-1} on the east beach (profiles 14–19) to 21 my^{-1} at the eastern end of west beach (profiles 34, 35) to 2 my^{-1} just east of the western rock arm (profiles 84, 85). The average across all profiles within the MMR site is 16.6 my^{-1} or one order of magnitude higher than the historic rate. Profiles 34 to 36 have retreated between 152 to 146 m and while 2nd order polynomial trend lines have a slightly better R^2 value and optical fit (Figure 17) over the last few years than linear trends, there are no indications that the barrier has reached a more stable position in this retreated position.

In fact, the barrier at these profiles is positioned landwards of the marsh cliff which is also still eroding and this erosion will increase wave power on the barrier which is therefore highly likely to roll back further.

At the soft cliffs of Happisburgh [70], lowering of the lower intertidal foreshore in front of defences was identified as the driver for accelerated coastal catch-up that has overtaken what was deemed to be a 'natural' trajectory of retreat. As suggested in an earlier study for the historic period [43] and evidenced as an example in Figure 9 for the time post-breach, there is very little change in elevation on the lower intertidal platform to either drive the coastal catch-up process or accompany it. This would point to sea level rise as being the main driver for the overall catch-up process.

Based on historic progression and retreat rates together with the length of time the beach has been held in place for, a catch-up distance of 100 m was suggested in Section 2.1. Using a rate of sea level rise of 0.002 my^{-1} since the 1950s and the estimate of 0.65 m retreat per 0.001 m of sea level rise [15] would similarly deliver a catch-up distance of ~90 m. All profiles east of profile 47 have retreated by more than 100 m with profile 34 by 152 m. This mismatch could be due to the historic rates based on maps being too low, that extrapolating historic retreat rates is not an appropriate method to estimate catch-up distances or that published rates of retreat in relation to sea level rise are not applicable to the MMR site.

The most likely reason for roll-back distances observed so far and to be expected into the future are the fundamental changes to the barrier beach post-breach. Natural barriers tend to roll back as a closed unit, and in a swash aligned [14,15] or sediment rich drift aligned setting any local patterns of barrier lowering and breaching are repaired through natural processes within a short period of time [42]. There are no historic reports or indications from historic maps that the Medmerry barrier was breached and developed an inlet and neither, for example, has this been the case for the longer, more drift aligned southern coast of Dungeness [71]. In contrast, the artificial breach has changed the sediment dynamics by first removing 7200 m^3 over a length of ~230 m and creating new accommodation space for shingle to migrate landwards along the new channel, drawing in beach sediment from about a hundred metres to the west and east and thus creating conditions for this section to roll back due to reduced CSA. On the west side of the breach, this started to change the coastal alignment to more swash alignment in that section (a rotation of ~20°) reducing sediment loss which pushed longshore transport and CSA loss onto the next section, creating a process of alongshore progressing roll-back as the next section started to become more swash-aligned. On the east beach on the other hand, the loss of CSA into the area along the channel had little time to change the plan-shape before wholesale roll-back took place. However, the barrier breakdown shown at the east beach is not due to further sediment loss alongshore but through temporary loss into shore parallel channels. The removal of the sediment and creation of the wide opening are what differentiates MMR from the natural breach at Porlock where the barrier remains largely unchanged since the breach in 1996 [18]. This suggests, based on only this one comparison, that a smaller breach channel to start its natural development together with leaving the excavated sediment in the system close to the channel could avoid the large scale changes observed at MMR, albeit at the risk of the smaller breach closing again [45].

Thus far, the progressing roll-back has rotated the coast line towards being more swash aligned. The average shoreline orthogonal from the western rock arm to the breach is 215°, in line with the dominant wave direction. The process has also moved the remaining CSA on top of the marsh surface, where it generally sits above MHWS level. Both of these outcomes contribute to a reduction in longshore transport through reducing the wave angle and reducing the opportunity for hydrodynamic processes to move this sediment by being largely out of reach under normal conditions. The remaining CSA will ensure future roll-back under hydrodynamic conditions that are likely to happen on an annual basis, in particular as the remaining CSA appears to be too small to lead to crest build-up. Along most parts of the west beach, the land drops landwards (Figure 2 and profile 79 in Figure 3

Article

Topological and Morphological Controls on Morphodynamics of Salt Marsh Interiors

Ben R. Evans [1], Iris Möller [1,2] and Tom Spencer [1,*]

[1] Cambridge Coastal Research Unit, Department of Geography, University of Cambridge, Downing Place, Cambridge CB2 3EN, UK; bre24@cam.ac.uk (B.R.E.); moelleri@tcd.ie (I.M.)
[2] Department of Geography, Museum Building, Trinity College Dublin, Dublin 2, Ireland
* Correspondence: ts111@cam.ac.uk

Abstract: Salt marshes are important coastal environments and provide multiple benefits to society. They are considered to be declining in extent globally, including on the UK east coast. The dynamics and characteristics of interior parts of salt marsh systems are spatially variable and can fundamentally affect biotic distributions and the way in which the landscape delivers ecosystem services. It is therefore important to understand, and be able to predict, how these landscape configurations may evolve over time and where the greatest dynamism will occur. This study estimates morphodynamic changes in salt marsh areas for a regional domain over a multi-decadal timescale. We demonstrate at a landscape scale that relationships exist between the topology and morphology of a salt marsh and changes in its condition over time. We present an inherently scalable satellite-derived measure of change in marsh platform integrity that allows the monitoring of changes in marsh condition. We then demonstrate that easily derived geospatial and morphometric parameters can be used to determine the probability of marsh degradation. We draw comparisons with previous work conducted on the east coast of the USA, finding differences in marsh responses according to their position within the wider coastal system between the two regions, but relatively consistent in relation to the within-marsh situation. We describe the sub-pixel-scale marsh morphometry using a morphological segmentation algorithm applied to 25 cm-resolution maps of vegetated marsh surface. We also find strong relationships between morphometric indices and change in marsh platform integrity which allow for the inference of past dynamism but also suggest that current morphology may be predictive of future change. We thus provide insight into the factors governing marsh degradation that will assist the anticipation of adverse changes to the attributes and functions of these critical coastal environments and inform ongoing ecogeomorphic modelling developments.

Keywords: wetland; salt marsh; degradation; satellite time series; self-organisation; morphodynamic feedback; geospatial

1. Introduction

Salt marshes represent a major component of low-lying sedimentary coastal systems and occur across the world [1]. Over recent decades, salt marshes have attracted increasing attention, with much research being focused on the services and functions they provide [2]. Salt marshes exhibit an extremely high biodiversity [3] and primary productivity [4]. They attenuate wave energy and contribute significantly to the protection provided by natural foreshores from high waves and water levels threatening coastal communities [5,6]. Marshes are a sink for atmospheric carbon [7–9], while providing a habitat for many endangered or threatened species and nursery areas for commercial fish stock species [10,11]. They also have cultural value as areas for recreation and tourism. In the UK, over the last 150 years map and aerial imagery suggest an expansion of marsh areas in northern England, as against areal loss in the south, attributed to regional variations in sediment supply [12]. It has, however, proven difficult to ascertain patterns of marsh areal change and controlling factors over the latter half of the twentieth century. The East Anglian coast (Figure 1) is thought to be a region with high rates of wetland loss (e.g., [13]), but in reality rates and types of marsh loss have exhibited great spatial variability (e.g., [14]). Furthermore, achieving precise estimates of changes in marsh area has been shown to be challenging by the few large-scale UK inventories attempted [15–17].

The position of a marsh system within a broader context of the coastal zone exerts controls on factors such as sediment or nutrient import and export, tidal flushing and residence times, and forces exerted by tidal currents. The connectivity between intertidal wetland areas and offshore deep channel zones is crucial to water, sediment, and nutrient exchange and thus to the morphological evolution of marshes [18].

The position of a marsh parcel within the surrounding system, and the position of a point on the marsh within individual parcels, modulate local-scale responses. There has long been recognition that elevation–sedimentation relationships vary with scale. For example, single-tide sediment deposition decreases with distance from tidal channels, while surface elevation provides an important marsh-wide control over annual to decadal timescales [19]. Kearney and Rogers [20] previously used logistic regression to predict internal platform integrity changes in marshes at a regional scale in Chesapeake and Delaware Bays, USA. They demonstrated empirical relationships between changes in marsh surface condition and factors such as distance up-estuary and position within a marsh parcel. The marsh systems on the UK East coast have a different context (tidal range, position within tidal frame, sedimentology, vegetation community) to those studied by Kearney and Rogers [20] but we are able to draw comparisons between the topological relationships presented here and their findings.

The morphology of the marsh, described by the spatial distribution of landscape units (at a scale of metres) such as vegetated platforms, salt pans, creeks, and large channels, is the integrative result of historic morphodynamics [21]. Morphology is also thought to exert a control on future changes through biogeomorphic feedback [22], while the interactions between topography and hydrodynamic forces have been extensively explored from a numerical perspective [23]. From an empirical perspective, a relationship between the functional form of marsh margins and erosion rates has been demonstrated [24].

Of particular, and most immediate, interest for landscape management are the loci of greatest dynamism; the most important to understand when considering future ecosystem service provision are those exhibiting (or likely to exhibit) erosion. This study aims to assess the decadal morphodynamics of salt marsh systems on the east coast of the UK, evaluate the role of topological and morphological factors in determining the observed changes, and provide understanding of the controls on salt marsh morphological evolution to support ecosystem management and the development of models that combine ecological and physical functioning. We present landscape-scale statistical models relating such changes to easily derived spatial parameters at scales from the regional (tens of kilometres) to local (metres). Such understanding will help with the prediction of locations likely to exhibit degradation accompanied by concomitant losses of ecosystem services. This will thereby facilitate targeted management interventions to protect the ecological and physical functioning of these important coastal ecosystems.

2. Materials and Methods
2.1. Study Area

The coastline of East Anglia, UK, is bounded by the Humber estuary to the north and the Thames estuary to the south (Figure 1). The region is, in many parts, densely populated. The population in the coastal districts of Suffolk and Norfolk exceeds 600,000 (Office for National Statistics GB 2016 census data—www.ons.gov.uk/census accessed on 23 October 2018). A considerable amount of variability occurs along this stretch of coast in terms of the hydrodynamic and sedimentary contexts. The mean spring tidal range (MSTR) varies from 6.18 m at Immingham on the Humber to a minimum of 1.94 m at Lowestoft, Suffolk, before increasing again further south (ntslf.org accessed on 10 December 2020).

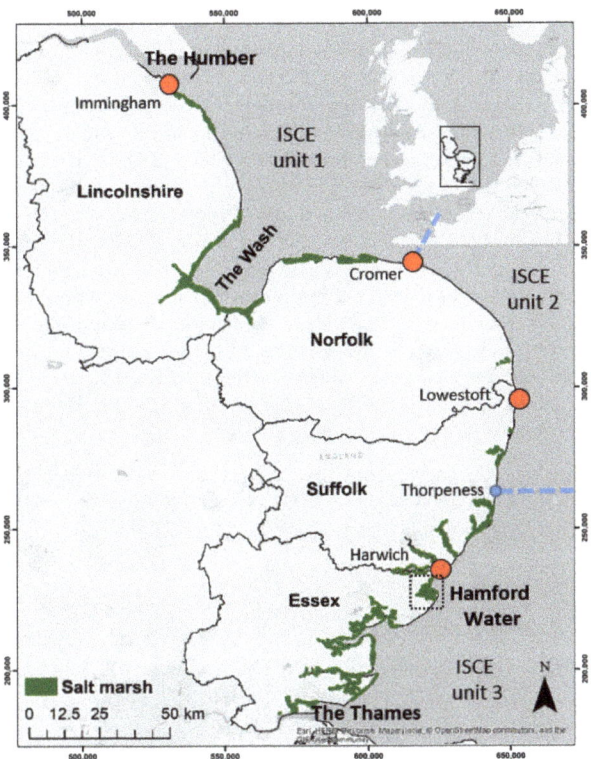

Figure 1. Study region of East Anglia, UK, showing areas where marsh is present [17] and indicating locations referenced in the text. Blue dashed lines denote the boundaries of ISCE units after [25]. Red dots denote standard ports with tide gauge records.

Pethick and Leggett [25] partitioned the region into three Integrated Scale Coastal Evolution (ISCE) units. The Northern ISCE includes the eroding glacial cliffs north of the Humber, which provide sediment inputs for the sandy shorelines in Lincolnshire and the infilling embayment of The Wash. The ISCE includes the spit and barrier island system of the north Norfolk coast as far east as Cromer. The second ISCE is dominated by cliffs composed of glacial sands and gravels and lies between Cromer and Thorpeness. The third, southerly, unit comprises numerous estuaries and inlets sitting within a large embayment and characterised by silt or clay sediments [26]. The region contains some 14,406 ha of salt marsh [17] of diverse character and setting; open coast, embayment, back-barrier, and estuarine marshes are represented [27]. Suffolk and Essex have both experienced a net loss of marsh area in the second half of the twentieth century [15] while The Wash embayment, between Norfolk and Lincolnshire, represents a long-term sediment sink [28] and continues to infill [26], with attendant increases in marsh area [24]. At the regional scale, none of these systems can be thought of as 'sediment starved'.

2.2. Morphological Change

We address controls on morphodynamic change within marsh interiors comprising the complex morphologies of vegetated surfaces, creeks, pools, and pans that lie landward of the seaward margin of the marsh as a whole. We use satellite imagery to estimate changes in vegetation distributions within these areas, from which we infer morphological changes. This inference is based on well-established elevational controls on intertidal vegetation establishment [29], which have been thoroughly ground-referenced for NW Europe by

Suchrow and Jensen [30]. In inferring morphological change, we assume that all surfaces of sufficient elevation to support vegetation become colonised, while those that are too low do not.

Changes in the extent of vegetation within marsh interiors were estimated using a modified trend analysis of the Landsat archive, which represents the longest appropriate satellite time series available (1984–present). Imagery dating between 1985 and 2016 was used in this study. The exact time period over which the metric is calculated will vary slightly between pixels due to the different acquisition dates of imagery over certain areas and cloud cover precluding the use of some pixels (see https://osf.io/mgsyz/).

A metric was derived, denoted δP_{veg}, that can be interpreted as representing the percentage change in vegetation cover within any given pixel over the timeframe of the satellite observations. As such, it reflects the temporal variations in the areal unvegetated–vegetated marsh ratio (UVVR) within each 30 m by 30 m pixel. The UVVR could be considered a geomorphic metric that has itself been shown to be related to marsh vulnerability [31]. The methodological workflow we use is summarised in Figure 2 and is detailed extensively in Appendix A.

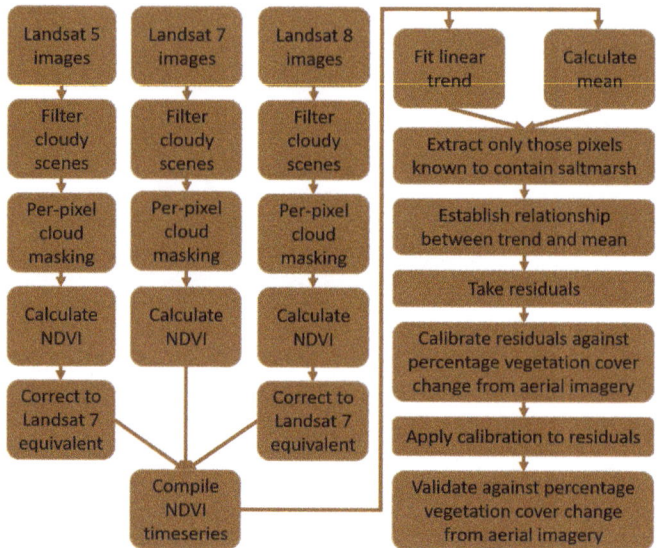

Figure 2. Summary of workflow used to derive δP_{veg} metric.

In Google Earth Engine [32], the Normalised Difference Vegetation Index (NDVI), a proxy for the amount of chlorophyll (and therefore vegetation) present, was computed for all scenes within the Landsat archive for the study region up to 2016. Conceptually, the NDVI for a pixel in a satellite image can be considered to be a function of the percentage of that pixel covered by vegetation and the nature of the vegetation within that pixel. A change in the NDVI reflects a change in the percentage vegetation cover within the pixel, with the signal potentially being modulated by any attendant changes in community composition (and therefore spectral signature) and the vigour of the vegetation present. Lopes et al. [33] evaluted a number of vegetation indices for the monitoring of salt marsh extent and condition in Portugal based on the Landsat archive and concluded that NDVI performed best, with a seasonally varying goodness-of-fit [34] typically exceeding 0.9 at one location and 0.75 at another, where a perfect classification would result in a value of 1.

NDVI values were cross-calibrated to account for differences in radiomemtric response between different Landsat sensors before a linear trend was computed over the time series for each pixel. A relationship between the coefficients of the trend and the mean NDVI over the time series was found, which was removed by taking the residuals of the regression fit between the slope of the trend line and the mean NDVI ($R^2 = 0.22$, $p \leq 0.001$). The resulting residuals were standardised and calibrated against 25cm Environment Agency aerial photography from 1992 and 2013/14. Calibration was achieved by the visual assessment of the aerial photography subsets extracted for a random sample of satellite pixels (n = 83) stratified to represent the full range of observed standardised residual trend coefficents. For each satellite pixel area, 50 points were randomly distributed and each was manually classified as either coinciding with vegetated or unvegetated surfaces in both the 1992 and 2013/14 aerial photography. For each year, the percentage of satellite pixel area that was vegetated in the aerial photography was then calculated based on the counts in each surface cover class. A strong relationship was found between the satellite-derived residuals and the photography-based estimates of change in vegetation cover ($R^2 = 0.87$, $p \leq 0.001$), implying that changes in vegetation extent dominate changes in δP_{veg}. The calibration sample was drawn from the entire study region. δP_{veg} varies in the range -100% to $+100\%$, where -100% represents a change from fully vegetated to fully bare and $+100\%$ the opposite. The method was validated against a sample of pixels representative of the full range of calibrated estimates (n = 100) but drawn from a local subset area (Hamford Water, Essex) to obviate the effect of any large-scale (e.g., latitudinal) signal that may have been present within the calibration. The δP_{veg} metric performed well, with an RMSE of 11.9% of full scale ($\pm 100\%$).

2.3. Topological and Morphological Metrics

Two metrics were derived to describe the topology of a location within a marsh and two morphological metrics were developed to describe the distribution of landscape units within a single Landsat pixel area.

2.3.1. Geomorphic Setting

The geomorphic setting of the marsh, meaning its context within the wider coastal system, was represented as a cost function, denoted Cost Distance (CD), describing how difficult it would be for a parcel of water originating offshore to reach any given location within a marsh. Thus, for example, interior marsh areas towards the head of estuaries are more 'costly' to reach (less well connected to the offshore) than the seaward margins of open coast marshes. Without a full simulation of tidal exchanges against which to calibrate flow pathways, the CD metric is not expected to behave in an isomorphic manner with actual tidal exchanges. Rather, CD values are internally consistent and represent a scale of relative connectivity within the study domain.

The area between the 10 km offshore limit and the land was represented on a 10 m grid and divided into four zones. For ease, we denote these 'subtidal', 'intertidal', 'supratidal', and 'terrestrial', while recognising that they do not conform strictly to these descriptions. Intertidal, for example, would ordinarily refer to elevations between the lowest and highest tides experienced. In the UK, this range would extend well below 0 m Ordnance Datum Newlyn (ODN), which approximates mean sea level but is used here as the lower bound of the 'intertidal' zone (see below). The landward limit was defined by the UK Environment Agency Second Generation Shoreline Management Plan as segments vector layer(SMP2), which typically reflects the line of engineered defences. Costs to traverse each cell of the grid were based on distances, with the cells in each zone given different weighting factors. Areas below 0 m ODN were denoted 'subtidal' and were assigned a cost according to their euclidean distance in metres from the offshore boundary.

An 'intertidal' zone was defined as areas between 0 m ODN and the level of the highest astronomical tide (HAT). Elevations were derived from the Environment Agency 2 m-resolution LiDAR composite product (2008) resampled to the 10 m grid. Since spatially resolved data describing HAT were not available, modelled MSTR values [35] were extrapolated to intersect the shoreline and an $0.7\times$ MSTR was used to approximate the level of HAT. Our comparison of the levels thus estimated and known levels at the four standard ports in the study region (Immingham, Cromer, Lowestoft, and Felixstowe) suggests that this approximation tends to slightly overestimate (order of 10 cm) the level of HAT. The dependency of intertidal wetland development on tidal range is well documented, with equivalent landforms occurring at higher levels relative to the mean sea level in macrotidal settings than in microtidal ones [27,36]. The elevation range available for the development of intertidal landforms can be described as an 'accommodation range'. The DEM elevations above 0 m ODN were therefore normalised to reflect the spatial variability in accommodation range, which was itself approximated as 0.5× MSTR. This produced a normalised elevation (NE) raster that did not exhibit substantial dependency on tidal range and was used to scale the resulting cost functions for the intertidal zone.

A 'supratidal' zone was defined as areas above HAT but seaward of the SMP2 vector marking the terrestrial limit. Such areas may still be inundated and therefore permit water flow during exceptional events, so this zone was given a uniform but very high cell cost relative to the other zones. A 'terrestrial' zone landward of engineered defences was modelled as impassable for tidal waters.

The zones were combined to produce an overall cost surface raster which was converted to a cost-distance raster where each cell value represents the cumulative cost to reach it by the least-cost path from the 10 km offshore limit of the domain. The weightings for each zone were manually adjusted to produce the best achievable visual replication of expected flow routes for tidal waters to reach a given location through complex channel networks. Figure 3 shows a schematic cross-shore transect from the engineered defence to the 10 km offshore limit of the domain (top panel). Per-cell and cumulative costs are plotted in red, with the levels of 0 m ODN and HAT also indicated. The four zones upon which the overall cost surface was based are indicated along with their final weighting functions (where D is the horizontal distance in metres and NE is the normalised elevation). The lower panel of Figure 3 shows examples of the least-cost paths calculated for random pixels superimposed on both the local per-pixel cost surface and aerial photography to demonstrate the ability of the method to reproduce expected flow routes.

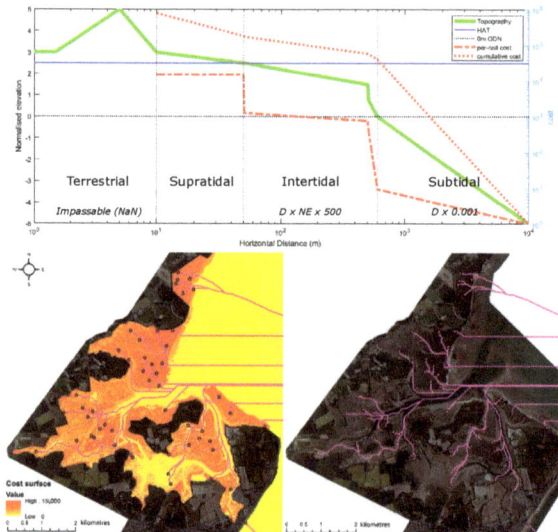

Figure 3. Schematic representation of topography and associated costs (**top**). The four zones and their associated cost weighting functions are identified. Example from Hamford Water, Essex, of per-cell costs (**bottom left**) and aerial photograph for reference (**bottom right**). Pink lines on maps are example least-cost paths derived for a random selection of pixels. See Figure 1 for location.

2.3.2. Distance from Creek/Edge of Marsh Parcel

This measure represents the well-established tendency for sediments to be deposited rapidly once creek banks become overtopped during inundation, leading to the development of creek levees and limited deposition rates in areas away from cliffed seaward margins [37,38]. To represent this dynamic, a measure of distance from a creek or the edge of a marsh parcel was used. To facilitate analysis at scales commensurate with the size of Landsat pixels used for other variables (30 m by 30 m), a reduced resolution product representing offshore or large-creek margins of marsh parcels was derived from the Environment Agency's salt marsh extent layer [17]. Large creeks were defined as those wider than the diagonal of a Landsat pixel (ca. 42.5 m), since these are the units for which internal morphological changes were measured. Creeks and pools narrower than 42.5 m were removed using a 21.25 m outer buffer on the polygons of the salt marsh extents layer, followed by the dissolving of any overlaps thus created and 21.25 m inner buffer operations. This spatial resolution limit, imposed by the buffering process, effectively disregards the smaller creeks, which nevertheless perform important system functions. This fact must be taken into account when interpreting the findings, and we comment further on this aspect in the discussion. The other metrics used, including δP_{veg}, are not sensitive to spatial resolution limits in the same manner.

Landward limits of the marsh polygons were removed by extracting only those portions of perimeter lines that were greater than 30 m (1 landsat pixel) from the SMP2 vector, ensuring that distances do not represent those from the landward limit. For each parcel, the euclidean distance from the edge was then calculated on a 30 m grid aligned to that used for δP_{veg} estimation. The metric is henceforth referred to as Euclidean Distance (ED).

2.3.3. Integrity of Marsh Platform

The first morphological metric describes the integrity of the marsh platform by the proportion of each 30 m satellite pixel's area that contains undissected vegetated marsh areas. It is referred to as pCore.

The Morphological Spatial Pattern Analysis (MSPA—[39]) tool, supplied within the GUIDOS toolbox [40], is a morphological segmentation algorithm designed to assess habitat connectivity and fragmentation—for example, in forest ecosystems [41,42] or for planning of green infrastructure [43]. MSPA operates on a binary raster of 'foreground' and 'background' pixels, where foreground represents the habitat or land cover type of interest. It classifies foreground pixels according to how many other foreground pixels they are adjacent to and a distance parameter controlling the width of areas considered to be 'egde' because they are close to background pixels. Pixels are allocated to one of seven foreground classes (core, edge, perforation, bridge, loop, branch, and islet) and a background class. Each of these classes can also have an attribute describing whether it is entirely surrounded by other foreground classes (internal) or with connectivity through adjacent background classes to the edge of the raster (external). Loops and bridges can additionally be defined as appearing independently or within edges or perforations. The result is 22 possible types of feature that are extracted from the binary raster. In this context, foreground pixels represent vegetated marsh platform areas while background pixels correspond to bare sediments, channels, and pools. Although these classes were originally designed to describe habitat connectivity features, analogues can be readily defined for most classes in the context of fine-scale saltmarsh morphology (Table 1). MSPA was applied to a 25 cm-resolution binary raster derived from the Environment Agency's salt marsh extents layer [17], which describes recent (2008–2010) marsh morphology. Core areas were defined as parts of vegetated marsh greater than the MSPA edge width parameter (2.5 m) from a background area. The pCore metric was the aggregation of both internal and external MSPA 'core' classes for a given satellite pixel area.

Table 1. Outline of the landform classes produced by MSPA and their interpretation in the context of fine-scale salt marsh morphology (internal: no background connectivity to raster edge; external: background connectivity to raster edge).

Feature	Classification Rule	Interpretation
Background	Background pixels	Salt pans or pools if internal, channel or mudflat if external
Core	Areas greater than the edge distance from nearest background pixel	Large, coherent marsh areas
Edge	Areas within the edge distance of background pixels	Margins of core areas with channel connectivity
Perforation	Edge pixels entirely enclosing an area of background pixels	Margins of salt pans or pools without channel connectivity
Branch	Strip less than twice the edge distance wide that joins to a core area at one end	Narrow extensions from core areas
Islet	Foreground area too small to contain any core area	Small, isolated marsh fragments
Bridge	Strip less than twice the edge distance wide that joins two core areas	Narrow causeway between larger coherent marsh areas
Bridge in Edge	Bridge joining two areas of edge class	As above but for edge areas
Bridge in Perforation	Bridge joining two areas of perforation class	Narrow strip of marsh separating marsh areas that are distinct but entirely contained within a salt pan or pool
Loop	Strip less than twice the edge distance wide that joins to the same core area at both ends	Narrow strip of marsh enclosing a salt pan or pool
Loop in Edge	Strip less than twice the edge distance wide that joins to the same edge area at both ends	Narrow strip of marsh enclosing a salt pan or pool
Loop in Perforation	Strip less than twice the edge distance wide that joins to the same perforation area at both ends	Narrow strip of marsh enclosing a smaller salt pan or pool within a larger one

2.3.4. Limitations to Tidal Connectivity

The second morphological metric describes the proportion of pixel area comprised of unvegetated areas and their periphery that are unconnected to the drainage network; it is denoted pUncon. It is also derived from the MSPA segmentation and reflects pools or pans and their periphery that do not have connectivity via channels to the offshore domain. The pUncon metric was computed as the aggregation of the 'internal' MSPA classes, including unvegetated areas.

An example area of the MSPA segmentation for six adjacent satellite pixels is shown in Figure 4, with the respective values for the pCore and pUncon metrics. These two morphological metrics are interpreted as describing the marsh morphology within a data-space that separates, at its extremes, between contiguous, undissected marsh platform (high pCore), marsh areas that are heavily fragmented by creek networks (low pCore, low pUncon), and areas that have a high density of salt pans and pools (low pCore, high pUncon). The inset graph on Figure 4 illustrates the position of the depicted pixels within this data-space. The processes leading to these morphologies are likely to be different, as are their likely future evolutionary trajectories. Creek networks, particularly low-order ones, are typically stable in the platform once established [44], and maintain a dynamic equlibrium with the tidal prism [45]. Interior areas of intact marsh platforms may remain so or become punctuated by pools or pans [46–48], with the density of pans being related to the tidal range and sediment type at a national scale in the UK [49] and the elevation and distance from marsh edge at a site scale [47].

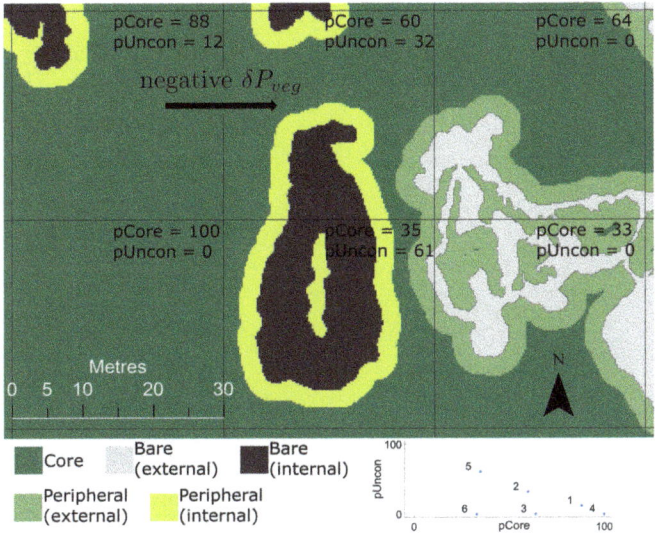

Figure 4. TMSPA segmentation for six adjacent 30 m satellite pixels showing the aggregated classes used to compute the pCore and pUncon metrics. Metric values of each pixel are provided and plotted within the data-space in the inset graph. Pixels are numbered 1–3 across the top row and 4–6 across the bottom row.

2.4. Probability of Observing Marsh Degradation

Marsh degradation was considered to have occurred for pixels where the δP_{veg} was negative. For each of the topological and morphological metrics, the probability of a location exhibiting degradation was computed from the proportion of pixels where $\delta P_{veg} < 0$ in each of 100 equal intervals across the observed ranges of the four topological or morphological metrics described above (CD, ED, pCore, pUncon). Least-squares regression analyses were used to establish relationships for each of the metrics between the observed probabilities of degradation and interval centre points.

3. Results
3.1. Morphodynamic Change

δP_{veg} was estimated for approximately 180,000 30 m pixels, amounting to approximately 16,200 ha of marsh. An example of the resulting metric for about 600 ha of salt marsh in Hamford Water, Essex, is presented in Figure 5 to illustrate the degree of spatial variability observed in changes to marsh integrity over relatively small spatial scales. The inset histogram shows the distribution of estimates across the entire study domain from the Humber to the Thames, which can be seen to be normal but with a mean somewhat above zero, suggesting a dominance of vegetation establishment within the domain, even though this is not necessarily evident within the Hamford Water subset depicted. The overall probability of degradation for the entire dataset was 0.144 for the approximate time period 1985–2016.

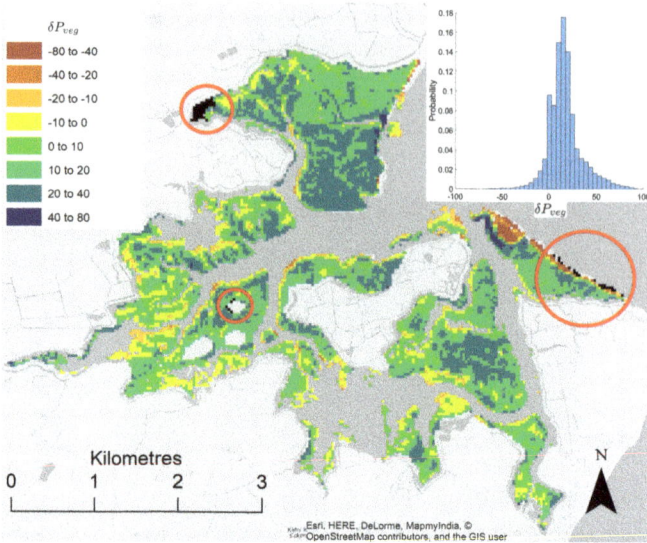

Figure 5. δP_{veg} estimates for approximately 600 ha of marsh in Hamford Water, Essex, between 1985 and 2016. Inset histogram shows the distribution of estimates across the entire study domain between the Humber and the Thames (16,200 ha). Red circles highlight the locations of pixels (black) excluded from the regression analysis of probability of degradation against Cost Distance (CD).

3.2. Topological and Morphological Relationships

No significant regression relationship was found between Cost Distance (CD) and the probability of degradation when using the entire dataset. The CD parameter, however, has very long tails to its distribution, particularly at the upper end of the scale. At the lower end, these pixels represent the seaward limit of open-coast marsh areas, while at the upper end they are mainly high, supratidal regions towards the heads of estuaries or around islands of high ground. These locations may not be expected to experience the same controls on marsh morphodynamics as the majority of interior and estuarine marsh areas, so might confound the regression analysis for such areas. Areas with exceptionally low CD values coincide with the seaward margins of open coast marshes, which have the potential to retreat [14] and advance rapidly [24]. Values of δP_{veg} in such areas therefore tend towards extreme values and reflect changes in marginal position more than changes in marsh platform integrity. Where CD is exceptionally high, δP_{veg} values are associated with the upland boundary and may again not reflect changes in marsh platform integrity but rather shifts between terrestrial and halophytic vegetation communities, which may have completely different reflectances. The extremities of the CD distribution were discarded where $CD \leq 500,000$ and $CD \geq 1,400,000$. 91% of the population was retained, and all the locations excluded within Hamford Water are marked, for illustration purposes, as black pixels within the red circles on Figure 5. With the extremities of the distribution excluded, a significant positive linear relationship between CD and the probability of degradation was found (Adjusted $R^2 = 0.37$, $p \leq 0.001$—see Figure 6, Panel A). The low positive coefficient suggests that, as CD increases—implying a reduction in tidal connectivity to offshore waters—the probability of marsh degradation increases slightly. CD values do not represent real-world physical quantities. For instance, a doubling of CD could occur because of multiple different combinations of increased horizontal distance and/or elevation. The precise coefficients of this relationship are therefore not readily interpretable beyond their sign and approximate magnitude.

A second-order polynomial relationship was found between Euclidean Distance (ED) and the probability of degradation, whereby areas with a low ED exhibit moderate probabilities of degradation in the order of 0.1, with this probability declining to a minimum of less than 0.05 at around 350 m before increasing again with ED to values in excess of 0.3 at distances of 1200 m. The relationship is significant at $p \leq 0.001$, and the high adjusted R^2 of 0.76 suggests that ED is an important determinant of changes in condition (Figure 6, Panel B). The ED metric is directly comparable to that used by Kearney and Rogers [20] to predict changes in marsh condition, and the regression fit from their study is superimposed on the figure for comparison.

Significant relationships were also found between both pCore and pUncon and the probability of degradation (Figure 6, panels C and D, respectively). The former relationship implies a decrease in the probability of degradation with increasing values of the pCore, although very high values of pCore become associated with increased probabilities of degradation again. With high adjusted R^2 values of 0.63 for pCore, the proportion of a pixel that is core vegetated marsh area is strongly related to changes in marsh condition. Pixels containing salt pan features were relatively rare within the dataset, with n = 13,157, representing 9.2% of all pixels. The regression only included those pixels where pUncon > 0. The relationship is significant with an R^2 value of 0.63, suggesting a strong positive relationship between the proportion of an area that comprises salt pans and their peripheral marsh features and the history of morphological evolution.

Summaries of all four regression relationships are provided in Table 2.

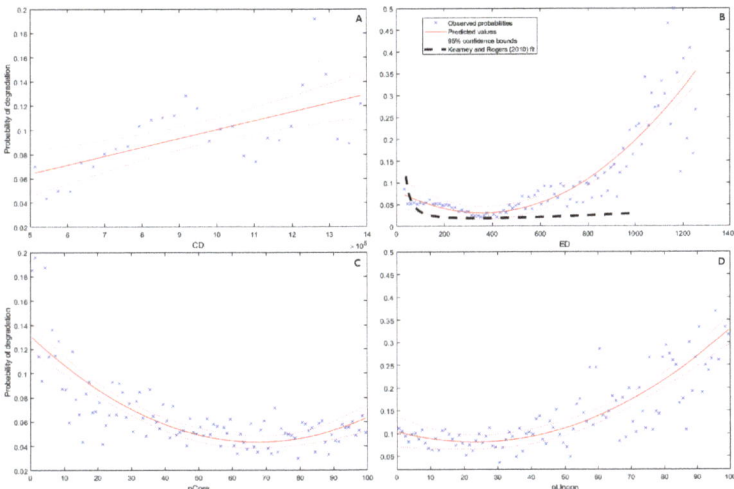

Figure 6. Probability of degradation against topological and morphological metrics. CD panel (**A**), ED panel (**B**), pCore panel (**C**), and pUncon panel (**D**). Relationship observed for ED by Kearney and Rogers [20] depicted on panel (**B**) for comparison. All relationships are significant at $p \leq 0.001$.

Table 2. Summary of regression models between topological or morphological metrics and the probability of marsh degradation.

	Adjusted R^2	x	x^2	f-Stat	p-Value
CD	0.37	7.3×10^{-8}	N/A	17.4	≤ 0.001
ED	0.76	-2.9×10^{-4}	4.0×10^{-7}	147	≤ 0.001
pCore	0.63	-2.6×10^{-3}	1.9×10^{-5}	85.7	≤ 0.001
pUncon	0.63	-2.0×10^{-3}	-4.2×10^{-5}	83.9	≤ 0.001

4. Discussion
4.1. Morphodynamic Change

The regional data for the Humber to Thames study area show an overall trend towards increasing marsh platform integrity over time, with rapid increases in integrity being much more common than rapid losses (inset to Figure 5). This pattern is, in part, a result of the rapid infilling and marsh advance that occurred in The Wash embayment during the observation period (1985–2016), where rates of margin advance up to 75 m per year were observed between 1992 and 2014 [24]. This established a large area of marsh that is included in the analysis and is associated with very high values of δP_{veg}. The pattern of increase and decrease in internal platform integrity is much patchier elsewhere, as seen for Hamford Water (Figure 5).

A degree of bias towards positive values of δP_{veg} was introduced by the choice of a marsh presence/absence mask from relatively late in the study period. Phelan et al. [17] base their mapping on data from 2008 to 2010. This implies that areas that may have contained marsh early in the study period, but which became completely unvegetated prior to 2008 and would produce negative δP_{veg}, will have been excluded from the analysis. A visual assessment of the aerial photography from 2013/14 and 1992 suggests that this phenomenon was rare within the region. The scale of negative changes in the overall horizontal extent of the marshes over the study period, relative to the Landsat pixel size, is typically small. Only isolated pixels at the seaward limits of some open-coast marshes are likely to have been affected by this bias [24]. Our findings support the idea that vegetated areas of marsh platform have the potential to increase in platform integrity much more rapidly than they deteriorate. This is likely the result of the potential for the rapid colonisation of large horizontal extents of unvegetated surfaces that accrete to a critical elevation to support seedling survival [29] near-simultaneously because of their very low gradients. Conversely, during erosive phases sediment loss is likely to be more gradual due to biostabilisation [50,51], and is also likely to be more localised in areas of high hydrodynamic stress. Assuming that morphological change can be inferred from vegetation extent change, the data suggest that, in marsh interiors at least, accretionary processes tend to outpace erosional ones.

We address change over a single time period only. Our methodology is not, therefore, able to detect regime shifts or abrupt changes as distinct from more gradual trends that result in the same δP_{veg} value. A natural development of our work, as the data archives become longer and denser, would be to incorporate temporal segmentation approaches similar to those used by the LandTrendr algorithm [52,53]. This would allow us to investigate whether the topological and morphological controls on abrupt regime shifts differ from those on gradual changes. Such work is beyond the scope of the current study.

4.2. Geomorphic Setting (CD)

No significant relationship was found when considering probability of degradation across the entire range of CD. This is likely because CD has a large range between 3.9×10^5 and 3.1×10^6, with over 90% of values falling in the interval 5.0×10^5 and 1.4×10^6. The upper end of the distribution in particular is therefore very sparse. This leads to very small numbers of pixels being represented in each of the 100 intervals across the CD distribution. With the relatively low prevalence of degradation in the order of 10% within the entire dataset, these small samples at high CD values often fail to represent any degraded pixels, resulting in probabilities of degradation of zero. Even if some degraded pixels are sampled, the resulting probability estimate is unlikely to be usefully precise while the sample size remains below about 50 pixels. Furthermore, the areas where $CD > 1.4 \times 10^6$ are typically high-elevation areas which are likely to be supratidal and may therefore be expected to be responding to different processes controlling their dynamics when compared to the intertidal marsh areas that are of principal interest here. Similarly, the data density is very low where $CD < 5.0 \times 10^5$, as these areas represent the seaward limits of open-coast marshes. The observations in these areas are likely to be dominated by the wave-driven erosion of the marsh margin rather than the internal marsh changes that δP_{veg} represents. The probabilities of degradation in these areas are relatively high, aligning well with the observations of the widespread retreat of open coast marsh margins in the region [24]. Excluding such areas from the analysis is therefore justifiable, as it enables insight into dynamics in the intertidal zone that are otherwise masked by variance in other areas that are either artefactual or likely to arise from a different suite of processes to those types of marsh interior processes that this study seeks to assess.

When the range of CD was limited to the interval 5.0×10^5 and 1.4×10^6, the regression analysis showed a significant positive linear relationship between CD and the probability of a pixel showing degradation. Low CD values are associated with minimum probabilities of degradation (Panel A, Figure 6). This implies that the interiors of open-coast marshes experience little degradation, while those towards the head of estuaries or tidal inlets are more susceptible. This aligns well with the conceptualisation of sediment sources for this study region, which is dominated by minerogenic marshes [26] and offshore tidal waters are the primary source of allochthonous input to support marsh elevations [54]. Those areas of marsh that are least tidally connected (high CD) are shown to be the most vulnerable, since the delivery of sediments is most restricted in these areas. This finding contrasts with those of Kearney and Rogers [20], who observe an increasing probability of degradation at shorter distances up-estuary. This is because the domain that they studied on the east coast of the US has much more significant riverine inputs and the locations of sedimentation are therefore fluvially, rather than tidally, dominated. Additionally, the Chesapeake Bay (US) marshes are highly organogenic, with the upper marsh sediment total organic content being reported to be around 80% at Rhode River [55], which implies that autochthonous accumulation dominates. By comparison, the UK east coast marshes rely more heavily on allochthonous inputs with much lower total organic contents than those of the US, at around 15% [56]. The relationship we find between CD and the probability of degradation is relatively weak ($R^2 = 0.37$), reflecting the fact that other factors, likely occurring at smaller scales, may be more significant. These may include the controls represented by the other ED, pCore, and pUncon metrics in this study, but also factors such as proximity and the magnitude of fluvial sediment loads that we have been unable to address here. The strength of the relationship may also arise, in part, from the failures of the simplified CD metric to perfectly represent tidal connectivity within the domain. Nevertheless, given the size of the region considered, the heterogeneity of marsh settings represented and the methodological limitations, the fact that any relationship emerges implies that the position of a marsh within the wider coastal setting is an important control on its vulnerability to sediment starvation and subsequent degradation. The contrast between our findings and those of Kearney and Rogers [20] suggests that the marsh position is not, however, a diagnostic parameter, since its effect varies between regions. Rather, it modulates the impacts of larger-scale geomorphological contexts (that may be considered as boundary conditions at the scale of the analysis presented here), such as sediment sources and delivery pathways. This finding implies that empirical attempts to predict morphological change in coastal wetlands must be nested within a hierarchy of process understanding in order to ensure that outcomes are appropriate for a particular location. Not all regions behave equally.

4.3. Distance from Creek/Edge of Marsh Parcel (ED)

The relationship established between Euclidean Distance (ED) and probability of degradation is significant and stronger ($R^2 = 0.76$) than that found for CD. It is also non-linear with initially high probabilities at short distances that decline to a minimum around 350 m before increasing dramatically. There is a notable similarity with the relationship observed in Chesapeake and Delaware Bays (black dashed line on Figure 6). The initial decline observed here is somewhat less rapid than that found by Kearney and Rogers [20], and beyond 400 m there is a strong increase in the probability of degradation with increasing ED at a rate that exceeds that found by Kearney and Rogers [20].

The inter-regional similarity observable regarding ED suggests that topological factors controlling marsh stability at scales below those represented by CD (i.e., within-marsh scales rather than within-estuary scales) may be operating in very similar fashions between regions, although the differences in the rates of decline and increases in degradation probability around the 350 m minima suggest a possible dependence on the scale/size of the marsh systems being observed. Marsh parcels are substantially smaller in the UK than in the USA example, where ED values of up to about 100 km were observed, although the goodness of fit above about 1 km declines. Differences in drainage network morphologies may also contribute. For the context of the east coast of the UK, the initial decline in probabilities can be interpreted, in part, as a function of the scale of channel identified in the basemap used for the distance calculations. Only major creeks exceeding 42.5 m width were included. Where the ED values are very low, the degradation measured by δP_{veg} could have a component that reflects the marginal erosion of the banks of large channels, where fetch is sufficient for wave-driven erosion to become significant in determining the spectral change within the pixel over the study period. Thereafter, however, it still appears that marsh vulnerability decreases with increasing distance from these major channels. This could be associated with the increasing drainage density of smaller creeks (not resolved by the ED metric used here), leading to shorter unchannelised lengths, a greater preponderance of levee-effects [19], and ultimately a greater potential for the drainage of and allochthonous sediment import to marsh areas within 350 m of a major channel. Beyond this distance, the probability of degradation increases again, which we attribute to declining drainage density and efficiency, leading to decreasing potential for tidal flushing, drainage, and sediment import as distances from the primary tidal channels continue to increase. Internal marsh areas without efficient drainage and a long way from major channels tend to experience relatively little elevation gain from external sources [57] and, particularly in the context of relative sea level rise, vegetation experiences increasing water and salt stress, potentially leading to die-back and substrate collapse [58]. This phenomenon is observable within the region and is illustrated by the hotspots of negative δP_{veg} in marsh interior areas shown in Figure A1 within the Appendix A.

4.4. Percentage Core Areas (pCore)

pCore is based on a 25 cm spatial resolution and therefore resolves differences in marsh morphology at a sub-pixel scale in terms of δP_{veg}. The same is true for pUncon. The relationship observed whereby the probability of degradation decreases to a minimum at pCore values of around 70% before levelling off or increasing slightly implies that fragmented areas of marsh (low pCore) reflect a history of greater marsh degradation. This implies that more degraded areas of marsh may continue to degrade at a faster rate than areas of platform with a high integrity. As a marsh platform becomes fragmented, pCore declines and the perimeter–area ratio of the remaining marsh parcels increases, providing a greater effective marginal length that may be vulnerable to erosion by hydrodynamic forces. The stability of the morphological state therefore decreases with increasing fragmentation, representing a positive morphodynamic feedback controlling marsh degradation. The slight increase in probability at very high pCore values may reflect the tendency for marsh areas that are separated from minor creeks by only a few metres to begin to degrade as a result of water stress [58], which Ursino et al. [59] showed can increase rapidly away from channels. Additional contributors to marsh degradation occurring at high pCore values may be reduced sediment inputs [19,57] or increased salt stress [60] in the interiors of marsh parcels.

4.5. Percentage of Unconnected Areas (pUncon)

The relationship between pUncon and the probability of degradation is significant, with a R^2 value of 0.63. The form of the relationship takes an almost opposite form to that for pCore, with higher values of pUncon being associated with higher probabilities of degradation. pCore and pUncon are somewhat negatively correlated to each other

(R = −0.11, $p \leq 0.001$), so this inverse relationship may in part reflect the same processes as are discussed with reference to pCore. The analysis for pUncon, however, incorporates only those marsh pixels where pans or pools are present, which represents a small subset of the dataset (9.2%). As such, this analysis allows for the isolation of behaviours exclusively in areas where pans are observed. Areas with a higher pUncon and therefore a greater proportion of pan-related features exhibit higher probabilities of degradation. Notably, for fragmentation identified by the pUncon metric, the maximum probabilities of degradation observed are much higher (≈0.5) than those calculated on the larger dataset of pCore (≈0.2), where low metric values also indicate fragmentation. Low pCore values, by contrast, largely reflect fragmentation by creek networks and bare surfaces connected to them. The difference in magnitudes of probability identified by the two regression relationships implies that the presence of pans indicates a much more vulnerable landscape configuration than one fragmented by creeks. Neumeier et al. [61] identified the life cycle of pans in Canadian marshes whereby they undergo a phase of active expansion before achieving maturity. The data presented here also support the conclusion that pans have a tendency to expand over decadal timescales. The analysis cannot identify causality, however. It is possible that the presence of pans establishes a feedback encouraging their subsequent expansion as the marsh develops [48]. Questions also remain over the causes of initial pan formation, with some theories suggesting that event-based phenomena, such as smothering of vegetation by rafted debris, may cause pans to develop. French et al. [62] noted that pan densities are lower on the more enclosed of the backbarrier marshes in Norfolk, where less debris may be rafted into the marshes over shorter seaward margins. Their finding is correlative but Pethick [47] argues that a mechanism for pan initiation on mature marshes must exist. Whatever the cause of pan initiation, our findings suggest that, once established, marsh areas containing pans are highly vulnerable compared to other areas. It is possible, therefore, that stochastic events, such as debris rafting, could initiate a long-term landscape vulnerability. In contrast, pans may simply be diagnostic of other conditions such as relative sea level changes, tidal range, or coastal configuration, rather than morphodynamic drivers in their own right [49]. If pans are not, in themselves, morphodynamic drivers, then our findings would suggest that the external controls causing pan formation continue to cause subsequent expansion and the conclusion that panned landscapes are vulnerable stands. Further work is needed to address the question of controls on salt pan development to better understand the fundamental causes of this vulnerability.

5. Conclusions

Our findings show that there exist certain overarching controls on the vulnerability of salt marshes to degradation at a range of scales. We demonstrate this observation through the application of a systematic spatial analysis of a simple, satellite-image-derived measure of change. By applying this methodology at the regional scale and across a range of estuarine, backbarrier, embayment, and open coast settings, we illustrate the nature of these controls more clearly than has hitherto been possible.

This work has presented an inherently scalable method for monitoring the platform integrity of salt marsh surfaces at a sub-pixel scale that is easily adapted to incorporate current and future data sources (such as imagery from the more recently launched Sentinel 2 satellites). The δP_{veg} metric presented here is a continuous variable representing change in marsh surface integrity over a given time period. It therefore provides substantially more statistical possibilities than the MSCI [20] or than we have explored in this study.

We express topological and morphological factors at a range of scales as metrics describing the connectivity of tidal waters, position within marsh, marsh platform integrity, and the prevalence of salt pans or pools. We demonstrate that all of these are significantly related to the morphodynamic evolution of marshes. This spatial hierarchy of morphological controls may continue to be applicable at both larger and smaller scales than are addressed here. The presence of controls at larger scales is shown by the finding of contrasting relationships between geomorphic setting and marsh degradation in this study and that of [20]. We hypothesise that this difference arises from regional-scale contrasts in climate, biota, sediment supply, and sea-level history that cause fundamental differences in the processes by which the marsh systems function and evolve. At a whole-marsh scale, however, responses to the distance from the marsh margin seem to be fairly consistent between regions, suggesting commonality in some of the processes governing marsh dynamics. At a smaller scale than is considered here, a variety of factors may become important, such as the spatial distribution of vegetation types [46,63] or phenotypes [64], which may determine sediment erodibility.

We have presented aggregated relationships that emerge at a regional scale. Overall, these suggest that marsh areas that are already exhibiting some form of fragmentation that lie far from the nearest creek and towards the heads of estuaries and inlets are the most likely to exhibit degradation. The prediction of changes in a particular location remains challenging. No relationships were found between the continuous values of δP_{veg} itself and any of the predictors presented here using basic statistical techniques. Only when the dimensionality of the dataset is reduced to probabilities do aggregated relationships emerge. The large number of parameters influencing marsh dynamics, the multiple scales of processes involved, and the complex interactions between them means that statistical prediction of internal marsh changes will require methods capable of capturing the interactions and high dimensionality that are inherent to such natural systems. Further work is needed to explore the potential of more sophisticated statistical techniques drawn from machine learning domains to synthesise datasets such as the one presented here into location-specific values of parameters describing the sign and magnitude of predicted marsh evolution.

Author Contributions: Conceptualization, B.R.E.; methodology, B.R.E., I.M. and T.S.; software, B.R.E.; validation, B.R.E.; formal analysis, B.R.E.; investigation, B.R.E.; resources, B.R.E., I.M. and T.S.; data curation, B.R.E.; writing—original draft preparation, B.R.E.; writing—review and editing, B.R.E., I.M. and T.S.; visualization, B.R.E..; supervision, I.M. and T.S.; project administration, I.M. and T.S.; funding acquisition, I.M. and T.S. All authors have read and agreed to the published version of the manuscript.

Funding: This research was funded by European Commission's Seventh Framework Programme (grant number 607131) and was conducted within the Foreshore Assessment using Space Technology (FAST) project. Further funds have been provided by the Isaac Newton Trust and the UKRI Natural Environment Research Council (NERC) grant RESIST-UK (grant number NE/R01082X/1). The APC was funded by the Cambridge Coastal Research Unit.

Data Availability Statement: The data supporting the analyses presented here are available on an Open Science Framework repository. Doi:10.17605/OSF.IO/MGSYZ.

Acknowledgments: We would like to thank our colleagues on the FAST project for their assistance, particularly that of Edward Morris. We are also grateful for the support and equipment provided by the UKRI NERC Field Spectroscopy Facility in Edinburgh.

Conflicts of Interest: The authors declare no conflict of interest.

Abbreviations

The following abbreviations are used in this manuscript:

CD	Cost distance
ED	Euclidean distance
HAT	Highest astronomical tide
ISCE	Integrated scale coastal evolution
L_5	Landsat 5
L_7	Landsat 7
L_8	Landsat 8

MSCI	Marsh surface condition index
MSPA	Morphological spatial pattern analysis
MSTR	Mean spring tidal range
NDVI	Normalised difference vegetation index
NE	Normalised elevation
ODN	Ordanace datum Newlyn
pCore	Percentage 'core' areas
pUncon	Percentage 'unconnected' areas
RMSE	Root-mean-squared error
SMP2	Second-generation shoreline management plan
UVVR	Unvegetated–vegetated ratio
δP_{veg}	Change in percentage vegetation cover within pixel

Appendix A. Methodology for Estimation of Marsh Platform Integrity Changes from Satellite Observations

The Normalised Difference Vegetation Index (NDVI), a dimensionless index taking values between -1 and 1, is a proxy for the amount of chlorophyll (and therefore vegetation) present, with higher values indicating more chlorophyll. The NDVI is the normalised ratio between reflectance in the red and near-infrared bands. Healthy vegetation produces positive index values (approaching one) [65]. Conceptually, the NDVI for a pixel in a satellite image can be considered to be a function of the percentage of that pixel covered by vegetation and the nature of the vegetation within that pixel. Applying an assumption of approximate stationarity in the reflectance of the bare sediments, changes in the percentage vegetation cover within the pixel are reflected in a change in NDVI, with the signal potentially being modulated by any attendant changes in the community composition (and therefore spectral signature) and vigour of the vegetation present.

Summer NDVI is relatively insensitive to the successional stage of the vegetation within this study region, while being lower for pioneer stages than mature stages during winter. Field spectroscopy was conducted at Tillingham, Essex, throughout the period 2015–2016. A total of 58 pioneer spectra and 103 mature marsh spectra were collected using an SVC HR1024i spectroradiometer and calibrated reference panel. The resulting hemispherical-conical reflectance factors were convolved to Landsat-8 band responses, from which NDVI was calculated. Pioneer vegetation (dominated by *Salicornia* and *Spartina* species) has similar Landsat-8 NDVI in summer (June-October) to the perennial marsh canopy (t-test, $p \geq 0.05$). However, the near-complete dieback of pioneer vegetation leads to the exposure of bare sediment and therefore lower winter NDVIs.

In Google Earth Engine [32], all scenes intersecting the study area were extracted from the Landsat archives for Landsat-5, -7, and -8 at a spatial resolution of 30 m, providing coverage between 1985 and 2018 (excluding Landsat-7 images subsequent to the failure of the scan line corrector on 31 May 2003). Level 1 Top-of-Atmosphere images were imported and filtered for cloud cover based on their metadata cloud score and subsequently on a per-pixel basis using the Simple Cloud Score algorithm. Thresholds for excluding data were set at 20% for both stages. NDVI was computed for all the remaining pixels of all images.

Differences in sensor response, and the NDVI values derived from them, are widely recognised [66] and have been shown to produce bias in time series analysis if combined without corrections being applied [67]. NDVI images were corrected for different sensor responses to produce a consistent time series of Landsat-7-equivalent NDVI values. Landsat-8 scenes were corrected using the cross-calibration derived by Roy et al. [68]. No existing cross-calibration was available for Landsat 5. To calculate a calibration function pixels were identified that fell within large areas of established marsh (those exceeding 1500 m^2 in the UK salt marsh extent map [17]) and more than 42.4 m (the diagonal of a 30 m Landsat pixel) from the edge of the marsh area. These were considered likely to be 'pure', fully vegetated locations. All the Landsat 5 and Landsat-7 scenes were selected for the period between the launch of Landsat-7 on 15 April 1999 and 31 May 2003. This process resulted in a total of 3747 pixels being selected for the cross-calibration using 5 Landsat-5 scenes and 40 Landsat-7 scenes. The per-pixel mean NDVI values were compared using a second-order polynomial, since a degree of saturation occurred in the Landsat-5 sensor when compared to Landsat-7 ($p \leq 0.0001$, $R^2 = 0.756$). The cross-calibration functions applied are detailed in Table A1.

Table A1. Cross-calibration functions to correct NDVI from Landsat-5 (L_5) and Landsat-8 (L_8) [68] to Landsat-7 (L_7) equivalence prior to time series analysis.

Transformation	Function	R^2
L_5 to L_7	$L_7 = 0.085 + (0.460 L_5) + (0.247 L_5^2)$	0.756
L_8 to L_7	$L_7 = -0.011 + 0.969 L_8$	0.906

The corrected Landsat-7-equivalent time series of NDVI images was processed in the Google Earth Engine to produce per-pixel linear trend coefficients. These trend coefficients were weakly related to the mean NDVI for the pixel over the entire time series ($R^2 = 0.22$, $p \leq 0.001$). This was interpreted as arising either from a CO_2 fertilisation signal causing vegetation in general to become 'greener' throughout the time series. Alternatively, it may reflect a pixel-scale morphological control on change in vegetation distribution, whereby pixels with higher platform integrity tend to increase their integrity more than those with lower integrity. Either of these effects would confound the investigation of topological controls. The relationship was therefore removed by using the residuals of the linear fit in Equation (A1) where $\delta N / \delta t$ denotes the NDVI trend and $\bar{N}$ denotes the mean NDVI. The residuals were subsequently standardised.

$$\delta N / \delta t = 0.011254 \bar{N} - 0.001430 \quad (A1)$$

Standardised residuals were converted into sub-pixel estimates of percentage change in vegetation cover (henceforth δP_{veg}) by calibration against geo-referenced vertical aerial photography supplied by the UK Environment Agency. The observed range of the standardised residuals was divided into 100 equal intervals and one pixel was selected at random within each interval. Some intervals towards the tails of the distribution contained no pixels, precluding their inclusion. In total, 83 pixels were selected. Pixels were clipped from the earliest available aerial photography (1992, panchromatic, 25 cm resolution) and from colour photography from 2013/2014 (20 cm resolution).

In Matlab, 50 random points were generated per Landsat pixel image pair (1992 and 2013/14), and sequentially superimposed on each image. A single operator visually assessed the surface cover and allocated each point as either vegetated or not vegetated. Manual assessment and attribution is assumed to provide the highest achievable accuracy in this context. A total of 4150 points were manually attributed for each year. From the proportions of vegetated and unvegetated points in an individual Landsat pixel area, the percentage vegetation cover was estimated. The difference between the percentage of the pixel area that was vegetated in 2013/14 compared to 1992 was calculated. A linear relationship was found between the standardised residuals and the change in vegetation cover. The linear relationship between the change in percentage vegetation cover between 1992 and 2013/14 estimated from aerial photography and the standardised residuals of the NDVI trend analysis (R_{trend}) is given in Equation (A2). The R-squared value of 0.87 implies that the change in vegetated area is the major contributor to changes in the residual trend. The unexplained variance is likely the result of other factors not accounted for by vegetation extent alone, such as species compositional change.

The method outlined above produces estimates of change in marsh platform integrity as continuous values between ±100%. This offers many statistical possibilities that will be explored in future work. For the purposes of the current study, estimates were thresholded at zero to produce a binary gain/loss indicator allowing for the alignment of statistical methods with the work of Kearney and Rogers [20], who discerned between pixels that were either degraded or not degraded.

$$\delta P_{veg} = 17.953 R_{trend} + 17.616 \tag{A2}$$

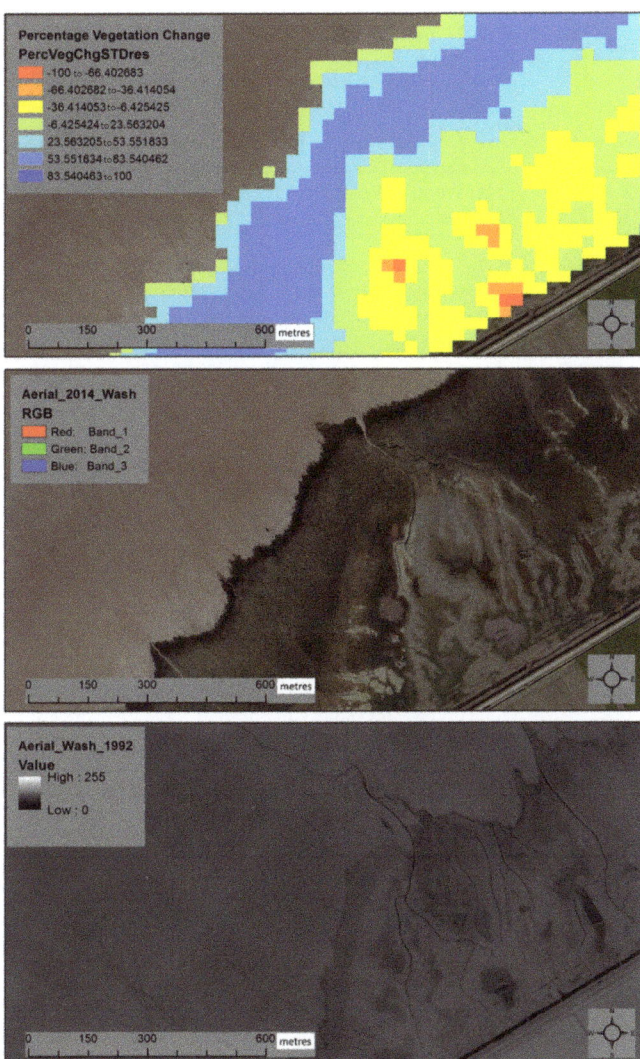

Figure A1. Estimated changes in percentage vegetation cover derived from the Landsat time series (**top**), with aerial photography from 2014 (**middle**) and 1992 (**bottom**) for comparison.

The performance of the calibrated δP_{veg} method was evaluated at a more local scale than the entire study domain in case large scale spatial dependency associated with, for example, latitude was a significant factor affecting calibration. The area selected for validation was Hamford Water, Essex, a tidal inlet containing approximately 600 ha of marsh that has been shown to exhibit a wide variety of morphodynamic behaviours in close spatial proximity to each other [69]. Analysis up to the point of manual calibration was repeated using only Hamford Water as the domain to establish locally derived residual trends which were classified into ten classes using a Jenks Natural Breaks algorithm. The largest contiguous area for each class was identified and from that area ten pixels were selected at random for validation, providing 100 pixels representing a range of morphological behaviours. These were analysed by manual point attribution from aerial photography following the same method as previously outlined. The change in percentage vegetation cover from manual point attribution was compared to δP_{veg} estimated from the regional-scale analysis, producing a root mean square error (RMSE) of 11.9% of full range (−100% to +100% change).

References

1. McOwen, C.; Weatherdon, L.; Bochove, J.W.; Sullivan, E.; Blyth, S.; Zockler, C.; Stanwell-Smith, D.; Kingston, N.; Martin, C.; Spalding, M.; et al. A global map of saltmarshes. *Biodivers. Data J.* **2017**, *5*, e11764. [CrossRef]
2. Friess, D.A.; Yando, E.S.; Alemu I, J.B.; Wong, L.W.; Soto, S.D.; Bhatia, N. Ecosystem Serices and Dissserices of Mangrove Forests and Salt Marshes. In *Oceanography and Marine Biology: An Annual Review*; CRC Press: Boca Raton, FL, USA, 2020; pp. 58:107–58:142.
3. Mitsch, W.J.; Gosselink, J.G. *Wetlands*, 3rd ed.; Wiley: New York, NY, USA, 2000; p. 920.
4. McLeod, E.; Chmura, G.L.; Bouillon, S.; Salm, R.; Björk, M.; Duarte, C.M.; Lovelock, C.E.; Schlesinger, W.H.; Silliman, B.R. A blueprint for blue carbon: Toward an improved understanding of the role of vegetated coastal habitats in sequestering CO2. *Front. Ecol. Environ.* **2011**, *9*, 552–560. [CrossRef]
5. Möller, I.; Spencer, T.; French, J.R.; Leggett, D.J.; Dixon, M. Wave transformation over salt marshes: a field and numerical modelling study from North Norfolk, England. *Estuarine Coast. Shelf Sci.* **1999**, *49*, 411–426. [CrossRef]
6. Möller, I. Quantifying saltmarsh vegetation and its effect on wave height dissipation: Results from a UK East coast saltmarsh. *Estuarine Coast. Shelf Sci.* **2006**, *69*, 337–351. [CrossRef]
7. Burden, A.; Garbutt, R.; Evans, C.; Jones, D.; Cooper, D. Carbon sequestration and biogeochemical cycling in a saltmarsh subject to coastal managed realignment. *Estuarine Coast. Shelf Sci.* **2013**, *120*, 12–20. [CrossRef]
8. Chmura, G.L. What do we need to assess the sustainability of the tidal salt marsh carbon sink? *Ocean. Coast. Manag.* **2013**, *83*, 25–31. [CrossRef]
9. Roner, M.; Alpaos, A.D.; Ghinassi, M.; Marani, M.; Silvestri, S.; Franceschinis, E. Spatial variation of salt-marsh organic and inorganic deposition and organic carbon accumulation: Inferences from the Venice lagoon, Italy. *Adv. Water Resour.* **2016**, *93*, 276–287. [CrossRef]
10. Boesch, D.F.; Turner, R.E. Dependence of fishery species on salt marshes: The role of food and refuge. *Estuaries* **1984**, *7*, 460. [CrossRef]
11. Costa, M.J.; Costa, J.; de Almeida, P.R.; Assis, C.A. Do eel grass beds and salt marsh borders act as preferential nurseries and spawning grounds for fish? An example of the Mira estuary in Portugal. *Ecol. Eng.* **1994**, *3*, 187–195. [CrossRef]
12. Ladd, C.J.; Duggan-Edwards, M.F.; Bouma, T.J.; Pagès, J.F.; Skov, M.W. Sediment Supply Explains Long-Term and Large-Scale Patterns in Salt Marsh Lateral Expansion and Erosion. *Geophys. Res. Lett.* **2019**, *46*, 11178–11187. [CrossRef]
13. Hughes, R.G.; Paramor, O.A.L. On the loss of saltmarshes in south-east England and. *J. Appl. Ecol.* **2004**, *41*, 440–448. [CrossRef]
14. van der Wal, D.; Pye, K. Patterns, rates and possible causes of saltmarsh erosion in the Greater Thames area (UK). *Geomorphology* **2004**, *61*, 373–391. [CrossRef]
15. Burd, F. *Erosion and Vegetation Change on the Salt Marshes of Essex and North Kent between 1973 and 1988*; Technical Report; Nature Conservancy Council: Peterborough, UK, 1992.
16. Cooper, N.J.; Cooper, T.; Burd, F. 25 years of salt marsh erosion in Essex: Implications for coastal defence and nature conservation. *J. Coast. Conserv.* **2001**, *7*, 31–40. [CrossRef]
17. Phelan, N.; Shaw, A.; Baylis, A. *The Extent of Saltmarsh in England and Wales: 2006–2009*; Environment Agency: Bristol, UK, 2011.
18. Vandenbruwaene, W.; Meire, P.; Temmerman, S. Formation and evolution of a tidal channel network within a constructed tidal marsh. *Geomorphology* **2012**, *151–152*, 114–125. [CrossRef]
19. French, J.R.; Spencer, T. Dynamics of sedimentation in a tide-dominated backbarrier salt marsh, Norfolk, UK. *Mar. Geol.* **1993**, *110*, 315–331. [CrossRef]
20. Kearney, M.S.; Rogers, A.S. Forecasting sites of future coastal marsh loss using topographical relationships and logistic regression. *Wetl. Ecol. Manag.* **2010**, *18*, 449–461. [CrossRef]
21. Allen, J. Simulation models of salt-marsh morphodynamics: Some implications for high-intertidal sediment couplets related to sea-level change. *Sediment. Geol.* **1997**, *113*, 211–223. [CrossRef]
22. Da Lio, C.; D'Alpaos, A.; Marani, M. The secret gardener: Vegetation and the emergence of biogeomorphic patterns in tidal environments. *Philos. Trans. Ser. Math. Phys. Eng. Sci.* **2013**, *371*. [CrossRef]
23. D'Alpaos, A.; Lanzoni, S.; Marani, M.; Rinaldo, A. Landscape evolution in tidal embayments: Modeling the interplay of erosion, sedimentation, and vegetation dynamics. *J. Geophys. Res. Earth Surf.* **2007**, *112*, 1–17. [CrossRef]
24. Evans, B.R.; Möller, I.; Spencer, T.; Smith, G. Dynamics of salt marsh margins are related to their three-dimensional functional form. *Earth Surf. Process. Landforms* **2019**, *44*, esp.4614. [CrossRef]

25. Pethick, J.; Leggett, D. The morphology of the Anglian coast. In *Coastlines of the Southern North Sea*; Hillen, R., Verhagen, H., Eds.; American Society of Civil Engineers (ASCE): Reston, VA, USA, 1993; pp. 52–64.
26. Pye, K.; French, P. *Erosion and Accretion Processes on British Saltmarshes: Volume Three*; Technical Report; Cambridge Environmental Research Consultants: Cambridge, UK, 1993.
27. Allen, J. Morphodynamics of Holocene salt marshes: A review sketch from the Atlantic and Southern North Sea coasts of Europe. *Quat. Sci. Rev.* **2000**, *19*, 1155–1231. [CrossRef]
28. Kestner, F. The Old Coastline of the Wash. *T Geogr. J.* **1962**, *128*, 457–471. [CrossRef]
29. Balke, T.; Stock, M.; Jensen, K.; Bouma, T.J.; Kleyer, M. A global analysis of the seaward salt marsh extent: The importance of tidal range. *Water Resour. Res.* **2016**, *52*, 3775–3786. [CrossRef]
30. Suchrow, S.; Jensen, K. Plant species responses to an elevational gradient in German North Sea salt marshes. *Wetlands* **2010**, *30*, 735–746. [CrossRef]
31. Ganju, N.K.; Defne, Z.; Kirwan, M.L.; Fagherazzi, S.; D'Alpaos, A.; Carniello, L. Spatially integrative metrics reveal hidden vulnerability of microtidal salt marshes. *Nat. Commun.* **2017**, *8*, 14156. [CrossRef]
32. Gorelick, N.; Hancher, M.; Dixon, M.; Ilyushchenko, S.; Thau, D.; Moore, R. Google Earth Engine: Planetary-scale geospatial analysis for everyone. *Remote Sens. Environ.* **2017**, *202*, 18–27. [CrossRef]
33. Lopes, C.L.; Mendes, R.; Caçador, I.; Dias, J.M. Assessing salt marsh extent and condition changes with 35 years of Landsat imagery: Tagus Estuary case study. *Remote Sens. Environ.* **2020**, *247*, 111939. [CrossRef]
34. Hargrove, W.W.; Hoffman, F.M.; Hessburg, P.F. Mapcurves: A quantitative method for comparing categorical maps. *J. Geogr. Syst.* **2006**, *8*, 187–208. [CrossRef]
35. ABPMer. Atlas of Marine Energy Resources. 2008. Available online: http://www.renewables-atlas.info/ (accessed on 5 May 2015).
36. French, J. Tidal marsh sedimentation and resilience to environmental change: Exploratory modelling of tidal, sea-level and sediment supply forcing in predominantly allochthonous systems. *Mar. Geol.* **2006**, *235*, 119–136. [CrossRef]
37. French, J.R.; Spencer, T.; Murray, A.L.; Arnold, N.S. Geostatistical analysis of sediment deposition in two small tidal wetlands, Norfolk, UK. *J. Coast. Res.* **1985**, *11*, 308–321.
38. Reed, D.J.; Spencer, T.; Murray, A.L.; French, J.R.; Leonard, L. Marsh surface sediment deposition and the role of tidal creeks: Implications for created and managed coastal marshes. *J. Coast. Conserv.* **1999**, *5*, 81–90. [CrossRef]
39. Soille, P.; Vogt, P. Morphological segmentation of binary patterns. *Pattern Recognit. Lett.* **2009**, *30*, 456–459. [CrossRef]
40. Vogt, P. GUIDOS: Tools for the assessment of pattern, connectivity, and fragmentation. In Proceedings of the EGU General Assembly 2013, Vienna, Austria, 7–12 April 2013; Volume 15, p. 13526.
41. Ostapowicz, K.; Vogt, P.; Riitters, K.H.; Kozak, J.; Estreguil, C. Impact of scale on morphological spatial pattern of forest. *Landsc. Ecol.* **2008**, *23*, 1107–1117. [CrossRef]
42. Saura, S.; Vogt, P.; Velázquez, J.; Hernando, A.; Tejera, R. Key structural forest connectors can be identified by combining landscape spatial pattern and network analyses. *For. Ecol. Manag.* **2011**, *262*, 150–160. [CrossRef]
43. Chang, Q.; Liu, X.; Wu, J.; He, P. MSPA-Based Urban Green Infrastructure Planning and Management Approach for Urban Sustainability: Case Study of Longgang in China. *J. Urban Plan. Dev.* **2015**, *141*, A5014006. [CrossRef]
44. French, J.R.; Stoddart, D.R. Hydrodynamics of saltmarsh creek systems: Implications for marsh morphological development and material exchange. *Earth Surf. Process. Landforms* **1992**, *17*, 235–252. [CrossRef]
45. Friedrichs, C.T.; Perry, J.E. Tidal salt marsh morphodynamics: A synthesis. *J. Coast. Res.* **2001**, *27*, 7–37.
46. Adam, P. *Saltmarsh Ecology*; Cambridge University Press: Cambridge, UK, 1990; p. 461.
47. Pethick, J. The distribution of salt pans on tidal salt marshes. *J. Biogeogr.* **1974**, *1*, 57–62. [CrossRef]
48. Yapp, R.H.; Johns, D.; Jones, O.T. The salt marshes of the Dovey Estuary. *J. Ecol.* **1917**, *5*, 65–103. [CrossRef]
49. Goudie, A. Characterising the distribution and morphology of creeks and pans on salt marshes in England and Wales using Google Earth. *Estuarine Coast. Shelf Sci.* **2013**, *129*, 112–123. [CrossRef]
50. Murray, A.B.; Knaapen, M.A.; Tal, M.; Kirwan, M.L. Biomorphodynamics: Physical-biological feedbacks that shape landscapes. *Water Resour. Res.* **2008**, *44*. [CrossRef]
51. Spencer, T.; Möller, I.; Rupprecht, F.; Bouma, T.J.; van Wesenbeeck, B.K.; Kudella, M.; Paul, M.; Jensen, K.; Wolters, G.; Miranda-Lange, M.; Schimmels, S. Salt marsh surface survives true-to-scale simulated storm surges. *Earth Surf. Process. Landforms* **2016**, *41*. [CrossRef]
52. Kennedy, R.E.; Yang, Z.; Cohen, W.B. Detecting trends in forest disturbance and recovery using yearly Landsat time series: 1. LandTrendr—Temporal segmentation algorithms. *Remote Sens. Environ.* **2010**, *114*, 2897–2910. [CrossRef]
53. Kennedy, R.; Yang, Z.; Gorelick, N.; Braaten, J.; Cavalcante, L.; Cohen, W.; Healey, S. Implementation of the LandTrendr Algorithm on Google Earth Engine. *Remote Sens.* **2018**, *10*, 691. [CrossRef]
54. Reed, D.J. Sediment dynamics and deposition in a retreating coastal salt marsh. *Estuarine Coast. Shelf Sci.* **1988**, *26*, 67–79. [CrossRef]
55. Kirwan, M.L.; Langley, J.A.; Guntenspergen, G.R.; Megonigal, J.P. The impact of sea-level rise on organic matter decay rates in Chesapeake Bay brackish tidal marshes. *Biogeosciences* **2013**, *10*, 1869–1876. [CrossRef]
56. Reef, R.; Schuerch, M.; Christie, E.K.; Möller, I.; Spencer, T. The effect of vegetation height and biomass on the sediment budget of a European saltmarsh. *Estuarine Coast. Shelf Sci.* **2018**, *202*, 125–133. [CrossRef]

57. Temmerman, S.; Govers, G.; Wartel, S.; Meire, P. Spatial and temporal factors controlling short-term sedimentation in a salt and freshwater tidal marsh, scheldt estuary, Belgium, SW Netherlands. *Earth Surf. Process. Landforms* **2003**, *28*, 739–755. [CrossRef]
58. Reed, D.J. The impact of sea-level rise on coastal salt marshes. *Prog. Phys. Geogr.* **1990**, *14*, 465–481. [CrossRef]
59. Ursino, N.; Silvestri, S.; Marani, M. Subsurface flow and vegetation patterns in tidal environments. *Water Resour. Res.* **2004**, *40*. [CrossRef]
60. Shen, C.; Zhang, C.; Xin, P.; Kong, J.; Li, L. Salt Dynamics in Coastal Marshes: Formation of Hypersaline Zones. *Water Resour. Res.* **2018**, *54*, 3259–3276. [CrossRef]
61. Neumeier, U.; Poulin, P.; Roge, M.; Morisette, A.; Huard, A.M. Morphology and evolution of salt marsh pans in the lower St. Lawrence Estuary. In Proceedings of the Coastal Dynamics, Arcachon, France, 24–28 June 2013, pp. 1275–1286.
62. French, J.; Spencer, T.; Stoddart, D.R. *Backbarrier Salt Marshes of the North Norfolk Coast: Geomorphic Developments and Response to Rising Sea-Levels*; Discussion Papers in Conservation; Ecology and Conservation Unit, Univeristy College London: London, UK, 1990; Volume 54, pp. 1–3.
63. Ford, H.; Garbutt, A.; Ladd, C.; Malarkey, J.; Skov, M.W. Soil stabilization linked to plant diversity and environmental context in coastal wetlands. *J. Veg. Sci.* **2016**, *27*, 259–268. [CrossRef]
64. Bernik, B.; Pardue, J.; Blum, M. Soil erodibility differs according to heritable trait variation and nutrient-induced plasticity in the salt marsh engineer Spartina alterniflora. *Mar. Ecol. Prog. Ser.* **2018**, *601*, 1–14. [CrossRef]
65. Rouse, J.; Haas, R.; Schell, J.; Deering, D. *Monitoring The vernal Advancement and Retrogradation (Green Wave Effect) of Natural Vegetation*; Progress Report RSC 1978-1; Remote Sensing Center, Texas A&M Univ: College Station, TX, USA, 1973; p. 93.
66. Ke, Y.; Im, J.; Lee, J.; Gong, H.; Ryu, Y. Characteristics of Landsat 8 OLI-derived NDVI by comparison with multiple satellite sensors and in-situ observations. *Remote Sens. Environ.* **2015**, *164*, 298–313. [CrossRef]
67. Sulla-Menashe, D.; Friedl, M.A.; Woodcock, C.E. Sources of bias and variability in long-term Landsat time series over Canadian boreal forests. *Remote Sens. Environ.* **2016**, *177*, 206–219. [CrossRef]
68. Roy, D.; Zhang, H.; Ju, J.; Gomez-Dans, J.; Lewis, P.; Schaaf, C.; Sun, Q.; Li, J.; Huang, H.; Kovalskyy, V. A general method to normalize Landsat reflectance data to nadir BRDF adjusted reflectance. *Remote Sens. Environ.* **2016**, *176*, 255–271. [CrossRef]
69. Evans, B. Processes Governing Saltmarsh Morphodynamics Methodological Challenges and Spatial Variability. Master's Thesis, Department of Geography, University of Cambridge, Cambridge, UK, 2011.

Article

Sand Net Device to Control the Meanders of a Coastal River: The Case of the Authie Estuary (France)

Anh T. K. Do [1,2,*], Nicolas Huybrechts [1] and Philippe Sergent [1]

- [1] Cerema, HA Research Team, 134 rue de Beauvais, 60200 Compiegne, France; nicolas.huybrechts@cerema.fr (N.H.); Philippe.Sergent@cerema.fr (P.S.)
- [2] Faculty of Water Resources Engineering, The University of Da Nang (UD)—University of Science and Technology, 54 Nguyen Luong Bang Str, Danang 50000, Vietnam
- * Correspondence: dtkanh@dut.udn.vn or thi-kim-anh.do@cerema.fr

Abstract: The Authie estuary is characterized by an important southern sand spit and a northern shoreline subject to strong erosion due to the meandering of the coastal river. In order to reduce this erosion, a new soft coastal defence, namely the sand net device (SND), has been implemented inside the Authie estuary. It consists of several nets assembled in an inverted V creating a porous structure and thus trapping sand as shoreline protection. However up to now, little proof has been provided on the explicit influence of this SND on the hydrodynamic pattern and associated morphodynamics. In this paper, field surveys of morphological developments combined with numerical modelling (Telemac-2D/3D) analyze the influence of the SND into flow pattern and morphodynamics. In situ monitoring clearly points out sedimentation around the SND and a deepening of the main channel. Modelling results show that, without SND, erosion is observed around its location. With a SND implemented, the velocity has been reduced and created a deviation in its direction by a circulation around the SND location. The impact area of the structure is around 500 m in both directions, upstream and downstream part.

Keywords: sand net device; Authie estuary; meandering river; erosion; sedimentation

1. Introduction

Estuary mouths generally feature complex interactions between waves, tides, wave-induced currents that vary with tidal range and fluvial discharge. These systems disrupt the longshore drift and sediment supply [1]. Along sandy coasts, estuary mouths are often characterized by sand accumulation in the form of sand bars or of a sand spit that develops across the estuary [2,3]. The continuing development of a spit across the estuary mouth, usually in the direction of the prevailing littoral drift, frequently results in the erosion of the downdrift estuary shore due to the migration of the main estuary channel [4]. In addition to the effects of natural forcing factors, sediment accumulation and/or shore erosion at an estuary mouth can be increased or be conversely reduced due to human actions that modify estuarine hydrodynamics and sediment dynamics (man-induced changes in river discharge, land reclamation, river bank stabilization, coastal defense structures) [5].

One typical example of interaction between coastal sand spit and neighbouring river is the shallow Authie estuary located in the English Channel (Figure 1a). The Authie mouth consists of an important south sand spit prograded seawards and northward and a north bank subject to strong erosion, and a large zone of saltmarshes in the middle part of the estuary. This estuarine mouth is largely blocked by the prominent sand spit and intertidal/subtidal platform, and this has forced the main channel to migrate along the northern shore and adjacent shoreline [4].

The last severe dune erosions of Authie estuary occurred in 2011 and 2018. The meander has approached the northern shore and eroded the dunes under the combined action of currents and waves [6]. In order to prevent such events, a new soft coastal defence system

has been implemented to reduce erosion inside the Authie estuary. It consists of a porous groyne which aims to trap sediment inside net layers and to thus create a sandy deposit as shoreline protection. Up to now, the efficiency of this sand net device (SND) has not been documented. The objective of this contribution is thus to analyze the influence of this SND on the flow pattern and morphodynamic of the estuary. The characteristics of the studied configuration and the implemented SND are first presented. The SND influence is studied with field surveys combined with numerical modelling. Field survey allows to quantify the bed evolution around the implemented device. A 3D numerical flume experiment is developed to characterize the drag coefficient induced by the SND. Finally, a 2D large scale model of the estuary serves to analyse the morphodynamic evolution and the impact on flow circulation with or without the SND in order to highlight its effects.

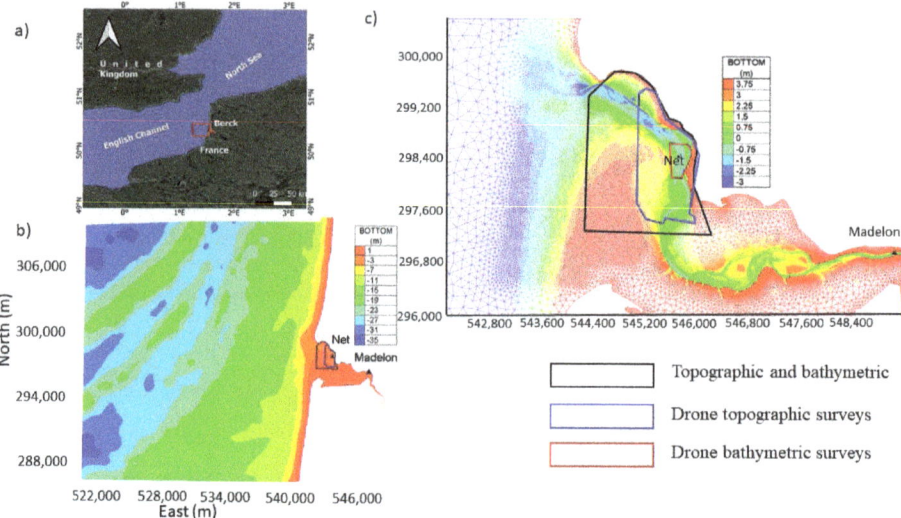

Figure 1. Location of Authie estuary and survey stations (**a**); model domain in numerical model (**b**); and areas of topographic and bathymetric surveys (**c**).

2. Authie Estuary

The Authie Estuary, located in the eastern English Channel near the town of Berck-sur-Mer (Figure 1a), is a small macrotidal estuary exhibiting a relatively large intertidal zone. The total length of the main river is 98 km and the river drains a low-gradient Mesozoic limestone plateau catchment of approximately 985 km^2 that supplies very limited sediment to the coastal zone due to the nature of the bedrock geology [4,7]. The river discharge is quite low and ranging from 4 m^3/s in summer to 13 m^3/s in spring with an average of 10 m^3/s [7]. The estuary mouth is affected by large tidal range within 8.5 m and 4.9 m for spring and neap tides, respectively. This large tidal amplitude is responsible for strong tidal currents up to 1 m/s at the mouth during spring tides and even up to 1.5 m/s seaward of the estuary mouth and in the adjacent coastal zone [8,9]. The tidal ranges decrease to 4 m and 1.8 m, respectively, 7 km inland (at La Madelon habour). The coastal/nearshore zone is characterized by a shore-parallel circulation dominated by northward-directed flood currents [10].

The Authie estuary has endured infilling of sand from the English Channel [7,8,11] and describes a typical geomorphological structure. The coast to the south has both prograded seawards and northwards over time (6.1 m/yr between 2005–2012; ref. [4,7]) and the northward progradation has been accompanied by the development of a very extensive intertidal and subtidal platform and spit. The progressive extension of this major accumulation protects the inner estuary from wave action and it thus favors the development of mudflats and saltmarshes [12]. The estuary mouth is largely blocked by the prominent sand spit and intertidal/subtidal platform, and this has forced the main channel of the Authie to flow along the northern shore of the estuary mouth and adjacent shoreline [4]. The dune erosion at the northern shoreline (Figure 2a) is induced by river meandering [6]. Large portions of the inner estuary have been polderized during the last centuries, which resulted in increased sedimentation and seaward saltmarsh progression [7,8].

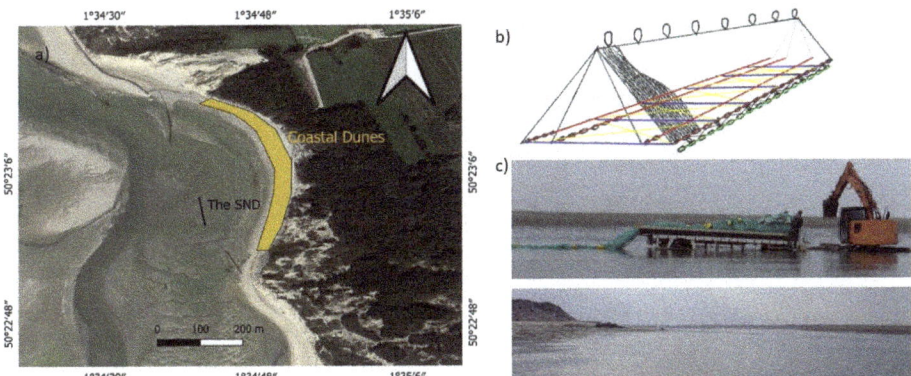

Figure 2. Location of the SND (**a**); schematic of the device: layers of nets assembled in inverted V, buoy to raise the device with the tide (**b**); and the SND in reality (**c**).

3. Materials and Methods
3.1. Large Scale Demonstrator of Sand Net Device (SND)

The implemented hydraulic structure (Figure 2a) is a soft engineering solution developed by the company S-Able by Michon [13], which applied for the patent. It consists of several nets assembled looking as a pyramid or a tepee to create a porous structure and associated turbulent dissipation (Figure 2b). The feets of the nets are maintained by chains and anchors, whereas the deployment of the net head on rising and falling tide is completed by floating buoys (Figure 2c). As discussed by Sergent et al. [6] the device may be considered as a porous groyne with two effects: shielding and sediment trapping. Between the shoreline and the sand spit, the river is usually meandering between two branches: one main channel near the sand spit and a secondary channel near the shoreline. The river returned to the secondary branches in 2011 and 2018. The principle is thus to install the SND at the entrance of the secondary branch of the river. The reduction of the flow velocity around the nets allows sediment trapping. The sediment deposit and the additional energy losses induced in the secondary branch will favour the flow inside the main branch where we want to maintain the coastal river. The sediment accumulation thus forms a protection to reduce the erosion pattern. Such a first device was installed in 2014 and raised in 2017 [6] but with limited morphodynamic monitoring. In 2019, a new SND was installed and a more complete field monitoring has been achieved. The length of the installation is 108 m and its width 1.5 m. The installation of the sand nets inside the secondary branch was performed on 27 March in 2019. In the part near the shoreline, the nets rely on the sandbank and they are progressively introduced inside the channel using a truck having at the end of the installation wheels almost completely in the water (about 0.5–1 m in depth, Figure 2c). When the water depth is sufficiently high so that the buoys are able to raise the nets completely, the SND height reaches up to 1.1 m.

3.2. In Situ Surveys

The field monitoring consists of different types of topographic and bathymetric surveys (Table 1). The topographic monitoring is performed by drones and covers the area defined by the blue line in Figure 1c.

Table 1. The different topographic and bathymetric data.

Data	Date of Surveys	Area	Data in the Channel of River
Topography and bathymetry	15 February 2019	Black line	Yes
Topography	20 March 2019	Blue line	No
Bathymetry	18 April 2019	Red line	Yes
Topography and bathymetry (Lidar)	30April 2019	Whole bay and shoreline	No
Topography	4 July 2019	Blue line	No
Bathymetry	4 July 2019	Red line	Yes
Topography	2 September 2019	Blue line	No

The drone monitoring provides Digital Elevation Models (DEMs) in the right bank of Authie from the river to beyond the summit of the dune and in the left bank of Authie from the river until the end of the defined area. A first survey was carried out before the installation of the SND: 20 March 2019. Other drone surveys have occurred on 4 July 2019 and 2 September 2019.

The DEMs are constructed from drone flight involving the measurement of grounding points for the georeferencing of topographic measurements. The main channel of the Authie estuary, located in the middle, is permently immersed (i.e., at low tide) and it is not covered. The expected accuracy of the DEMs is 5–10 centimetres (horizontal or vertical) outside the vegetated area and up to 25 cm (horizontally) on the left bank of the Authie.

As the drone sensor is blind below the water surface, the topography is completed by observations of bathymetry around the riverbed. Two surveys have been conducted in February and October 2019 (black line in Figure 1c) whereas more local surveys around the nets have been conducted in April and July 2019 (red line in Figure 1c). The different bathymetry surveys have been conducted with a single beam sounder mounted on a vessel. In addition, an airborne Lidar survey has been conducted by local authorities in April 2019. The Lidar survey covers the whole bay of Authie and the shoreline from Bay of Somme to bay of Canche. Bed elevation in both intertidal and subtidal areas are measured by the airborne sensor.

Besides, tide and velocity measurements were conducted in 2017 and 2019. The most complete data was collected in 2017 with both velocity and water level whereas only water levels were measured in 2019. Water levels are measured at two locations within Authie estuary (Net and Madelon see Figure 1c) and velocity data are available near the location of the SND.

3.3. Numerical Experiments

Two different models are set up using the open source TELEMAC-MASCARET modelling system (hereafter the TMS, version V8P1). The TMS has been widely used to simulate the hydrodynamic flow and associated sediment transport dynamic in fluvial zones [14,15] or coastal areas [16–18]. Trials have been performed inside an experimental flume (Ifremer at Boulogne sur Mer) of 4 m wide. The water depth has been remained constant at 2 m and the upstream flow velocity has been imposed from 0.6 to 1 m/s. The drag coefficient has been estimated from a force measurement on the device. However, to estimate how the drag coefficient of the SND evolves with the tidal range, numerical experiments are conducted. The studied SND in both experimental and numerical flume is similar as the one deployed in situ: 1.5 m in baseline length and 1.1 m in height.

The dimension of the numerical domain is 200 m in length, 4 m in width. The numerical model is based on Telemac 3D which solves the Navier-Stokes equations. Concerning the turbulence model, the k-ϵ model is selected. The distance between the nodes is about

0.1 m in the horizontal planes and with 18 sigma planes uniformly distributed for the vertical resolution. The same number of planes is used for all the simulations. On similar configurations, Tassi et al. [19] points out that the mesh convergence is reached for 18 planes. A simulation has been performed with 24 planes and the differences in the variables (depth and velocity) are lower than 1%.

The time step is 0.05 s and the duration of each simulation is 30 min to reach a steady flow. In the numerical model, the SND is considered as a bottom step without permeability. It serves to provide a first simple estimation of the energy losses induced by the sand net device. In reality, it could correspond to a device full of sandy deposit. As boundary condition, the velocity is imposed upstream whereas the water depth is imposed downstream. The velocity is kept constant to 0.8 m/s whereas six different values of the water depth ranging between 0.9 and 6 m are imposed in order to analyze how the drag coefficient evolves with the tidal level. The drag coefficient is estimated as

$$C_d = \frac{p_{t1} - p_{t2}}{0.5 \rho U_1^2} \quad (1)$$

where p_{t1}, p_{t2} are the total pressure upstream and downstream the SND; C_d is the drag coefficient; ρ is water density and U_1 is the velocity upstream.

3.4. Large-Scale Numerical Model

The hydrodynamic model (TELEMAC-2D) is based on the depth-averaged shallow water equations for momentum and continuity [20]. The unstructured model mesh, created using Bluekenue grid generation software has variable resolution, being relatively fine (8–10 m) around the SND and coarser (200–250 m) at offshore parts. The horizontal grid contains 80.305 nodes and 158.189 triangular elements.

The computational domain of the model has been developed to represent the Authie estuary which includes the open sea (23 km in wide and 24 km in length), the estuary and a part of the upstream river (Figure 1b). The model has been forced here with tidal elevations and tidal velocities at the offshore boundaries and a constant river flow rate of 10 m³/s at the inland river boundary.

At the maritime boundary, astronomical tide elevation and tidal currents are reconstructed using the European Shelf atlases (TXPO, ref. [21]) as a superposition of harmonic waves [22] for each of the nodes of the offshore boundary (Equation (2)).

$$H_{tide} = H_0 + \sum_n H_n f_n \cos(\sigma_n t - g_n + V_n - u_n) \quad (2)$$

where H_{tide} is the tidal height; H_0 is the mean height of the water level; n is the harmonics number; H_n is the mean amplitude of the n-wave; f_n is the nodal correction for the amplitude; σ_n is the frequency; t is the time; g_n is the phase lag of the equilibrium tide; V_n is the astronomic argument; and u_n is the nodal correction for the phase lag. Similar relationships are used for the velocity.

The bathymetry interpolated on the mesh comes from different sources: offshore from the SHOM (Service Hydrographique Marine), Lidar data collected in April 2019 nearshore and inside the bay. More detailed bathymetric data inside the estuary area and the net area is used (survey of February 2019). During the simulations, a time step of 5 s is used for all the simulations. An initial spin-up simulation of 30 days is achieved to initialize the hydrodynamic variables.

The sediment transport module (GAIA), Audouin et al. [23] is internally coupled with the hydrodynamics (TELEMAC-2D). The bed friction is predicted using the bed roughness prediction by van Rijn. [24]. The Soulsby-van Rijn transport formula [25] is used here to estimate the total transport rate (bed load + suspended load) without considering bed slope correction and morphological factor. The total bed roughness can be decomposed into a grain roughness k'_s, a small-scale ripple roughness k_r, a mega-ripple component k_{mr}, and a dune roughness k_d.

$$k_s = k'_s + \sqrt{k_r^2 + k_{mr}^2 + k_d^2} \qquad (3)$$

Both small scale ripples and grain roughness have an influence on the sediment transport laws, while the mega-ripples and dune roughness only contribute to the hydrodynamic model (total friction, ref. [26,27]). In the bed roughness feed-back method, the total bed roughness calculated by GAIA is sent to Telemac-2D.

Influence of waves and wind are not reckoned in this study. The SND is installed behind the sand spit and it is thus protected from the waves except during stormy events. Here, it is proposed to focus on a short-term period (1 month). For such a short-term period, the tide and the flowrate can be considered as the main forcing.

First, the hydrodynamic simulation is carried out considering a fixed bed to assess its accuracy. As proposed by Huybrechts et al. [16,17], no calibration is performed since the friction coefficients are provided by the van Rijn formula. Then, the hydrodynamic model is coupled with sediment transport and morphological evolution. The results of the fixed bed simulation are used as initial conditions for the coupled simulation. The coupled simulation (Telemac 2D and Gaia) are conducted with and without the SND. The simulation times of all sediment transport is 45 days (3 neap-spring cycles) starting from 15 February 2019 as the initial bathymetry before net implementation.

The presence of structure is often treated by an additional drag force for instance for tidal turbines [28,29] or even for bridge piers [20]. Similarly it is proposed to reckon the energy losses induced by the SND by a drag force inside the model.

The position of the SND inside the mesh has been defined as a soft line meaning that nodes are placed along a defined line during the building of the mesh. The drag force is applied on these nodes using a polygon. In this way, the representation of the SND is less sensitive to the mesh resolution.

The drag force is applied as a source term added to momentum equation taking into account the orientation of the SND. The drag force equation is adjusted from Joly et al. [28]. The two components along x and y direction of drag force are indicated below.

$$F_{D,x} = -\frac{1}{2} H_{net} C_D U \mid U \mid \cos(\theta) \qquad (4)$$

$$F_{D,y} = \frac{1}{2} H_{net} C_D V \mid U \mid \sin(\theta) \qquad (5)$$

where C_D is a drag coefficient that can be extracted from the numerical flume ex-periment, θ is the orientation of the central axis of the SND, in this case $\theta = -30°$ (0 is north oriented), Hnet is the height of the net (1.1 m) and U and V are the velocity (east and north component).

The drag coefficient is assumed to be independent of the flow orientation. The flow orientation only has an influence on the final force. For a South-North oriented SND, the $F_{D,y}$ is null and the $F_{D,x}$ will be maximum for a flow-oriented East-West. More flume or numerical experiments would be necessary to build a more complete relationship of the drag coefficient (depth ratio, flow angle, ...).

4. Results and Discussion

This section first presents the results and discussions of observed morphodynamics around the SND. Second, the results of estimation of the drag coefficient by 3D numerical experiments are presented and discussed. Third, the validated results of 2D large-scale models are presented. Finally, Sections 4 and 5 are used to present and discuss about the influence of the SND on residual currents and morphodynamics based on the large-scale model. These provide valuable insight into the influence of the SND on the flow pattern and morphodynamic of the Authie estuary.

4.1. In Situ Observed Morphodynamic around the SND

Measured topographic evolutions are illustrated in (Figure 3). The location of the SND is represented by a black line. A few days before the installation of the SND (Figure 3a, 20 March), width of the river is 70 m. The sand spit is moving from west to east and it is pushing the river to the shoreline. The configuration 3 months after the installation is represented in (Figure 3b). It appears that the river width has become narrow in the vicinity of the device (width = 25 m). The sand spit on the west has also been reduced. Around the net, sedimentation has effectively occurred. Between 3 and 6 months, a more stable configuration around the net is observed. The channel seems stabilized and maintained away from the shoreline.

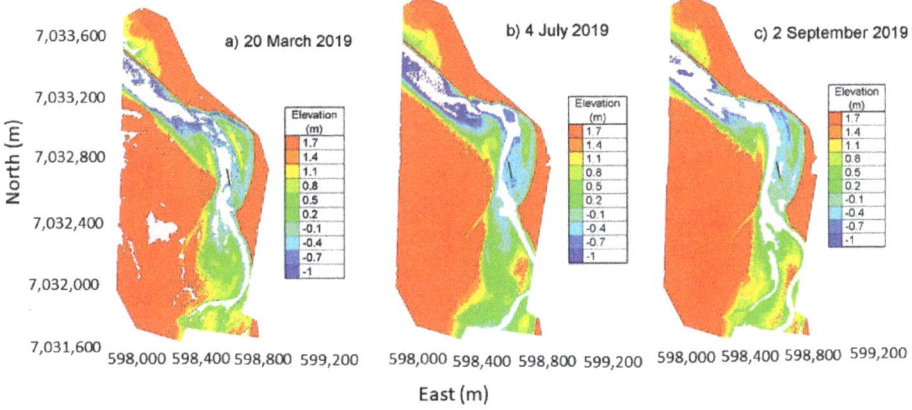

Figure 3. Topographic surveys by drone: (**a**) at 20 March 2019; (**b**) at 4 July 2019 and (**c**) at 2 September 2019. SND was installed 27 March 2019 indicating by the black line.

The erosion-sedimentation pattern inside the channel around SND is analyzed based on local bathymetry surveys (Figure 4). Figure 4a depicts the temporal change in the erosion/sedimentation pattern in the channel between February 2019 to October 2019 whereas Figure 4b,c display bed elevation at two cross sections, T1 downstream the nets and T2 at net location. Positive values of Dz indicates sedimentation whereas negative values indicate erosion.

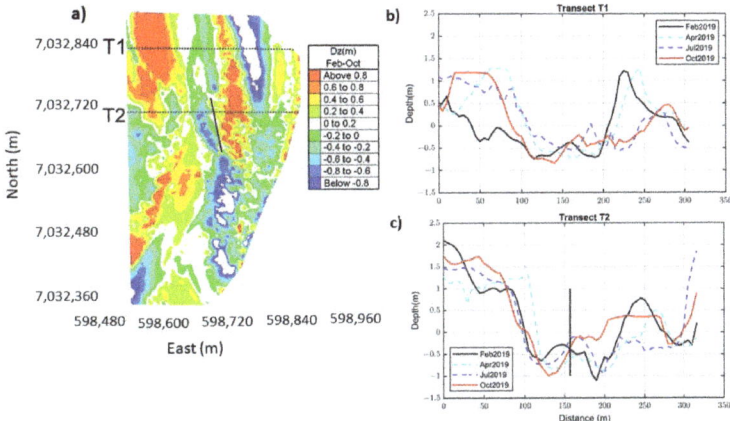

Figure 4. (**a**) Bed level changes during period February 2019 and October 2019; (**b**) Cross transect T1 and (**c**) Cross transect T2 at the SND. The back lines depict the location of the SND.

In Figure 4a, an important sedimentation is noticed on the east side of the SND whereas erosion has occurred at the west provides more details about the bed evolution. For T1 and T2, a growth of the sand spit is first observed between February to April. Erosion has occurred on both sides of the net during this period. In fact, this period corresponds to a mixed configuration: 1.5 months of natural evolution before the sand net installation and one month with the SND. Between April and July, sedimentation has occurred around the SND and a deepening of the channel has occurred between the net and the sand spit (Figure 4b). Between July and September, similar patterns are observed: erosion of the riverbed on the west, sedimentation on the eastern side of the SND. Figure 5 points out that these morphological changes are associated with a shift of the main channel orientation. The yellow line in Figure 5 indicates the thalweg line of −0.8 m of the main channel. In February (Figure 5a), two deep channels are observed with their junction near the net. In October (Figure 5b), only the channel at the west remains and the river is blocked between the sand spit and the sandy deposits generated around the SND.

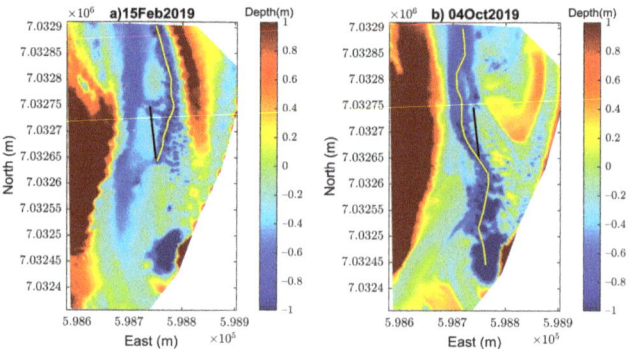

Figure 5. Detail bathymetry around the SND at: (**a**) 15 February 2019; (**b**) 4 October 2019. The yellow lines depict as the thalweg line of −0.8 m of the main channel. The back lines depict the location of the SND.

4.2. Estimation of the Drag Coefficient Induced by the SND Using the 3D Numerical Experiments

The flow pattern predicted by the 3D numerical experiments is illustrated for the 2 m depth configuration (Figure 6) for both components: along channel (X component) and vertical component (W component). Due to the step effect, the presence of the device induces a reduction of the flow section and an increase of the flow velocity. For the configuration of 2 m in water depth, the flow velocity increases from 0.8 to 2 m/s. A drop in the free surface elevation is also noticed across the SND (Figure 6). Just behind the step, a low velocity zone is present which is favorable to sedimentation. The drag coefficient estimated from the experimental flume is 3 for the 2 m depth configuration whereas it reaches 3.6 in our numerical experiment. The measured velocity inside the experimental flume is also increasing from 0.8 to 1.6 m/s. The maximum velocity is reached behind the SND in both experimental and numerical flumes. In the in-situ and experimental configurations, the device is porous. A part of the flow goes through the device leading to a smaller velocity increase above the porous device and a smaller energy loss (total pressure drop). The representation of the SND by a bathymetric step thus probably tends to over-estimate the flow acceleration and the associated drag coefficient. In situ, the velocity inside the SND is decreasing which should result in sediment deposit that progressively reduces the porosity. Effectively after one month, the in situ SND can be almost full on sandy deposit [6].

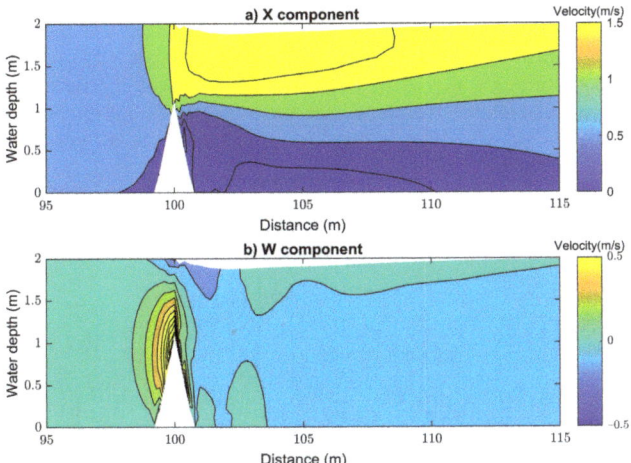

Figure 6. Along (**a**) and vertical velocities (**b**) with water depths in numerical experiment induced by the SND.

The evolution of the drag coefficient for the different studied water depths is plotted in Figure 7 in regard of the section ratio before the device and on the device. As the width is constant it corresponds to the ratio of the upstream water depth by the water depth at the step. High water depth leads to less section reduction and less energy losses. It corresponds to high tide configuration. The energy losses increase as power 4 with the water depth ratio. This relationship is conformed with the classical formula of energy losses induced by flow section reduction [30]. From Figure 7, the drag coefficient evolves from 0.3 to 35. The energy losses induced by the device is maximum for low water depth which correspond to the peaks of current during the ebb and the flood and thus when the sediment transport is significant. Figure 7 provides an estimation of the range of values for the drag coefficient requested to build the large scale 2D numerical model.

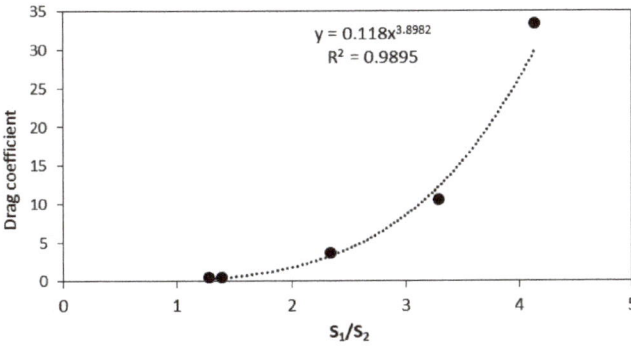

Figure 7. Relationship between drag coefficient and the area ratio from flume numerical, S1 corresponds to the flow area upstream and S2 corresponds to the flow area above the sand nest crest.

4.3. Validation of the 2D Hydrodynamic Model

The performance of the large-scale model has been assessed using data collected in May 2017 (water level and velocity). Figure 8 illustrates the comparison between observed and simulated water levels and velocities for a period of 30 days in May 2017. Model performance is quantified through root mean square error (RMSE), and predictive skill (SS) introduced by Willmott. [31]. The model score of water level indicates a high value of SS of 0.97 with RMSE of 0.22 m at the Net location. The score of velocity shows a bit overestimate with a value of SS of 0.7 and the RMSE is 0.32 m/s. In general, the model results are able to follow the measurements throughout the neap–spring tidal cycle quite closely. The peak velocity at Net location indicates also a good agreement between observation and simulation.

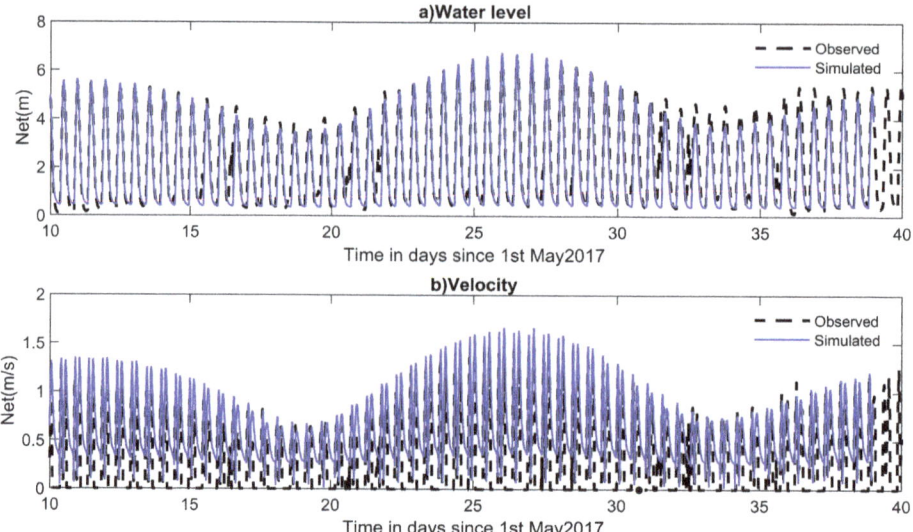

Figure 8. Results of water level (**a**) and velocity (**b**) validation at the Net location.

4.4. Influence of the Sand Net on the Residual Current

A 45 days simulation has been performed with or without the SND to evaluate its influences on the bed evolution and associated modifications of the residual currents.

Residual current is estimated over one tidal cycle representing either neap tide or spring tide with and without drag force (Figure 9). Downstream oriented residual currents dominate in both spring (Figure 9a,c) and neap tide (Figure 9b,d) but its magnitude in spring tides is stronger than in neap tides. For the simulation with the drag force, impacts are noticed on the eastern side of the SND in both spring and neap tide. During spring tides (Figure 9c), two branches in the flow pattern are observed creating a zone with low velocity between them (0.05 m/s). However, the velocity is slightly higher at the area of the left side of the SND (0.4 m/s). During neap tides, main branches still maintain around SND but with reduced velocity on the east branch due to influence of the SND.

Residual currents over spring and neap tidal cycle are also extracted at transect T2, cross-section throughout the nets (Figure 10). A large reduction in residual current at the SND is observed both in spring and neap tide. During neap tide, the residual current has been reduced from 0.14 m/s to 0.04 m/s whereas it reduces from 0.25 m/s to 0.07 m/s during the spring tide. Compared to the case without SND, the residual current is divided into two peaks with SND. The residual current increases and reaches the first peak in front of SND (west side, or left side, at distance 100–150 m, Figure 10). Then it decreases due to the SND and forms another peak of velocity on the east side of SND at a distance about 200 m. From Figures 9 and 10, it appears that the core of the SND is creating the region of low velocity behind it.

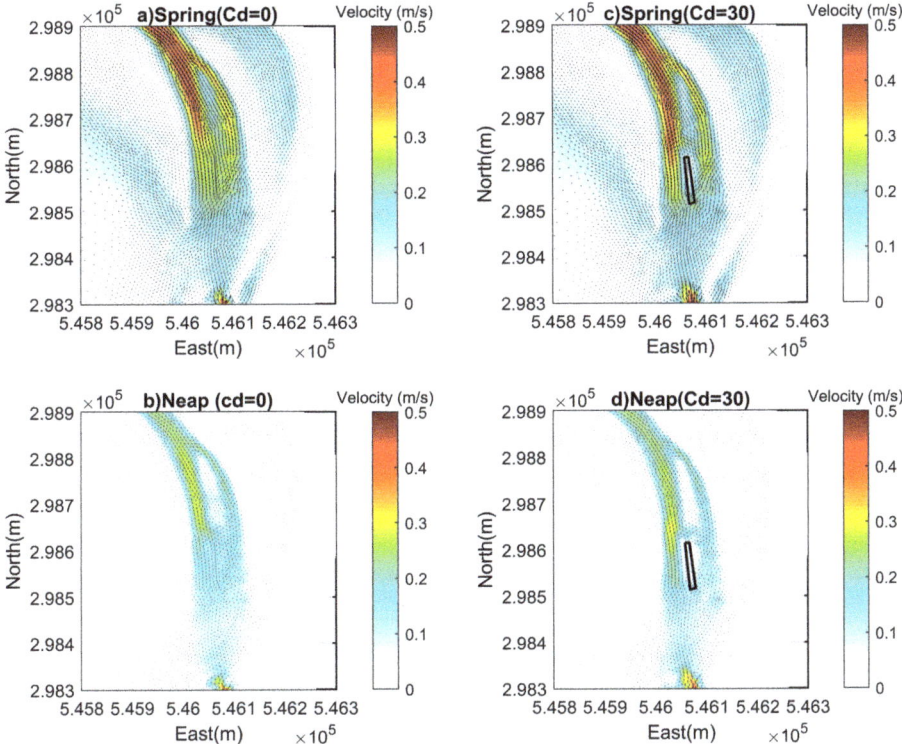

Figure 9. Residual current with and without the SND during spring tide (**a,c**) and during neap tide (**b,d**). The back lines depict the location of the SND.

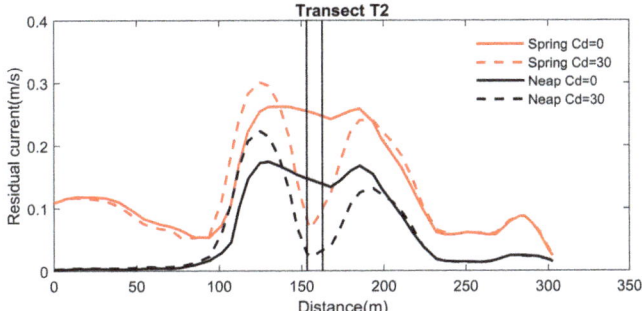

Figure 10. Residual current at cross transect T2 (the SND is located at a distance of 153 m corresponding the reduction zone in velocities indicating by vertical black line).

4.5. Influence of Sand Net Installation on Morphodynamics

Due to the changes in hydrodynamics caused by the SND, morphological development is altered (Figure 11). The effect of SND is stretched out over approximately 400 m along the channel in both directions (upstream and downstream from the net location) with the difference in bed level changes larger than 2 cm.

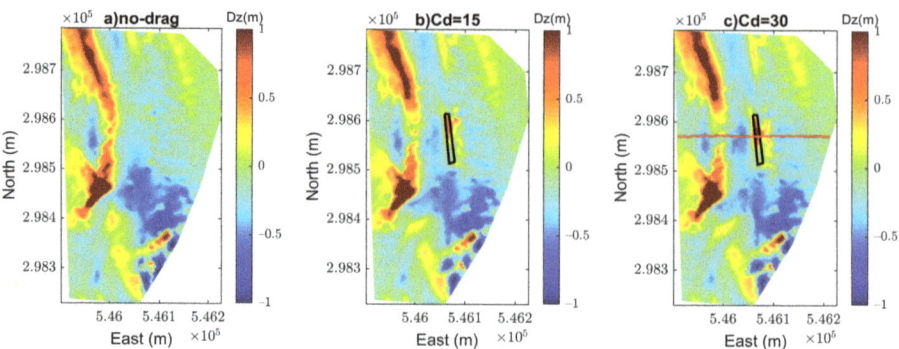

Figure 11. Erosion/sedimentation with different drag coefficients: (**a**) without drag coefficient Cd = 0; (**b**) with drag coefficient Cd = 15; (**c**) with drag coefficient Cd = 30. The black line depicts the location of the SND and the red line indicates location of transect T2. Postive values of Dz indicates sedimentation whereas negative values indicate erosion.

Figure 11 presents the evolution of bathymetry after 45 days simulation considering different drag coefficients (without drag Cd = 0; Cd = 15, and Cd = 30 based on the range of drag coefficient from numerical flume, Section 4.2). The figure illustrates that the SND has contributed to accretion on the right bank of the channel (the area on the right side of the SND) and a deepening of the main channel on the left side of the nets. This erosion/sedimentation pattern displays the same behavior from observed bathymetry (Figure 4a). The model predicts a reduction in velocity and a slight deviation flow around at this location (Figures 9 and 10). This phenomenon leads to a deposition that can be observed behind the sand net and develops further downstream as can be seen in Figure 11b,c. A higher drag force coefficient creates more sedimentation because of more reduction in velocity induced by the SND as shown in Figure 12 (Bed level changes at transect T2). With a drag coefficient of 30, an accretion of approximate 0.8 m is observed behind the SND whereas it reduces to about 0.2 m with a drag of 15 and it shows an erosion of (−0.2 m) in case without drag force (without SND). The deposition behind the SND results from reduction in velocity is observed, this result is quite well comparative with observed bathymetry in Figure 4a. The model confirms that the SND has induced the deposition behind its location and it has an effect on circulation by creating a deflation in current.

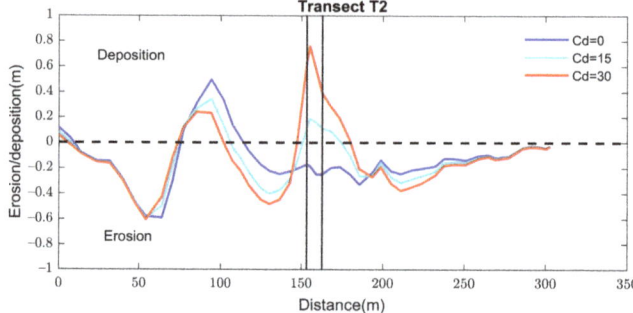

Figure 12. Erosion/sedimentation at the transect T2 with different drag coefficients.

5. Conclusions

A new soft engineering solution, namely the sand net device (SND), has been implemented in the Authie estuary in order to prevent bank erosion by a meandering of a coastal river. The paper presents the evolution of the morphodynamic over 3 and 6 months after the implementation. In situ monitoring clearly points out sedimentation around the SND and a deepening of the main channel. It has thus successfully maintained the river on its western branch. Numerical modeling allows further analysis and separation of the influence of the SND. From numerical experiments, values of the drag coefficient induced by the SND have been estimated within 0.3 to 30 according to the water depth (high tide corresponds to low drag coefficient). Since the strongest tidal currents have been noticed with low water depth, the strongest energy losses during high transport rate periods. After one and half month, the large-scale model predicts deposition around the SND and modification of the flow circulation.

The large-scale numerical results with SND indicate that, while the nets are able to reduce energy within the study area with a radius effectiveness of around 500 m both directions, upstream and downstream part. The velocity has been reduced and created a deviation in its direction by a circulation around the SND location. The morphological development shows a potential sedimentation around the SND location.

The main patterns are correctly reproduced by the model which could be then used to test different SND configurations. Even if some development could be forecast as 3D modelling and inclusion of waves for longer time scale (year). The way to address the drag force once the SND is full of sand also needs further investigation.

The presence of waves and their subsequent modification has been ignored from this study. The morphological changes are only considered for a short-term period. Consequently, the impact of the nets on long-term morphological development is left for further study.

Author Contributions: Conceptualization, all; methodology, N.H. and A.T.K.D.; software, N.H. and A.T.K.D.; validation, N.H. and A.T.K.D.; formal analysis, N.H. and A.T.K.D.; investigation, N.H.; data treatment, N.H.; writing—original draft preparation, N.H. and A.T.K.D.; writing—review and editing, N.H., A.T.K.D. and P.S.; visualization, A.T.K.D.; supervision, N.H. and P.S.; project administration, N.H. and P.S.; funding acquisition, N.H. and P.S. All authors have read and agreed to the published version of the manuscript.

Funding: This research is part of the ENDURE project funded by Interreg 2 Seas programme 2014–2020 co-funded by the European Regional Development Fund.

Institutional Review Board Statement: Not applicable.

Informed Consent Statement: Not applicable.

Data Availability Statement: The data presented in this study are available on request from the corresponding author. A part of data is not publicly available due to belong to the 3rd party data.

Acknowledgments: The authors gratefully acknowledge the Service d'Hydrographique et d'océanographique de la Marine (SHOM) and the Reseau d'Observations du Littoral Normandie et Haut de France for providing bathymetric and topographic data for this study. The CA2BM is also acknowledged for providing their data and their help to conduct field surveys. This work has been achieved during the Endure (Ensure Dune Resilience) led by Norfolk County Council (https://www.endure.eu.com/, accessed on 22 July 2021).

Conflicts of Interest: The authors declare no conflict of interest. Any role of the funders in the design of the study; in the collection, analyses or interpretation of data; in the writing of the manuscript, or in the decision to publish the results.

References

1. Ridderinkhof, W.; Hoekstra, P.; Van der Vegt, M.; De Swart, H.E. Cyclic behavior of sandy shoals on the ebb-tidal deltas of the Wadden Sea. *Cont. Shelf Res.* **2016**, *115*, 14–26. [CrossRef]
2. Morales, J.A.; Borrego, J.; Jiménez, I.; Monterde, J.; Gil, N. Morphostratigraphy of an ebb-tidal delta system associated with a large spit in the Piedras Estuary mouth (Huelva Coast, Southwestern Spain). *Mar. Geol.* **2001**, *172*, 225–241. [CrossRef]
3. Monge-Ganuzas, M.; Evans, G.; Cearreta, A. Sand-spit accumulations at the mouths of the eastern Cantabrian estuaries: The example of the Oka estuary (Urdaibai Biosphere Reserve). *Quat. Int.* **2015**, *364*, 206–216. [CrossRef]

4. Hesp, P.A.; Ruz, M.H.; Hequette, A.; Marin, D.; Da Silva, G.M. Geomorphology and dynamics of a traveling cuspate foreland, Authie estuary, France. *Geomorphology* **2016**, *254*, 104–120. [CrossRef]
5. Bastos, L.; Bio, A.; Pinho, J.L.S.; Granja, H.; da Silva, A.J. Dynamics of the Douro estuary sand spit before and after breakwater construction. *Estuar. Coast. Shelf Sci.* **2012**, *109*, 53–69. [CrossRef]
6. Sergent, P.; Huybrechts, N.; Smaoui, H. Large Scale Demonstrator of Fishing Nets Against Coastal Erosion of Dunes by Meanders in Authie Estuary (Côte D'Opale—France). In *Estuaries and Coastal Zones in Times of Global Change*; Springer: Singapore, 2020; pp. 573–593.
7. Dobroniak, C. Morphological evolution and management proposals in the Authie Estuary, northern France. In Proceedings of the Dunes Estuaries, Koksijde, Belgium, 19–23 September 2015; Volume 2205, pp. 537–545.
8. Anthony, E.J.; Dobroniak, C. Erosion and recycling of aeolian dunes in a rapidly infilling macrotidal estuary: The Authie, Picardy, northern France. *Geol. Soc. Lond. Spec. Publ.* **2000**, *175*, 109–121. [CrossRef]
9. Dobroniak, C.; Anthony, E.J. Short-term morphological expression of dune sand recycling on a macrotidal, wave-exposed estuarine shoreline. *J. Coast. Res.* **2002**, *36*, 240–248. [CrossRef]
10. Cartier, A.; Héquette, A. Variation in longshore sediment transport under low to moderate conditions on barred macrotidal beaches. *J. Coast. Res.* **2011**, *Special Issue 64*, 45–49. Available online: http://www.jstor.org/stable/26482130 (accessed on 22 July 2021).
11. Marion, C.; Anthony, E.J.; Trentesaux, A. Short-term (≤2 yrs) estuarine mudflat and saltmarsh sedimentation: High-resolution data from ultrasonic altimetery, rod surface-elevation table, and filter traps. *Estuar. Coast. Shelf Sci.* **2009**, *83*, 475–484. [CrossRef]
12. Deloffre, J.; Verney, R.; Lafite, R.; Lesueur, P.; Lesourd, S.; Cundy, A.B. Sedimentation on intertidal mudflats in the lower part of macrotidal estuaries: Sedimentation rhythms and their preservation. *Mar. Geol.* **2007**, *241*, 19–32. [CrossRef]
13. Michon, D. Dispositif et Système de Protection Contre L'érosion du Littoral. EP 2585640 B1, 6 September 2017.
14. Wang, L.; Shi, Z.H.; Wang, J.; Fang, N.F.; Wu, G.L.; Zhang, H.Y. Rainfall kinetic energy controlling erosion processes and sediment sorting on steep hillslopes: A case study of clay loam soil from the Loess Plateau, China. *J. Hydrol.* **2014**, *512*, 168–176. [CrossRef]
15. Langendoen, E.J.; Mendoza, A.; Abad, J.D.; Tassi, P.; Wang, D.; Ata, R.; El kadi Abderrezzak, K.; Hervouet, J.M. Improved numerical modeling of morphodynamics of rivers with steep banks. *Adv. Water Resour.* **2016**, *93*, 4–14. [CrossRef]
16. Huybrechts, N.; Villaret, C.; Lyard, F. Optimized predictive two-dimensional hydrodynamic model of the Gironde estuary in France. *J. Waterw. Port Coast. Ocean. Eng.* **2012**, *138*, 312–322. [CrossRef]
17. Huybrechts, N.; Villaret, C. Large-scale morphodynamic modelling of the Gironde estuary, France. *Proc. Inst. Civ. Eng. Marit. Eng.* **2013**, *166*, 51–62. [CrossRef]
18. Santoro, P.; Fossati, M.; Tassi, P.; Huybrechts, N.; Van Bang, D.P.; Piedra-Cueva, J.I. A coupled wave–current–sediment transport model for an estuarine system: Application to the Río de la Plata and Montevideo Bay. *Appl. Math. Model.* **2017**, *52*, 107–130. [CrossRef]
19. Tassi, P.; Villaret, C.; Huybrechts, N.; Hervouet, J.M.N. Numerical modelling of 2D and 3D suspended sediment transport in turbulent flows. In Proceedings of the Seventh AIRH Symposium River Coastal an Estuarine Morphodynamics, Beijing, China, 6–8 September 2011
20. Hervouet, J.-M. *Hydrodynamics of Free Surface Flows: Modelling with the Finite Element Method*; John Wiley and Sons Ltd.: West Sussex, UK, 2007, 340p.
21. Egbert, G.D.; Erofeeva, S.Y. Efficient inverse modeling of barotropic ocean tides. *J. Atmos. Ocean. Technol.* **2002**, *19*, 183–204. [CrossRef]
22. Schureman, P. *Manual of Harmonic Analysis and Prediction of Tides*; US Government Printing Office: Washington, DC, USA, 1958; Volume 4.
23. Audouin, Y.; Benson, T.; Delinares, M.; Fontaine, J.; Glander, B.; Huybrechts, N.; Kopmann, R.; Leroy, A.; Pavan, S.; Pham, C.-T.; et al. Introducing GAIA, the brand new sediment transport module of the TELEMAC-MASCARET system. In Proceedings of the XXVIth TELEMAC-MASCARET User Conference, Toulouse, France, 15–17 October 2019.
24. Van Rijn, L.C. Unified view of sediment transport by currents and waves. II: Suspended transport. *J. Hydraul. Eng.* **2007**, *133*, 668–689. [CrossRef]
25. Soulsby, R. *Dynamics of Marine Sands*; Thomas Telford: Telford, London, 1997.
26. Villaret, C.; Hervouet, J.M.; Kopmann, R.; Merkel, U.; Davies, A.G. Morphodynamic modeling using the Telemac finite-element system. *Comput. Geosci.* **2013**, *53*, 105–113. [CrossRef]
27. Brakenhoff, L.; Schrijvershof, R.; Van Der Werf, J.; Grasmeijer, B.; Ruessink, G.; Van Der Vegt, M. From ripples to large-scale sand transport: The effects of bedform-related roughness on hydrodynamics and sediment transport patterns in delft3d. *J. Mar. Sci. Eng.* **2020**, *8*, 892. [CrossRef]
28. Joly, A.; Pham, C.T.; Andreewsky, M.; Saviot, S.; Fillot, L. Using the DRAGFO subroutine to model Tidal Energy Converters in Telemac-2D. In *Telemac User Club 2015*; Science and Technology Facilities Council: Warrington, UK, 2015.
29. Ross, L.; Sottolichio, A.; Huybrechts, N.; Brunet, P. Tidal turbines in the estuarine environment: From identifying optimal location to environmental impact. *Renew. Energy* **2021**, *169*, 700–713. [CrossRef]
30. Crane. *Flow of Fluids Through Valves, Fittings, and Pipe*; Technical Paper No. 410 th Printing, 197414 th Printing; Crane Ltd.: Ongar, UK, 1974.
31. Willmott, C.J. On the validation of models. *Phys. Geogr.* **1981**, *2*, 184–194. [CrossRef]

Article

Influence of Sand Trapping Fences on Dune Toe Growth and Its Relation with Potential Aeolian Sediment Transport

Christiane Eichmanns * and Holger Schüttrumpf

Institute of Hydraulic Engineering and Water Resources Management, RWTH Aachen University, Mies-van-der-Rohe-Straße 17, 52074 Aachen, Germany; schuettrumpf@iww.rwth-aachen.de
* Correspondence: eichmanns@iww.rwth-aachen.de; Tel.: +49-241-80-25264

Abstract: This study provides insights into dune toe growth around and between individual brushwood lines of sand trapping fences at the dune toe of coastal dunes using digital elevation models obtained from repeated unmanned aerial vehicle surveys. Prevailing boundary conditions, especially sediment supply, as well as the porosity and arrangement of the installed sand trapping fences significantly influence the effectiveness of different configurations of sand trapping fences. The dune toe growth is significant immediately after constructing a new sand trapping fence and decreases over time. According to the results presented in this study, for sand trapping fences that have been in place longer, the protruding branch height and the porosity of the remaining branches play a minor role in trapping sand. Sand trapping fences with lower permeability favour localized coastal dune toe growth directly at their brushwood lines, whereas fences with higher porosity allow for more sediment deposition further downwind. The trend in dune toe changes can be roughly predicted by integrating potential sediment transport rates calculated with hourly meteorological data.

Keywords: field experiments; nature-based solutions; sand trapping fences; dune toe volume changes; foredune recovery; unmanned aerial vehicle

Citation: Eichmanns, C.; Schüttrumpf, H. Influence of Sand Trapping Fences on Dune Toe Growth and Its Relation with Potential Aeolian Sediment Transport. *J. Mar. Sci. Eng.* **2021**, *9*, 850. https://doi.org/10.3390/jmse9080850

Academic Editor: Achilleas Samaras

Received: 21 June 2021
Accepted: 27 July 2021
Published: 6 August 2021

Publisher's Note: MDPI stays neutral with regard to jurisdictional claims in published maps and institutional affiliations.

Copyright: © 2021 by the authors. Licensee MDPI, Basel, Switzerland. This article is an open access article distributed under the terms and conditions of the Creative Commons Attribution (CC BY) license (https://creativecommons.org/licenses/by/4.0/).

1. Introduction

Coastal dunes are a natural barrier against storm surges and act as a sediment resource in case of erosive storm events, thereby offering protection for the low-lying hinterland against flooding and sea-level rise [1–4]. Furthermore, they have a natural protective function within the framework of nature conservation and serve for recreation [5]. However, the coastal dune system, in particular the foredune, is complex and highly dynamic as natural processes drive the dune development [5,6]. Long-term coastal dune development results from the sum of erosive processes due to hydrodynamic forces during storm surges and accretive processes due to aeolian sediment transport processes, resulting in growing or eroding coastal dunes [4,7,8]. Additionally, coastal management interventions like beach nourishments, installing sand trapping fences, the presence of vegetation, the sediment grain size, or the beach width can, amongst others, influence the development of the coastal dunes [4,6,9–13].

To support the restoration and maintenance of beach and dune systems, accurate knowledge of beach-dune interaction and the effectiveness of coastal protection measures to strengthen coastal dunes is required [5,14,15]. Generally, a good empirical understanding of dune erosion and wave-dune interaction processes exists and has been extensively studied [8,16–18]; however, the prediction of dune growth is a significant challenge due to the complexity of influencing factors, e.g., coastal dune formation, aeolian sediment transport, vegetation, or sediment moisture. These factors and their interaction make the understanding of the morphological and volumetric changes of the dune system a major challenge when utilizing building with nature methods for designing coastal protection measures [6,19,20]. The literature on aeolian sediment transport can, e.g., be found in

BAGNOLD (1941) [21], VAN RIJN AND STRYPSTEEN (2019) [7], BAAS AND SHERMAN (2006) [20] or SHERMAN et al. (2012) [22].

Where a positive sediment supply exists, sand trapping fences as a widely used nature-based solution can often be found along the coastline of barrier islands at the seaward dune slope close to the dune toe. They are part of the coastal protection measures [2,23].

Generally, fences control air and water flow, sediments, and direct people flow or animals [24]. Depending on their purpose, they can be differentiated into two different types: wind fences and sand-trapping fences [24–26]. Wind fences are mainly used in arid and desert regions and aim to reduce wind velocity, prevent wind-induced erosion, and, e.g., protect transport infrastructure or monetary assets against heavy wind or sediment loads [26–29]. On the other hand, in coastal regions, sand trapping fences are placed with the following purposes: rehabilitating eroded areas from storm surges or blowouts in the coastal dunes, for reinforcement of the coastal dune toe, for protecting transport infrastructure or monetary assets from drifting sand, to control human access to nature reserve, and to initiate the formation of coastal dunes by supporting the selective deposition of sand [30,31]. While wind velocity reduction has already been extensively studied for wind fences [27,30,32,33], only a few detailed studies, e.g., [23–25,31,34–37], about sand trapping fences for initiating and facilitating the establishment of the dune toe are available. There is currently a research demand on sand-trapping fences in coastal areas for the position relative to the beach profile, the porosity and height of the fence, and the arrangement of the fence [25,36].

In this work, sand trapping fences with the primary aim to strengthen the dune toe are considered. Figure 1a shows an aerial photograph of the sand trapping fence on Norderney with brushwood lines parallel and orthogonal to the coastal dunes and Figure 1b a close-up of the sand trapping fence from the viewpoint of the coastal dunes showing sand being trapped in between the brushwood lines.

Figure 1. (a) Aerial drone photograph of the sand trapping fence consisting of brushwood on the study site of Norderney and (b) a close-up of the sand trapping fence seen from the coastal dunes, showing sand being trapped in between the brushwood lines (9 March 2021).

The individual brushwood lines generally reduce the wind velocity, so that sediment can accumulate at the individual brushwood lines. These processes initiate and facilitate the dune toe development [38].

Currently, the design of these sand trapping fences on the East Frisian islands, i.e., the arrangement of the brushwood lines parallel and orthogonal to the coastal dunes, the position of the brushwood lines relative to the dune profile as well as the porosity and the height of the sand trapping fences is based on empirical knowledge, creating further uncertainties for implementing these coastal protection measures [36].

This study presents insights into the effectiveness of different sand trapping fence configurations to contribute to the formation of the dune toe. Thus, the results will help to improve and adapt methods for nature-based solutions of foredune restoration in coastal areas.

Therefore, during field campaigns from May 2020 until March 2021, we monitored the terrain elevation heights of two different study sites to gain more insight into the dune toe development influenced by different configurations of a sand trapping fence. As a result, the following research goals are set:

(1) Determination of the porosity of the different sand trapping configurations.
(2) Description of the temporal changes of dune toe volume and dune profiles at the sand trapping fence under consideration of the prevailing boundary conditions.
(3) Evaluation of the different sand trapping fence configurations to trap sand effectively.
(4) Investigation on the relation between dune toe volume changes and potential aeolian sediment transport.

First, the regional settings, the coastal protection measures, and the study sites are described in detail. After describing the applied methodology, the results are presented and discussed. Finally, the manuscript concludes with a discussion and an outlook.

2. Regional Setting and Coastal Protection Measures

The East Frisian Islands, see Figure 2, form a natural barrier island system in the German North Sea. The development and the shape of these sandy natural barrier islands are continuously changing as part of a highly dynamic morphological system due to the sea level rise, varying sediment availability, sandbar relocations, and storm surges [39,40]. For a detailed study on beach-dune systems near tidal inlets the readers are referred to SILVA (2019) [13].

The whole barrier island system stretches over ~90 km. Six main tidal inlets dissect the islands, see Figure 2a [2,41]. Between this island system and the mainland (distance ~3–20 km) extensive areas with tidal flats exist.

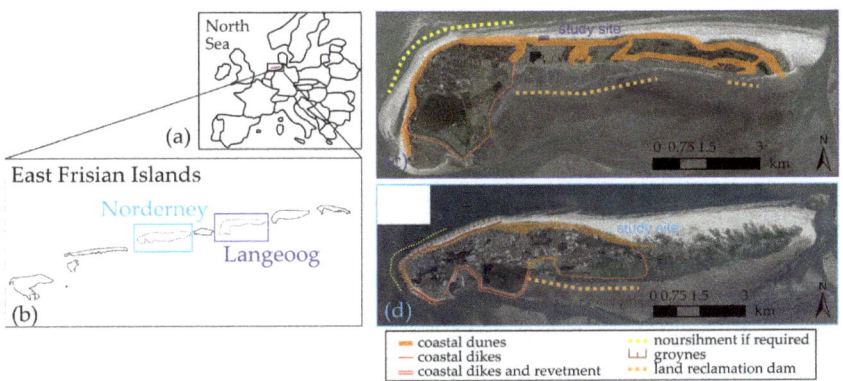

Figure 2. (**a**) Location of the East Frisian Islands along the North Sea coast in Germany, (**b**) showing the East Frisian Islands, (**c**) study site Langeoog, and (**d**) study site Norderney (with permission from © GeoBasis-DE/ BKG, 2021 [42], data obtained from [2,42]).

The East Frisian Islands are influenced by tidal energy as well as wave energy and can be categorized as mesotidal barrier islands with semi-diurnal tides and a tidal range of around T_R ~2.5 m (Norderney, Riffgat) up to T_R ~2.7 m (Langeoog, port entrance) [43–45]. As the tide rises, the tidal basins are filled, and they are emptied again as the tide falls [46]. Incoming waves generally run in from the directions between northwest and southwest; only the northwest components of waves are incident on the study site [47].

Figure 3a shows the hourly averaged wind data at the weather station Norderney at the height of 11 m above the ground and (b) Spiekeroog (see Figure 3b) at the height of 14 m above the ground. The wind data from 1 May 2020 to 31 March 2021 are depicted as a wind rose. Over the measured time period, a significant southwest component of the wind with magnitude wind velocities of up to ~20 m/s and mainly oblique offshore wind conditions concerning the coastline were recorded. The oblique onshore wind occurred less frequently but, on average, reached higher wind velocities [48]. The strong southwesterly wind conditions have little effect on the local water level at both study sites, whereas the less frequent but strong northwesterly wind has a longer fetch length and can lead to higher water levels locally.

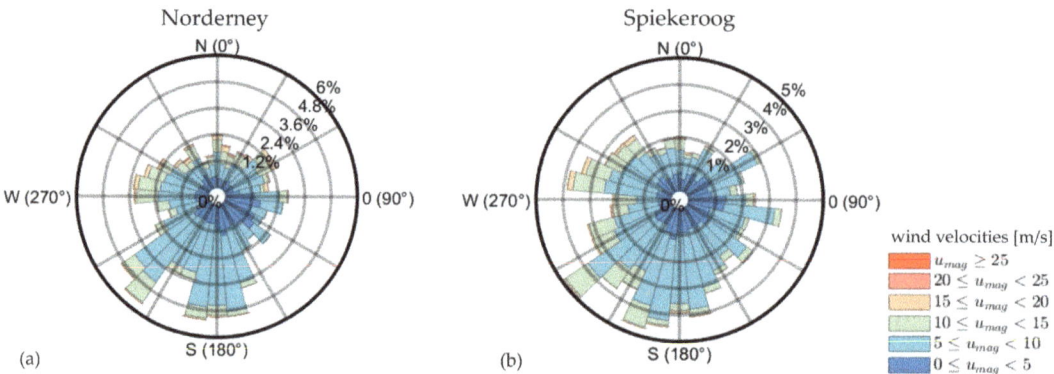

Figure 3. Hourly averaged wind velocities and wind directions from the weather station (**a**) Norderney and (**b**) Spiekeroog from 1 May 2020 to 31 March 2021 (wind data obtained from [48]).

Both weather stations provide similar results, with Spiekeroog always tending to measure higher magnitude wind velocities than Norderney. This is because the nearby urban area attenuates wind velocities from Norderney's weather station.

The East Frisian island Langeoog (see Figure 2b) covers ~20 km^2, and its morphology generally consists of a natural sandy beach followed by foredunes and older dune landscapes. The fully established foredune is ~ 20 m high and partially covered with the European Marram grass (*Ammophila arenaria*) [2,36]. The island has a coastal dike line of 5.5 km (red line) in the southwest and a coastal dike line (red line) of 0.3 km in the south, while coastal dunes (orange areas) over ~20.3 km protect the coastline from the southwest side of the island northward towards the east. A little part of the coastline is additionally protected by dike revetments (red double line) in the west. In the northwest of the island, sand nourishments are carried out if required (yellow dotted line). The study site Langeoog is located north of the island at the dune toe, see Figure 2b. The beach comprises quartz sand with a median grain size of d_{50} = 218 µm [36]. The beach has a relatively steep slope with m ~ 1:50. The beach width W [m], indicated as the distance between a defined water level (average of the high tide level MHW or average of the low tide level MNW) and the dune toe level (z = +3 mNHN [49,50]), varied from ~300 m during MNW = −1.3 mNHN [43] to ~70 m during MHW = +1.4 mNHN [43]. When the sand trapping fences were investigated in this study, the dry beach width was always W > 50 m. In July 2020, beach nourishments with a sand volume of V = 700.000 m^3 at Pirolatal on Langeoog island, 1.5 km west of the study site, were conducted.

With an area of ~26 km^2, Norderney (see Figure 2 ©) is the second-largest East Frisian island. It has coastal dunes (orange areas) stretching over ~12.1 km from the southwestern side of the island northward towards the isl'nd's center with heights up to 20 m. The coastal dunes are also in part covered with *Ammophila arenaria*. The beach slope m ~ 1:200 is much lower on Norderney than on Langeoog. The coastline is over ~10 km protected by coastal dikes (red line) in the south. Additionally, the dike line is partly protected by revetments (red double line) and massive groynes (brown line). In the northwest of the island, sand nourishments are carried out if required (yellow dotted line) [2]. The study site Norderney is also located in the north of the island at the dune toe, see Figure 2c, and had a dry beach width W ~ 320 m (MHW = +1.2 mNHN, [43]) over the measuring time.

During low tide (MNW = −1.3 mNHN [43]) the beach width can increase up to $W \sim 550$ m. The study site Norderney is located north of the island at the dune toe, see Figure 2c. Sand trapping fences installed in the past surround the investigation area [2,28].

3. Sand Trapping Fences

3.1. Description of Studied Sand Trapping Fences

Sand trapping fences on the East Frisian Islands are generally constructed in late spring after the storm surge season is over and before the peak tourist season has started by the Lower Saxony Water Management, Coastal Protection and Nature Conservation Agency (NLWKN). The sand trapping fences on Norderney and on Langeoog were installed at the dune toe in July 2019 and May 2020, respectively.

Many participants, also consisting of students and trainees, participated in constructing the sand trapping fence on Norderney. Therefore, the sand trapping fence installed on Norderney is less homogeneous than Langeoog's sand trapping fence installed by a few experienced employees of NLWKN [51]. The sand trapping fences are made out of locally available brushwood positioned in the sand in parallel and orthogonal arrangements to the coastal dunes. The branches are buried about ~0.5 m into the ground and then protrude about ~1.8 m from the ground. The bundles of brushwood on both study sites differ from each other as; for Langeoog, long, thin, straight birch twigs were used, and on Norderney, rather knob-thick, curved branches were used.

3.2. Sand Trapping Fence Configurations

Figure 4 shows an aerial drone photograph of the sand trapping fence at the dune toe at the study site of Langeoog. The sand trapping fence is stretched over a length of ~120 m and has four different configurations. The configurations differ in their arrangement of parallel and orthogonal brushwood lines to the coastal dunes and the number of bundles of brushwood used per running meter n [bb/m], see Figure 4. The red polygons delimit the individual fields 1–12, west, and east. A green polygon shows a field in which sediment deposition is not influenced by the sand trapping fence and which serves as a reference for further analysis. This reference field is located ~40 m east of field 12, ensuring that the sand trapping fence does not influence the wind field according to DONG et al. [28]. The sand trapping fence is characterized by thirteen brushwood lines (brown lines in Figure 4) arranged orthogonal to the coastal dunes and three brushwood lines (orange and yellow lines in Figure 4) parallel to the coastal dunes. The brushwood lines orthogonal to the coastal dunes have an average length of ~6 m, except for configuration 4, with an average length of ~3 m. There the deflectors at the dune toe are missing. Three parallel brushwood lines stretch over ~30 m each and intersect with the orthogonal brushwood lines. Configuration 1 consists of brushwood lines parallel ($n = 2$ bb/m) and orthogonal ($n = 3$–4 bb/m) to the coastal dunes. The westerly exposed configuration 1 is followed by configuration 2, consisting only of orthogonal brushwood lines ($n = 3$–4 bb/m) to the coastal dunes. Configuration 3 has the most densely set of parallel brushwood lines with $n = 5$ bb/m. Most eastward, configuration 4 lies with orthogonal brushwood lines with an average length of ~3 m. Offshore of the sand trapping fence *Ammophila arenaria* of varying heights (with a medium height of about 0.5 m) and irregularities in the topography were present in config. 2–4, see Figure 4. The vegetation covered maximum 3.0% of the investigated study area.

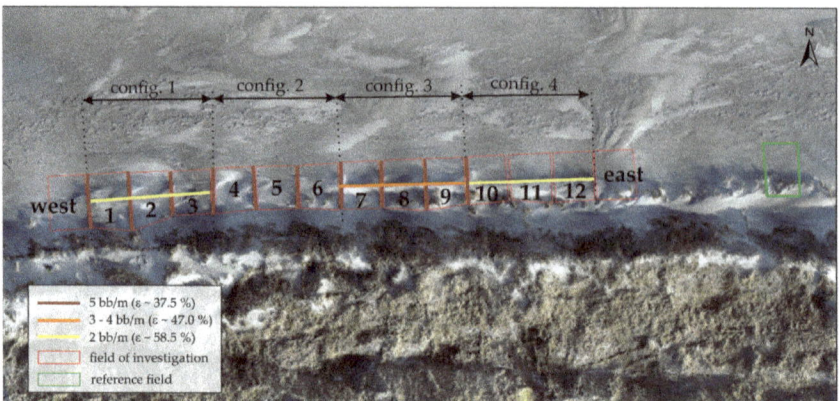

Figure 4. Aerial photograph of the sand trapping fence at the study site of Langeoog showing the four different configurations differing in their arrangement of brushwood lines parallel and orthogonal to the coastal dunes and the number of bundles of brushwood per running meter n [bb/m] and their porosity ε [%], respectively. The red polygons delimit fields 1–22, the fields west and east, and a green polygon the reference field.

In Figure 5, an aerial drone photograph of the sand trapping fence at the study site of Norderney is shown. The red polygons delimit the individual fields 1–22, west, and east. A reference field, located ~75 m east of field 22, ensures no influencing effects of the sand trapping fence on the wind profile [27]. The reference field is located where the upper endings of brushwood lines of a sand trapping fence installed in the past exist. This sand trapping fence is already fully filled with sand, and the brushwood bundles protrude around 2–5 cm above the ground. Zhang et al. (2010) [26], from their findings in wind tunnel experiments, stated that behind a porous fence with a height of h = 3 cm, the saltating sand particles reach a maximum length of four times the fence height behind the porous fence in main wind direction for wind velocities up to u = 9 m/s. Even for higher wind velocities, see, e.g., Ning et al. (2020) [32], who investigated the fence height effect on sand trapping in field experiments, it is assumed that the effect of this sand trapping fence is locally limited and therefore can be neglected for further analysis.

The sand trapping fence stretches over ~240 m. The configurations 1*, 2*, 3*, and 4* generally correspond to the configurations on Langeoog. However, for configurations 1*, 3*, and 4*, two parallel brushwood lines to the coastal dunes were installed, resulting in different field sizes between the brushwood lines. These fields are ~10 m wide, except for the first two fields in the west, which are ~20 m wide. The average length of the orthogonal brushwood lines is ~16 m. Furthermore, the arrangement of the configurations is different with configuration 3* followed by configuration 1*, configuration 4*, and configuration 2*, seen from west to east. When wind approaches from west or east, the outer fields have a potentially higher sediment supply since the sediment transport in the inner fields is attenuated by the brushwood bundles, resulting in a potentially lower sediment supply. Between the individual lines of brushwood only small spots of *Ammophila arenaria*, mainly in config. 4* and config 2*, were present, see Figure 5. The total coverage of the area with vegetation was maximum 3.5% at this study site.

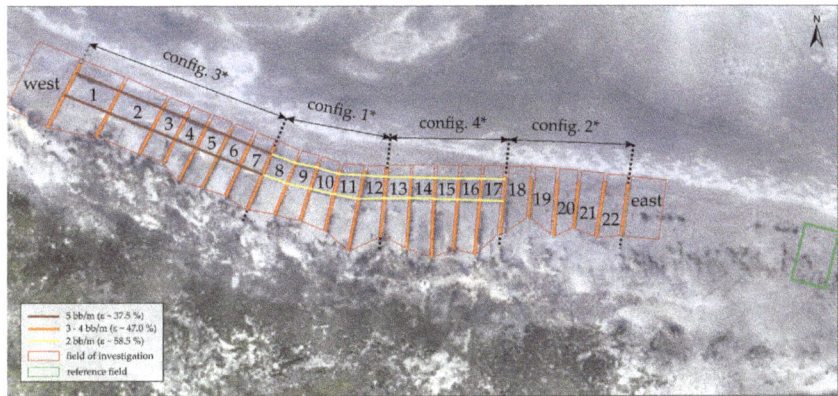

Figure 5. Aerial photograph of the sand trapping fence at the study site of Norderney showing the four different configurations differing in their arrangement of brushwood lines parallel and orthogonal to the coastal dunes and the number of bundles of brushwood per running meter n [bb/m] and their porosity ε [%], respectively. The red polygons delimit fields 1–22, the fields west and east, and a green polygon the reference field.

3.3. Sand Trapping Fence Porosity

In this section, the porosity of the sand trapping fences is determined, in addition to the number of brushwood bundles used per running meter n [bb/m]. It is necessary for the comparability of the results to determine the different porosities as the installation of the sand trapping fences was executed differently and furthermore, different types of branches were used, see Section 3.1, and therefore, the comparability of the results must be ensured.

In Figure 6, a standardized section of 45 cm × 45 cm of the sand trapping fence with (a) a low porosity with 5 bb/m, (b) a medium porosity with 3–4 bb/m, and (c) a high porosity with 2 bb/m is shown using the example of the study site Norderney.

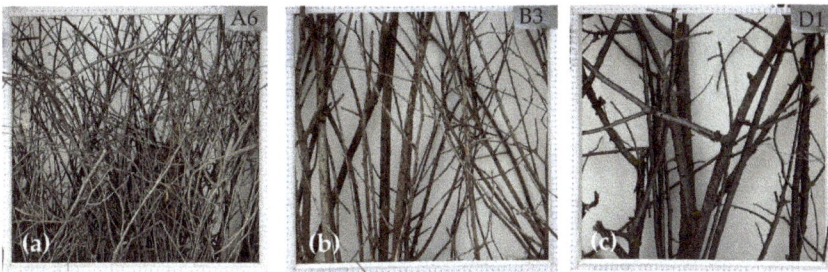

Figure 6. (a) Standardized section of the sand trapping fence with 5 bb/m, (b) standardized section of the sand trapping fence with 3–4 bb/m, (c) standardized section of the sand trapping fence with 2 bb/m.

The photographs were processed with the MATLAB (R2018b, version 9.510.944444) Color Thresholder Application [52]. The application offers four different color spaces for creating a mask to threshold the images. The color space red, green, blue (RGB) was chosen to create the masks, as the results were more precise than those obtained by the other color spaces. The color channel values, representing the color spaces of the brushwood bundles, were selected manually to segment the photographs. The image mask covers the regions overlaid by the brushwood branches in black, increasing the contrast to the background in white. Afterward, the masked images were converted into binary images. The small areas of black that were entirely surrounded by white color were removed to reduce the noise using the salt and pepper noise reduction filter [53]. The sand trapping fence's porosity was determined by the ratio of black pixels of the noise-cleared image to the total number of pixels in the image [54]. Figure 7 shows (a) the masked image, (b) the binary image, and (c) the porosity clearance of the standardized section from configuration 2* of the sand trapping fence on Norderney with n = 3–4 bb/m.

Figure 7. Result of image processing to determine the sand trapping fence's porosity with (**a**) the masked image, (**b**) the binary image, and (**c**) the noise cleared image of the standardized section (configuration 2*) of the sand trapping fence on Norderney with n = 3–4 bb/m.

The applied approach was validated by processing photographs of a defined number of brushwood branches (one up to five branches) with a known surface area. Therefore, the surface area was determined by measuring the length and width of the branches. As the branches show many irregularities in their geometry, the comparison between the results obtained by MATLAB and the measured lengths and widths contains uncertainties. However, with a mean error of the surface area $error_{mean}$ ~ 0.11, a minimum error of $error_{min}$ ~ 0.03, and a maximum error of $error_{max}$ ~ 0.14, the applied approach shows good results for the validation case.

In Table 1, the date of installation of the sand trapping fence, the configuration type, the number of parallel brushwood lines to the coastal dunes k [-], the total length of parallel L_1 [m] and orthogonally L_2 [m] arranged brushwood lines, the number of used brushwood bundles for the parallel n [bb/m] and orthogonally i [bb/m] arranged brushwood lines to the coastal dunes, the dates at which the photographs were taken, the section of the sand trapping fence (lower or upper part), the average porosities of the brushwood bundles for the parallel ε_n [%] and orthogonally ε_i [%] arranged brushwood lines and the average porosity for each configuration $\bar{\varepsilon}$ [%] are shown. The porosity was calculated out of several (between 4 and 21) photographs of the same configuration. The mean value of the porosity $\bar{\varepsilon}$ [%] for each field of the sand trapping fence was determined from the porosities of the orthogonally and parallel brushwood bundles of this field, weighed by their length.

Note that the photographs were taken on different dates. As time progresses, more and more sand can accumulate at the brushwood lines of the sand trapping fence. Thus, the photographs taken later depict more of the upper section of the sand trapping fence, where the porosity is lower than the photographs taken earlier, which depict more of the lower section of the sand trapping fence, where the porosity is higher.

Generally, it becomes clear that with increasing brushwood bundles per running meter, the porosity decreases. What is striking in Table 1 is the difference between the determined porosities of the sand trapping fence on Langeoog and Norderney for the same configuration with an equal number of brushwood bundles per running meter. A possible explanation might be that different people installed the sand trapping fences, as discussed in Section 3.2. Furthermore, different types of brushwood bundles were used. The diversity of the brushwood bundles makes it challenging to build sand trapping fences with nearly identical characteristics. This underlines the importance of determining the porosity of the sand trapping fences to interpret their efficiency consistently. When comparing the individual islands to each other, it is better to compare the porosities instead of using brushwood bundles.

Table 1. Summary of sand trapping fence characteristics of Langeoog and Norderney comprising the date of installation of the sand trapping fence, the configuration type, the number of parallel brushwood lines to the coastal dunes k [-], the total length of parallel L_1 [m] and orthogonally L_2 [m] arranged brushwood lines, the number of used brushwood bundles for the parallel n [bb/m] and orthogonally i [bb/m] arranged brushwood lines to the coastal dunes, the dates at which the photographs were taken, the section of the sand trapping fence (lower or upper part), the average porosities of the brushwood bundles for the parallel ε_n [%] and orthogonally ε_i [%] arranged brushwood lines and the average porosity for each configuration $\bar{\varepsilon}$ [%].

Study Site, Date of Installation	Config. Type	k [-]	$L_1 + L_2$ [m]	n [bb/m]	i [bb/m]	Date of Photograph	Section	ε_n [%]	ε_i [%]	$\bar{\varepsilon}$ [%]
Langeoog, May 2020	1	1	30 + 24	~2	~3	26/05/2020 *	lower	33	24	29
	4		30 + 15	~2	~3	26/05/2020 *	lower	33	24	30
	2		0 + 24	~3	~3	14/03/2021	upper	-	24	24
	3		30 + 24	~5	~3	26/05/2020 *	lower	12	24	17
Norderney, July 2020	1*	2	100 + 96	~2	~3–4	10/03/2021	upper	61	51	
						01/08/2019 *	lower	49	43	51
							average	55	47	
	4*		100 + 81	~2	~3–4	10/03/2021	upper	74	51	
						01/08/2019 *	lower	50	43	55
							average	62	47	
	2*		0 + 93	~3–4	~3–4	10/03/2021	upper	-	51	
						01/08/2019	lower		43	47
							average		47	
	3*		180 + 128	~5	~3–4	10/03/2021	upper	42	51	
						01/08/2019 *	lower	33	43	41
							average	37.5	47	

* Project partner NLWKN provided photographs.

4. Materials and Methods

4.1. Experimental Instrumentation

The field campaigns employed an unmanned aerial vehicle (UAV, manufacturer DJI Phantom 4 with real-time kinematic). The UAV is equipped with a one-inch complementary metal-oxide-semiconductor sensor camera with a resolution of 20 megapixels to obtain ortho-image data and a real-time kinematic function to gain spatial coordinates. For detailed technical information on the UAV, the readers are referred to the drone's user manual [55]. The UAV surveys were conducted on Langeoog from 20 May 2020 to 12 March 2021 and on Norderney from 24 August 2020 to 9 March 2021. The weather conditions were different from sunny and windless to stormy and cloudy.

Two flight plans on Norderney and four flight plans on Langeoog with varying flight altitudes between 20 m and 100 m (distance above the coastal dunes) were performed using the DJI Pilot app. The camera took photographs with 70% and 80% forward and lateral overlap, respectively. The flight velocity was kept low and varied around an average velocity of ~4 m/s.

The drone's georeferenced ortho-images generally achieve an accuracy of 1 cm + 1 ppm (root mean square error) horizontally and 1.5 cm + 1 ppm vertically [55]. Four visible checkpoints were installed with coded target markers distributed within the study site to evaluate the precision of the derived digital elevation model (DEM). These checkpoints' exact positions were also registered using the global navigation satellite system JAVAD GNSS Receiver SigmaD with an accuracy of 1 cm + 1 ppm (root mean square error) horizontally and 1.5 cm + 1 ppm vertically [56].

4.2. Structure from Motion Processing of UAV Images and Data Precision

The structure from motion processing of UAV images was performed using Agisoft Metashape Pro (version 1.6.5; 64 bit) [57] to obtain digital elevation models. The following steps were subsequently performed: (i) importing of photographs and camera positioning, (ii) conversion of the coordinate systems from Universal Transverse Mercator (UTM) World Geodetic System 1984 (WGS 84) with the geoid height Earth Gravitational Model 1996 (EGM 96) to UTM ETRS 89 with German Geoid height GCG 2016, (iii) image alignment at the high/highest accuracy level; (iv) gradual selection of study site, (v) checkpoint positioning, (vi) optimization of camera alignment, (vi) generation of the dense point cloud with high/medium accuracy and application of the moderate filter for calculating the depth maps, (vii) DEM and orthophotographs generation from the dense point cloud. The final UAV-derived DEM reached an averaged resolution of ~3.5 cm/pixel. Additionally, the measured checkpoints gave coordinates in UTM WGS 84 with ellipsoidal heights converted into UTM ETRS89 with GCG 2016 heights.

The difference in x-, y-, and z-direction between the markers in the DEM obtained by the UAV and the measured checkpoints gave mean distances for the study site Langeoog of 0.023 m, 0.032 m, and 0.059 m for x, y, and z, respectively. For Norderney, the UAV flew at higher altitudes, resulting in mean distances of $x = 0.051$ m, $y = 0.047$ m, and $z = 0.085$ m.

4.3. Analysis Method for Evaluating the Dune Toe Growth

The coastal beach-dune system can be divided into five cross-shore horizontal elevation slices: (1) bed, (2) foreshore, (3) intertidal beach, (4) dry beach, and (5) coastal dunes with (6) sand trapping fence, see Figure 8. The dune toe level separates the dry beach (5) from the coastal dunes (5). The dune toe level at the East Frisian Islands is defined at $z = +3$ mNHN [49].

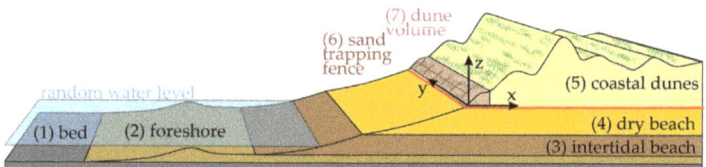

Figure 8. Schematic sketch of the coastal beach-dune system (adapted from [5]).

In the following, the dune volume (7), see Figure 8, was defined as the volume of sand above a fixed horizontal plane in the z-direction and a vertical boundary in the x-direction (approximately ~3 m onshore of the orthogonal deflectors of the sand trapping fence). In addition, the horizontal z-plane was chosen to be at least at dune toe level and at the same time ~3 m onshore of the sand trapping fence's deflectors, see Figures 4 and 5. Thereby, it was ensured that the sand trapping fences directly influence the observed study site at the dune toe.

Therefore, the chosen dune volume is defined depending on the chosen boundary planes and does not represent the whole coastal dune volume.

In addition to calculating the dune volume around the sand trapping fence, the dune volume between the orthogonally arranged brushwood lines was also determined for each field individually. Thereby, a comparison of the different configurations to each other is possible.

The dune volumes at different times were calculated using ArcGIS (version 10.5.1; 64 bit) [58]. For this purpose, the formatted. *xyz* digital elevation model derived from Agisoft Metashape Pro [57] was converted to a database, added to the map as a layer, and the obtained multipoint input features were converted to a raster. Afterward, shape polygons were defined for the different areas of interest, and then the three-dimensional (3D) Analyst surface volume tool was applied to obtain the dune volumes over a standardized section V/A [m^3/m^2]. Finally, the interpolate shape tool was used to obtain the cross-sectional and longitudinal dune profiles.

4.4. Calculation Procedure of Potential Aeolian Sediment Transport

The saturated aeolian sediment transport rate q_s [kg/m/hr] is calculated by a modified Bagnold model [21,59]:

$$q_s = \begin{cases} 3600 \cdot \alpha_B \cdot \sqrt{\dfrac{d_{50}}{d_{50,ref}}} \cdot \dfrac{\rho_a}{g} \cdot (u_*^3 - u_{*t}^3) & \text{for } u_* > u_{*t} \\ 0 & \text{for } u_* > u_{*t} \end{cases} \quad (1)$$

For the Bagnold factor, a value of $\alpha_B = 2$ was chosen to represent naturally graded sand [21,22]. The mean particle size was defined with d_{50} = 218 µm [36], and the reference sediment diameter was $d_{50,ref}$ = 250 µm as a standard value for dune sand [60]. The air density was chosen as ρ_a = 1.2 kg/m³ and the gravitational acceleration as g = 9.81 m/². u_* [m/s] is the shear velocity and u_{*t} [m/s] is the critical shear velocity, at which transport of dry sand is initiated [18]. The shear velocity is assumed to be constant over an hourly interval. According to SARRE (1989) [61], these simplifications in the determination of potential aeolian transport rates are not critical, whereas other transport-limiting factors, such as surface moisture or vegetation, are of greater importance in coastal areas [6]. Except for wind velocity, all parameters in Equation (1) are considered constant over time. It implies that the sediment transport rate depends solely on the variability of the wind [22,60,62,63].

The potential transport rates represent the maximum transport rates as transport limiting factors like surface roughness, vegetation, shells, surface slope, and fetch effects are neglected [59,62,64–66]. The fetch effect increases sediment transport rates with increasing fetch length downwind until an equilibrium condition is reached. Thus, a fetch length shorter than the critical fetch length can result in lower transport rates [65,67]. On narrow beaches, the critical fetch is often not reached, leading to limited aeolian sediment transport conditions depending on the incoming wind direction [50,68]. Numerous authors found that the critical fetch distance F [m] ranges from seven to tens of meters [7,65,69–71]. As the dry beach widths of Norderney $W \sim 320$ m and Langeoog $W \sim 70$ m were wider over the measuring period than the critical fetch distance with $F \sim 50$ m, see Section 2, we assume no influence on potential sediment transport by reduced fetch lengths.

It is necessary to know the aerodynamic roughness length or a measured vertical wind profile to determine the shear velocity [72]. However, since the roughness length varies temporally and spatially, it is not useful to use it for this work [72,73]. In contrast, HSU (1974) [74] proposed the following relationship for predicting shear velocity for dry beach areas from routine hourly wind observations at meteorological weather stations:

$$u_* = 0.037 \cdot u_{10}. \quad (2)$$

The wind velocity measured 10 m above ground is given with u_{10} [m/s]. The equation is based on field data from numerous study sites [5,74]. The critical shear velocity is given with:

$$u_{*t} = A \cdot \sqrt{\left(\dfrac{\rho_s}{\rho_a} - 1\right) \cdot g \cdot d_{50}}, \quad (3)$$

where A [-] is an empirical constant (here: 0.11) [21,75] and ρ_s = 2650 kg/m³ is the density of sand grains. With the given parameters for Langeoog [36], the critical shear velocity at the study site can be calculated as u_{*t} = 0.24 m/s. Since Langeoog and Norderney are sedimentologically similar, the same mean grain size and the same critical shear velocity is assumed for Norderney, respectively.

The sum of the potential transport rates calculated accordingly to Equation (1) over the measured time series gives the total sediment transport depending on the angle of prevailing wind direction relative to the coastline. For total cross-shore sediment transport $Q_{cross-shore}$ [m³/m], see Equation (4), and for total longshore sediment transport $Q_{longshore}$ [m³/m], see Equation (5):

$$Q_{cross-shore} = \frac{1}{\rho_b} \sum_{i=1}^{k} q_i \cdot \sin(\gamma - O) = \frac{1}{\rho_b} \sum_{i=1}^{k} q_i \cdot \sin(dd_j) \quad (4)$$

$$Q_{longshore} = \frac{1}{\rho_b} \sum_{i=1}^{k} q_i \cdot \cos(\gamma - O) = \frac{1}{\rho_b} \sum_{i=1}^{k} q_i \cdot \cos(dd_j) \quad (5)$$

where γ [°] is the angle between wind direction and north, O [°] is the orientation of the coastline, dd_j [°] is the difference between the wind direction and the coastal orientation, and ρ_b [kg/m³] is the bulk density of sand. The bulk density ρ_b = 1600 kg/m³ was chosen as VAN RIJN (2019) [59] used the value for the Dutch coast and STRYPSTEEN (2019) [5] for the Belgian coast. The total number of hours in the measured time series is represented by k [-] [5,76]. To compare predicted potential dune volume changes (as a function of potential sediment transport) with measured dune volume changes, the angle of the wind to the coastline is considered by the sinus and cosine function. In Figure 9, the explained approach is applied for both study sites showing the different angles. For the coastline of Langeoog and Norderney, an orientation of $O_{Langeoog}$ = 88° and $O_{Norderney}$ = 110° to the north is assumed, respectively.

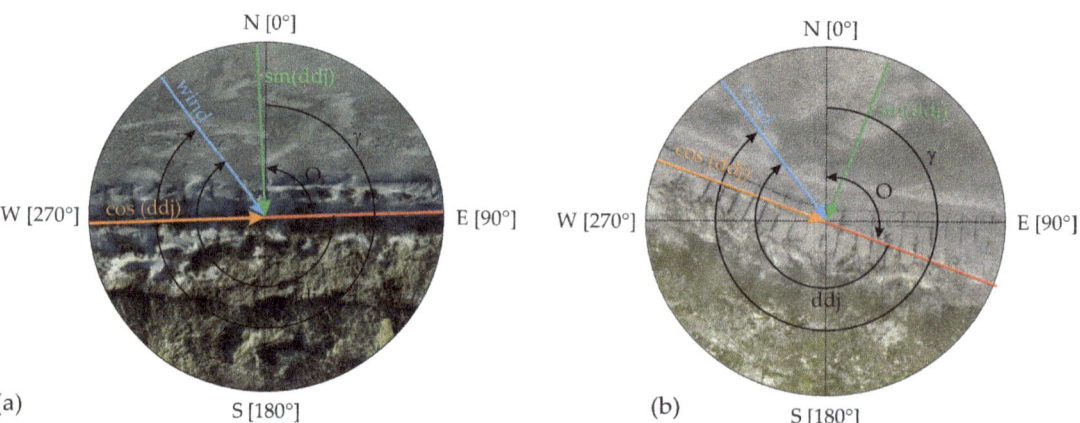

Figure 9. Orientation of the coastline of (**a**) the study site of Langeoog and (**b**) Norderney. Green arrows show the onshore directions of aeolian sediment transport towards the coastal dunes, the angles O [°] show the wind direction (concerning the north), and dd_j [°] the angles between the coastal orientation and the wind direction (methodology adapted from [5]).

5. Results and Discussion of Topographic Data
5.1. Dune Volume Changes

Figure 10 shows the orthophotographs with elevation heights ranging from 3 mNHN up to 8 mNHN of Langeoog's sand trapping fence on 20 May 2020, 15 June 2020, 27 August 2020, 26 October 2020, 14 December 2020, and 12 March 2021. As the terrain surface height increases, the colormap changes from (light) green to (light) orange to red. The upper boundary of the green area to the north represents the dune toe level. Immediately after finishing the construction of the sand trapping fence on 19 May 2020, the first drone survey was conducted on 20 May 2020. Therefore, Figure 10a, represents the initial condition of the dune volume at the dune toe. In Figure 10b–f, sand has accumulated at the brushwood lines of the sand trapping fence as time passes.

Figure 10 shows that the terrain elevation's continuous and relatively uniform growth is evident from the contours parallel to the coastal dunes. Furthermore, it seems that the coastal dunes in the west are already more developed compared to the coastal dunes in the east. It becomes clear that the dune toe level continued to move towards the North Sea at least 0.3 m but at most 3.9 m. Especially during late autumn, the individual fields between the brushwood lines were filled with sand.

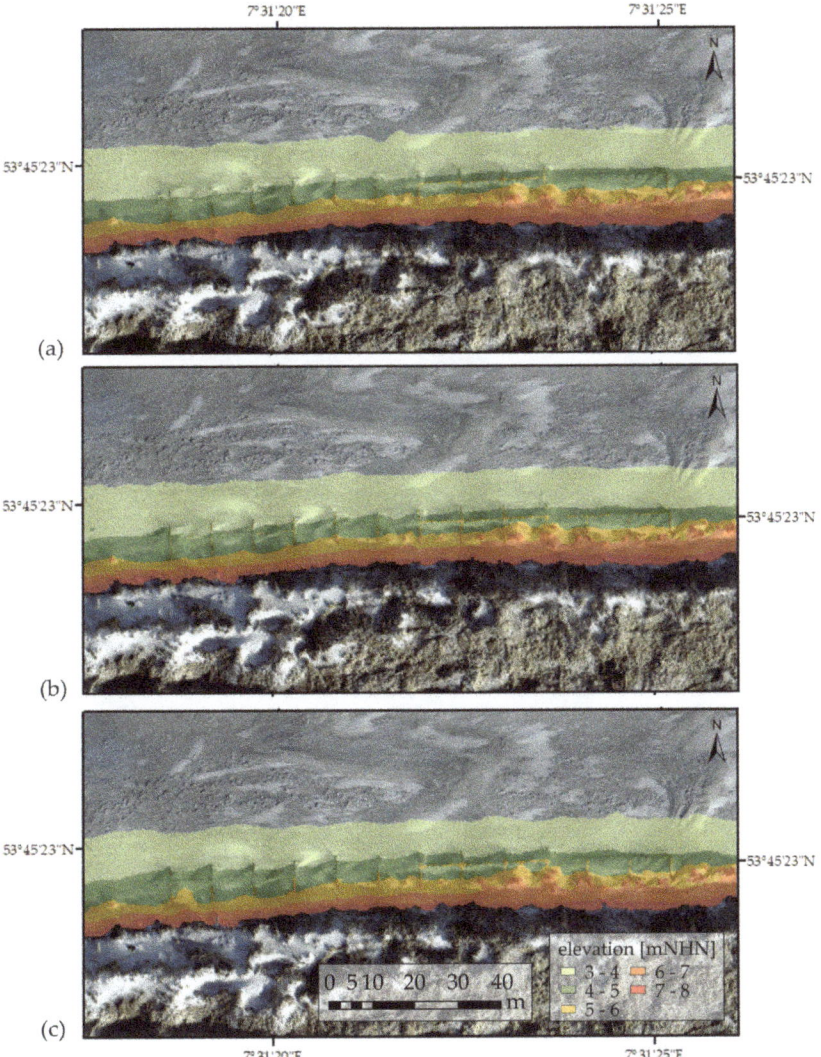

Figure 10. *Cont.*

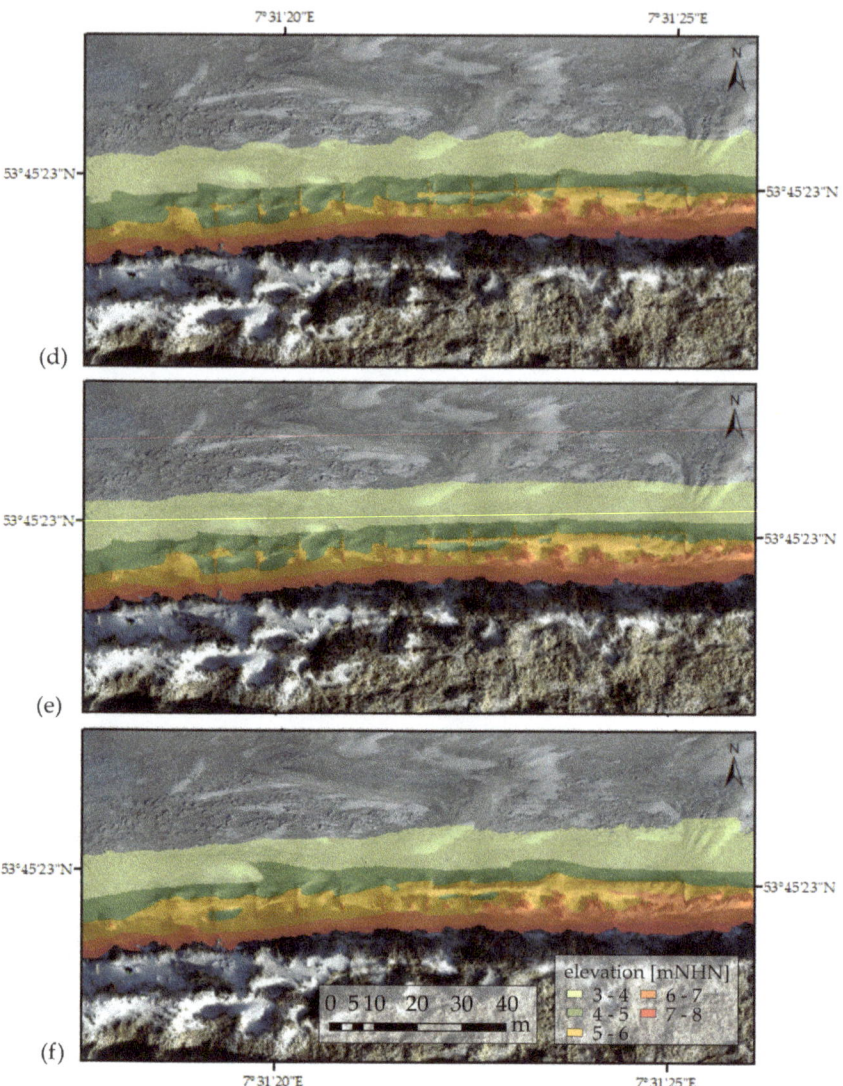

Figure 10. (**a**) Orthophotograph with digital elevation heights from 3 to 8 mNHN of study site Langeoog on 20 May 2020, (**b**) on 15 June 2020, (**c**) on 27 August 2020, (**d**) Orthophotograph with digital elevation heights from 3 to 8 mNHN of study site Langeoog on 26 October 2020, (**e**) on 14 December 2020, (**f**) on 12 March 2021.

To highlight the areas of sedimentation and erosion, Figure 11 shows the different elevation heights derived from the DEM of the study site of Langeoog from 20 May 2020 compared to 12 March 2021. Areas of erosion are displayed in blue colors, whereas sedimentation areas are shown in red colors. The white colors indicate areas where the elevation change is smaller than the threshold of measurement uncertainty (~10 cm).

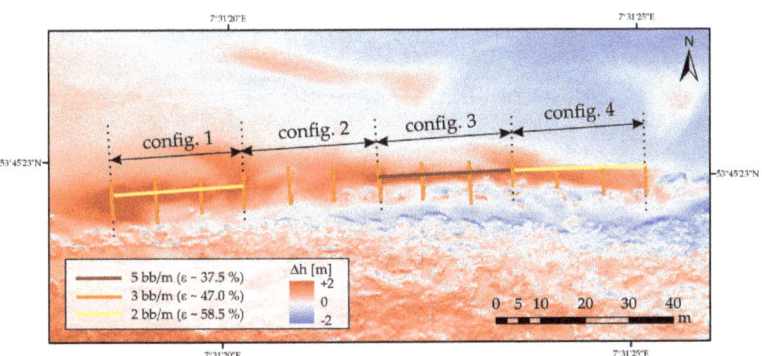

Figure 11. Differences in elevation heights derived from the DEM of study site Langeoog between 20 May 2020 and 12 March 2021.

It is clearly visible that a particularly large amount of sand accumulated at the individual lines of brushwood of the sand trapping fence. Large areas on the beach, onshore of the sand trapping fence, have grown as time passes, initiating the dune toe growth. Over the measured time period, the surface elevation grew up to Δh_{max} = +1.75 m. However, erosion areas also exist on the beach onshore and offshore of the sand trapping fence (Δh_{min} = −1.25 m), see Figure 11. The different configurations have each experienced varying degrees of growth:

- Configuration 1: In the first three fields to the west, an average sand volume of $\Delta V / A_{config \cdot 1} \sim 0.71$ m^3/m^2 has accumulated over the whole time period, implying that the amount of accumulated sand is 13% higher compared to the mean of all configurations ($\Delta V / A_{config \cdot 1-4} \sim 0.63$ m^3/m^2). The first field exposed to the west trapped the highest amount of sand with $\Delta V / A_{field1} \sim 0.80$ m^3/m^2 (Δh_{field1} = + 1.75 m). As time passed, sand has accumulated both at the parallel and orthogonal lines of brushwood and onshore of the sand trapping fence's deflectors, meaning that the dune toe shifted onshore towards the north.
- For configuration 2, only moderate accumulation of sand up to $\Delta h_{config \cdot 2, max}$ = +1.39 m has occurred at and between the orthogonally arranged deflectors and onshore of the sand trapping fence close to the dune toe. An average sand volume of $\Delta V / A_{config \cdot 2}$ = 0.60 m^3/m^2 has accumulated over the measuring time.
- Configuration 3: Predominantly, sand has accumulated at the parallel lines of brushwood and the onshore deflectors. There is hardly any accumulation present offshore of the parallel brushwood lines towards the coastal dunes. Thus, areas of erosion are more likely to be found here. This configuration recorded the lowest growth over the whole measuring time with a sand volume of $\Delta V / A_{config \cdot 3}$ = 0.56 m^3/m^2. The sand accumulated up to $\Delta h_{config \cdot 3}$ = +1.42 m.
- For configuration 4, extensive growth of the sediment pockets between the orthogonally arranged brushwood bundles offshore of the parallel brushwood line has been recorded, with heights up to $\Delta h_{config \cdot 4, max}$ = +1.25 m. The sand volume on the lee side grew faster than the dune volume on the luv side. The configuration has the second-largest growth rate with an accumulated sand volume of $\Delta V / A_{config \cdot 4}$ = 0.66 m^3/m^2 over the measured time. However, there are extensive erosion areas on the beach, and the dune toe level has not increased significantly.

A closer look at the standardized sand volume changes per defined area at each measuring time shows that the different configurations differ in the amount of accumulated sand, see Figure 12. For configuration 1–4, the results are shown as boxplots containing three fields for each configuration, in Figure 12a–d. The red lines within the boxplots represent the median values of dune toe volume change. In Figure 12e, the fields west and east, and in Figure 12f the reference field is shown, respectively.

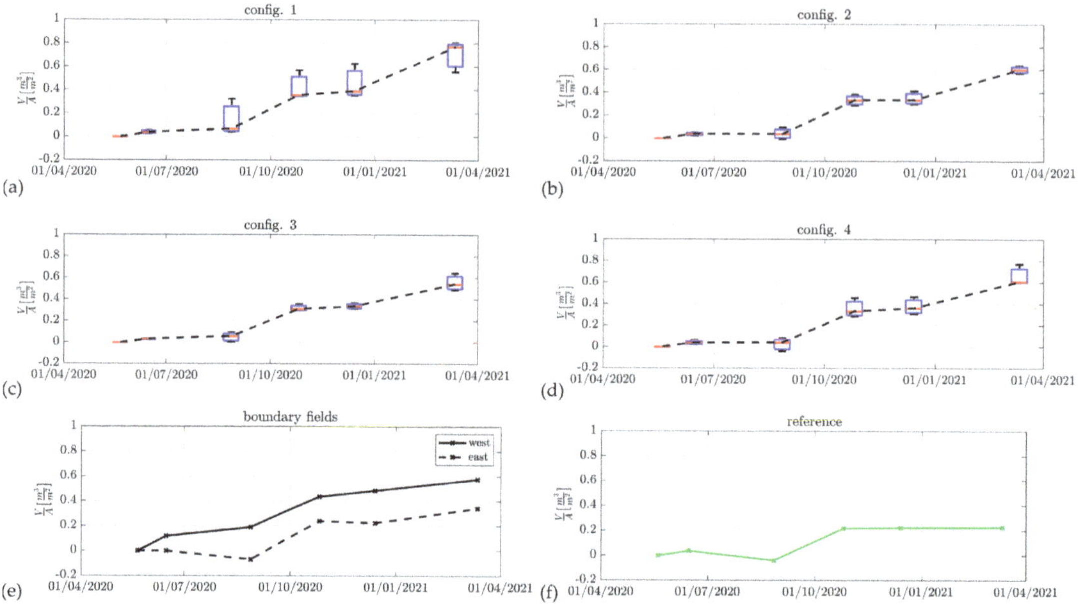

Figure 12. (**a**–**d**) Dune volume changes per area V/A [m^3/m^2] over time for the different sand trapping configurations as well as (**e**) the most westward and the most eastward fields. (**f**) Reference field on the study site Langeoog.

The measured values were connected linearly over time, even though this may deviate from reality. However, no measurement results are available for the time interval between, and thus, the trend of the volume changes at the sand trapping fence becomes visible.

The growth rate for all areas was highest from 27 August 2020 to 26 October 2020 and 14 December 2020 to 12 March 2021, whereas only small growth rates were present from 15 June 2020 to 27 August 2020. The areas in the west of the sand trapping fence and of configuration 1 increased over the entire measurement period, whereby the field exposed to the west had a more substantial increase at the beginning during summer compared to configuration 1 and a lower increase from 14 December 2020 to 12 March 2021.

The areas east of the sand trapping fence and configurations 2–4 showed a very similar trend: firstly, slight sedimentation occurred, followed by erosion processes from 15 June 2020 to 27 August 2020. A renewed increase, which stagnated in the meantime (26 October 2020 to 14 December 2020), then increased until 12 March 2021 again, followed. The sand volume of configuration 4 almost reached the final dune volume of configuration 1.

Figure 4f shows the amount of sand deposited at the study site without a sand trapping fence, which during the whole period of the investigations amounts to $V/A \sim 0.2$ m^3/m^2. This might be due to the natural development of the coastal dunes. Comparing the results of the reference field, see Figure 4f, to the results of the other fields, it is noted that the sand trapping fence has a positive influence on trapping sand at the dune toe as much more sand has been trapped at the brushwood lines than without any brushwood bundles. The reference field has a similar volume change over time compared to the east field. This indicates that, directly east of the sand trapping fence, its effect on the deposition of sediment has already vanished.

The coastal dunes are already more established at the eastern end than the western end, see Figure 13. This might explain more rapid growth at the western end than at the eastern end, given that dune growth tends to follow a sigmoid growth curve [12,77]. HOUSER et al. (2015) [77] conducted field measurements at the northern Gulf of Mexico (Santa Rosa Island, Florida and Galveston Island, Texas) and found that for predicting the evolution of a barrier island's foredune height a parameterized sigmoid growth curve can be applied. These results are supported by DALYANDER et al. (2020) [12], who developed an empirical dune growth model to predict the evolution of the foredune of a barrier island for the example of the Dauphin Island (Alabama). This could influence the observed variability in sediment accumulation independently of the sand trapping configurations.

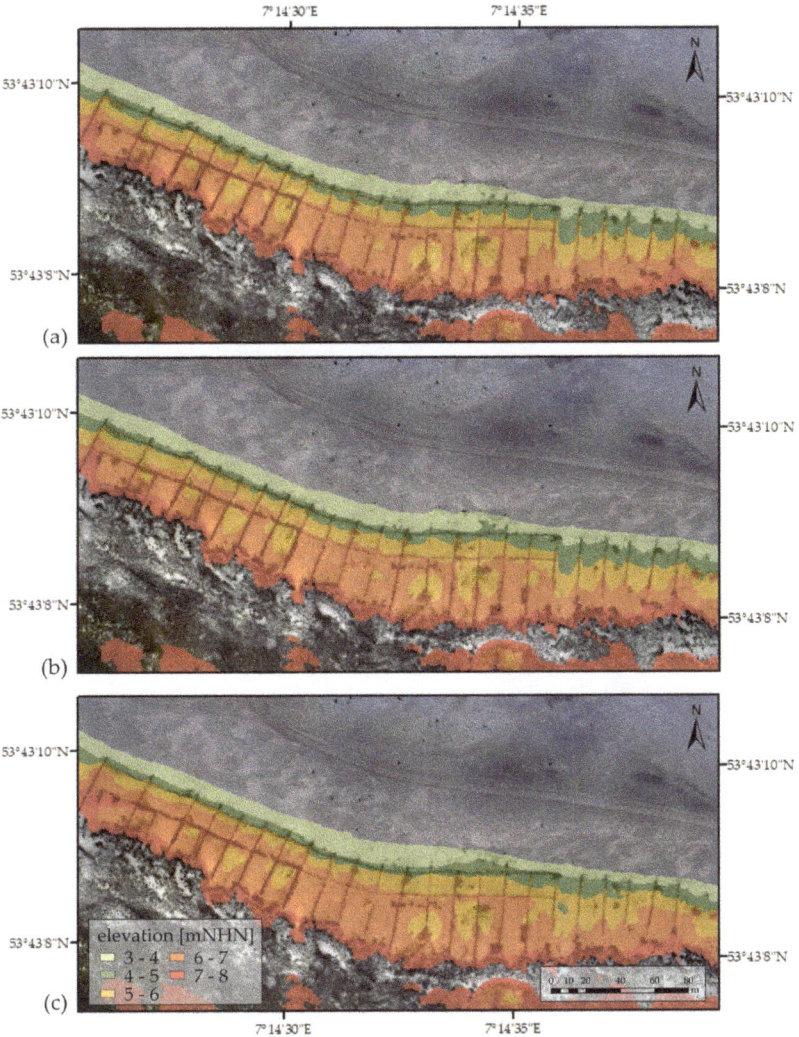

Figure 13. (a) Orthophotograph with digital elevation heights from 3–8 mNHN of study site Norderney on 24 August 2020, and on (b) 12 December 2020, (c) Orthophotograph with digital elevation heights from 3–8 mNHN of study site Norderney on 9 March 2021.

Figure 13 shows the orthophotographs with elevation heights ranging from 3 mNHN up to 8 mNHN of Norderney's sand trapping fence on 24 August 2020, 12 December 2020, 9 March 2021, respectively. The first orthophotograph from 27 August 2020 depicts the sand trapping fence's condition approximately one year after its installation. At this date, sand has already been deposited at the sand trapping fence.

Figure 13 reveals an increase in the dune toe level from 24 August 2020 to 9 March 2021. The dune toe level shifted onshore towards the north, a minimum of at least 0.2 m and a maximum of 2.9 m.

Over the measured time period, the surface elevation grew up about $\Delta h_{max} = +1.20$ m, see Figure 14. Only little areas directly along the brushwood lines offshore show erosion, see Figure 14. The different configurations have experienced the following degrees of growth:

- Configuration 3*: The area onshore of the sand trapping fence on the beach and between the two parallel brushwood lines has grown significantly. The areas offshore of the second parallel brushwood lines are essentially unchanged. Only the field exposed to the west shows accumulated sand. The growth for configuration 3* was generally very homogeneous with heights up to $\Delta h_{config \cdot 3*} = +1.16$ m. A sand volume of $\Delta V/A_{config \cdot 3*} = 0.18$ m^3/m^2 has accumulated over the measuring time.
- Configuration 1* recorded the lowest sand volume change with a value of $\Delta V/A_{config \cdot 3*} = 0.04$ m^3/m^2 over measuring time. Both onshore and offshore fields have developed very similarly over time. The dune toe level increased significantly over the measuring time.
- Configuration 4*: A sand volume of $\Delta V/A_{config \cdot 4*} = 0.09$ m^3/m^2 has accumulated over the whole measuring time. The development of the fields largely corresponds to the development of configuration 1*, whereas the dune toe level increased less.
- In configuration 2*, a sand volume of $\Delta V/A_{config \cdot 2*} = 0.27$ m^3/m^2 has accumulated over the measuring time. The dune toe level has grown only a little. The fields between the orthogonal brushwood lines were filled homogenously, whereby the fields exposed to the east recorded the most significant increase with $\Delta h_{config \cdot 3*} = +1.20$ m.

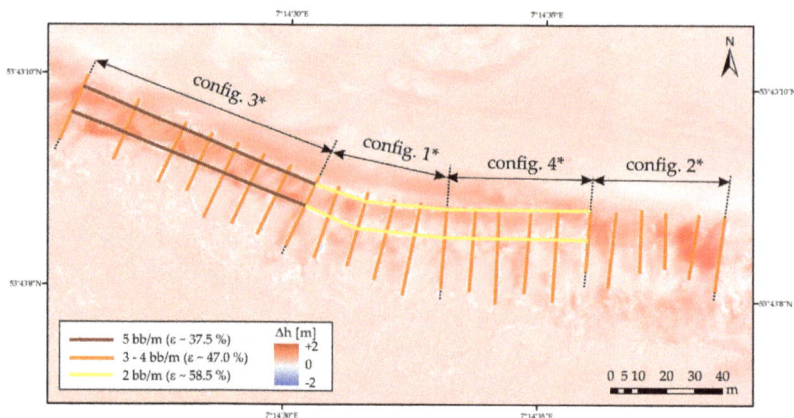

Figure 14. Differences in elevation heights derived from the DEM of study site Norderney between 24 August 2020 and 9 March 2021.

Figure 15 shows the corresponding standardized sand volume changes per area at each measuring time for Norderney.

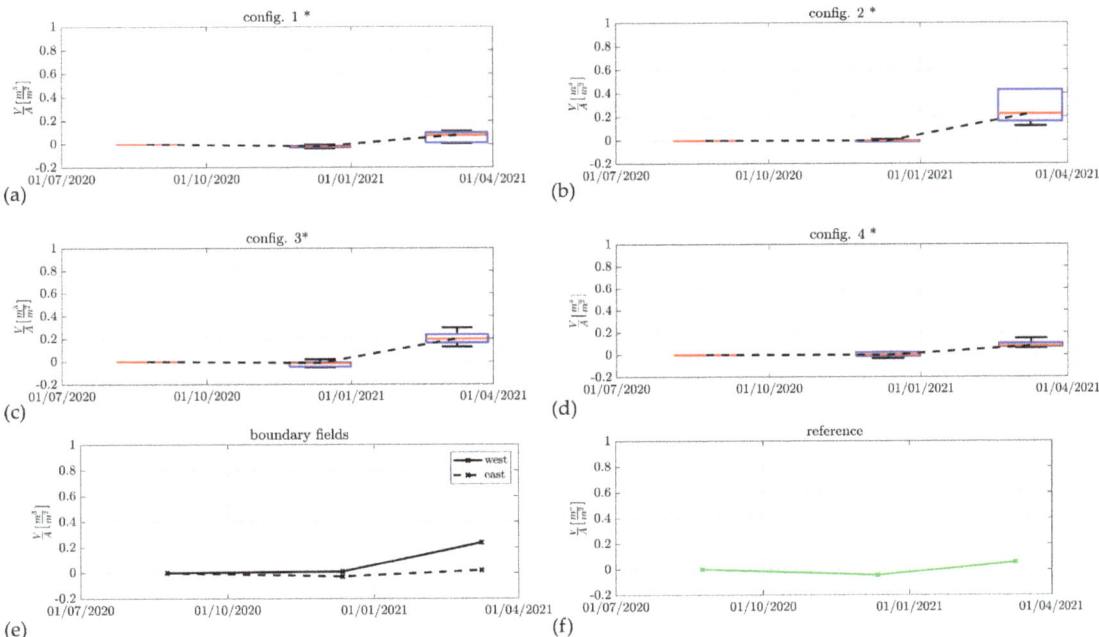

Figure 15. (**a**–**d**) Dune volume changes per area V/A [m^3/m^2] over time for the different sand trapping configuration as well as (**e**) the most westward and the most eastward fields. (**f**) Reference field on the study site Norderney.

In general, the trends of sand volume changes are very similar for all configurations. From 25 August 2020 to 12 December 2020; a slight stagnation or even a decrease in the sand volume occurred. It is followed by a considerable increase in sand volume from 12 December 2020 to 9 March 2021, with the most substantial increase for configuration 2* and configuration 3*. These configurations with the fields in the west accumulated the most sediment in total.

The reference field without any sand trapping fence, see Figure 5, shows a similar trend of volume change over the measurement period as for the east field. The comparison between the reference field without any sand trapping fence and the fields with sand trapping fence confirm the effectiveness of the sand trapping fences to initiate the growth of the dune toe.

When evaluating the sand volume changes of the different configurations on Norderney and Langeoog, the different initial and boundary conditions have to be considered. Therefore, the results of both study sites are not directly comparable: firstly, the configurations are arranged differently to each other depending on their location, see Section 3.2. Secondly, Langeoog's and Norderney's coastlines are orientated differently to the north, see Figure 9, resulting in different onshore and longshore wind conditions, see Figure 3. In addition, the beaches have different profiles and are different in size, see Section 3.1. The investigated sand trapping fence on Norderney are directly surrounded by earlier installed sand trapping fences whereas, on Langeoog, the next sand trapping fence is several hundred meters away. As stated above, the sand trapping fence on Norderney was established earlier than on Langeoog, and therefore, any incipient coastal dune growth has likely already occurred, explaining slower growth rates.

Moreover, the effectiveness of the sand trapping fence is influenced by independent morphological events such as the migration of ridges. For example, on Langeoog, it can be seen that erosion took place on the beach and, thus, resulted in potentially lower sand volume changes close to the erosive area of the beach, see Figure 11.

5.2. Development of the Longshore Dune Profile Influenced by Sand Trapping Fences

Figure 16a shows the longshore dune profiles onshore and Figure 16b offshore of the sand trapping fence of the study site Langeoog on 20 May 2020, 15 June 2020, 27 August 2020, 26 October 2020, 14 December 2020, and 12 March 2021. The y-axis shows the distance alongshore, and the z-axis the height. Both distances are standardized along their individual maximum length and height, respectively. The dashed lines in Figure 16 indicate the brushwood lines arranged orthogonal to the coastal dunes.

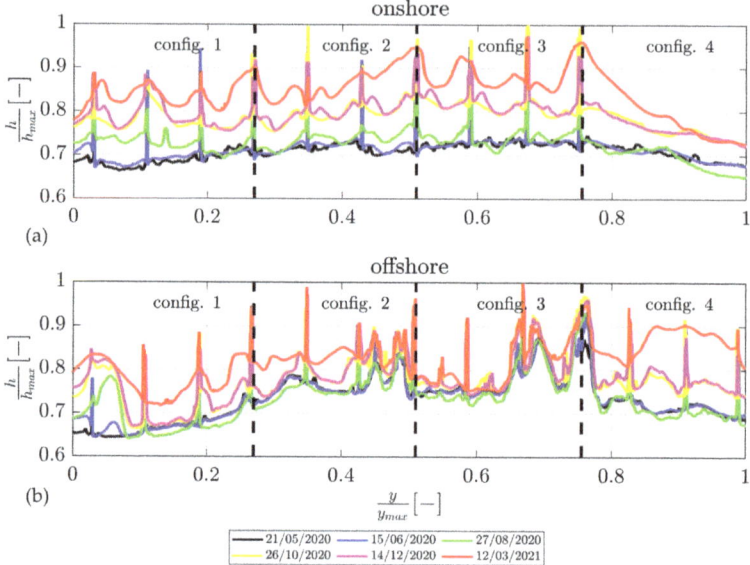

Figure 16. (a) Longshore profiles onshore and (b) offshore of the sand trapping fence of the study site Langeoog on 20 May 2020, 15 June 2020, 27 August 2020, 26 October 2020, 14 December 2020, and 12 March 2021. The dashed lines divide the study site into individual configurations.

The following can be seen even more clearly: firstly, the sand accumulates at the brushwood lines upwards before the sand accumulates in width, as also observed by NING et al. (2020) [31]. Exposed fields with potentially higher sediment transport brushwood lines can trap more sand than other fields without any exposed position.

In Figure 17, onshore fields show higher growth compared to the offshore fields. Areas that have grown remarkably onshore are not necessarily areas with significant growth offshore. Configuration 4* has experienced the most growth of all configurations.

It becomes clear that growth has occurred primarily from 12 December 2020 to 9 March 2021. The area between the two parallel brushwood lines, see Figure 17b, has grown, particularly in configuration 3* and configuration 2*.

5.3. Development of the Cross-Shore Dune Profile Influenced by Sand Trapping Fences

Figure 18 shows the cross-shore dune profiles of all four configurations over the measuring period. A representative cross-shore profile positioned in the middle of a field for each configuration is displayed. The cross-shore distance and the height are standardized along their individual maximum length and height, respectively. For configurations 1, 2, 3, the cross-shore brushwood lines can be recognized at about half of the distance cross-shore. Configuration 2, however, has no cross-shore brushwood lines.

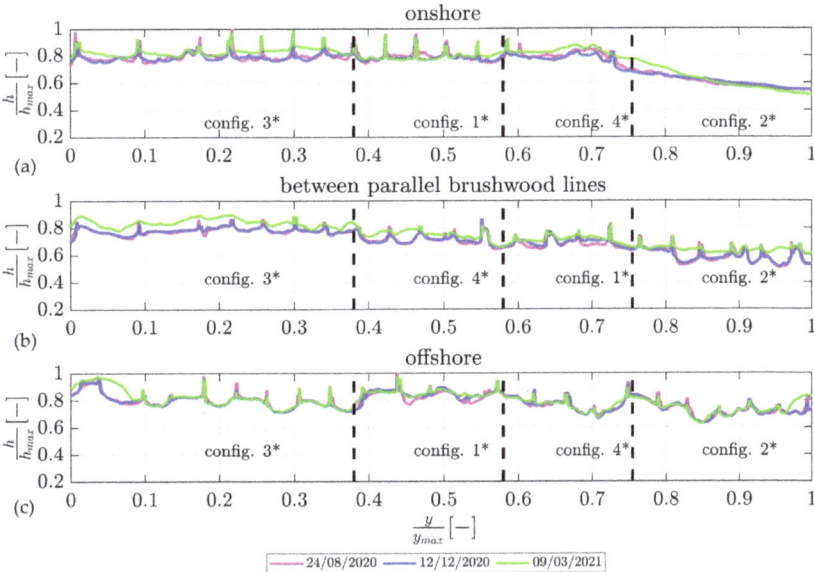

Figure 17. (**a**) Longshore profiles onshore, (**b**) between parallel brushwood lines, and (**c**) offshore of study site Norderney on 24 August 2020, 12 December 2020, and 9 March 2021. The dashed lines divide the study site into individual configurations.

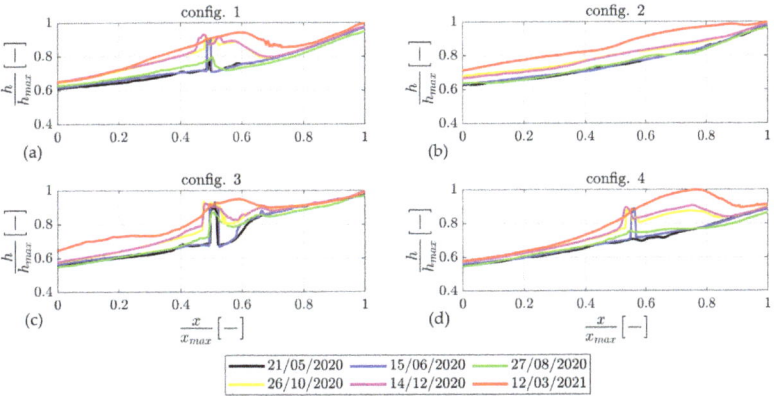

Figure 18. Cross-shore dune profiles of (**a**) config. 1, (**b**) config. 2, (**c**) config. 3, and (**d**) config. 4 of study site Langeoog on 20 May 2020, 15 June 2020, 27 August 2020, 26 October 2020, 14 December 2020, and 12 March 2021.

Configuration 2 indicates a relatively continuous growth in height distributed cross-shore. Configurations 1–3 show very similar growth, with configurations 1 and 3 showing more growth onshore than offshore. Configuration 4 shows especially growth offshore towards the coastal dunes.

In Figure 19, the cross-shore dune profiles for the study site Norderney are shown, respectively.

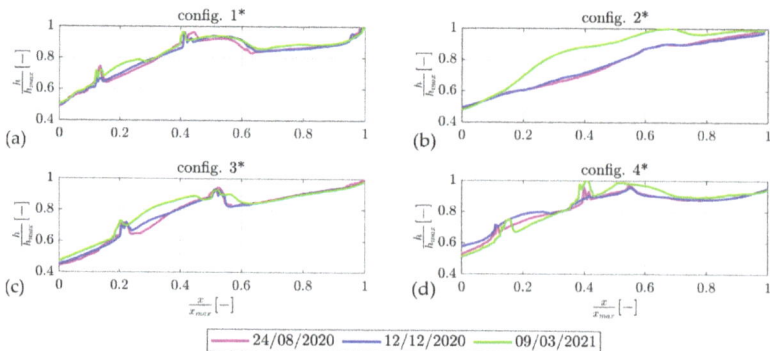

Figure 19. Cross-shore dune profiles of (**a**) config. 1, (**b**) config. 2, (**c**) config. 3, and (**d**) config. 4 of study Norderney on 24 August 2020, 12 December 2020, and 9 March 2021.

For configuration 2*, the growth occurred in the natural dune shape. Configurations 1*, 3*, 4* show very similar dune growth. First, the area offshore is filled with sand, propagating onshore. Configuration 4*, without any orthogonally arranged deflectors at the dune toe, showed a slower increase in the dune toe level compared to the other configurations.

The brushwood lines arranged parallel to the coastal dunes with higher porosity (see Figures 4 and 5) have allowed growth further in cross-shore direction than those with lower porosity, where local growth directly at the brushwood line has been greatly increased. Furthermore, it is suggested that the orthogonally arranged deflectors at the dune toe favour an accretion of sand at the dune toe.

6. Discussion

The spatial distribution of the vegetation *Ammophila arenaria* and the ratio of vegetated and total area were determined by using ArcGIS (version 10.5.1; 64 bit) [58]. With the help of orthophotographs, vegetation was identified and its area share was calculated. During the measurement period, the vegetation cover varied between 0.8–3.0% (Langeoog) and between 1.2–3.5% (Norderney), respectively. As generally acknowledged in the literature, the presence of vegetation significantly affects sand trapping at coastal foredunes by increasing the surface roughness, which promotes sediment deposition and incipient dune formation [30,78–81]. There is a strong correlation between dune morphodynamic and vegetation, which considerably varies in time and space due to influencing factors such as rainfall or temperature [37,82,83]. As the vegetation area is locally limited and relatively scarce for both study sites, we expect this to have little effect on the sediment deposition as compared to the effect of the sand trapping fence.

The brushwood bundles on both study sites differ from each other in their porosity and stem characteristics, especially stem diameter, see Section 3.1. At present, we are not aware that the stem diameter has a significant influence on sediment transport and subsequence trapping efficiency, especially since, in scientific research, the fence's porosity was identified as the major influence on these parameters (e.g., [25,26,32,79,84]).

Beach nourishments usually enlarge the beach width and thereby the fetch length over the beach increases as well [85]. Furthermore, rates of aeolian sediment transport depend on the grain size and the amount of shell fragments [85,86], see Equations (1) and (3). This means that, e.g., coarser grains would lead to a potentially lower sediment transport rate. Since many long-term effects of nourishments are still not fully understood, these nourishments could influence the development of the coastal dunes [6,9]. This, in turn, leads to further uncertainty in calculating the potential sediment transport rates, see Figures 21 and 22, since beach nourishments are not considered in these calculations. However, their influence is expected to be only small since over the measuring period, the fetch length was always greater than the critical fetch length. Furthermore, the sediment supply was sufficient for aeolian sediment transport before and after the beach nourishments took place.

Another uncertainty when discussing the results is the natural development of coastal dunes [77]. This phenomenon can superimpose or interact with the trapping efficiency of newly installed sand trapping fences.

6.1. Trap Efficiency of Different Sand Trapping Fence Configurations

In Figure 20, the sand volume changes from August 2020 to March 2021 (197 days) on Langeoog (dark colors) and Norderney (light colors) are shown. On the y-axis the sand volume changes per square meter over 197 days are shown. On the x-axis in Figure 20a the average porosities $\bar{\varepsilon}$ [%] of parallel and orthogonal brushwood lines are shown, whereas in Figure 20b the x-axis depicts the configuration number. The outwardly exposed fields showed a particular large accumulation of sand, see Figures 12 and 15, most likely due to the increased supply of sediment compared to the other fields.

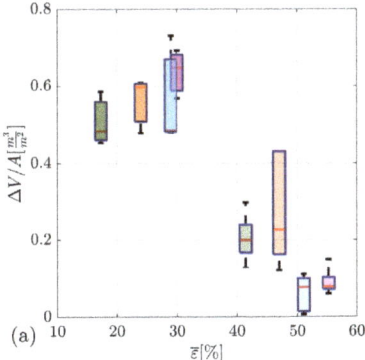
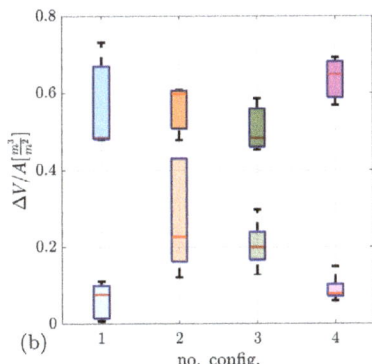

Figure 20. Sand volume changes from August 2020 to March 2021 (197 days) of different sand trapping configurations on Langeoog (darker colors) and Norderney (brighter colors) presented as a boxplot based on (**a**) their average porosity $\bar{\varepsilon}$ [%] and (**b**) their configuration type 1 (blue), type 2 (orange), type 3 (green), and type 4 (purple).

It can be seen in Figure 20a that, for configurations 1–4, a greater dune toe growth was recorded than for configurations 1*–4* comparing the same time period from August 2020 to March 2021. Norderney shows significantly lower sand volume changes over time than Langeoog. It seems reasonable that the potential growth rate is particularly high directly after finishing the construction of a new sand trapping fence like on Langeoog because the branches stick out high from the sand and have a lower porosity near the ground, see Section 3.3. As time passes, more sand has already accumulated at the brushwood lines, meaning that only the upper part of the sand trapping fence with a higher porosity sticks out at the top. This probably slows down the growth rate.

In Figure 20b, the sand volume changes are plotted over the different configurations, showing that a similar configuration on Langeoog leads to a different result on Norderney. This implies that the prevailing boundary conditions like sediment supply or the age of the installed sand trapping fence (height and porosity of the remaining branches) have a strong influence on the different configurations' effectiveness, see also Section 5.1.

6.2. Correlation between Dune Volume Changes and Potential Aeolian Sediment Transport

Coastal dune growth is significantly related to potential aeolian sediment transport [5–7]. Studies of coastal dune development typically focus on measuring short-term transport processes at timescales of hours to days [5,36,61,87]. These studies often show good results between predicted and observed potential aeolian sediment transport [21,36].

Coastal dune development is also commonly studied by measuring long-term topographical changes on timescales of months to years and related to sediment transport equations [7,74,88,89]. Long-term aeolian sediment transport from the beach towards the coastal dunes is generally predicted by integrating hourly meteorological data, such as wind velocity and direction from meteorological weather stations, see Section 4.4. At these timescales, results related to dune volume changes have so far been subject to significant uncertainties [5,61]. However, KEIJSERS et al. (2014) [89] and DE VRIES et al. (2016) [6] have found good correlations on annual to decadal timescales for wide beaches $W > 200$ m. Strypsteen (2019) [5] found dune growth primarily determined by aeolian sediment transport from the beach on a decadal timescale.

We examined the possible correlation between dune growth influenced by sand trapping fences and potential aeolian sediment transport rates on the timescale of months. As of date, it is not clear which wind directions and associated potential sediment transport contribute to dune toe growth or erosion. Therefore, it is a frequent practice to examine different possible mechanisms according to onshore and cross-shore wind directions, see, e.g., STRYPSTEEN (2019) [5]. We, therefore, present three different methods, which differ in whether erosion or accumulation of sand is favoured depending on the wind direction:

- Method 1: Cross-shore onshore aeolian sediment transport rates, see Equation (4), are solely used to explain coastal dune toe growth.
- Method 2: Cross-shore onshore and longshore aeolian sediment transport rates, see Equations (4) and (5), are used to calculate coastal dune toe growth.
- Method 3: Onshore wind conditions initiate dune toe growth, whereas all wind directions offshore lead to dune erosion.

In Figures 21 and 22, these methods are applied for the study sites Langeoog and Norderney, respectively. A positive trend means dune volume growth; a negative trend means dune volume erosion. The blue line represents the dune volume changes based on the weather station Norderney and the dotted blue line based on the weather station Spiekeroog over the measuring time interval. In the following section, only the measurement results of the wind station Norderney are described in more detail since these correspond better with the measured values. Furthermore, Spiekeroog's results are a multiple of Norderney's results. The orange line indicates the observed dune volume changes derived in Section 5.1. Over the whole measuring time, there was no storm surge measured by FEDERAL MARITIME AND HYDROGRAPHIC AGENCY [90], reaching the dune toe level suggesting that aeolian processes solely and sand trapping caused a change in dune volume.

It is clearly visible that method 1 and method 2 show similar and good results in predicting the trend of the dune toe volume change for the study site Langeoog, whereas method 1 shows even better results.

Over the measured time interval, a total dune volume change of $V/A_{method1} = 5.3$ m^3/m^2 for method 1, $V/A_{method2} = 9.5$ m^3/m^2 for method 2, and of $V/A_{method3} = 3.7$ m^3/m^2 for method 3 was predicted.

For method 1 the average dune growth is approximately 20% of the potential aeolian sediment, whereas for method 2 approximately 10% of the potential aeolian sediment is deposited. Time intervals of a positive dune toe volume change for the predicted model agree well with areas of dune growth in the observed model. Obviously, and as can be clearly seen in Figure 21, the dune volume change is not equal to the potential sediment transport, assuming that all sediment accumulates at the sand trapping fence. Either not all sediment that is potentially transported by onshore winds to the dune toe is sedimented, and the potential sediment transport is overestimated due to the necessary simplifications made in its calculation, especially neglecting shells, sand moisture, and salt crusts.

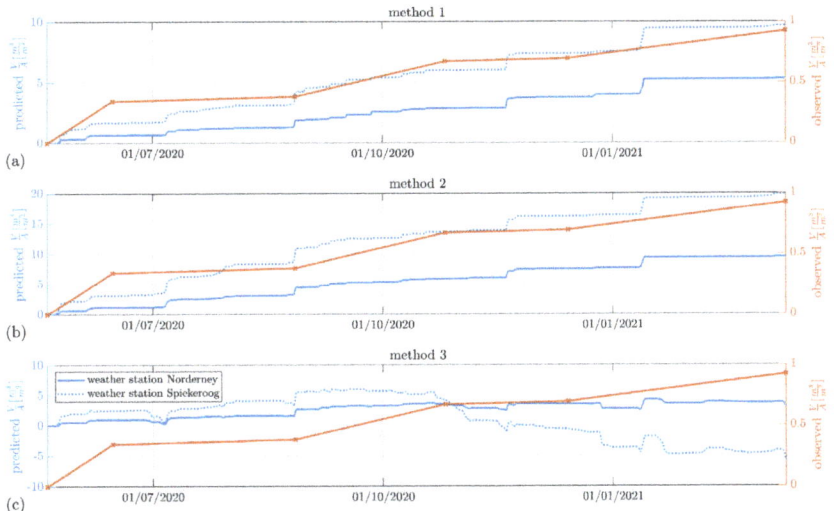

Figure 21. Predicted dune volume changes based on the transportation Equations (4) and (5) obtained by the wind data from weather station Norderney (blue line) and Spiekeroog (dotted blue line), and observed dune volume changes (orange line) for study site Langeoog applying (**a**) method 1, (**b**) method (2), and (**c**) method (3).

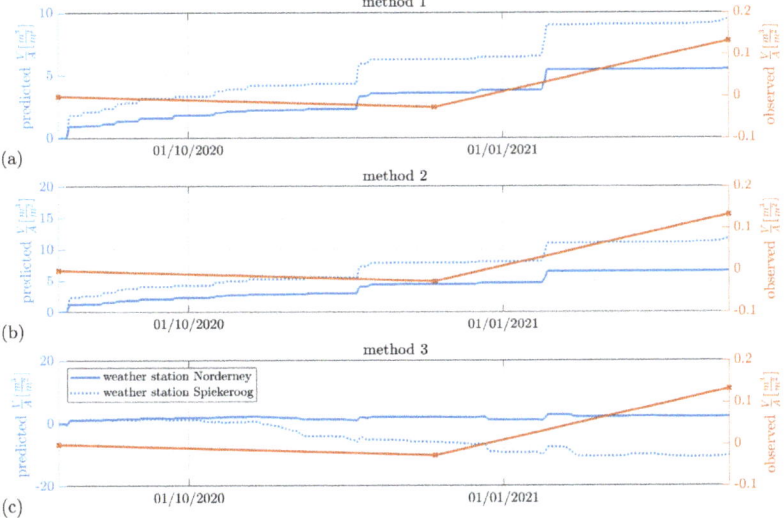

Figure 22. Predicted dune volume changes based on the transportation Equations (4) and (5) obtained by the wind data from weather station Norderney (blue line) and Spiekeroog (dotted blue line), and observed dune volume changes (orange line) for study site Norderney applying (**a**) method 1, (**b**) method (2), and (**c**) method (3).

Method 3 would suggest erosion and a decrease in dune volume. However, this erosion is most likely prevented by the sand trapping fences and a sheltering effect of the dunes landward of the dune toe.

For Norderney, the results have no significant correlation between predicted and measured values for the whole duration of the measurements. However, the final state again corresponds to the trend of volume change for method 1 and method 2. It should, however, be noted that only three measuring points are available. The growing pattern of coastal dunes following a sigmoid growth curve ([12,77]) may also explain why, for Norderney, the observed volume changes do not correlate to potential aeolian sediment transport since the growth of coastal dunes is a product of both potential transport and sand trapping.

In general, the assumption can be made that with a sufficiently long measurement period and many measurements of dune volumes, the cross-shore aeolian sediment transport rates (method 1) and additionally longshore sediment transport rates (method 2) are an appropriate approach to predicted the dune volume changes at sand trapping fences, especially for incipient coastal dune growth.

7. Conclusions and Outlook

This study provided the insights into monitoring coastal dune toe growth around and in between individual lines of brushwood of a sand trapping fence with different configurations. This work presented the results of field experiments conducted on the East Frisian islands Langeoog and Norderney, analyzing topographical changes at the dune toe influenced by a sand trapping fence as time passes. The following conclusions can be drawn from the results presented in this work:

- It is clearly visible that a particularly large amount of sand accumulated at the individual lines of brushwood of the sand trapping fence.
- In exposed fields of newly constructed sand trapping fences with potentially higher sediment supply from the beach, brushwood lines can trap more sand than in fields in the center of the sand trapping fence.
- The brushwood lines arranged parallel to the coastal dunes with a higher porosity have allowed for growth further towards the coastal dunes. For those with lower porosity, growth has been greatly increased directly at the brushwood lines.
- The orthogonally arranged deflectors at the dune toe can favour an accretion of sand at the dune toe.
- The dune growth potential at the sand trapping fence is greatest shortly after construction of the sand trapping fence and declines over time.
- The growing pattern of coastal dunes follows a sigmoid growth function with a more established coastal dune on Norderney than on Langeoog.
- For the sand trapping fence that has been in place longer, the protruding branch height and the porosity of the remaining branches seem to play a minor role for trapping sediment.
- The prevailing boundary conditions like sediment supply as well as the height and the porosity of the brushwood bundles strongly influencing the effectiveness of the different sand trapping configurations.
- In general, with a sufficiently long measurement period and number of measurements of topographical changes, the calculations of the cross-shore aeolian sediment transport rates according to method 1, or also considering longshore sediment transport rates according to method 2, is an appropriate approach to predict the trend in dune toe volume changes at sand trapping fences, especially for incipient dune formation.
- The dune toe growth of coastal dunes influenced by sand trapping fences is a product of both potential transport and sand trapping.

Repeated UAV surveys provide an accurate method to study detailed changes in dune toe volume on a timescale of months to years. We strongly recommend extending the knowledge of the influence of sand trapping fences on aeolian sediment transport and dune toe development in standardized wind tunnel experiments to gain quantitative data.

Author Contributions: Conceptualization, C.E.; methodology, C.E.; formal analysis, C.E.; investigation: C.E., data processing, C.E., resources, H.S.; original draft preparation, C.E.; review and editing, H.S.; visualization, C.E.; supervision, H.S.; project administration, H.S.; and funding acquisition, C.E., H.S. and others. All authors have read and agreed to the published version of the manuscript.

Funding: This research was funded by the German Federal Ministry of Education and Research (BMBF) within the project ProDune (grant number 03KIS125) that was initiated in the framework of the German Coastal Engineering Research Council (KFKI).

Institutional Review Board Statement: Not applicable.

Informed Consent Statement: Not applicable.

Data Availability Statement: Not applicable.

Acknowledgments: The authors thank the project partner Lower Saxony Water Management, Coastal Protection and Nature Conservation Agency for installing the sand trapping fences, their help in attaining permission to conduct the field experiments, and for sharing their expertise in the project support group. The authors thank the administration of the National Park Wadden Sea of Lower Saxony for the permission to conduct the field experiments on the East Frisian Islands. We, furthermore, thank the technical staff and student assistants of the IWW for their help in conducting the field experiments.

Conflicts of Interest: The authors declare no conflict of interest. The funders had no role in the study's design; in the collection, analyses, or interpretation of data; in the writing of the manuscript, or in the decision to publish the result.

References

1. Kystdirektoratet. Aeolian Sediment Transport and Natural Dune Development, Skodbjerge, Denmark, Skodbjerge, Denmark. Lemvig.: Interreg. North Sea Region. Building with Nature. 2020. Available online: https://northsearegion.eu/media/12719/aeolian-sediment-transport-and-natural-dune-development-skodbjerge-denmark.pdf (accessed on 21 June 2021).
2. Generalplan Küstenschutz Niedersachsen: Ostfriesische Inseln, Küstenschutz Band 2.; Niedersächsischer Landesbetrieb für Wasserwirtschaft, Küsten- und Naturschutz (Lower Saxony Water Management, Coastal Protection and Nature Conversation Agency), Ed. 2010. Available online: https://www.nlwkn.niedersachsen.de/startseite/hochwasser_kustenschutz/kustenschutz/generalplane_fur_insel_und_kustenschutz/generalplan-kuestenschutz-45183.html (accessed on 21 June 2021).
3. Peters, K.; Pohl, M. *Kuratorium für Forschung im Küsteningenieurwesen (German Coastal Engineering Research Council). Die Küste (The Coast), Issue 88, EAK 2020. Empfehlungen für die Ausführung von Küstenschutzwerken durch den Ausschuss für Küstenschutzwerke der Deutschen Gesellschaft für Geotechnik e.V. und der Hafenbautechnischen Gesellschaft e.V. (Recommendations for Coastal Protection Structures. Working Group 'Coastal Protection Structures' as a Joint Commitee of the German Port Geotechnical Society and the German Port Technology Association)*, 3rd ed.; Westholsteinische Verlagsanstalt Boyens & Co.: Heide, Germany, 2020.
4. Hesp, P. Foredunes and blowouts: Initiation, geomorphology and dynamics. *Geomorphology* **2002**, *48*, 245–268. [CrossRef]
5. Strypsteen, G. Monitoring and Modelling Aeolian Sand Transport at the Belgian Coast. Ph.D. Thesis, KU LEUVEN, Brugge, Belgium, 2019.
6. De Vries, S.; Southgate, H.N.; Kanning, W.; Ranasinghe, R. Dune behavior and aeolian transport on decadal timescales. *Coast. Eng.* **2012**, *67*, 41–53. [CrossRef]
7. Bagnold, R.A. *The Physics of Blown Sand and Desert Dunes*; Springer: Dordrecht, The Netherlands, 1941.
8. Van Thiel de Vries, J.S.M. Dune Erosion during Storm Surges. Ph.D. Thesis, Technische Universität Delft, Amsterdam, The Netherlands, 2009.
9. Staudt, F.; Gijsman, R.; Ganal, C.; Mielck, F.; Wolbring, J.; Hass, H.C.; Goseberg, N.; Schüttrumpf, H.; Schlurmann, T.; Schimmels, S. The sustainability of beach nourishments: A review of nourishment and environmental monitoring practice. *J. Coast Conserv.* **2021**, *25*. [CrossRef]
10. Martínez, M.L.; Hesp, P.A.; Gallego-Fernández, J.B. (Eds.) Coastal Dune Restoration: Trends and Perspectives. In *Restoration of Coastal Dunes*; Springer: Berlin/Heidelberg, Germany, 2013; pp. 323–339. ISBN 978-3-642-33444-3.
11. Hanley, M.E.; Hoggart, S.; Simmonds, D.J.; Bichot, A.; Colangelo, M.A.; Bozzeda, F.; Heurtefeux, H.; Ondiviela, B.; Ostrowski, R.; Recio, M.; et al. Shifting sands? Coastal protection by sand banks, beaches and dunes. *Coast. Eng.* **2014**, *87*, 136–146. [CrossRef]
12. Dalyander, P.S.; Mickey, R.C.; Passeri, D.L.; Plant, N.G. Development and Application of an Empirical Dune Growth Model for Evaluating Barrier Island Recovery from Storms. *J. Mar. Sci. Eng.* **2020**, *8*, 977. [CrossRef]
13. Galiforni Silva, F. Beach-Dune Systems Near Inlets: Linking Subtidal and Subaerial Morphodynamics. Ph.D. Thesis, University of Twente, Enschede, The Netherlands, 2019.
14. Short, A.D.; Hesp, P.A. Wave, Beach and Dune Interactions in Southeastern Australia. *Mar. Geol.* **1982**, 259–284. [CrossRef]
15. Arens, S.M. Rates of aeolian transport on a beach in a temperate humid climate. *Geomorphology* **1996**, *17*, 3–18. [CrossRef]
16. Van Rijn, L.C. Coastal erosion and control. *Ocean Coast. Manag.* **2011**, *54*, 867–887. [CrossRef]
17. D'Alessandro, F.; Tomasicchio, G.R. Wave–dune interaction and beach resilience in large-scale physical model tests. *Coast. Eng.* **2016**, *116*, 15–25. [CrossRef]
18. Schweiger, C.; Kaehler, C.; Koldrack, N.; Schuettrumpf, H. Spatial and temporal evaluation of storm-induced erosion modelling based on a two-dimensional field case including an artificial unvegetated research dune. *Coast. Eng.* **2020**, *161*, 103752. [CrossRef]

19. Sutton-Grier, A.; Gittman, R.; Arkema, K.; Bennett, R.; Benoit, J.; Blitch, S.; Burks-Copes, K.; Colden, A.; Dausman, A.; DeAngelis, B.; et al. Investing in Natural and Nature-Based Infrastructure: Building Better Along Our Coasts. *Sustainability* **2018**, *10*, 523. [CrossRef]
20. Baas, A.C.W.; Sherman, D.J. Spatiotemporal Variability of Aeolian Sand Transport in a Coastal Dune Environment. *J. Coast. Res.* **2006**, *225*, 1198–1205. [CrossRef]
21. Van Rijn, L.C.; Strypsteen, G. A fully predictive model for aeolian sand transport. *Coast. Eng.* **2019**, *156*. [CrossRef]
22. Sherman, D.J.; Li, B.; Ellis, J.T.; Farrell, E.J.; Maia, L.P.; Granja, H. Recalibrating aeolian sand transport models. *Earth Surf. Process. Landf.* **2013**, *38*, 169–178. [CrossRef]
23. Grafals-Soto, R. Understanding the Effetcs of Sand Fence Usage and the Resulting Landscape, Landforms and Vegetation Patterns: A New Jersey Example. Ph.D. Thesis, University of New Brunswick, New Brunswick, NJ, USA, 2010.
24. Grafals-Soto, R.; Nordstrom, K. Sand fences in the coastal zone: Intended and unintended effects. *Environ. Manag.* **2009**, *44*, 420–429. [CrossRef] [PubMed]
25. Li, B.; Sherman, D.J. Aerodynamics and morphodynamics of sand fences: A review. *Aeolian Res.* **2015**, *17*, 33–48. [CrossRef]
26. Zhang, N.; Kang, J.-H.; Lee, S.-J. Wind tunnel observation on the effect of a porous wind fence on shelter of saltating sand particles. *Geomorphology* **2010**, *120*, 224–232. [CrossRef]
27. Dong, Z.; Luo, W.; Qian, G.; Wang, H. A wind tunnel simulation of the mean velocity fields behind upright porous fences. *Agric. For. Meteorol.* **2007**, *146*, 82–93. [CrossRef]
28. Dong, Z.; Chen, G.; He, X.; Han, Z.; Wang, X. Controlling blown sand along the highway crossing the Taklimakan Desert. *J. Arid Environ.* **2004**, *57*, 329–344. [CrossRef]
29. Hotta, S.; Horikawa, K. Function of Sand Fence Placed in Front of Embankment. In Proceedings of the 22nd Conference on Coastal Engineering 2–6 July 1990, Delft, The Netherlands, 2–6 July 1990; pp. 2754–2767. [CrossRef]
30. Adriani, M.J.; Terwindt, J.H.J. *Sand Stabilization and Dune Building*; Government Publishing Office: Hague, The Netherlands, 1974; ISBN 9012004985.
31. Ning, Q.; Li, B.; Ellis, J.T. Fence height control on sand trapping. *Aeolian Res.* **2020**, *46*, 100617. [CrossRef]
32. Yu, Y.; Zhang, K.; An, Z.; Wang, T.; Hu, F. The blocking effect of the sand fences quantified using wind tunnel simulations. *J. Mt. Sci.* **2020**, *17*, 2485–2496. [CrossRef]
33. Lima, I.A.; Araújo, A.D.; Parteli, E.J.R.; Andrade, J.S., Jr.; Herrmann, H.J. Optimal Array of Sand Fences; 2017. Available online: http://arxiv.org/pdf/1702.05114v1 (accessed on 21 June 2021).
34. Anthony, E.J.; Vanhee, S.; Ruz, M.-H. An assessment of the impact of experimental brushwood fences on foredune sand accumulation based on digital elelvation models. *Ecol. Eng.* **2007**, *31*, 41–46. [CrossRef]
35. Ruz, M.-H.; Anthony, E.J. Sand trapping by brushwood fences on a beach-foredune contact: The primacy of the local sediment budget. *Zeitschrift für Geomorphologie* **2008**, *52*, 179–194. [CrossRef]
36. Eichmanns, C.; Schüttrumpf, H. Investigating Changes in Aeolian Sediment Transport at Coastal Dunes and Sand Trapping Fences: A Field Study on the German Coast. *JMSE* **2020**, *8*, 1012. [CrossRef]
37. Sanromualdo-Collado, A.; Hernández-Cordero, A.I.; Viera-Pérez, M.; Gallego-Fernández, J.B.; Hernández-Calvento, L. Coastal Dune Restoration in El Inglés Beach (Gran Canaria, Spain): A Trial Study. *REA* **2021**, 187–204. [CrossRef]
38. Gerhardt, P. Im Auftrage des Kgl. Preuss. In *Handbuch des Deutschen Dünenbaues*; Johannes, A., Paul, B., Alfred, J., Eds.; Verlagsbuchhandlung Paul Parey: Berlin, Germany, 1990.
39. Reise, K. Coast of change: Habitat loss and transformations in the Wadden Sea. *Helgol. Mar. Res.* **2005**, *59*, 9–21. [CrossRef]
40. De Groot, A.V.; Oost, A.P.; Veeneklaas, R.M.; Lammerts, E.J.; van Duin, W.E.; van Wesenbeeck, B.K. Tales of island tails: Biogeomorphic development and management of barrier islands. *J. Coast Conserv.* **2017**, *21*, 409–419. [CrossRef]
41. Hillmann, S.; Blum, H.; Thorenz, F. *National Analysis—Germany Lower Saxony.: Niedersächsischer Landesbetrieb für Wasserwirtschaft, Küsten und Naturschutz (Lower Saxony Water Management, Coastal Protection and Nature Conservation Agency)*; NLWKN: Lower Saxony, Germany, 2019.
42. Federal Agency for Cartography and Geodesy. *Geodaten der Deutschen Landesvermessung. Bundesamt für Kartographie und Geodäsie (Federal Agency for Cartography and Geodesy)*; Federal Agency for Cartography and Geodesy: Leipzig, Germany. Available online: http://sg.geodatenzentrum.de/web_public/nutzungsbedingungen.pdf (accessed on 29 March 2021).
43. Bundesamt für Schifffahrt und Hydrographie. *Gezeitenkalender 2021: Hoch- und Niedrigwasserzeiten für die Deutsche Bucht und Deren Flussgebiete*; Bundesamt für Schifffahrt und Hydrographie: Hamburg, Germany, 2020.
44. Thorenz, F.; Kuratorium für Forschung im Küsteningenieurwesen (German Coastal Engineering Research Council). Die Küste (The Coast), Issue 74, EAK; *Coastal Flood Defence and Coastal Protection along the North Sea Coast of Niedersachsens*; Kuratorium für Forschung im Küsteningenieurwesen (German Coastal Engineering Research Council): Hamburg, Germany, 2008.
45. Hayes, M.O. *Barrier Island Morphology as a Function of Tidal and Wave regime: Barrier Islands from the Gulf of St. Lawrence to the Gulf of Mexic*; Academic Press: New York, NY, USA, 1979; pp. 1–27.
46. Niemeyer, H.D. Long Term Morphodynamical Development of the East Frisian Island and Coast. In Proceedings of the 24th International Conference on Coastal Engineering, Kobe, Japan, 23–28 October 1994.
47. Hagen, R.; Freund, J.; Plüß, A.; Ihde, R. (Eds.) *Validierungsdokument EasyGSH-DB Nordseemodell. Teil: UnTRIM2–SediMorph–UnK*; Federal Waterways Engineering and Research Institute: Karlsruhe, Germany, 2019.
48. DWD. Climate Data Center. 2021. Available online: https://cdc.dwd.de/portal/ (accessed on 1 April 2021).

49. Ladage, F. *Vorarbeiten zu Schutzkonzepten für die Ostfriesischen Inseln—Morphologische Entwicklung um Langeoog im Hinblick auf die verstärkten Dünenabbrüche vor dem Pirolatal*; NLWKN: Norderney, Germany, 2002.
50. Donker, J.; van Maarseveen, M.; Ruessink, G. Spatio-Temporal Variations in Foredune Dynamics Determined with Mobile Laser Scanning. *JMSE* **2018**, *6*, 126. [CrossRef]
51. Lower Saxony Water Management, Coastal Protection and Nature Conversation Agency. *Documentation of the Configuration of the Installed Sand Trapping Fences on Langeoog and Norderney*; Lower Saxony Water Management, Coastal Protection and Nature Conversation Agency: Hannover, Germany, 2020.
52. *MATLAB, Version 9.510.944444 (R2018b)*; The MathWorks Inc.: Natick, MA, USA, 2018.
53. Azzeh, J.; Zahran, B.; Alqadi, Z. Salt and Pepper Noise: Effects and Removal. *Int. J. Inform. Vis.* **2018**, *2*, 252. [CrossRef]
54. Image Analyst. Image Segmentation Tutorial Image Analyst (2021). Image Segmentation Tutorial. MATLAB Central File Exchange 2021. Available online: https://www.mathworks.com/matlabcentral/fileexchange/25157-image-segmentation-tutorial (accessed on 21 June 2021).
55. DJI. Phantom 4 RTK: Product Specifications. Available online: https://www.dji.com/de/phantom-4-rtk/info (accessed on 31 March 2021).
56. Javad. JAVAD Global Navigation Satellite System (GNSS) Receiver SigmaD-G3D: Data Sheet GNSS Receiver Sigma-3. Available online: http://download.javad.com/manuals/ (accessed on 31 March 2021).
57. *AgiSoft Metashape Professional. Version 1.6.5 Build 11249, 64 Bit*; AgiSoft Metashape Professional: St. Petersburg, Russia, 2020. Available online: https://www.agisoft.com/downloads/installer/ (accessed on 27 July 2021).
58. ESRI ArcGIS Desktop. Version 10.5.1, 64 Bit. ESRI: 2017. Available online: https://www.esri.com/en-us/arcgis/products/arcgis-pro/overview/ (accessed on 27 July 2021).
59. Van Rijn, L.C. Aeolian Transport over a Flat Sediment Surface. *Aeolian Transp.* **2019**. Available online: www.leovanrijn-sediment.com (accessed on 27 July 2021).
60. Nickling, W.G.; McKenna Neumann, C. (Eds.) *Aeolian Sediment Transport*, 2nd ed.; Springer: Dordrecht, The Netherlands, 2009; ISBN 978-1-4020-5718-2.
61. Sarre, R.D. Aeolian sand drift from the intertidal zone on a temperate beach: Potential and actual rates. *Earth Surf. Process. Landf.* **1989**, *14*, 247–258. [CrossRef]
62. De Vries, S. *Physics of Blown Sand and Coastal Dunes*; Delft University of Technology: Delft, The Netherlands, 2013.
63. Dong, Z.; Liu, X.; Wang, H.; Wang, X. Aeolian sand transport: A wind tunnel model. *Sediment. Geol.* **2003**, *161*, 71–83. [CrossRef]
64. Davidson-Arnott, R.; Yang, Y.; Ollerhead, J.; Hesp, P.; Walker, I.J. The effects of surface moisture on aeolian sediment transport threshold and mass flux on a beach. *Earth Surf. Process. Landf.* **2007**, *33*, 55–74. [CrossRef]
65. Delgado-Fernandez, I. A review of the application of the fetch effect to modelling sand supply to coastal foredunes. *Aeolian Res.* **2010**, *2*, 61–70. [CrossRef]
66. Hoonhout, B.; de Vries, S. Field measurements on spatial variations in aeolian sediment availability at the Sand Motor mega nourishment. *Aeolian Res.* **2016**, *24*, 93–104. [CrossRef]
67. Bauer, B.O.; Davidson-Arnott, R.; Hesp, P.A.; Namikas, S.L.; Ollerhead, J.; Walker, I.J. Aeolian sediment transport on a beach: Surface moisture, wind fetch, and mean transport. *Geomorphology* **2009**, *105*, 106–116. [CrossRef]
68. Bauer, B.O.; Davidson-Arnott, R.G. A general framework for modeling sediment supply to coastal dunes including wind angle, beach geometry, and fetch effects. *Geomorphology* **2003**, *49*, 89–108. [CrossRef]
69. Lynch, K.; Jackson, D.W.T.; Cooper, J.A.G. Aeolian fetch distance and secondary airflow effects: The influence of micro-scale variables on meso-scale foredune development. *Earth Surf. Process. Landforms* **2008**, *33*, 991–1005. [CrossRef]
70. Davidson-Arnott, R.G.; MacQuarrie, K.; Aagaard, T. The effect of wind gusts, moisture content and fetch length on sand transport on a beach. *Geomorphology* **2005**, *68*, 115–129. [CrossRef]
71. Spies, P.-J.; McEwan, I.K. Equilibration of saltation. *Earth Surf. Process. Landf.* **2000**, *25*, 437–453. [CrossRef]
72. Davidson-Arnott, R.; Law, M.N. Measurement and Prediction of Long-Term Sediment Supply to Coastal Foredunes. *J. Coast. Res.* **1996**, *12*, 654–663.
73. Field, J.P.; Pelletier, J.D. Controls on the aerodynamic roughness length and the grain-size dependence of aeolian sediment transport. *Earth Surf. Process. Landf.* **2018**, *43*, 2616–2626. [CrossRef]
74. Hsu, S.A. Computing Eolian sand Transport from routine weather data. In Proceedings of the 14th Conference on Coastal Engineering, Copenhagen, Denmark, 24–28 June 1974; pp. 1619–1626. [CrossRef]
75. Shao, Y.; Lu, H. A simple expression for wind erosion threshold friction velocity. *J. Geophys. Res.* **2000**, *105*, 22437–22443. [CrossRef]
76. Nickling, W.G.; Davidson-Arnott, R. (Eds.) *Aeolian Sediment Transport on Beaches and Coastal Sand Dunes*; Canadian Coastal Science and Engineering Association: Guelph, ON, Canada, 1990.
77. Houser, C.; Wernette, P.; Rentschlar, E.; Jones, H.; Hammond, B.; Trimble, S. Post-storm beach and dune recovery: Implications for barrier island resilience. *Geomorphology* **2015**, *234*, 54–63. [CrossRef]
78. Keijsers, J.; de Groot, A.V.; Riksen, M. Vegetation and sedimentation on coastal foredunes. *Geomorphology* **2015**, *228*, 723–734. [CrossRef]
79. Miri, A.; Dragovich, D.; Dong, Z. Wind-borne sand mass flux in vegetated surfaces—Wind tunnel experiments with live plants. *CATENA* **2019**, *172*, 421–434. [CrossRef]

80. Cohn, N.; Hoonhout, B.; Goldstein, E.; de Vries, S.; Moore, L.; Durán Vinent, O.; Ruggiero, P. Exploring Marine and Aeolian Controls on Coastal Foredune Growth Using a Coupled Numerical Model. *JMSE* **2019**, *7*, 13. [CrossRef]
81. Hacker, S.D.; Zarnetske, P.; Seabloom, E.; Ruggiero, P.; Mull, J.; Gerrity, S.; Jones, C. Subtle differences in two non-native congeneric beach grasses significantly affect their colonization, spread, and impact. *Oikos* **2012**, *121*, 138–148. [CrossRef]
82. Durán, O. Vegetated Dunes and Barchan Dune Fields. Ph.D. Thesis, Universität Stuttgart, Stuttgart, Germany, 2007.
83. Durán, O.; Moore, L.J. Vegetation controls on the maximum size of coastal dunes. *Proc. Natl. Acad. Sci. USA* **2013**, *110*, 17217–17222. [CrossRef]
84. Arens, S.M.; Baas, A.C.W.; Van Boxel, J.H.; Kalkman, C. Influence of reed stem density on foredune development. *Earth Surf. Process. Landf.* **2001**, *26*, 1161–1176. [CrossRef]
85. Van der Wal, D. Effects of fetch and surface texture on aeolian sand transport on two nourished beaches. *J. Arid Environ.* **1998**, *39*, 533–547. [CrossRef]
86. Jackson, N.L.; Nordstrom, K.F. Aeolian sediment transport and landforms in managed coastal systems: A review. *Aeolian Res.* **2011**, *3*, 181–196. [CrossRef]
87. Jackson, N.L.; Nordstrom, K.F. Aeolian transport of sediment on a beach during and after rainfall, Wildwood, NJ, USA. *Geomorphology* **1997**. [CrossRef]
88. Delgado-Fernandez, I. Meso-scale modelling of aeolian sediment input to coastal dunes. *Geomorphology* **2011**, *130*, 230–243. [CrossRef]
89. Keijsers, J.G.S.; Poortinga, A.; Riksen, M.J.P.M.; Maroulis, J. Spatio-temporal variability in accretion and erosion of coastal foredunes in the Netherlands: Regional climate and local topography. *PLoS ONE* **2014**, *9*, e91115. [CrossRef]
90. Bundesamt für Schifffahrt und Hydrographie. *Berichte zu Sturmfluten und Extremen Wasserständen: Nordsee*; Bundesamt für Schifffahrt und Hydrographie: Hamburg, Germany, 2021.

Article

Climate Change Impacts on Coastal Wave Dynamics at Vougot Beach, France

Pushpa Dissanayake [1,*], Marissa L. Yates [2], Serge Suanez [3], France Floc'h [4] and Knut Krämer [1]

[1] Coastal Geology and Sedimentology, Institute of Geosciences, 24118 Kiel, Germany; knut.kraemer@ifg.uni-kiel.de
[2] Saint-Venant Hydraulics Laboratory, University Paris-Est and Cerema, 49-78401 Chatou, France; marissa.yates@cerema.fr
[3] Université de Bretagne Occidentale, CNRS, LETG UMR 6554, Institut Universitaire Européen de la Mer, 29280 Plouzané, France; serge.suanez@univ-brest.fr
[4] Université de Bretagne Occidentale, CNRS, LGO UMR 6538, Institut Universitaire Européen de la Mer, 29280 Plouzané, France; france.floch@univ-brest.fr
* Correspondence: pushpa.dissanayake@ifg.uni-kiel.de

Citation: Dissanayake, P.; Yates, M.L.; Suanez, S.; Floc'h, F.; Krämer, K. Climate Change Impacts on Coastal Wave Dynamics at Vougot Beach, France. *J. Mar. Sci. Eng.* **2021**, *9*, 1009. https://doi.org/10.3390/jmse9091009

Academic Editor: Achilleas Samaras

Received: 1 September 2021
Accepted: 10 September 2021
Published: 15 September 2021

Publisher's Note: MDPI stays neutral with regard to jurisdictional claims in published maps and institutional affiliations.

Copyright: © 2021 by the authors. Licensee MDPI, Basel, Switzerland. This article is an open access article distributed under the terms and conditions of the Creative Commons Attribution (CC BY) license (https://creativecommons.org/licenses/by/4.0/).

Abstract: Wave dynamics contribute significantly to coastal hazards and were thus investigated at Vougot Beach by simulating both historical and projected future waves considering climate change impacts. The historical period included a major storm event. This period was projected to the future using three globally averaged sea level rise (SLR) scenarios for 2100, and combined SLR and wave climate scenarios for A1B, A2, and B1 emissions paths of the IPCC. The B1 wave climate predicts an increase in the occurrence of storm events. The simulated waves in all scenarios showed larger relative changes at the beach than in the nearshore area. The maximum increase of wave energy for the combined SLR and wave scenarios was 95%, while only 50% for the SLR-only scenarios. The effective bed shear stress from waves and currents showed different spatial variability than that of the wave height, emphasizing the importance of interactions between nearshore waves and currents. Increases in the effective bed shear stress (combined scenarios: up to 190%, and SLR-only scenarios: 35%) indicate that the changes in waves and currents will likely have significant impacts on the nearshore sediment transport. This work emphasizes that combined SLR and future wave climate scenarios need to be used to evaluate future changes in local hydrodynamics and their impacts. These results provide preliminary insights into potential future wave dynamics at Vougot Beach under different climate change scenarios. Further studies are necessary to generalize the results by investigating the wave dynamics during storm events with different hydrodynamical conditions and to evaluate potential changes in sediment transport and morphological evolution due to climate change.

Keywords: wave impacts; sea level rise; macro-tidal coast; Delft3D; SWAN; numerical modelling

1. Introduction

Waves are one of the dominant forcing factors in coastal systems, regulating hydrodynamics and inundation risks and driving sediment transport and morphological changes [1–5]. Waves can cause significant episodic morphological changes during extreme events, and the resultant changes may be partially recoverable or may lead to long-lasting changes of coastal systems [6–11]. Future climate change scenarios are expected to intensify wave impacts with increases in sea levels and increases in the frequency and intensity of extreme events [1,12–16]. Wave impacts may therefore cause significant coastal hazards affecting local morphology, infrastructure, and industries such as tourism.

Coastal systems are important socio-economic and environmental zones. About 10% of the world's population live in coastal zones [17], which contain many of the world's megacities and important infrastructure [14], while also hosting diverse flora and fauna [18].

Ample recreation opportunities in coastal zones attract tourists, generating millions of euros annually for local communities (e.g., around the Wadden Sea [19]). In Europe (http://www.eurosion.org/reports-online/eurosionspecial.pdf, accessed on 15 April 2021), between 500 and 1000 billion euros are invested annually in the 500 m coastal band, and 16% of the European population (70 million people) lives in a coastal community. The existence of sustainable coastal systems depends on management policies, which need to be developed based on comprehensive understanding of the system's response to present and future forcing scenarios [14]. Numerous approaches are used to enhance the understanding of coastal systems under different climate change scenarios, supporting efforts to conserve these unique areas [15].

In the past, most studies of future coastal hazards have focused on the impacts of sea level rise (SLR) on coastal erosion (e.g., using the Bruun Rule [20]) or on flooding risks (e.g., "bathtub" approach of passive flooding [21]). In general, SLR is expected to increase the impacts of waves on beaches, since larger waves will reach the original shoreline and propagate farther inland [22]. However, the impacts of SLR on beaches depend strongly on the nearshore and beach characteristics, and it is widely accepted that the hydrodynamic and morphological response depends strongly on the local environment [23]. SLR is not the only physical process impacting coastal hazards, and more recent work highlights the importance of simulating the interactions between changes in water levels and waves, specifically in evaluating extreme water levels during coastal flooding events [15,24,25].

Projections of future hydrodynamic forcing in coastal systems have high uncertainties that must be evaluated using probabilistic approaches [12,26,27]. The IPCC (Intergovernmental Panel of Climate Change) Fifth Assessment Report [12] estimated global mean sea level rise in 2100 for four different emissions scenarios, called Representative Concentration Pathways (RCPs). For each RCP, the median and likely range of global mean sea level rise was calculated based on simulations from 21 process-based models. Projected future wave climates indicate the occurrence of more intense storm events and changes in the average and mean wave conditions in some areas, with high regional variability [13,24,27]. Downscaling of global general circulation models (GCMs) may be used to generate nearshore wave conditions, but these approaches are intensive [15,24] and may be difficult to put in place in many coastal environments. Where reliable projections of wave conditions are not yet available, Banno and Kuriyama [26] projected historical wave time series to the future using statistics calculated from different climate change scenarios. In the present study, this method was used to make projections of future wave climates at a local study site, while adopting the global mean and range of SLR estimates from the IPCC [12].

Numerical models are widely used to simulate wave dynamics and the subsequent impacts of water levels and currents in coastal systems at various spatiotemporal scales [3,28,29]. For example, the impacts of climate variability on waves and alongshore sediment transport patterns in the Anapa bay-bar coastline in the Black Sea were simulated over the period 1979–2017 using MIKE SW [29]. The results showed that swell waves increased from the SSE direction and decreased from the WSW direction. This caused spatially variable changes in the swell contribution to sediment dynamics, leading to different erosion and sedimentation patterns along the coastline. Using SWASH, Medellín et al. [30] simulated wave runup on the Yucutan coast of Mexico with present and future (2030–2054) forcing scenarios, including the influence of both SLR (global mean change) and changes in the wave climate (using a statistical approach based on the RCP8.5 scenario). The simulation results showed spatial variability in changes in the wave dynamics, with no significant increases in the storm impact regime between the present and future conditions unless SLR was also considered. To estimate accurately the impacts of SLR, the authors concluded that it should be incorporated in the mean sea level prior to performing numerical wave runup simulations, rather than simply adding it to the resulting wave-induced water levels. Furthermore, when studying large-scale wave climate trends, Dodet et al. [31] used Wavewatch3 (WW3) to simulate decadal-scale wave climate variability in the north-east Atlantic Ocean over 57 years (1953–2009). They observed that wave heights decreased from high (55°) to low (35°) latitudes, with a significant increase in Hs_{90} at northern latitudes (55°), reaching up to 1.2 m (0.02 m/year) during the study period.

These studies demonstrate the capacity of numerical models to investigate wave dynamics in different environments and forcing conditions. However, simulations of wave conditions are sensitive to the wind forcing and the parameterization of wave dissipation. In addition, climate change impacts on wave dynamics depend strongly on the geographical location of interest, due to both the regional variability in climate changes (e.g., SLR, wind forcing, and wave conditions) and the particularities of each site (e.g., nearshore bathymetry, tidal regime, and morphological changes). In the long run, coastal-scale and site-specific studies are necessary for developing local-scale management policies. In this study, historical and future wave dynamics were simulated at Vougot Beach, France, at high spatiotemporal scales, using the SWAN model [32] coupled with the Delft3D model [33].

Vougot Beach is a macrotidal environment, located in north Brittany (France). Nearshore hydrodynamic observations (wave heights and water levels) were recorded during several field campaigns [9] and wave heights simulated with the WW3 model are available offshore of the study area with a spatial resolution of up to 600 m [34]. Previously, the in situ measurements were compared with the offshore simulated waves from WW3 to investigate the wave hydrodynamics at this coast [9]. In the current study, a local-scale model propagating waves to the nearshore zone and beach, including the highly variable nearshore bathymetry, was developed. With a validated model, potential future changes in wave dynamics can be investigated at high spatiotemporal resolution by forcing the model with the projected waves and water levels based on climate change scenarios. Existing studies along this coast have not addressed these aspects, which are of utmost importance for policy makers to identify the suitable management strategies to mitigate coastal hazards. In addition, few studies of the combined impacts of future SLR and wave climate changes exist on macrotidal beaches [35].

The main objective of this study was to compare historical and future local wave dynamics at Vougot Beach with high spatiotemporal resolution and to evaluate potential changes caused by climate change impacts. The novelty of the approach is in simulating wave dynamics for an observed wave time series and the future projection of the same wave time series by considering the effects of both SLR and the impacts of future emissions scenarios on the local wave climate. It was hypothesized that future climate change scenarios will increase wave dynamics at this coast, thus increasing the vulnerability to coastal hazards and the risks of erosion and flooding.

To achieve this, Section 2 describes the study area and field data, and Section 3 details the applied approach. The results are presented in Section 4, with a discussion of the limitations of the current study and suggestions for future work in Section 5. Finally, the conclusions of the study are presented in Section 6, including the general applicability of this work.

2. Study Site
2.1. Location

Vougot Beach is located in the community of Guisseny, France (Figure 1a,b). This coastal zone is one of the elements composing a vast landscape unit identified as the "coastal bench of the northern coast of Plateau of Leon" [36], creating complex local bathymetry and hydrodynamics at the study site (Figure 1d). The coastal bench is a string of low coastal regions (altitudes < 15 m, all elevation and depth values are referred to the French datum: NGF (nivellement général de la France). A submarine scarp between 10 m and 40 to 60 m depth delimits the outer edge of a large platform with reefs and islets (3 to 6 km wide), on which Holocene sandy accumulations form the current beach/dune systems, such as Vougot Beach [37–39]. These reefs and inlets determine the complex morphology of the foreshore and offshore zones of Vougot Beach, causing complex nearshore hydrodynamics (i.e., wave and currents) [10]. In recent decades, the dune at the eastern part of the beach (Figure 1d, corresponding to the study site here) has experienced chronic retreat reaching

0.7 m/year [40]. The study area (Figure 1d) is relatively protected from waves originating in the west to the northwest by the platform scattered with islets and reefs that emerge at low tide, such as Karreg Hir, Golhédoc or Enez Du (Figure 1c).

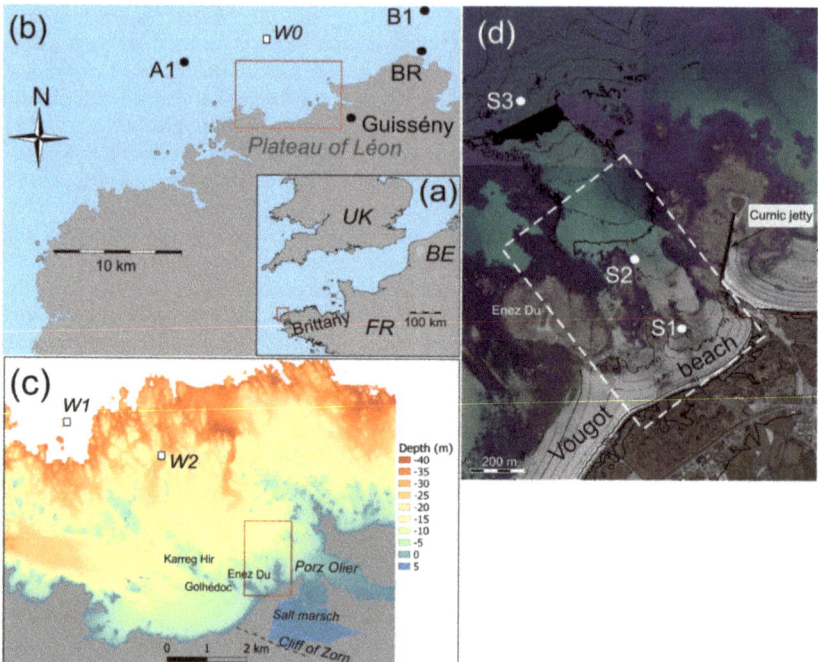

Figure 1. Location of Vougot beach on the north coast of Finistere in Brittany, France (**a**) in the municipality of Guisseny (**b**), showing the Brignogan wind measuring station from Météo France (BR: 48.68° N 4.33° W), and the offshore corner points (A_{G1} and B_{G1}) of the coarse-grid model domain (G1 in Figure 4). Topo-bathymertry of the northern coast of Finistère (**c**), including the study site (digital elevation model Litto3D–Finistère 2014, produced by IGN and SHOM, https://diffusion.shom.fr/pro/risques/litto3dr-finistere-2014.html, accessed on 22 January 2015) W1 (48.67° N 4.53° W, 44 m depth) and W2 (48.65° N 4.39° W, 23 m depth) are the locations of waves. Satellite image of Vougot Beach (**d**) indicating the study area (dashed white rectangle) and the location of the pressure sensors (S1, S2 and S3). Red rectangles show the spatial extent of each subsequent inset.

The macrotidal range, reaching 8.4 m for astronomical tides, is responsible for the large intertidal beach surface, which can expose more than 400 m in the cross-shore at low tide. The most energetic waves come from the west to north sector with an average significant wave height (Hs) between 1 and 1.5 m, and an average peak period (Tp) between 9 and 10 s. The largest storm wave heights and periods (respectively $\geq$10 m and 8 s) occur between December and February [10]. During spring, the waves are less energetic (35% of waves with Hs = 2–4 m and Tp = 8–12 s), before an increase in fall with Hs reaching up to 10 m approximately 20% of time. Wind data recorded at the Brignogan Météo France station (BR, Figure 1b) show that the most frequent annual winds are from the south to west sector, with a moderate north–east component. The strongest wind velocities (>8 m/s more than 30% of the time) blowing from north–west to south–west occur generally during winter (December to February, generating mainly west–northwest waves (96%) [10]. During the summer (June to August), winds are much weaker (generally $\leq$ 4.5 m/s), before increasing again in the fall.

2.2. Data

In this study, observations of water levels, wave characteristics, wind data, and bathymetry were retrieved from existing databases and field studies covering a period from 7 January to 18 February 2013, during which major storms impacted Vougot Beach [9].

Three pressure sensors S1, S2, and S3 (OSSI-010-003C, Ocean Sensor Systems Inc.®, accuracy ± 1.5 cm) were deployed to measure water levels and wave characteristics in the nearshore region of Vougot Beach (Figure 1d). Each sensor was set to a recording frequency of 5 Hz to measure water level variations with high temporal resolution. S1 and S2 were deployed at 0.7 m and 2.5 m depth, representing the mid and lower zones of the intertidal beach, respectively. Therefore, S1 and S2 emerged out of the water twice a day during low tide. S3 measured water levels farther offshore in 12.0 m depth, and thus remained permanently submerged.

The OSSI pressure data were corrected for the (1) atmospheric mean sea level pressure recorded at the Brignogan Météo France station (BR in Figure 1b) and (2) non-hydrostatic pressure following linear wave theory [41,42]. The mean surface elevation was extracted using a 10 min moving average. The wave spectrum and wave-averaged parameters were calculated from the Fourier transform (1024 data points over the incident gravity wave band, between 0.04–0.4 Hz). A Hamming window was applied to the signal (with zero values at the end) and 15 min [43] averages were calculated for several contiguous spectra with 50% overlap to avoid leakage issues related to a signal that was not perfectly periodic. The mean spectral wave parameters, i.e., significant wave height (Hs) and the equivalent spectral mean period, were computed in each frequency band [44].

The predicted astronomical tides at A_{G1} and B_{G1} (see Figure 1b) were obtained from the tidal database of European Shelf 2008 (ES2008) using the online tool Delft Dashboard, (https://publicwiki.deltares.nl/display/DDB/Delft+Dashboard, accessed on 15 December 2020). During the analysis period, the average phase difference between locations A_{G1} and B_{G1} was about 10 min, and the spring and neap tidal ranges were approximately 7.5 m and 2.4, respectively (Figure 2a). The maximum tidal anomaly (TA: total water level—astronomical tide) reached up to 1.1 m during the storm event that occurred around 6 February 2013, caused primarily by storm surge at this water depth.

Hindcast wave time series were obtained from the HOMERE wave database, generated with the spectral wave model WW3 (see Boudière et al. [34] for more details). Wave characteristics were extracted at locations W1 (48.67° N 4.53° W) and W2 (48.65° N 4.39° W), in 44 m and 23 m depth, respectively (Figure 1c). During the six-week analysis period from 7 January–18 February 2013, more than 4 storm events showed Hs exceeding 4 m at the deeper water location (W1, Figure 2b), including one event with Hs exceeding 6 m, with large waves arriving primarily from the northwest.

Wind measurements used in this study were provided by Météo France at the Brignogan station (BR, Figure 1b). Strong winds during the study period primarily originated from the northwest (Figure 2c), and the wind velocities often exceeded 8 m/s, occasionally reaching 15 to 20 m/s during the most extreme events (i.e., 6 February 2013).

The bathymetry data were collected from two sources. The first set was a high-resolution (1 m × 1 m) bathymetry from the digital elevation model Litto3D® (https://diffusion.shom.fr/pro/risques/litto3dr-finistere-2014.html, accessed on 22 January 2015), produced by the IGN and SHOM using measurements from 2013. These data spanned about 6 km in the cross-shore direction, extending to about 40 m depth (Figure 1c). The second dataset was obtained from the GEBCO 08 (General Bathymetric Chart of the Oceans) bathymetry database through Delft Dashboard. These data had a very coarse spatial resolution (~600 m) around the study area, and were therefore only used for water depths greater than 35 m to span the region between the Litto3D bathymetry and the offshore limit of the model domain.

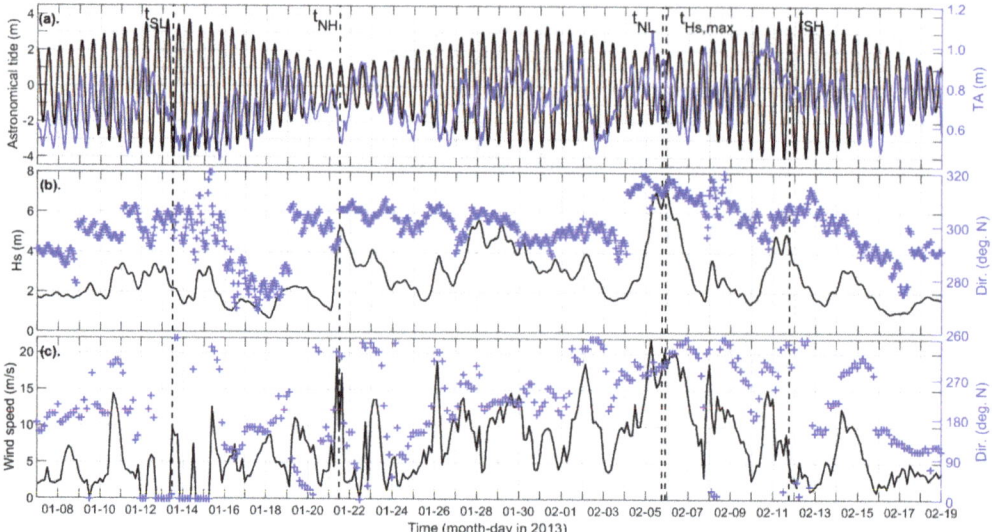

Figure 2. Data used for the numerical simulations. (**a**) Predicted astronomical tide at A_{G1} (red line) and B_{G1} (black line). Note that the red line is not visible because there was only a 10 min phase shift between the time series at A_{G1} and B_{G1}. The blue line is the derived tidal anomaly (TA) at S3 (Figure 1d). (**b**) Significant wave height (black line) and direction (blue crosses) at W1 (Figure 1b) from the WW3 model. (**c**) Measured wind speed (black line) and direction (blue crosses) at BR (Figure 1b).

3. Approach

To study the impacts of climate change on the nearshore hydrodynamics at Vougot Beach, a series of numerical simulations were carried out using past observations and hindcast simulations of water levels, waves, and winds. The same time series was projected into the future using SLR projections to adapt the water level and a statistical approach to project the wave time series to the future.

3.1. Future Scenarios

3.1.1. Sea Level Rise

Existing global and regional sea level rise scenarios were assessed to select the water level scenarios to be used in this study. The 5th Assessment Report of IPCC estimated the median global mean sea level rise to be 0.74 m (ranging from 0.53–0.98 m) in 2100 following the RCP8.5 [12]. The RCP8.5 was selected since it is the most pessimistic concentration pathway scenario ('business as usual'). The median and range of expected values in 2100 were calculated from the results of the process-based projections from 21 Coupled Model Intercomparison Project phase 5 (CMIP5) Atmosphere–Ocean General Circulation Models (AOGCMs). At the regional scale, the Integrated Climate Data Center (ICDC) provides predictions of local sea level rise rates, and offshore of the study site, the closest projection location estimates approximately 0.67 m of sea level rise in 2100 (also following the RCP8.5). This value falls within the range of global SLR estimates, and thus, the three values of global SLR estimates provided in the IPCC report were retained for the analyses here: SLRmin = 0.53 m, SLRavg = 0.74 m, and SLRmax = 0.98 m. The recent 6th Assessment Report updated global mean SLR estimates by 2100 (e.g., intermediate, SSP2-4.5: 0.44–0.77 m and very high, SSP5-8.5: 0.63–1.01 m emissions scenarios), and the values retained in this study are consistent with the updated predictions.

3.1.2. Wave Climate

To estimate the impacts of climate change on the wave field, a statistical approach was adopted following Banno and Kuriyama [26]. They suggested that projected changes in the wave field can be estimated by adjusting past wave time series with the predicted changes in the wave statistics (i.e., mean, standard deviation, log-normal distribution). Their approach was applied to project a six-week time period during the 2012–2013 winter to the future by adjusting the significant wave height (Hs), peak wave period (Tp), wave direction (θ), and directional spreading (σ_θ). Given the limitations of the time period and spatial coverage of existing wave databases, this analysis was carried out in two steps using two different wave databases to estimate projected changes in offshore wave conditions and the appropriate transfer function to transform offshore waves to nearshore waves (at W1: 48.67° N 4.53° W, Figure 1c).

The projected changes in the offshore wave conditions (at W0: 48.69° N 4.52° W, Figure 1b) were estimated using the database created by Laugel [45], who simulated wave conditions in the North Atlantic using a dynamical downscaling approach. A hindcast period from 1961–2000 and a forecast period from 2061–2100 were simulated using the spectral wave model TOMAWAC [46], which was run with the same model configuration for both time periods (see Laugel [45] for more details). Concerning the wind forcing conditions, two different scenarios were considered: for the hindcast period, the results of ARPEGE-CLIMAT global climate model simulations [47] and for the forecast period, projected scenarios following the emissions scenarios A1B, A2, and B1 [48]. In this study, two relatively pessimistic emissions scenarios were selected to generate the wave projections to investigate the scenarios causing the largest potential changes.

The difference between the hindcast and forecast periods was estimated by calculating: the log-normal distribution of Hs during the two time periods (considering changes in the mean and extreme values), and the mean and standard deviation of T_p, θ, and σ_θ. The hindcast wave time series were transformed by adjusting each value of Hs, T_p, θ, and σ_θ to correspond to forecast values using the updated distributions, producing a 6-week long future time series at the offshore point W0 (Figure 1b).

In the second step, linear transformation functions (for Hs, T_p, θ, and σ_θ) were calculated using the past observations at W0 and W1 to estimate the transformed wave time series at W1 (Figures 1c and 3). Using this approach, Hs exceeded 6 m during one event in the hindcast time series, while it exceeded this threshold during three events in the B1 forecast time series. A1B and B1 had larger wave heights than A2, with B1 showing the largest wave heights overall. Dominant wave directions were fairly similar in all forecasts compared with the past waves (Figure 3b–e).

3.2. Numerical Modelling

The Delft3D model was used to simulate the local hydrodynamics at Vougot Beach with high spatiotemporal resolution. After calibrating the model with past observations, changes in the local hydrodynamics were evaluated for different scenarios of the projected SLR and wave climate changes.

3.2.1. Delft3D

Delft3D is an open-source model that has shown skill in simulating wave dynamics for a wide range of case studies [3,11,49]. Delft3D is a three-dimensional model based on a finite difference approach [33,50,51]. In this analysis, a depth-averaged approach (2DH) was used. The wave dynamics were simulated by online wave coupling with the wave model, SWAN [32], which allows simulating wave–current interactions at a specified time interval. A 1 h interval was used to capture the tidal variation, even though the temporal resolution of the wind and wave data was 3 h. At a complex study site such as Vougot Beach, with high bathymetric variability and a macrotidal regime, it is important to include wave–current interactions to simulate accurately wave dynamics.

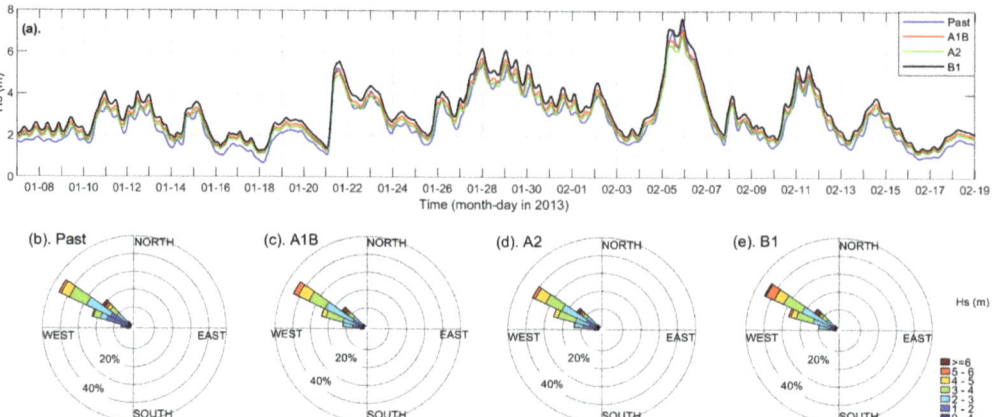

Figure 3. Comparison of (**a**) wave height and wave roses during the (**b**) historical period from 7 January–18 February 2013, and (**c**) A1B, (**d**) A2, and (**e**) B1 future wave projections at W1.

3.2.2. Model Domains and Boundary Forcing

A nested modelling approach was used to initiate the model offshore in deep-water conditions (G1 domain) and to refine progressively the model grids to simulate high spatial resolution wave dynamics in the nearshore region (G3 domain in Figure 4a and Table 1). The large-scale, coarse-grid G1 domain was used to simulate only the astronomical tide to provide the appropriate boundary conditions for the G2 domain, including the tidal phase difference between A_{G2} and B_{G2} (Figure 4b). Wave–current interactions were then simulated in the G2 and G3 domains with progressively finer grids.

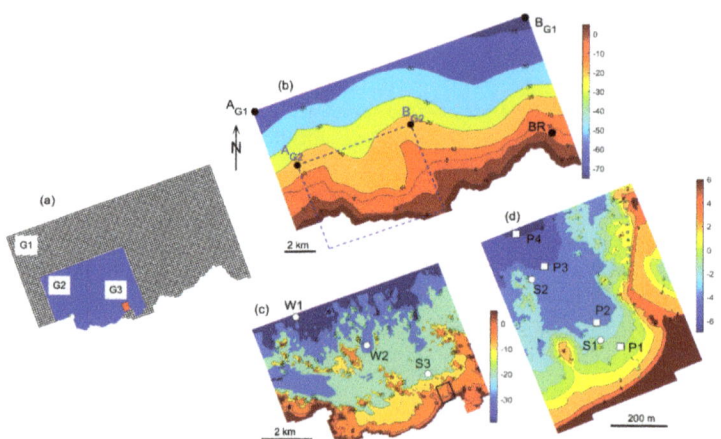

Figure 4. Model setup: (**a**) nested model grids, G1, G2, and G3; (**b**) bathymetry of the large-scale G1 grid, astronomical tides were obtained at A_{G1} and B_{G1} from the ES2008 tidal database, BR is the Brignogan wind station, the dashed blue line indicates the extent of the G2 grid, and A_{G2} and B_{G2} are the locations where the simulated water levels were extracted for G2. (**c**) Bathymetry of the G2 grid, where W1 and W2 indicate the wave data points from WW3 (HOMERE database), S3 is the offshore pressure sensor, and the black square indicates the extent of the G3 grid. (**d**) Bathymetry of the study area (G3), where S1 and S2 are nearshore pressure sensors and P1 to P4 are the selected locations to analyze the wave dynamics.

Table 1. Characteristics of the G1, G2, and G3 model domains (Figure 4).

Model Domain	Spatial Extent (Alongshore × Cross Shore in km)	Grid Type	Grid Resolution (Alongshore × Cross Shore in m)
G1	20 × 10	rectilinear	200 × 200
G2	8 × 6	curvilinear	40–50 × 20–60
G3	0.5 × 0.7	curvilinear	9 × 4–5

The model bathymetries were created using the two sources of data. The G1 bathymetry (200 m × 200 m, the same scale as the model grid) was based on the GEBCO 08 (https://publicwiki.deltares.nl/display/DDB/Delft+Dashboard, accessed on 15 December 2020) dataset and did not represent the strong bathymetric variations in the nearshore region (Figure 4b). The G2 and G3 bathymetries were constructed by interpolating the high-resolution (1 m × 1 m) digital elevation model Litto3D® (https://diffusion.shom.fr/pro/risques/litto3dr-finistere-2014.html, accessed on 22 January 2015) (Figure 4c,d) onto the 2 models' grids to capture the finer details of the bathymetric variations. However, the offshore area of G2 was not entirely covered by this dataset, and the data gaps were filled by triangular interpolation using neighboring available depth values (Figure 4c). The highest resolution grid, G3, represented the finer details of the bathymetry well, with a resolution of less than 10 m in the cross-shore and alongshore directions representing the jetty of Curnic and the reef at the eastern and western ends of the domain, respectively (see Figures 1d and 4d).

The G1 domain was forced with the astronomical tide level defined at A_{G1} and B_{G1} from the ES2008 (https://publicwiki.deltares.nl/display/DDB/Delft+Dashboard, accessed on 15 December 2020) tidal database (Figure 4b). In Delft3D, the water level was specified at the offshore boundary, while the water level gradients were specified for the lateral boundaries. This combination of boundary conditions generates tidal currents perpendicular to the lateral boundaries, following the direction of tidal propagation (see details in Roelvink and Walstra [52]). The nested grid G2 was forced with both the total water levels (using the same approach as for G1) and the waves. The total water levels at the offshore corner points A_{G2} and B_{G2} were calculated as the sum of the simulated astronomical tide from G1 and TA at the pressure sensor at S3 (Figure 2a). For the wave boundary of G2, spatially uniform wave conditions were applied along the offshore boundary based on the wave characteristics estimated at W1. A JONSWAP spectrum (Joint North Sea Wave Project [53–55]) was used to specify the wave conditions at the boundary. G3 was nested in the G2 wave model, and thus the G3 boundary conditions were input directly from the G2 wave and water level simulations. The high-resolution G3 domain was, therefore, simulated including the effects of wave–current interactions with the tidal variations.

3.2.3. Model Simulations

The local hydrodynamics at Vougot Beach were investigated with observations from the 2012–2013 winter and with 7 different scenarios of potential changes in sea level and wave climate (Table 2).

The future SLR and wave climate scenarios were described in Section 3.1. The three SLR scenarios were simulated using the historical wave time series to investigate the relative impacts of only SLR on the wave dynamics along this coast. However, climate change will likely impact sea levels and wave climates simultaneously, so combined scenarios (SLR and waves) were developed considering four different combinations of SLR (min and max) and wave climate (A1B and B1) scenarios. Each simulation thus spanned the six-week analysis period from 7 January–18 February 2013, or the equivalent six-week period projected into the future.

Table 2. Summary of the water level and wave conditions used in each model simulation: (1) reference time period from 7 January–18 February 2013 and projected simulations considering (2, 3, 4) SLR-only and (5, 6, 7, 8) four different combinations of SLR and projected wave conditions.

Simulation	Scenario		Description
1	Reference		Water levels = astronomical tides at A_{G2} and B_{G2} + TA at S3 (Figure 1) Wave characteristics at W1 from WW3 (Figure 1) Wind data at BR, Brignogan (Figure 1)
2	Sea level rise	SLR_{min}	Only water level increased by 0.53 m: minimum of global range by IPCC [16]
3		SLR_{avg}	Only water level increased by 0.74 m: average of global range by IPCC [16]
4		SLR_{max}	Only water level increased by 0.98 m: maximum of global range by IPCC [16]
5	Combined sea level rise and future wave climate	SLR_{min} + A1B	Water level SLR_{min} Waves based on A1B of IPCC [16]
6		SLR_{max} + A1B	Water level SLR_{max} Waves based on A1B of IPCC [16]
7		SLR_{min} + B1	Water level SLR_{min} Waves based on B1 of IPCC [16]
8		SLR_{max} + B1	Water level SLR_{max} Waves based on B1 of IPCC [16]

3.3. Analysis

After simulating the reference period and the seven future scenarios, changes in the nearshore hydrodynamics (water levels, waves, and currents) were investigated at Vougot Beach. The results of the future simulations were compared to those of the reference simulation using the following analytical parameters: significant wave height as defined from the wave spectrum), wave spectral density, and effective bed shear stress.

(a) Wave spectral density

The wave spectral density (SD) represents the distribution of wave energy as a function of frequency and its shape depends on the processes of wave growth and decay, as well as interactions between different frequency bands. In this analysis, wave spectral density was estimated based on the JONSWAP spectrum [53,54].

$$SD(f) = \frac{\alpha g^2}{(2\pi)^4 f^5} exp\left[\frac{-5}{4}\left(\frac{f}{f_p}\right)^{-4}\right]\gamma^r \quad (1)$$

where, $r = exp\left[\frac{-(f-f_p)^2}{2\sigma^2 f_p^2}\right]$, $\sigma = \begin{cases} 0.07, f < f_p \\ 0.09, f \geq f_p \end{cases}$, α: Phillips constant (-), g: acceleration of gravity (m^2/s), f: wave frequency (Hz), γ: peak enhancement factor (3.3), σ: spectral width parameter (-), and t: time (s).

To evaluate changes in the wave spectral density, the average wave spectral density SD_{avg} (J/m^2/Hz) was calculated for each analysis period of length T (s) as:

$$SD_{avg} = \frac{1}{T}\int_0^T SD(f)dt \quad (2)$$

The relative change of the averaged wave spectral density with respect to the reference scenario $SD_{rel,i}$ was calculated for each future scenario, i as:

$$SD_{rel,i} = \left(\frac{SD_{avg,i} - SD_{avg,past}}{SD_{avg,past}} \right) \times 100\% \tag{3}$$

(b) Effective bed shear stress

The effective bed shear stress (τ_b) is an important parameter in an investigation the effects of wave dynamics in areas where both currents and waves strongly impact the hydrodynamics. This provides overall shear stress on the sea floor from both waves and currents, and their interactions, and determines local sediment transport, which will be investigated in the next phase of this study. The depth-averaged effective bed shear stress was calculated following the approach of Soulsby [56], using one standard function that can be adapted for different wave–current boundary layer models using different fitting coefficients (https://content.oss.deltares.nl/delft3d/manuals/Delft3D-FLOW_User_Manual.pdf, accessed on 19 May 2021). Of the several models available, the Fredsøe [57], boundary layer model was used in this study following the common approach [58]:

$$\vec{\tau_b} = \frac{|\vec{\tau_m}|}{|u|} \left(\vec{u} + \vec{u_s} \right) \tag{4}$$

$$|\vec{\tau_m}| = Y \left(|\vec{\tau_c}| + |\vec{\tau_w}| \right) \tag{5}$$

$$\tau_w = \frac{1}{2} \rho f_w u_w^2 \tag{6}$$

$$\tau_c = \rho C_D u^2 \tag{7}$$

where τ_m: bed shear stress of combined waves and currents (N/m^2), u: depth-averaged velocity (m/s), u_s: depth-averaged Stokes drift, Y: a fitting function for the wave–current boundary layer [59], τ_c: bed shear stress from currents alone (N/m^2), τ_w: bed shear stress from waves alone (N/m^2), ρ : water density (kg/m^3), f_w: friction factor (-), u_w: wave orbital velocity (m/s), and C_D: drag coefficient (-).

The average effective bed shear stress over the analysis period ($\tau_{b,avg}$) was calculated as,

$$\tau_{b,avg} = \frac{1}{T} \int_0^T \tau_b dt \tag{8}$$

(c) Statistical parameters

The model's skill in predicting water levels and wave heights was compared to the observations during the reference period, and then changes in the wave dynamics were estimated by comparing the future scenarios to the reference simulation using four statistical parameters (Equations (9)–(12)).

The coefficient of determination (R^2) was calculated to quantify the fraction of variance in each simulation corresponding to either the measurements or the reference simulation. This is defined as the squared value of the coefficient of correlation [59]:

$$R^2 = \left[\frac{\sum_{j=1}^n (x_j - \bar{x})(y_j - \bar{y})}{\sqrt{(x_j - \bar{x})(y_j - \bar{y})}} \right]^2 \tag{9}$$

where, x values represent the parameter time series (e.g., Hs) from either the measured data or the reference simulation and y values represent the simulated hindcast or forecast values, $\bar{x}$ and $\bar{y}$ indicate the mean values, and n is the number of time steps during the analysis period.

The root mean square difference (*RMSD*) quantifies the standard deviation of the differences between the simulations and either the measurements or the reference simulation:

$$RMSD = \sqrt{\frac{1}{n}\sum_{j=1}^{n}(x_j - y_j)^2} \qquad (10)$$

Smaller *RMSDs* imply better agreement between the observations and the model simulations (thus referred to as the *RMSE*: root mean square error), or smaller changes in future scenarios compared with the reference scenario.

The relative standard deviation (σ_{rel}) estimates the deviation between the reference and the future scenarios with respect to the averaged value ($\bar{\mu}$) of the normalised difference (μ_j).

$$\sigma_{rel} = \sqrt{\frac{1}{n}\sum_{j=1}^{n}(\mu_j - \bar{\mu})^2} \qquad (11)$$

$$\bar{\mu} = \frac{1}{n}\sum_{j=1}^{n}\mu_j \qquad (12)$$

where, $\mu_j = \frac{(y_j - x_j)}{x_j}$.

These statistics can be used to compare variations in wave dynamics (e.g., Hs, τ_b) among the scenarios and at different locations at Vougot Beach.

4. Results

4.1. Model Validation

The model's performance was validated by comparing the simulated water levels and wave heights with the measurements during the study period. Simulated water levels were compared with the water levels derived from the pressure sensor measurements at S1, S2, and S3 (Figure 5a–c). The water level variations varied significantly between each sensor as a function of the water depth.

To analyze the simulated hydrodynamics during characteristic periods of the tidal cycle at Vougot Beach, four dates throughout the analysis period were selected, representing spring-low (t_{SL}), neap-high (t_{NH}), neap-low (t_{NL}), and spring-high (t_{SH}) tidal conditions (columns in Figure 5a–c). The date of the peak storm wave height observed during this time period ($t_{Hs,max}$) was also selected for comparison. Around t_{SL}, the measured and simulated water levels agreed qualitatively well, except at S3, where the minima at spring-low water were slightly higher in the model than in the measurements (i.e., maximum difference ~0.3 m). Around t_{NH}, small differences in the measured and simulated water levels were observed at S1 during ebb tide. The largest differences in water levels at all locations were found around t_{NL} (S1~0.6 m, S2~0.5 m and S3~0.4 m) during the storm with the large wave heights. These differences may have been caused by modelling errors or by increases in errors in the sensor measurements in the surf and swash zones. The simulated water levels agreed better with the measurements during the flood phase of the tide because of the phase shift between the simulated and measured water level peak at high tide. Both of these phenomena may have an important role during storm events, particularly at S1. Around t_{SH}, the water level variations were similar to those around t_{SL}, with a slight overestimation of the maxima at S1 and the minima at S3.

The simulated water levels agreed well with the measurements with $R^2 > 0.97$ and $RMSE < 0.37$ m at S1, S2, and S3 (Figure 5d–f). The model was able to reproduce well the amplitude and phase of the measured water levels, with better agreement in deeper water (S3) than in shallow water (S1).

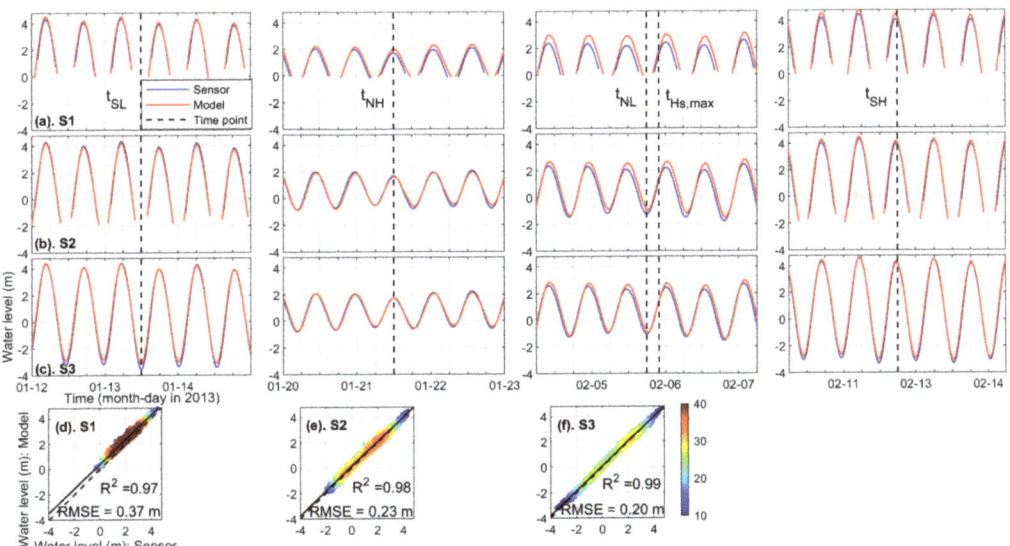

Figure 5. Comparison of the measured (blue) and the simulated (red) water levels at the pressure sensor locations: (**a**) S1, (**b**) S2, and (**c**) S3 (see Figure 4). For clarity, the comparisons were made around four time points (columns of a,b,c), t_{SL}: 2013–01–13 12:00 (spring-low water), t_{NH}: 2013–01–21 12:00 (neap-high), t_{NL}: 2013–02–05 18:00 (neap-low), t_{SH}: 2013–02–11 18:00 (spring-high), where the time of occurrence of the peak storm wave height is also indicated $t_{Hs,max}$: 2013–02–05 22:00 (just after t_{NL}). Scatter plots of measured and simulated water levels during the analysis period for (**d**) S1, (**e**) S2, and (**f**) S3, showing the calculated linear regression (solid line), perfect agreement (dashed line), and density of data points by percentage (color).

The wave height and directional distribution were analyzed qualitatively at the selected time points for the G2 (a) and G3 (b) domains (Figure 6). At all of the selected times, waves approached from the northwest. The largest wave heights (7.5 m) in the G2 domain were observed during the storm peak on 5 February 2013, in the middle of the flood phase of a neap tidal cycle (0.6 m at $t_{Hs,max}$). However, the largest waves propagating to the beach (G3 domain) occurred at spring-high tide (t_{SH}), when the offshore water level and wave height were about 3.5 m and 4.5 m, respectively. Given the high water level, the waves propagated farther shoreward before being dissipated, impacting higher elevations on the beach. On the contrary, during spring-low tide (t_{SL}), a large part of the study area became dry, limiting wave propagation to deeper water depths (>3.5 m). The tide level and its impact on wave propagation to the beach thus has an important role in controlling nearshore wave dynamics.

As noted previously, both simulated and measured wave heights at S1, S2, and S3 were modulated by the tide level. At the pressure sensor locations, the simulated wave heights were consistently larger than the measured wave heights (Figure 7a–c). The absolute differences ranged between 0.1–0.9 m (average = 0.4 m) at S1, 0.1–1.6 m (average = 0.6 m) at S2, and 0.8–1.4 m (average = 0.5 m) at S3, with slightly better agreement during some time periods (e.g., around t_{NH}). However, the simulated wave heights showed the same pattern of oscillations as in the data, indicating that the model correctly captured the phase of wave height changes relative to the tide level. The simulated wave heights at S1 agreed better with the data ($RMSE$ = 0.43 m) than at S2 (0.66 m), S3 (0.57 m), and W2 (0.57 m). This could be due to the fact that the vertical position of the S1 pressure sensor was more stable than the other two pressure sensors. At W2, the WW3 model predicted stronger tidal modulation than the present simulation with Delft3D, particularly during spring tide, thus the agreement between the two models improved during neap tide (Figure 7d). These differences may have also been caused by forcing the SWAN model with uniform offshore wave conditions.

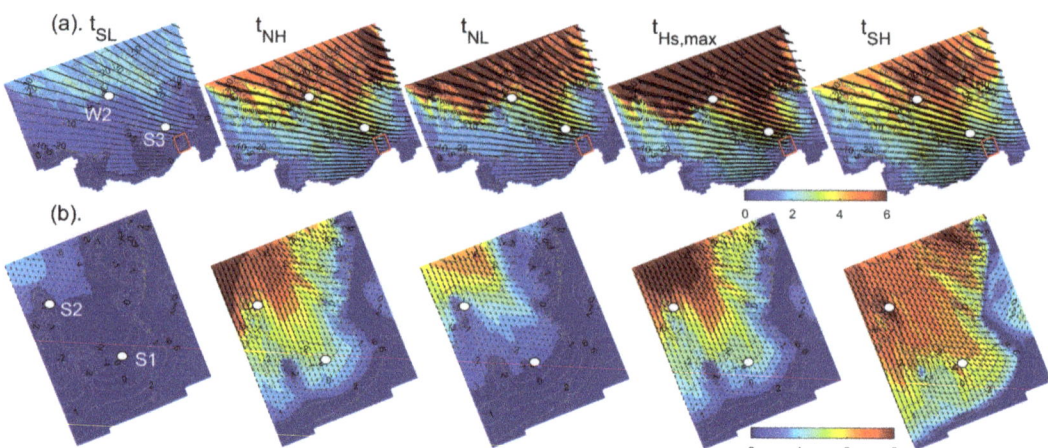

Figure 6. Wave height (color) and direction (vectors) in the G2 (**a**) and G3 (**b**) model domains at the selected five dates, t_{SL}: spring-low water, t_{NH}: neap-high, t_{NL}: neap-low, $t_{Hs,max}$: peak storm wave height, t_{SH}: spring-high. S1, S2, and S3 indicate the locations of the pressure sensors, and W2 indicates the location of the wave time series obtained from WW3. The red rectangles in (**a**) show the location of the G3 domain.

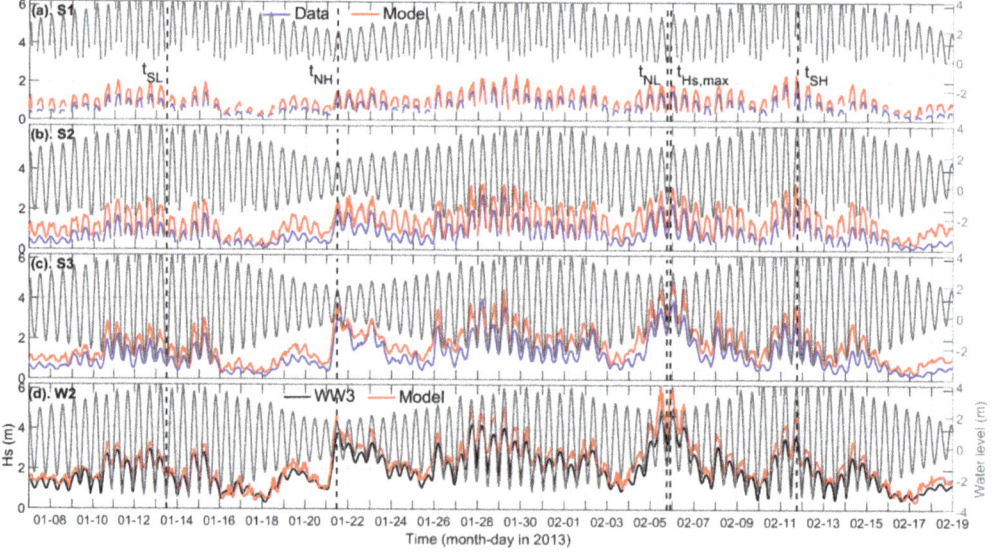

Figure 7. Comparison of the measured (blue) and the simulated (red) wave heights at the pressure sensor locations: (**a**) S1, (**b**) S2, and (**c**) S3 (see Figure 6). (**d**) Comparison of wave heights at W2 from WW3 (black line) and the present Delft3D model (red line). The gray line indicates the simulated water levels and the vertical dashed lines indicate the selected dates: t_{SL}: spring-low, t_{NH}: neap-high, t_{NL}: neap-low, $t_{Hs,max}$: peak storm wave height, and t_{SH}: spring-high water.

The model validation showed that the measured and simulated water levels agreed well, and that the tide level had a strong impact on nearshore wave heights (as expected on a macrotidal beach). The comparison of the simulated and measured wave height time series at the selected locations showed fair agreement (with *RMSE* ranging from 0.43–0.66). Overall, the reference simulation predicted large wave heights, which could be expected due to a number of reasons that are discussed in Section 5. For the remainder of this study, the simulated results presented in this section are used as the reference case, and all simulations of the future scenarios will be compared to these results to evaluate changes in nearshore hydrodynamics caused by SLR and wave climate changes.

4.2. Sea Level Rise

The first simulations of future scenarios considered SLR-only impacts (scenarios 2–4 in Table 2), and the historical wave time series was used as the input wave conditions. The simulated wave height distributions were qualitatively compared to the reference scenario at spring-low (t_{SL}) and spring-high (t_{SH}) tidal levels (Figure 8), representing the extreme tidal excursions and, thus, potential extremes in wave dynamics. The peak storm wave height at $t_{Hs,max}$ occurred in the middle of the flood phase of a neap tidal cycle and, thus, even though it corresponded to the largest offshore wave height (7.5 m at W1), it produced smaller waves in the nearshore region (e.g., at S1–S3: water depth up to 12 m) than at t_{SH} (4.5 m at W1, see Figure 6). The reference scenario showed the smallest wave height distributions at t_{SL} (Figure 8a) and t_{SH} (Figure 8b), and the maximum nearshore wave heights at t_{SL} increased as the sea level increases (Figure 8a, from left to right). However, at t_{SH}, the maximum nearshore wave heights increased up to SLR_{avg} and then decreased for SLR_{max} (Figure 8b), indicating larger wave energy dissipation in the G2 domain in the SLR_{max} simulation. Smaller wave heights propagated into the G3 domain (maximum depth ~6 m), causing the smallest wave heights at t_{SH} for the SLR_{max} scenario. The wave direction distributions were very similar for all four scenarios, indicating that the different SLR scenarios do not appear to have significant impacts on the observed nearshore wave refraction patterns for the selected incident wave directions, assuming no bathymetric changes. A large difference in wave refraction patterns was observed between two tidal levels (t_{SL} and t_{SH}) due to different incident wave conditions.

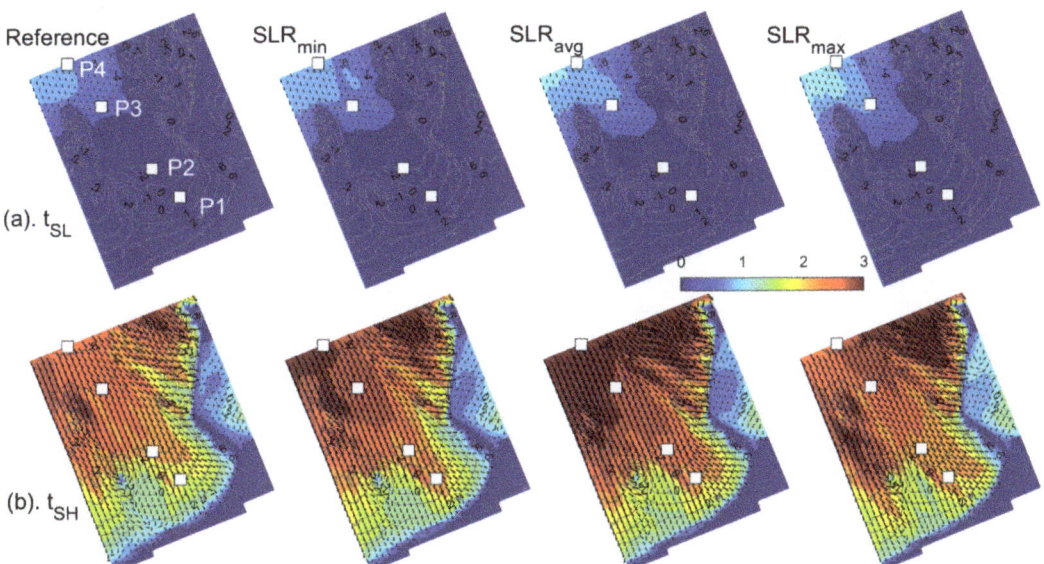

Figure 8. Simulated wave height distributions in the G3 domain for the reference, SLR_{min}, SLR_{avg}, and SLR_{max} scenarios for t_{SL}: spring-low water (**a**) and t_{SH}: spring-high water (**b**), indicating the analysis locations (white squares) P1 (0 m depth), P2 (2 m), P3 (4 m), and P4 (6.5 m).

The average wave energy density spectrum (SD_{avg}) was calculated for the reference analysis period from 7 January–18 February 2013 and for the future SLR scenarios at four selected locations along a cross-shore profile (P1–P4, see Figure 8). As the water depth increased from P1–P4, SD_{avg} increased, the spectral shape tended to be more skewed, and the spectral peak shifted toward lower frequencies from 0.04 Hz at P1 to 0.03 Hz at P4 for all scenarios (Figure 9). At the four selected points, the SLR simulations showed greater SD_{avg} relative to the reference simulation. In addition, SD_{avg} also increased with increasing SLR, which is coherent with increases in the spectral energy for increasing water depths. Overall, the differences in SLR scenarios appear to have marginal effects on the average spectral shape.

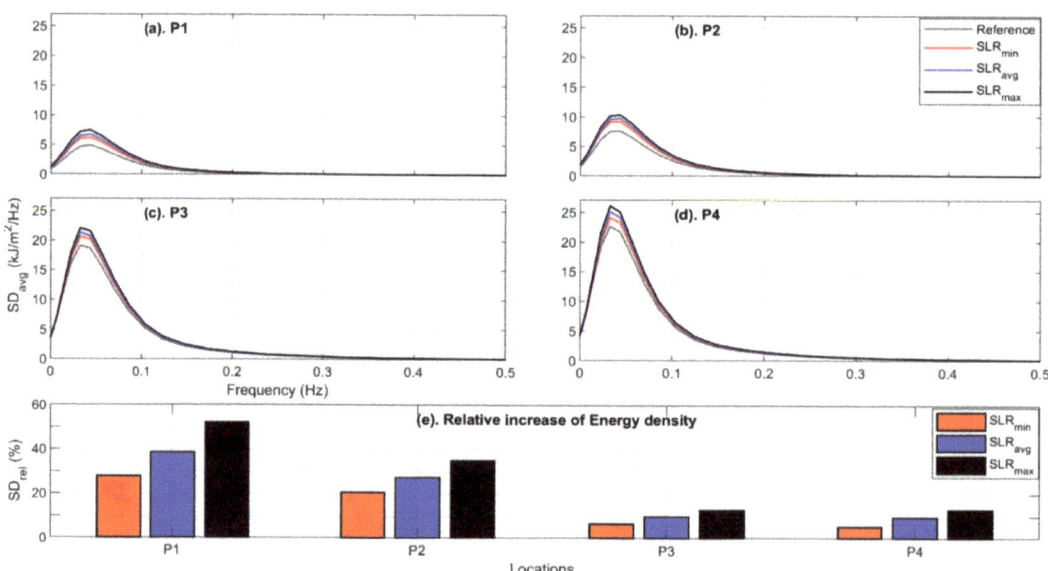

Figure 9. Average wave energy density spectrum (SD_{avg}: Equation (2)) during the analysis period from 7 January–18 February 2013 for the reference (gray line), SLR_{min} (red), SLR_{avg} (blue), and SLR_{max} (black) scenarios at P1: 0 m depth (**a**), P2: 2 m depth (**b**), P3: 4 m depth (**c**), and P4: 6.5 m depth (**d**) in the G3 domain (see Figure 8). (**e**) Relative increases in the wave energy density spectra with respect to the reference scenario (SD_{rel}: Equation (3)).

At each location, the relative change in the average spectral density (Figure 9e) increased with increased sea level (e.g., smallest and largest increases correspond to SLR_{min} and SLR_{max}, respectively). The shallowest location, P1, showed the largest increases (28% for SLR_{min}, 38% for SLR_{avg} and 52% for SLR_{max}) and was, thus, most strongly impacted by SLR. The impacts decreased with increasing water depth, showing a significant drop between P1 to P2, and even smaller impacts at P3 and P4, with increases of only 5–15%. As may be expected, SLR had the strongest effects on wave dynamics in shallow water.

4.3. Sea Level Rise and Future Wave Climates

Similar to the previous analysis, the combined effects of SLR and changes in the wave climate on the wave dynamics are shown at spring-low (t_{SL}) and spring-high (t_{SH}) tide (Figure 10) for the four combined scenarios (5–8, Table 2).

The simulation results showed increases in wave height for all four scenarios at both tide levels (Figure 10), with noticeable impacts of the effects of SLR. At t_{SL}, the wave heights increased with increased SLR. However, at t_{SH}, the changes due to SLR depended on the wave projection scenario. For A1B (offshore conditions: H_s = 4.3 m and $Dir.$ = 303°), the largest nearshore wave heights were observed for the SLR$_{max}$ simulation. The wave heights in the B1 scenarios were smaller than those of the A1B scenario. For B1 (offshore conditions: H_s = 4.7 m and $Dir.$ = 303°), the nearshore wave heights were fairly similar for SLR$_{min}$ and SLR$_{max}$. Therefore, changes in both wave height and direction resulted in different wave propagation processes (shoaling, refraction, and dissipation) as a function of SLR, with complex impacts on the overall wave dynamics.

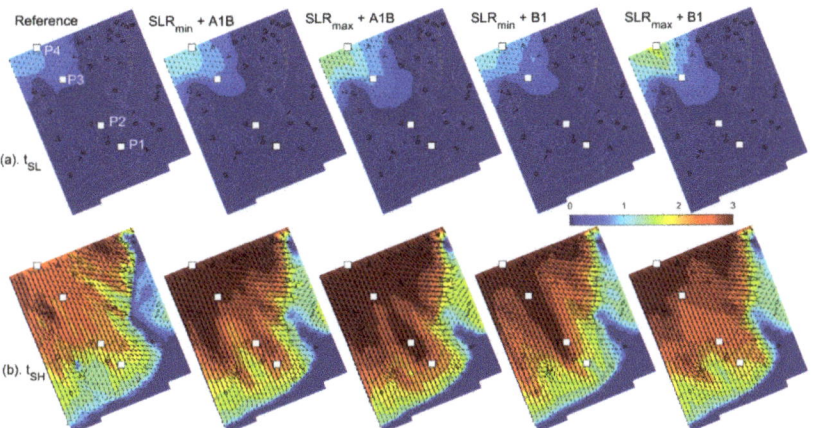

Figure 10. Simulated wave height distributions in the G3 domain for the reference, SLR$_{min}$ + A1B, SLR$_{max}$ + A1B, SLR$_{min}$ + B1, and SLR$_{max}$ + B1 scenarios at t_{SL}: spring-low water (**a**) and t_{SH}: spring-high water (**b**), indicating the analysis locations (white squares) P1 (0 m depth), P2 (2 m), P3 (4 m), and P4 (6.5 m).

The SD_{avg} of the combined A1B wave climate and SLR scenarios showed increases relative to the reference scenario (Figure 11), and these differences were larger than those observed for the SLR-only scenarios (Section 4.2, Figure 9). The largest increases in wave height occurred in shallow water (P1) and then decreased moving offshore into deeper water (P4). The SD_{avg} values for both A1B scenarios were significantly larger than that of the reference simulation, but the mean peak frequency remained similar. In contrast, the SD_{avg} for both B1 scenarios decreased relative to the reference simulation and showed an increase in the average peak frequency (up to 0.09 Hz, relative to 0.03 Hz, Figure 11a–d). Here, the nearshore wave conditions were impacted both by changes in wave propagation and transformation due to changes in the water level (and resultant currents) and by differences in the wave boundary conditions.

In contrast to the SLR scenarios (Section 4.2), SD_{rel} did not decrease monotonically with increasing water depth (Figure 11e). For example, for the SLR$_{min}$ + A1B scenario, P1 experienced the largest increase (62%) and P3 experienced the smallest increase (35%). The largest overall increases in SD_{rel} occurred for the SLR$_{max}$ + A1B scenario at all locations (maximum 95% at P1 and minimum 41% at P3). In contrast, SD_{rel} decreased for the SLR$_{min}$ + B1 scenario (maximum 29% at P3 and minimum 14% at P2). These results indicate that the larger offshore waves in the B1 wave climate dissipated more than those of the A1B wave climate, for both SLR scenarios. These results indicate that the combined SLR and the future wave climate scenarios caused complex changes in the nearshore wave dynamics that may be more strongly dominated by the wave climate than by SLR.

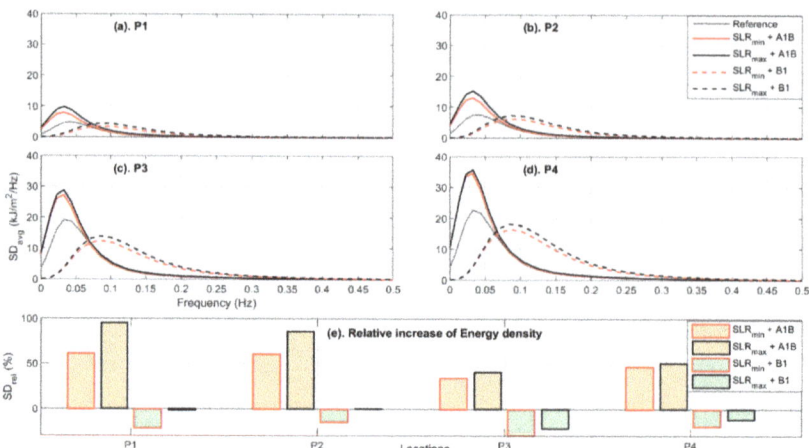

Figure 11. Average wave energy density spectrum (SD_{avg}) during the analysis period from 7 January–18 February 2013 for the reference (gray line), SLR_{min} + A1B (red), SLR_{max} + A1B (black), SLR_{min} + B1 (red-dashed), and SLR_{max} + B1 (black-dashed) at P1: 0 m depth (**a**), P2: 2 m depth (**b**), P3: 4 m depth (**c**), and P4: 6.5 m depth (**d**) in the G3 domain (see Figure 10). (**e**) Relative increase in the wave energy density spectra with respect to the reference scenario (SD_{rel}).

To investigate the impacts that the changes in wave and current dynamics may have on sediment transport processes, the average effective bed shear stress ($\tau_{b,avg}$) was evaluated (Figure 12). This term depends on the hydrodynamic forcing (waves and currents) and the local morphology. At P1, the reference scenario had the lowest bed shear stress (Figure 12a), which increased with increasing the sea level rise (SLR-only scenarios). A similar trend was observed at P2. In the reference scenario, P1 and P2 were submerged during only part of the tidal cycle. The length of the submerged periods increased with increasing SLR, resulting in higher $\tau_{b,avg}$ than the reference scenario. P3 and P4 were permanently submerged, and thus increases in sea level caused decreases in $\tau_{b,avg}$ relative to the reference. P3 experienced the highest $\tau_{b,avg}$ in all scenarios, as well as the largest variability during the analysis period (error bars, Figure 12). P3 is located in the nearshore zone, which is surrounded by shallower areas to the east and west (see bathymetry in Figure 4d), causing higher velocities and larger $\tau_{b,avg}$ than at the other three locations. The variability in changes in $\tau_{b,avg}$ as a function of SLR and wave climate scenarios makes it difficult to identify the causes of the changes. However, the combined A1B scenarios resulted in large increases in $\tau_{b,avg}$ at all locations. The large wave heights in the nearshore zone of the A1B scenarios caused higher velocities than in the B1 scenarios. The relative increase in $\tau_{b,avg}$ showed that P1 was most sensitive to changes in the water level and wave climate, and this effect decreased with increasing water depth (Figure 12b). At P3, both the SLR-only and combined scenarios caused small changes in $\tau_{b,avg}$ relative to the reference scenario. Therefore, the shallowest water depths at Vougot Beach showed the largest changes in waves in all future scenarios and may be the most vulnerable to wave impacts.

The statistical analyses of changes in wave height are summarized in Table 3. The effects of SLR on wave heights (Hs) increased in shallow water, as seen by the increases in the averaged normalized difference ($\overline{\mu}$) and the relative standard deviation (σ_{rel}). This trend increased with increases in sea level rise. The combined scenarios had stronger impacts on the wave height and, thus, showed lower correlation coefficients (R^2) and higher root mean square difference ($RMSD$) values than the SLR-only scenarios. Furthermore, the A1B scenarios had larger impacts on the nearshore wave heights than the B1 scenarios, and in both cases, the effect on wave heights increased with increasing SLR.

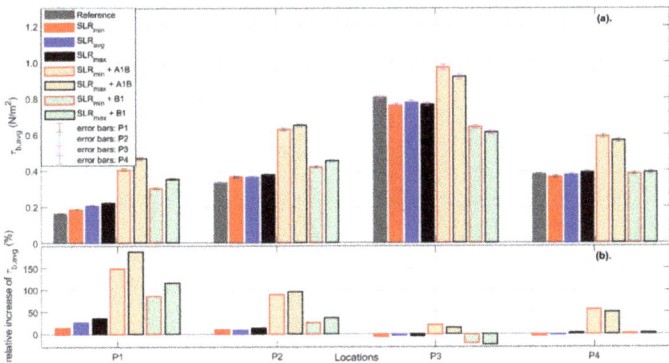

Figure 12. Average effective bed shear stress ($\tau_{b,avg}$) during the analysis period from 7 January–18 February 2013 (**a**) for the reference (gray bar), SLR_{min} (red), SLR_{avg} (blue), SLR_{max} (black), SLR_{min} + A1B (yellow red-enclosed), SLR_{max} + A1B (yellow black-enclosed), SLR_{min} + B1 (green red-enclosed), and SLR_{max} + B1 (green black-enclosed) at P1 (0 m depth), P2 (2 m), P3 (4 m), and P4 (6.5 m) on the G3 domain (see Figure 10). Standard error (standard deviation/ $\sqrt{}$number of time steps) is shown by error bars. Relative increase of $\tau_{b,avg}$ (**b**) is shown with the corresponding color bars.

Table 3. Statistical parameters comparing the difference between the reference and the future scenarios in wave height (*Hs*) at P1 (0 m depth), P2 (2 m), P3 (4 m), and P4 (6.5 m) (see location in Figure 10). R^2: correlation coefficient, *RMSD*: root mean square difference, $\overline{\mu}$: averaged normalised difference, σ_{rel}: relative standard deviation.

	Scenario	Parameter	Wave Height (Hs) Location			
			P1	P2	P3	P4
Sea level rise	SLR_{min}	R^2 (-)	0.93	0.94	0.92	0.94
		RMSD (m)	0.19	0.17	0.20	0.19
		$\overline{\mu}$ (-)	0.31	0.21	0.06	0.04
		σ_{rel} (m)	0.67	0.43	0.13	0.09
	SLR_{avg}	R^2 (-)	0.88	0.92	0.90	0.92
		RMSD (m)	0.25	0.22	0.24	0.22
		$\overline{\mu}$ (-)	0.43	0.30	0.08	0.05
		σ_{rel} (m)	0.90	0.59	0.15	0.11
	SLR_{max}	R^2 (-)	0.85	0.91	0.88	0.93
		RMSD (m)	0.31	0.26	0.27	0.23
		$\overline{\mu}$ (-)	0.53	0.38	0.10	0.07
		σ_{rel} (m)	1.10	0.73	0.17	0.11
Combined = sea level rise + future wave	SLR_{min} + A1B	R^2 (-)	0.90	0.89	0.87	0.87
		RMSD (m)	0.26	0.29	0.31	0.39
		$\overline{\mu}$ (-)	0.40	0.42	0.18	0.21
		σ_{rel} (m)	0.59	0.64	0.21	0.20
	SLR_{max} + A1B	R^2 (-)	0.84	0.86	0.84	0.84
		RMSD (m)	0.38	0.40	0.36	0.43
		$\overline{\mu}$ (-)	0.62	0.63	0.22	0.24
		σ_{rel} (m)	0.97	1.00	0.26	0.23
	SLR_{min} + B1	R^2 (-)	0.87	0.85	0.80	0.76
		RMSD (m)	0.19	0.27	0.33	0.43
		$\overline{\mu}$ (-)	0.24	0.34	0.13	0.21
		σ_{rel} (m)	0.46	0.58	0.29	0.32
	SLR_{max} + B1	R^2 (-)	0.81	0.82	0.77	0.75
		RMSD (m)	0.31	0.36	0.38	0.50
		$\overline{\mu}$ (-)	0.46	0.54	0.20	0.27
		σ_{rel} (m)	0.81	0.89	0.31	0.33

5. Discussion

The objective of this study was to evaluate the impacts of climate change on the coastal wave dynamics at Vougot Beach, including not only SLR, but also combined scenarios of SLR and wave climate changes to respond to the increasing need to investigate the interactions between these two factors [60]. Simulations were carried out for a 6-week period during the 2012–2013 winter (validation and reference period) and for the same 6-week period projected into the future using the selected SLR and wave climate scenarios (Table 2) to quantify the projected changes in the significant wave height Hs, the average wave energy density spectra SD_{avg}, and the effective bed shear stress τ_b. The simulation results showed the importance of both SLR and wave climate changes, and, in particular, interactions between the complex nearshore bathymetry and the macrotidal regime of the beach.

5.1. Macrotidal Beach Dynamics

The impacts of SLR and wave climate changes on the nearshore wave dynamics were most significant at high tide. This is particularly important for beach morphodynamics since changes in the hydrodynamic conditions at high tide have stronger impacts on beach and dune morphological changes [61–63]. Recent modelling studies of the predicted impacts of past and future storms on the morphology of a macrotidal beach also emphasized the importance of the water level on the impact of storm events [6,35]. However, Bennett et al. [35], stated that there is high variability between different sites, and while the SLR-only simulations in the current study were in agreement with their conclusion, the combined SLR and wave scenarios emphasized the importance of interactions between water levels and waves. Thus, although high spatial and temporal resolution modelling efforts are computationally expensive, they may provide evidence of the complexities of beach hydrodynamics, which have important impacts on beach and dune morphological changes.

5.2. Uncertainties in the Modelling Approach

The results presented here should not be interpreted as deterministic predictions of future beach hydrodynamics, but rather as a preliminary estimation of potential changes in nearshore hydrodynamics and their dependency on SLR and wave climate changes. This modelling approach depends on the accuracy of the model calibration and the forcing data, including, in particular, the predictions of future SLR and wave climate scenarios.

5.2.1. Model Calibration Uncertainties

The validation of the model simulations showed good agreement between the simulated and measured water levels (Figure 5), with high correlations ($R^2 > 0.97$) and low errors ($RMSE < 0.37$ m) between the two time series at the locations of the three pressure sensors. However, errors between the simulated and measured Hs were larger, with $RMSE$ ranging from 0.43–0.66 m (average difference in Hs ~ 0.5 m) at the three pressure sensors, and comparisons between Delft3D and WW3 estimated wave heights at the point W2 showed a $RMSD$ of 0.57 m. These differences may have been caused by errors in the numerical model or in the wave heights estimated from the pressure sensor measurements.

Errors in the numerical model may have been caused by a number of different factors including the model inputs, calibration, boundary conditions, bathymetric grid, and simulated physical processes. The input wave conditions were obtained from WW3 simulations at a grid point located in 44 m water depth, and errors between the in situ and WW3-simulated wave heights were not able to be estimated at this location. At a wave buoy located nearby in 60 m depth (Pierres Noires, buoy 62069), the estimated $RMSE$ and bias were 0.13 and 0.05 m, respectively [34].

In the model, the wave conditions were assumed to be constant along the offshore boundary, with a constant 40 m water depth, which likely caused the model to overestimate the wave height at the eastern end, which is shallower than the western end. The submarine scarp between 10 m and 40–60 m depth that delimits the outer edge of the large platform with reefs and islets was not well reproduced in the bathymetry data. The nearshore bathymetry was represented well with a high-resolution grid, but the offshore bathymetry may not have been represented accurately given the high spatial variability in the offshore zone at this site. The bathymetry remained constant in time, and the impacts of morphological changes on wave propagation were not considered. Finally, the SWAN model likely overestimates wave heights [28], and does not simulate accurately diffraction processes [64], which were therefore not included in the simulations. At Vougot Beach, diffraction may be important, and refraction and depth-induced processes may have also not been represented accurately enough.

The model was calibrated using bed friction and wave breaking parameters. Water level and currents in Delft3D are sensitive to the bed friction [65]. A Chézy coefficient of 60 m$^{1/2}$/s was selected following a sensitivity analysis of the water levels. Simulated wave heights in SWAN depend on the parameterization of the wave energy dissipation [28]. A friction coefficient of 0.06 m^2/s^3 and a wave breaking parameter of 0.65 were selected for the SWAN model by qualitatively comparing the simulated and measured wave heights. However, an extensive calibration and validation were not undertaken, and the simulated and observed wave heights showed fair agreement (Section 4.1). These values remained constant in all simulations, and only the relative changes between the reference and future scenarios were analyzed.

In addition to errors related to the numerical modelling, some of the differences between the simulated and measured wave heights may have been caused by errors in the wave height time series calculated from the pressure sensor measurements. The pressure sensors were located in 0.7 m (S1), 2.5 m (S2), and 12 m (S3) water depths, and S3 was the only sensor that remained permanently submerged. Sensors S1 and S2 were, thus, located in the surf zone, where waves may be highly nonlinear and even breaking. Linear reconstruction of wave heights from pressure sensors underestimates *Hs* in shallow water [66], leading to up to a 30% underestimation of individual wave heights near the breaking point [67,68]. Due to pressure attenuation at S3, only wave periods larger than around 3 s could be measured. This served as a high-frequency cutoff for the wave spectrum and may have shifted the computed significant wave height. Thus, the reconstruction method used to calculate the wave height at the pressure sensor locations, in addition to intrinsic instrument measurement errors, may have also contributed to the observed differences between the simulated and measured wave heights.

5.2.2. Projected SLR and Future Wave Time Series

It has been assumed that the primary driver of climate change impacts to the wave field comes from the meteorological forcing, and changes in the local bathymetry have not been considered. This study thus relied on accurate projections of sea level and local wave climate changes. The SLR predictions were global averages extracted from the 5th IPCC report [12], spanning the range of changes expected by 2100. Although global values were used in this study, regional-scale predictions fall within the global range (Section 3.1.1), and therefore the SLR predictions were assumed to be representative of expected future changes.

Future estimates of the wave climate are more difficult to obtain, in particular at local scales. At global scales, large differences exist in different wave forecasting models, as highlighted by the COWCLIP (Coordinated Ocean Wave Climate Project) project [29] and by the IPCC 5th Assessment Report [12], which assigned low confidence to wave projections. Thus, more recently, a series of ten new global wind-wave projection studies were completed using atmospheric forcing from the CMIP5 GCM simulations, highlighting that the uncertainties in wave predictions are dominated by climate model-driven uncertainties [69] leading to uncertainties of up to ~50% in single-method modelling studies. One must be careful in interpreting single, deterministic simulations of wave climate changes, thinking of these predictions as estimates of the possible changes in the local wave field.

The availability of ensemble averages of predicted wave fields at the global scale is useful for global-scale studies, but additional methods must be used to transform these wave conditions to local wave conditions. In this study, the statistics of the hindcast and forecast waves time series (using the dynamical downscaling approach of Laugel [45]) were used to estimate transfer functions to project the historical reference time series to the equivalent time series in 2100 (following Banno and Kuriyama [26]). A second set of linear transfer functions was used to transform these offshore wave conditions (W0) to the nearshore zone (W1) to use as input wave conditions in the Delft3D model. The estimates of future wave conditions could be improved by using ensemble averages of hindcast and future wave projections instead of the results from a single wave model. However, ensemble averages of future wave simulations are not yet readily available at worldwide scales, in particular in the nearshore zone. If ensemble averages of offshore waves exist, they must be propagated to the coastline, which requires setting up computationally intensive intermediate- to local-scale models or developing site-specific downscaling approaches.

5.3. Extension of the Modelling Approach

The availability of data for setting up, forcing, and calibrating numerical models (e.g., bathymetric and hydrodynamic measurements) is crucial to assess model performance and to obtain accurate results. The present modelling approach could be improved using extended offshore bathymetry data and measured offshore waves. This study was particularly focused on a six-week period during the 2012–2013 winter, but the study could be extended to investigate storm events with different hydrodynamic conditions (e.g., the energetic storms of the 2008 or 2013/2014 winter [70,71], events with different combinations of water levels and wave heights [6]) to generalize the conclusions presented here. Future work includes extending this work to evaluate the impacts on the beach and dune morphodynamics, including interactions between the hydrodynamics and changes in the nearshore bathymetry. This could facilitate improving the model predictions by considering temporal variations in the bathymetry, which were not considered here, as well as evaluating potential coastal erosion risks, dune breaching, and hinterland flooding. Lastly, the approach developed here can be applied to a wide variety of sites with sufficient bathymetric, wave, and water level observations to calibrate and validate the modelling approach before simulating future events using projections of future waves and water levels.

6. Conclusions

Wave dynamics at Vougot Beach were investigated using Delft3D to simulate a 6-week period in 2013 and seven projected scenarios in 2100, including three SLR-only scenarios and four combined SLR and wave climate change scenarios. The SLR-only scenarios showed that increased water levels allowed larger waves to propagate farther onshore, and the differences in wave heights were most significant in shallow water. The simulations of the combined SLR and wave scenarios showed the importance of evaluating the two effects simultaneously because the scenario showing the largest increases in nearshore wave heights did not correspond to the scenario with the largest offshore waves. Given the complex nearshore bathymetry and macrotidal regime of the beach, it is necessary to simulate the local-scale hydrodynamics with a high-resolution model to represent accurately the interactions between waves and water levels.

Future studies are required using improved wave projections, in particular in the nearshore environment, to gain a more comprehensive understanding of the potential changes in currents and waves, as well as their impacts. The approach presented here, as well as its extension to evaluate climate change impacts on nearshore sediment transport and morphological evolution, can thus be applied to other coastal systems to study local-scale changes in hydrodynamics and, ultimately, morphodynamics, providing useful information for beach management and policy makers.

Author Contributions: Conceptualization, P.D. and M.L.Y.; methodology, P.D. and M.L.Y.; software, P.D.; validation, P.D.; formal analysis, P.D. and M.L.Y.; investigation, P.D. and M.L.Y.; resources, P.D., M.L.Y. and S.S.; data curation, P.D., M.L.Y., S.S., F.F. and K.K.; writing—original draft preparation, P.D. and M.L.Y.; writing—review and editing, P.D., M.L.Y., S.S., F.F. and K.K.; visualization, P.D. and M.L.Y.; supervision, P.D., M.L.Y. and S.S.; project administration, P.D., M.L.Y. and S.S.; funding acquisition, P.D., S.S. and F.F. All authors have read and agreed to the published version of the manuscript.

Funding: This research was funded by German Research Foundation (DFG), grant number DI 2139/2-1 and the APC was funded by the same grant. The hydrodynamic survey was funded by the "Institut National des Sciences de l'Univers" (INSU-CNRS) in the framework of the French "Service National d'Observation" (SNO-DYNALIT). The equipment for hydrodynamic survey was funded by the Labex-Mer (ANR-10-LABX-19), and by an ISblue project, Interdisciplinary graduate school for the blue planet (ANR-17-EURE-0015).

Acknowledgments: This study is part of the MoDECS (Modification of Dune Erosion by adjacent Coastal Systems) project funded by German Research Foundation (DFG) under the grant number DI 2139/2-1. Field surveys at Vougot Beach were supported by the "Institut National des Sciences de l'Univers" (INSU-CNRS) in the framework of the French "Service National d'Observation" (SNO-DYNALIT), the Labex-Mer (ANR-10-LABX-19), and by an ISblue project, Interdisciplinary graduate school for the blue planet (ANR-17-EURE-0015). It was co-funded by a grant from the French government under the program "Investissements d'Avenir", the municipality of Guissény, Europe for Economic and Regional Development, the Regional Council of Brittany, and Finistère department as part of the CPER projects.

Conflicts of Interest: The authors declare no conflict of interest.

References

1. Chowdhury, P.; Behera, M.R. Effect of long-term wave climate variability on longshore sediment transport along regional coastline. *Prog. Oceanogr.* **2017**, *156*, 145–153. [CrossRef]
2. Harley, M.D.; Ciavola, P. Managing local coastal inundation risk using real-time forecasts and artificial dune placements. *Coast. Eng.* **2013**, *77*, 77–90. [CrossRef]
3. Hunt, S.; Bryan, K.R.; Mullarney, J.C. The effect of wind waves on spring-neap variations in sediment transport in two meso-tidal estuarine basins with contrasting fetch. *Geomorphology* **2017**, *280*, 76–88. [CrossRef]
4. Rosenberger, K.J.; Storlazzi, C.D.; Cheriton, O.M.; Pomeroy, A.W.M.; Hansen, J.F.; Lowe, R.J.; Buckley, M.L. Spectral Wave-Driven Bedload Transport Across a Coral Reef Flat/Lagoon Complex. *Front. Mar. Sci.* **2020**, *7*, 875. [CrossRef]
5. Yang, G.; Wang, X.H.; Zhong, Y.; Cheng, Z.; Andutta, F.P. Wave effects on sediment dynamics in a macro-tidal estuary: Darwin Harbour, Australia during monsoon season. *Estuar. Coast. Shelf Sci.* **2020**, *244*, 106931. [CrossRef]
6. Dissanayake, P.; Brown, J.; Sibbertsen, P.; Winter, C. Using a two-step framework for the investigation of storm impacted beach/dune erosion. *Coast. Eng.* **2021**, *168*, 103939. [CrossRef]
7. Dissanayake, P.; Brown, J.; Wisse, P.; Karunarathna, H. Effect of storm clustering on beach/dune evolution. *Mar. Geol.* **2015**, *370*, 63–75. [CrossRef]
8. Huang, S.Y.; Yen, J.Y.; Wu, B.L.; Shih, N.W. Field observations of sediment transport across the rocky coast of east Taiwan: Impacts of extreme waves on the coastal morphology by Typhoon Soudelor. *Mar. Geol.* **2020**, *421*, 106088. [CrossRef]
9. Suanez, S.; Romain, C.; Floc'h, F.; Blaise, E.; Ardhuin, F.; Filipot, J.F.; Cariolet, J.M.; Delacourt, C. Observations and Predictions of Wave Runup, Extreme Water Levels, and Medium-Term Dune Erosion during storm conditions. *J. Mar. Sci. Eng.* **2015**, *3*, 674–698. [CrossRef]
10. Suanez, S.; Cariolet, J.M.; Cancouët, R.; Ardhuin, F.; Delacourt, C. Dune recovery after storm erosion on a high-energy beach: Vougot beach, Brittany (France). *Geomorphology* **2012**, *139*, 16–33. [CrossRef]
11. Van Ormondt, M.; Nelson, T.R.; Hapke, C.J.; Roelvink, D. Morphodynamic modelling of the wilderness breach, Fire Island, New York. Part I: Model set-up and validation. *Coast. Eng.* **2020**, *157*, 103621. [CrossRef]
12. Church, J.A.; Clark, P.U.; Cazenave, A.; Gregory, J.M.; Jevrejeva, S.; Levermann, A.; Merrifield, M.A.; Milne, G.A.; Nerem, R.S.; Nunn, P.D.; et al. Sea Level Change. In *Climate Change 2013: The Physical Science Basis. Contribution of Working Group I to the Fifth Assessment Report of the Intergovernmental Panel on Climate Change*; Stocker, T.F., Qin, D., Plattner, G.-K., Tignor, M., Allen, S.K., Boschung, J., Nauels, A., Xia, Y., Bex, V., Midgley, P.M., Eds.; Cambridge University Press: Cambridge, UK; New York, NY, USA, 2013.
13. Mentaschi, L.; Vousdoukas, M.I.; Voukouvalas, E.; Dosio, A.; Feyen, L. Global changes of extreme coaszal wave energy fluxes triggered by intensified teleconnection patterns. *Geophys. Res. Lett.* **2017**, *44*, 2416–2426. [CrossRef]
14. Neumann, B.; Vafeidis, A.T.; Zimmermann, J.; Nicholls, R.J. Future coastal population growth and exposure to sea-level rise and coastal flooding—A global assessment. *PLoS ONE* **2015**, *10*, e0131375. [CrossRef]
15. Ranasinghe, R. On the need for a new generation of coastal change models for the 21st century. *Sci. Rep.* **2020**, *10*, 1–6. [CrossRef]

16. Vousdoukas, I.; Ranasinghe, R.; Mentaschi, L.; Plomaritis, T.A.; Athanasiou, P.; Luijendijk, A.; Feyen, L. Sand coastlines under threat of erosion. *Nat. Clim. Chang.* **2020**, *10*, 260–263. [CrossRef]
17. McGranahan, G.; Balk, D.; Anderson, B. The rising tide: Assessing the risks of climate change and human settlements in low elevation coastal zones. *Environ. Urban* **2007**, *19*, 17–37. [CrossRef]
18. Vendel, A.L.; Lopes, S.G.; Santos, C.; Spach, H.L. Fish assemblages in a tidal flat. *Braz. Arch. Biol. Technol.* **2003**, *46*, 233–242. [CrossRef]
19. De Jong, F.; Bakker, J.F.; van Berkel, C.J.M.; Dankers, N.M.J.A.; Dahl, K.; Gätje, C.; Marencic, H.; Potel, P. *Wadden Sea Quality Status Report, 1999*; Wadden Sea Ecosystem No. 9; Common Wadden Sea Secretariat, Trilateral Monitoring and Assessment Group, Quality Status Report Group: Wilhelmshaven, Germany, 1999.
20. Bruun, P.M. Sea level rise as a cause of shore erosion. *J. Waterw. Harb. Div.* **1962**, *88*, 117–130. [CrossRef]
21. Hinkel, J.; Lincke, D.; Vafeidis, A.T.; Perrette, M.; Nicholls, R.J.; Tol, R.S.J.; Marzeion, B.; Fettweis, X.; Ionescu, C.; Levermann, A. Coastal flood damage and adaptation costs under 21st century sea-level rise. *Proc. Natl. Acad. Sci. USA* **2014**, *111*, 3292–3297. [CrossRef] [PubMed]
22. Jiménez, J.A.; Sanchez-Arcille, A. Physical impacts of climatic change on deltaic coastal systems (II): Driving terms. *Clim. Chang.* **1997**, *35*, 95–118. [CrossRef]
23. Cooper, J.A.G.; Masselink, G.; Coco, G.; Short, A.D.; Castelle, B.; Rogers, K.; Anthony, E.; Green, A.N.; Kelley, J.T.; Pilkey, O.H.; et al. Sandy beaches can survive sea-level rise. *Nat. Clim. Chang.* **2020**, *10*, 993–995. [CrossRef]
24. O'Grady, J.G.; Hemer, M.A.; McInees, K.L.; Trenham, C.E.; Stephenson, A.G. Projected incremental changes to extreme wind-driven wave heights for the twenty-first century. *Sci. Rep.* **2021**, *11*, 8726. [CrossRef]
25. Vousdoukas, M.I.; Mentaschi, L.; Voukouvalas, E. Global probabilistic projections of extreme sea levels show intensification of coastal flood hazards. *Nat. Commun.* **2018**, *9*, 2360. [CrossRef]
26. Banno, M.; Kuriyama, Y. Prediction of future shoreline change with sea-level rise and wave climate change at Hasaki, Japan. In Proceedings of the 33rd International Conference of Coastal Engineering, Seoul, South Korea, 30 October 2014.
27. Hemer, M.A.; Fan, Y.; Mori, N.; Semedo, A.; Wang, X. Projected changes in wave climate from a multi-model ensemble. *Nat. Clim. Chang.* **2013**, *3*, 471–476. [CrossRef]
28. Boyd, S.C.; Weaver, R.J. Replacing a third-generation wave model with a fetch based parametric solver in coastal estuaries. *Estuar. Coast. Shelf Sci.* **2021**, *251*, 107192. [CrossRef]
29. Divinsky, B.O.; Kosyan, R.D. Influence of the climatic variations in the wind waves parameters on the alongshore sediment transport. *Oceanologia* **2020**, *62*, 190–199. [CrossRef]
30. Medellín, G.; Mayor, M.; Appendini, C.M.; Cerezo-Mota, R.; Jiménez, J.A. The Role of Beach Morphology and Mid-Century Climate Change Effects on Wave Runup and Storm Impact on the Northern Yucatan Coast. *Mar. Sci. Eng.* **2021**, *9*, 518. [CrossRef]
31. Dodet, G.; Bertin, X.; Taborda, R. Wave climate variability in the North-East Atlantic Ocean over the last six decades. *Ocean Model.* **2010**, *31*, 120–131. [CrossRef]
32. Booij, N.; Ris, R.C.; Holthuijsen, L.H. A third-generation wave model for coastal regions, Part I, Model description and validation. *J. Geophys. Res.* **1999**, *104*, 7649–7666. [CrossRef]
33. Lesser, G.; Roelvink, J.A.; Van Kester, J.A.T.M.; Stelling, G.S. Development and validation of a three-dimensional morphological model. *Coast. Eng.* **2004**, *51*, 883–915. [CrossRef]
34. Boudière, E.; Maisonidieu, C.; Ardhuin, F.; Accensi, M.; Pineau-Guillou, L.; Lepesqueur, J. A suitable metocean hindcast database for the design of marine energy converters. *Int. J. Mar. Energy* **2013**, *3*, E40–E52. [CrossRef]
35. Bennett, W.G.; Karunarathna, H.; Reeve, D.; Mori, N. Computational modelling of morphodynamic response of a macro-tidal beach to future climate variabilities. *Mar. Geol.* **2019**, *415*, 105960. [CrossRef]
36. Battistini, R. Le littoral septentrional du Léon: Principaux problèmes morphologiques. *Bull. L'association Géographes Français* **1953**, *30*, 58–71. [CrossRef]
37. Battistini, R. Description du relief et des formations quaternaires du littoral breton entre Brignogan et Saint-Pol-de-Léon (Finistère). *Bulletin d'Information du Comité Central d'Océanographie et d'Etude des Côtes* **1955**, *7*, 468–491.
38. Battistini, R.; Martin, S. La "Plate-forme à écueils" du Nord-Ouest de la Bretagne. *Norois* **1956**, *10*, 147–161. [CrossRef]
39. Guilcher, A.; Hallégouët, B. Coastal dunes in Brittany and their management. *J. Coast. Res.* **1991**, *7*, 517–533.
40. Suanez, S.; Cariolet, J.M.; Fichaut, B. Monitoring of Recent Morphological Changes of the Dune of Vougot Beach (Brittany, France) Using Differential GPS. *Shore Beach* **2010**, *78*, 37–47.
41. Bishop, C.T.; Donelan, M.A. Measuring waves with pressure transducers. *Coast. Eng.* **1987**, *11*, 309–328. [CrossRef]
42. Homma, M.; Horikawa, K.; Komori, S. Response characteristics of underwater wave gauge. *Coast. Eng. Jpn.* **1966**, *9*, 45–54. [CrossRef]
43. Pierson, W.J.; Marks, W. The power spectrum analysis of ocean-wave records. *Eos Trans. Am. Geophys. Union* **1952**, *33*, 834–844. [CrossRef]
44. IAHR Working Group on Wave Generation and Analysis. List of sea-state parameters. *J. Waterw. Port Coast. Ocean. Eng.* **1989**, *115*, 793–808. [CrossRef]
45. Laugel, A. Climatologie des états de mer en Atlantique nord-est: Analyse du Climat Actuel et des Evolutions Futures sous Scénarios de Changement Climatique, par Descente D'échelle Dynamique et Statistique. Ph.D. Thesis, Université Paris Est, Laboratoire d'Hydraulique Saint-Venant, Chatou, France, 2013.

46. Benoit, M.; Marcos, M.; Becq, F. Development of a third generation shallow-water wave model with unstructured spatial meshing. In Proceedings of the 25th International Conference on Coastal Engineering, Orlando, FL, USA, 2–6 September 1996; pp. 465–478.
47. Salas-Mélia, D.; Chauvin, F.; Déqué, M.; Douville, H.; Guérémy, J.F.; Marquet, P.; Planton, S.; Royer, J.F.; Tyteca, S. *Description and Validation of CNRM-CM3 Global Coupled Climate Modele*; Technical Report Note de centre GMGEC 103; CNRM: Toulouse, France, 2005.
48. Intergovernmental Panel on Climate Change (IPCC). *Climate Change 2007: The Physical Science Basis Summary for Policymakers*; IPPC: Geneva, Switzwerland, 2007; 18p.
49. Dissanayake, P.; Winter, C. Modelling the coastline orientation on storm erosion at the Sylt island, North Sea. In Proceedings of the Virtual Conference of Coastal Engineering, 6–9 October 2020. 36v, paper 20.
50. Stelling, G.S. On the construction of computational methods for shallow water flow problem. In *Rijkswaterstaat Communications*; Governing Printing Office: Hague, The Netherlands, 1984; Volume 35.
51. Stelling, G.S.; Lendertse, J.J. Approximation of Convective Processes by Cyclic ACI methods. In Proceedings of the 2nd ASCE Conference on Estuarine and Coastal Modelling, Tampa, FL, USA, 13–15 November 1991.
52. Roelvink, J.A.; Walstra, D.J. Keeping it simple by using complex models. *Adv. Hydrosci. Eng.* **2004**, *V1*, 1–11.
53. Donelan, M.A.; Hamilton, H.; Hui, W.H. Directional spectra of wind-generated waves. *Philos. Trans. R. Soc. Lond. A* **1985**, *315*, 509–562.
54. Hasselmann, K.; Barnett, T.P.; Bouws, F.; Carlson, H.; Cartwright, D.E.; Enke, K.; Ewing, J.A.; Gienapp, H.; Hasselmann, D.E.; Krusemann, P.; et al. *Measurements of Windwave Growth and Swell Decay during the Joint North Sea Wave Project (JONSWAP)*; Deutches Hydrographisches Institut, A8: Hamburg, Germany, 1973; pp. 1–95.
55. Nair, M.A.; Kumar, V.S. Wave spectral shapes in the coastal waters based on measured data off Karwar on the western coast of India. *Ocean. Sci.* **2017**, *13*, 365–378. [CrossRef]
56. Soulsby, R. *Dynamics of Marine Sands, a Manual for Practical Applications*; Thomas Telford: Teleford, UK, 1997.
57. Fredsøe, J. Turbulent boundary layer in wave-current interaction. *J. Hydraul. Eng.* **1984**, *110*, 1103–1120. [CrossRef]
58. Amoudry, L.O.; Souza, A.J. Deterministic coastal morphological and sediment transport modelling: A review and discussion. *Rev. Geophys.* **2011**, *49*, RG2002. [CrossRef]
59. Krause, P.; Boyle, D.P.; Bäse, F. Comparison of different efficiency criteria for hydrological model assessment. *Adv. Geosci.* **2005**, *5*, 89–97. [CrossRef]
60. Brooks, N.; Nicholls, R.; Hall, J. Sea Level Rise: Coastal Impacts and Responses. In *Expertise for WBGU on Oceans and Global Change*; WBGU: Berlin, Germany, 2006; p. 49.
61. Masselink, G. Simulating the Effects of Tides on Beach Morphodynamics. *J. Coast. Res.* **1993**, *SI 15*, 180–197.
62. Sabatier, F.; Anthony, E.J.; Héquette, A.; Suanez, S.; Musereau, J.; Ruz, M.H.; Regnauld, H. Morphodynamics of beach/dune systems: Examples from the coast of France. *Géomorphologie Relief Process. Environ.* **2009**, *15*, 3–22. [CrossRef]
63. Wright, L.D.; Nielsen, P.; Short, A.D.; Green, M.O. Morphodynamics of a macrotidal beach. *Mar. Geol.* **1982**, *50*, 97–127. [CrossRef]
64. Kim, G.H.; Jho, M.H.; Yoon, S.B. Improving the performance of SWAN modelling to simulate diffraction of waves behind structures. *J. Coast. Res.* **2017**, *SI 79*, 349–353. [CrossRef]
65. Hsu, Y.L.; Dykes, J.D.; Allard, R.A. *Evaluation of Delft3D Performance in Nearshore Flows*; Naval Research Laboratory, Ocean Dynamics and Prediction Branch, Stennis Space Center: Hancock, MS, USA, 2006.
66. Tsai, C.H.; Huang, M.C.; Young, F.J.; Lin, Y.C.; Li, H.W. On the recovery of surface wave by pressure transfer function. *Ocean. Eng.* **2005**, *32*, 1247–1259. [CrossRef]
67. Bonneton, P.; Lannes, D. Recovering water wave elevation from pressure measurements. *J. Fluid Mech.* **2017**, *833*, 399–429. [CrossRef]
68. Martins, K.; Blenkinsopp, C.E.; Almar, R.; Zang, Z. On the influence of swash-based reflection on surf zone hydrodynamics: A wave-by-wave approach. *Coast. Eng.* **2017**, *122*, 27–43. [CrossRef]
69. Morim, J.; Hemer, M.A.; Wang, X.L.; Cartwright, N.; Trenham, C.; Semedo, A. Robustness and uncertainties in global multivariate wind-wave climate projections. *Nat. Clim. Chang.* **2019**, *9*, 711–718. [CrossRef]
70. Masselink, G.; Castelle, B.; Scott, T.; Dodet, G.; Suanez, S.; Jackson, D.; Floc'h, F. Extreme wave activity during 2013/2014 winter and morphological impacts along the Atlantic coast of Europe. *Geophys. Res. Lett.* **2016**, *43*, 2135–2143. [CrossRef]
71. Ruju, A.; Filiplo, J.F.; Bentamy, A.; Leckler, F. Spectral wave modelling of the extreme 2013/2014 winter storms in the North-East Atlantic. *Ocean. Eng.* **2020**, *216*, 108012. [CrossRef]

Article

Two-Channel System Dynamics of the Outer Weser Estuary—A Modeling Study

Jannek Gundlach [1,*], Anna Zorndt [2], Bram C. van Prooijen [3] and Zheng Bing Wang [3,4]

[1] Ludwig-Franzius-Institute for Hydraulic, Estuarine and Coastal Engineering, Leibniz University Hannover, 30167 Hanover, Germany
[2] Federal Waterways Engineering and Research Institute (BAW), 22559 Hamburg, Germany; anna.zorndt@baw.de
[3] Faculty of Civil Engineering and Geosciences, Delft University of Technology, 2628 CN Delft, The Netherlands; B.C.vanProoijen@tudelft.nl (B.C.v.P.); z.b.wang@tudelft.nl (Z.B.W.)
[4] Deltares, P.O. Box 177, 2600 MH Delft, The Netherlands
* Correspondence: gundlach@lufi.uni-hannover.de

Citation: Gundlach, J.; Zorndt, A.; van Prooijen, B.C.; Wang, Z.B. Two-Channel System Dynamics of the Outer Weser Estuary—A Modeling Study. *J. Mar. Sci. Eng.* **2021**, *9*, 448. https://doi.org/10.3390/jmse9040448

Academic Editors: Pushpa Dissanayake, Jenifer Brown and Marissa Yates

Received: 10 March 2021
Accepted: 15 April 2021
Published: 20 April 2021

Publisher's Note: MDPI stays neutral with regard to jurisdictional claims in published maps and institutional affiliations.

Copyright: © 2021 by the authors. Licensee MDPI, Basel, Switzerland. This article is an open access article distributed under the terms and conditions of the Creative Commons Attribution (CC BY) license (https://creativecommons.org/licenses/by/4.0/).

Abstract: In this paper, we unravel the mechanisms responsible for the development of the two-channel system in the Outer Weser Estuary. A process-based morphodynamic model is built based on a flat-bed approach using simplified boundary conditions and accelerated morphological development. The results are analyzed in two steps: first, by checking for morphodynamic equilibrium in the simulations and second, by applying a newly developed method that interprets simulations based on categorization of the two-channel system and cross-sectional correlation analysis. All simulations reach a morphodynamic equilibrium and develop two channels that vary considerably over time and between the simulations. Variations can be found in the location and depth of the two channels, the development of the dominant channel over time and the alteration in the dominance pattern. The conclusions are that the development of the two-channel system is mainly caused by the tides and the basin geometry. Furthermore, it is shown that the alternation pattern and period are dependent on the dominance of the tides compared to the influence of river discharge.

Keywords: morphodynamics; Delft3D; long-term; two-channel

1. Introduction

The Weser estuary is one of the four estuaries in the German Bight. Its morphological pattern is characterized by a distinctive two-channel system in the Outer Weser part. This characteristic is relevant for the navigational access to the ports of Bremen and Bremerhaven [1]. In the late 19th century, a combination of increased navigational depth requirements and the limitation of navigational space due to morphological alternations [2] led to the construction of training walls and groynes [3,4] plus capital dredging [5]. Those anthropogenic interventions minimized the natural fluctuations in the position and dimensions of the two-channel system and permanently constrained the marine traffic to the main channel.

Morphology of estuaries and tidal inlet is governed by a complex combination of influences [6]. Roelvink and Reniers [7] question the scale/degree to which an estuarine bathymetry is forced by its own boundaries, such as dikes, headlands, unerodable layers, natural or man-made constraints. The most intrusive bathymetrical pattern is the appearance of tidal channels and shoals. Each estuary and tidal inlet has an individual arrangement of tidal features based on its forcing [8]. Nevertheless, large-scale features, such as the main channel(s), dividing shoals or branching side-channels, can be found commonly [9,10].

The advances in numerical modeling software [10–13] and rising computational capacity allow detailed morphodynamic investigations [7,14] and long-term morphodynamic simulations [15–17]. With these capacities given, it is now feasible to investigate reasons of the development of a two-channel system and morphodynamic alternations.

Contrary to systems like the Western Scheldt [18,19], not many numerical studies about the morphodynamics of the Weser Estuary have been published. Herrling et al. [20] investigated the present morphodynamics of the Weser Estuary with Delft3D, focusing on present day morphodynamics by assessing the feedback of sub- and intertidal area to the hydrodynamic drivers. Recently, the studies of Hesse [21] and Lojek [22] applied Delft3D for the Weser Estuary dealing with the estuarine turbidity maximum and storm surge influence on critical infrastructure, respectively. Models for simulation of sediment transport dynamics are used by the German Federal Waterways Engineering and Research Institute for environmental impact assessments, but these studies are seldomly published. For example, Kösters and Winter [23] used the model system Untrim [24] to simulate the transport of cohesive sediment of the Weser.

The key characteristic of the Weser Estuary is the two-channel system. The cause for this and its development is, however, poorly understood. Due to the many man-made interventions, an investigation of the natural behavior cannot be based on observations in the last century. Numerical modeling can, however, be used to explore the morphological development of the two-channel system by natural forcing. By imposing various forcing conditions, we can identify the mechanisms that are responsible for the two-channel system.

Previous studies have focused on the schematic reproduction of the natural long-term morphodynamic development of channels in geometrically constrained estuaries [18,19,25]. However, the Weser Estuary is different, as it is geometrically less constrained. The spatial range of possible channel patterns is larger and less intuitive. The aim of this study is to get insight into the driving factors responsible for the development and location of the two-channel system in the Outer Weser Estuary.

In order to achieve the defined goals of this study, three research questions are addressed:

1. Do, and if so, when do the simulations of the morphodynamics of the Weser estuary reach a morphological equilibrium?
2. Do two channels develop in the simulations, and if so, where (west vs. middle vs. east)?
3. Is one of the channels more dominant than the other and does it switch over time?

Study Area

The Weser estuary is one of the four German estuaries and is located in the German Bight. The estuarine part of the Weser is divided into the landward Lower Weser and the seaward Outer Weser and marks the entrance to the ports of Bremerhaven, Nordenhamm, Brake and Bremen (Figure 1). The freshwater discharge at the southern side has an annual average of 325 m^3/s and is rather constant over time. The Lower Weser is relatively narrow, while the Outer Weser shows a funnel shape that opens wide in the northwestern direction toward the North Sea. The sediments in the Outer Weser are mainly composed of fine sand, mixed with 5–20% of silt and clay at the surrounding tidal flats and locally, on the tidal flats close to the coastline, fine sand is mixed with >50% clay and silt (Geopotenzial Deutsche Nordsee [26]). The channel of the Lower and Outer Weser are mainly composed of fine and medium sand [27]. The estuarine morphology of the Weser shows the remarkable two-channel system in the Outer Weser and is still changing continuously [3]. Adjacently located to the Weser estuary is the Jade Bay, an almost parallel tidal inlet with no significant freshwater discharge. The Weser estuary channels are used for navigational purposes. In the past, the two-channel system showed a more pronounced main channel and a side channel with alternating behavior. For navigational purposes, starting 1917, training walls and groynes were constructed (indicated in yellow in Figure 1), stopping the alternation between the two channels and marking the end of a natural two-channel system [2,28]. These changes result in intensive maintenance dredging activities [29]. The constructions, channel deepening and maintenance dredging led to an increase of the tidal range from 0.3 m to almost 4 m at Bremen-Vegesack [28]. More information about the historical phenomena, the natural behavior and human interventions can be found in [2,4,28,30].

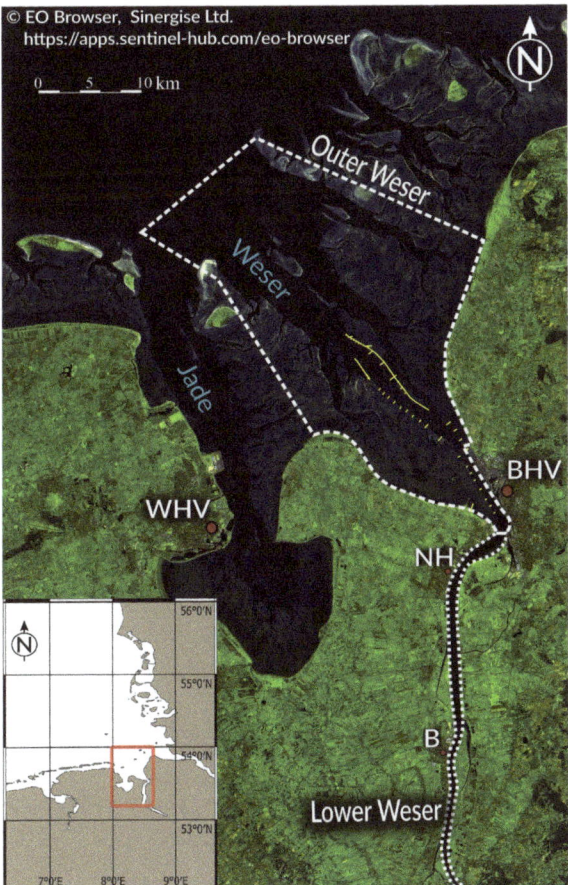

Figure 1. The Weser Estuary divided into the Outer Weser the Lower Weser and the adjacent Jade Bay. The cities of Bremerhaven (BHV), Nordenhamm (NH), Brake (B) and Wilhelmshaven (WHV) are indicated on the map for reference. The small map (Open Street Map) gives the location of the Weser Estuary in the German Bight and the satellite image taken from Copernicus Sentinel-2 (ESA) shows the present channel and shoal pattern in the Outer Weser with the constructed training walls and groynes marked in yellow.

2. Materials and Methods

2.1. The Flat-Bed Approach

Process-based flat-bed models have been widely applied for the production of channel and shoal patterns in tidal inlets and geometrically constrained estuaries [16,18,19,31]. This study differs from the previous ones in the sense that a wide estuary is modeled here and the applied model is steered by simplified boundary conditions.

In the application of a schematized Delft3D model, special attention is paid to the initiation of the model. For undisturbed natural morphological development, the influence of a discrete bathymetry needs to be minimized in order to allow unconstrained development. This is achieved by applying a flat bed as initial bathymetry [18,19]. The estuarine geometry is based on the available historical charts and kept fixed for the base case simulation.

2.2. Sediment Transport Formulation

In this study, Delft3D [32] is applied. Delft3D is a process-based model, including the FLOW- (for hydrodynamics) and MOR- (for morphodynamics) modules, which are essential for this study. The Delft3D-FLOW module is based on the Reynolds-averaged Navier–Stokes equations under the assumption of incompressible fluids, shallow water and Boussinesq approximation. These are solved on a curvilinear/structured grid with an implicit finite-difference scheme (as default), as shown by [32] and described in the manual [33].

Sediment transport is based on the Engelund–Hansen equation [34], which considers the total transport load as bedload transport only and is a good approximation for transport of noncohesive sediments as shown by prior studies [13,18,35]. Additionally, Reyns et al. [36] showed that the Engelund–Hansen transport formula works well in combination with the so-called MorFac approach [11], which will be discussed later. The bed elevation is dynamically updated at each hydrodynamic time step.

For bedload transport, bed slope effects can be considered by the factors α_{bs} (in local flow direction) and α_{bn} (normal to the local flow direction) as proposed by Bagnold [37] and Ikeda [38]. The bed slope factor in local flow direction α_{bs} is kept constant with the default value of 1 due to its limited influence [39] and will be not discussed further. However, the additional normal transport vector as presented by van Rijn [40] is a sensitive tuning parameter, which has a considerable influence on the developing morphology [41]. It is defined as:

$$\vec{S}_{b,n} = |S'_b| \alpha_{bn} \frac{u_{b,cr}}{|\vec{u}_b|} \frac{\partial z_b}{\partial n} \quad (1)$$

with $\vec{S}_{b,n}$ being the additional transport vector calculated by S'_b, the initial transport vector, α_{bn}, the user-defined coefficient for calibration, $u_{b,cr}$, the critical near-bed flow velocity, $\vec{u}_b$, the near-bed flow velocity and $\frac{\partial z_b}{\partial n}$, the bed slope normal to the flow direction.

The additional transport vector resulting from the calibrated α_{bn} value can compensate for artificially created steep slopes, too deep and narrow channels, which are caused by missing processes in the model formulations (e.g., avalanching mechanisms), simplified transport equations and potential numerical effects [42]. In particular, when simulating long-term morphodynamic development of channel and shoals in combination with morphological acceleration factors, as discussed later, the determination of the additional transport vector gains importance [18,43]. A detailed analysis of the function and effects of the slope factors is presented by Baar et al. [41]. By increasing α_{bn}, the bedload transport normal to the local flow direction is increased, leading to a generally smoother channel pattern. Following this tendency, high α_{bn} values might restrict realistic development of channels due to refilling from the channel banks. Therefore, α_{bn} should be chosen and treated carefully.

Additionally, as α_{bn} only influences the bedload transport, it has a different order of magnitude for the Engelund–Hansen transport formula, with 100% of the transport considered as bedload, in comparison to the van Rijn transport formula, where only about 10% of the transport is bedload [43]. For the Engelund–Hansen transport formula, applied in this study, a calibrated α_{bn} value of 7.5 is used in all simulations.

For the purpose of acceleration in the morphological development a morphological factor (MorFac) is used [11,12]. The MorFac accelerates morphological changes by multiplying the erosion and deposition fluxes per computational time-step with a constant or time varying value [33]. To speed up morphological simulations, various techniques can be used, based on the difference in time scales between the hydrodynamics and the morphodynamic response [44]. Simplifications can be made by schematizing the tide [44] or by using ensemble techniques to model the tides [45]. These studies indicate that reducing the tidal signal to a single tidal constituent is not sufficient. We therefore apply multiple tidal constituents in this study. Here, we follow the approach of the morphological factor as proposed by Roelvink [11] and later on used in other studies as well, e.g., [16,18,19,35,42]. In this approach, the bed level update per time step is multiplied by a factor, the so-called morphological factor. The approach is based on the assumption that the timing of the morphological change on intratidal scale is of minor importance. This implies that computing n times ebb flow and then n times flood flow results in the same morphology as computing n full tides (see Ranasinghe et al. [12] for a more detailed explanation).

Studies have shown that, depending on the application, a MorFac of up to 1000 can be used to simulate long-term morphodynamic development [36]. The attempt for a critical MorFac definition [12,36] resulted in a formula, inspired by the Courant condition, that relates the propagation speed of bed forms to the available cell size. For applications similar to the present one, MorFacs of up to 300 and 400 are documented [16,18,19].

Calculating a critical MorFac according to [36] leads to a critical MorFac in the order of 800, which is a high value in general. In this study, a MorFac of 400 is applied. Increasing/decreasing the MorFac corresponds with increasing/decreasing the time step for morphological modeling. Therefore, this numerical parameter needs to be selected based on requirements: A valid MorFac has to be small enough to satisfy two requirements related to respectively stability and accuracy of the simulations.

Regarding stability, MorFac values much larger than the chosen one may result into model instabilities meaning a violation of the stability criterion. The consequence of violating the stability requirement is that simulations cannot be carried out until the end. This can be an issue, especially with particular artificial initial conditions. An additional morphological stability criterion, the development of a morphological equilibrium, can be introduced. In this study, the morphological equilibrium is essential, in accordance with the investigation approach.

Regarding the accuracy criterion, it needs to be ensured that a further decrease of the MorFac will not affect model results. This prevents using a MorFac that overestimates sediment transport, leading to deeper channels, more exposed flats and less intertidal area.

The given MorFac value is applicable if the simulation is stable, a morphodynamic equilibrium develops and the resulting channel and shoal distribution does not vary significantly when applying smaller MorFacs. These aspects are analyzed by calculating the development of hypsometric curves of the model domain over time for the different MorFacs applied (50, 100, 200 and 400). Figure 2a presents the range of the resulting development of the hypsometric curves integrated over the model domain and plotted over time. Here, the same depth contour lines (indicated by the colors in Figure 2a are calculated in their cumulative percentage of appearance in the model domain (y-axis) for each of the MorFacs over time (x-axis). The span of the same contour lines between the different MorFacs is filled with the respective color (rather than the span of the depth range as typically seen). Additionally, the individual contour lines of the specific depths for the MorFac 400 are highlighted. The hypsometry starts with an unrealistic, artificial pattern, based on the uniform initial depth. During the MorFac simulations, each develops a channel and shoal pattern, changing the hypsometry in a similar way (small colored spans). At the end, a realistic distribution of the total area to different depth ranges is established, representing a realistic hypsometry. Figure 2b shows the individual hypsometric curves for the evaluated MorFacs after 2000 years of development as the cumulative percentage appearance (y-axis) of the developed depths (x-axis). The variations in the hypsometric development in Figure 2a are generally small with a local maximum of around 10%. Differences in the hypsometric curve at the end of the evaluation in Figure 2b are minimal. Hence, a decrease of the MorFac does not give different model results. Additionally, Figure 2a,b show a realistic hypsometry developed for all tested MorFacs. Thus, the accuracy requirements are fulfilled for the MorFac 400.

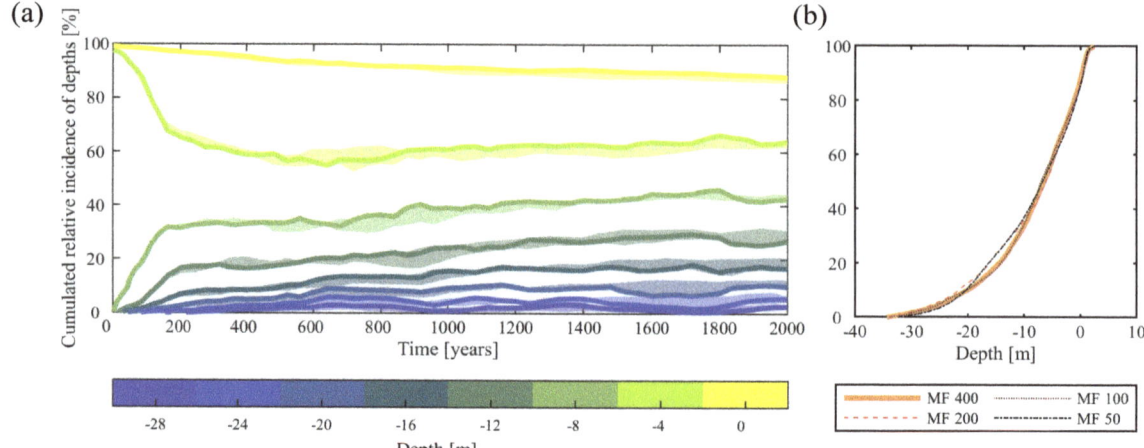

Figure 2. Validation of the morphological factor by (**a**) the development of cumulative relative incident (in [%]) of depth contour lines as the colored span of contour lines from the MorFacs 400, 200, 100, 50 (MorFac 400 in thick) and (**b**) the individual hypsometric curves after 2000 years.

2.3. Model Set-Up

A curvilinear rectangular grid is generated covering the Jade-Weser estuary from Bremen-Vegesack to a few kilometers into the North Sea (see Figure 3). Model boundaries are aligned to the historical land boundaries, which resemble the overall shape of the present ones. The grid cell resolution varies from around 10^3 m in the most outer North Sea part and around 10^2 m in the inner part of the model domain. The latter resolution is present in the area of interest. Both resolutions are based on the length scales of the channel and shoal features that can be found in the Weser estuary historically and at present.

The initial depth has a value of 7.34 m and is determined by the mean water depth of the Jade-Weser-area from a historical chart of the year 1878.

The model is steered by two open boundaries: The tidal constituents O1, K1, M2, S2, M4, MS4 and M6 on the northern model domain side and a constant river discharge on the southern end. The amplitudes and phases of the tidal constituents along the open boundary are extracted from a larger model (Jade-Weser-Elbe-Model) maintained by the Federal Waterway Engineering and Research Institute [46]. It is assumed that this tidal signal is representative for the historical tidal regime, based on the findings of schematized model studies [18,31]. The river discharge is 325 $\frac{m^3}{s}$ in alignment with the yearly averaged fresh water discharge historically [30] and at present [3].

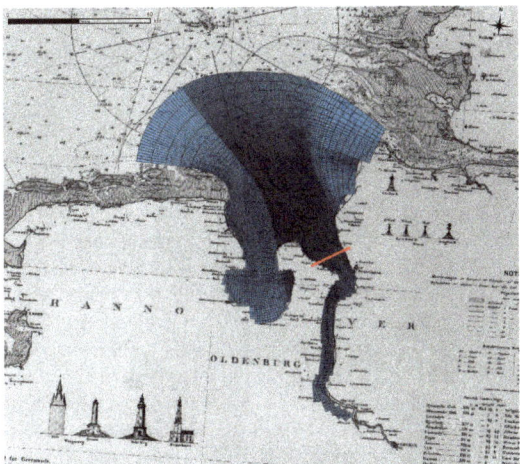

Figure 3. Model domain and grid—created on the basis of historical maps—with a background map from 1862. The cross-section 75, which is essential for the results and discussed later, is marked in red.

One noncohesive sediment fraction was used, as it was used in similar studies [18,19]. A 200 µm sand is in good agreement with the dominating sediment fraction in the Outer Weser area based on the data available in Geopotenzial Deutsche Nordsee [47]. The available sediment thickness varies between 25 and 35 m and is limited by a non-erodible Holocene layer [47].

2.4. Scenario Composition

A classification of estuaries from Boyd et al. [48] considers three main influences that shape an estuary: tides, waves and river discharge. For the German Bight, Kösters and Winter [23] looked at different combinations of tides, wind stress and waves to investigate resulting bottom shear stresses and morphodynamic changes. Furthermore, Herrling et al. [20] analyzed the effect of tides, wind-induced waves and currents as well as swells for the Outer Weser estuary. Their results suggest that the influence of wind stress and waves on the main channel morphodynamics can be neglected considering the schematization of this study. However, Herrling et al. [20] found that locally generated wind waves are influencing the morphodynamics of the inter- and supratidal area, which should be kept in mind, when looking at the results of this study. Nevertheless, these are not considered due to the anticipated spatial scale of this study and the simplified investigation approach. Therefore, five scenarios are defined (see Table 1).

Table 1. Scenario Composition Synthesis: Listing of the scenarios selected for investigation on the left, based on the different aspects of the tides and river discharge that are potentially responsible for the formation of a two-channel system. The affiliation of the scenarios to either tides or discharge is indicated by the dots within the columns in the middle, followed by a description of the effects the scenario en- or disables, respectively.

Scenario	Tides	Discharge	Description
No Kelvin Wave	•		No phase shift in the tidal constituents at the open boundary.
No Coriolis	•		No Coriolis effect included by setting the model latitude to zero.
Increased Tides	•		110% amplitude for tidal constituents (seasonal/long-term effects).
No Discharge		•	A constant discharge of 0 $\frac{m^3}{s}$ at the southern open boundary.
Max. Discharge		•	A constantly high discharge of 2000 $\frac{m^3}{s}$ is defined.

The funnel shape of the Weser estuary and previous studies [3,20,23] suggest that tides play the most important role in the morphodynamic development of the shoals and channels. Hence, special attention is paid to the tides. Two parts of the tides potentially influence the development of two-channel systems. The first part is the strength of the tides as such or relative to the river discharge. Variations in the tidal amplitude, based on seasonal or long-term effects, could lead to multiple conditions that are present for a limited time and individually support a western or an eastern channel in the Outer Weser Estuary, respectively. If each condition stabilizes a channel one site, the two-channel system could be based on two alternating tidal conditions (tidal range). Thus, by comparing a scenario simulation with a 10% increased tidal amplitude to the simulation with 0% increase (base case), it can be revealed if this hypothesis is true for the Outer Weser Estuary. Second, the spatial appearance based on deflections of the tides inside the estuary can lead to more pronounced channels on different sides of the estuary. Two main deflections are considered here: the Kelvin wave and the Coriolis effect. The latter deflects flows to the right, as the Weser Estuary is located at 53° north. The Kelvin wave is a result of this Coriolis-based deflection in the North Sea basin where a circular tidal wave propagation forms [49]. It causes a phase shift of the tidal wave in the German Bight, and thus at the offshore boundary of the Outer Weser. Both deflections might influence the location of a more dominant channel by pushing the ebb flow, flood flow or river discharge toward one side of the estuarine land boundaries. Consequently, a simulation without the Coriolis effect and one without the phase shift at the open boundary should reveal their effects on the two-channel system, respectively, when comparing their results to the base case simulation results, where both influences are included.

Additionally, two extreme river discharge cases are added to the scenario list.

The listed effects will be investigated in a three-step routine. First, the model setup is adapted such that the effect is included or not included. Second, a simulation is run. Third, the results of the scenario simulation are compared to the base case simulation, revealing the influence of the selected scenario on the channel and shoal development.

2.5. Postprocessing Methods

The development of the two-channel system and the corresponding morphological state is investigated by analyzing the temporal development of a cross-section regarding the dominance of western, eastern or middle channels. A novel method is to quantify the dominance of certain channel–shoal patterns in cross-sections (correlation analysis of (cross-)section evolution—CASE method). A small number (n) of cross-section types is determined from the baseline simulation (Figure 4a, with three exemplary cases) representing distinctive channel–shoal patterns with a certain feature, or a certain type of channel–shoal pattern. Each distinctive cross-section type defines a case, resulting in n cases that can optionally be organized in groups of equal channel–shoal pattern types (Figure 4b, with (blue = western dominance, yellow = equal dominance and red = eastern dominance)). All available cross-sections from different scenarios and/or different points in time are then correlated to these cases (schematized in Figure 4c), leading to n correlation coefficients between −1 and 1 for each point in time (Figure 4d). Based on the cross-section type with the maximum correlation, the dominant channel–shoal pattern is determined (Figure 4e). The degree of resemblance is further indicated by the correlation value (e.g., visualized by color intensity). This method is applied here to an exemplary cross-section, which lies within the center of the area in which the two channels occur (see Figure 3). From the base case scenario simulation, nine cross-section types are chosen (see Figure 4). Each of the nine cross-section corresponds to a morphological state of western channel dominance, equal channel dominance or eastern channel dominance (3 types each category). The base case is used for the definition of the cases due to its comparability with the scenario simulations. With this method, a time series of cross-sections is translated to a time series of dominance types for each scenario.

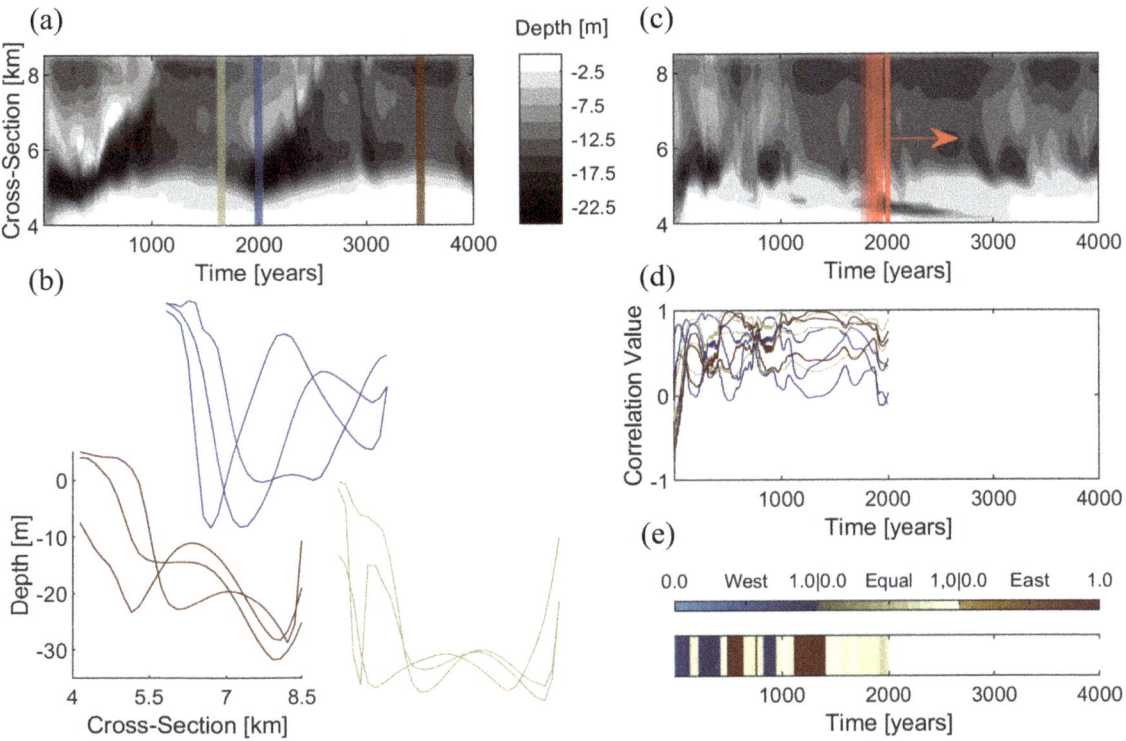

Figure 4. Graphical description of the CASE method with (**a**) the selection of representative cases, (**b**) the final nine cases for this study, (**c**) the correlation analysis over time, (**d**) the resulting correlation values and (**e**) the final result, where the morphological state is presented over time with the corresponding case (color) and its correlation value (color intensity).

To visually compare the temporal development of the two-channel system in the different scenarios, Hovmöller diagrams [50] are used which display the cross-section depths over time. Above each of those diagrams, a bar plot indicating the dominant two-channel type and the strength of the correlation calculated with the CASE method is displayed. The channel dominance categories are visualized by different colors (green for western, red for eastern and light yellow for equal dominance). Additionally, by showing the corresponding cross-correlation values through color intensity, plausibility of the respective category is indicated. With this approach of combining Hovmöller plots with results of the CASE method, a visual inspection of the temporal development of each scenario is combined with a quantitative classification of the corresponding morphological states.

3. Results

3.1. Base Case

The results of the base case simulation show a good representation in the Outer Weser estuary. A two-channel system clearly develops (see Figure 5) and remains morphodynamically active. The locations and depths of the channel are reasonable compared to naval charts. For the base case simulation, the criteria for morphodynamic equilibrium are reached after 650 years (the product of the hydrodynamic time and the MorFac) according to Figure 6. The results in Figure 6 are based on the hypsometric development of the area of interest (visualized in Figure 5b–f) and the cumulative bedload transport of the representative cross-section (indicated in Figure 3). Thus, for the base case, the first two research questions stated in the introduction can be confirmed.

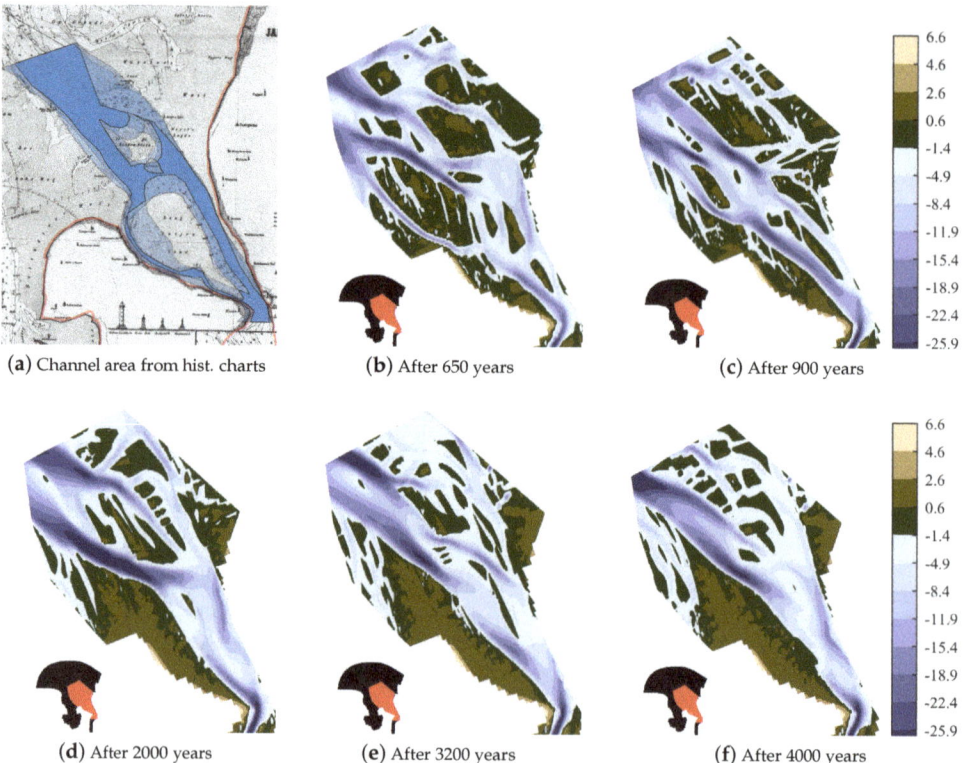

Figure 5. Simulation results of the base case. In (**a**), the locations of the tidal channel system from three historical charts (1812, 1859, 1870) are intersected. In (**b**–**f**), results of the morphological simulations are shown for different years, with channel depths in blue and shoals in earth colors.

The equilibrium point is shown in Figure 5b, where a number of side channels exist in addition to the two main channels. Afterward, the established two-channel system remains morphodynamically active and switches between two clearly separated channels (Figure 5c,e) and two almost unified channels (Figure 5d,f). Furthermore, an alternation of the location of the deepest channel can be found in the results, which connects to the third research question. Figure 7 visualizes the alternation applying the CASE method. Looking at the reversed Hovmöller diagram, the western channel is more prominent. Additionally, a channel and shoal scheme is present repetitively. First, a deep and wide channel develops on the western side (beginning–1200 years, 1850–2600 years and 3000–3100 years), followed by the development of an eastern channel (1250–1700 years, 2800–2950 years and 3200–3800 years), which becomes more dominant as the western channel becomes shallower at the same time. With respect to the third research question, there is a more dominant channel and even an alternation of the latter is found. This is approved by the correlation analysis (top of Figure 7), where the recurrent pattern of the prevailing western dominance (green) and eastern dominance (red) is illustrated. Additionally, there are periods where neither of the channels is more dominant (yellow). Overall, correlation values are high (>0.75) after initiation.

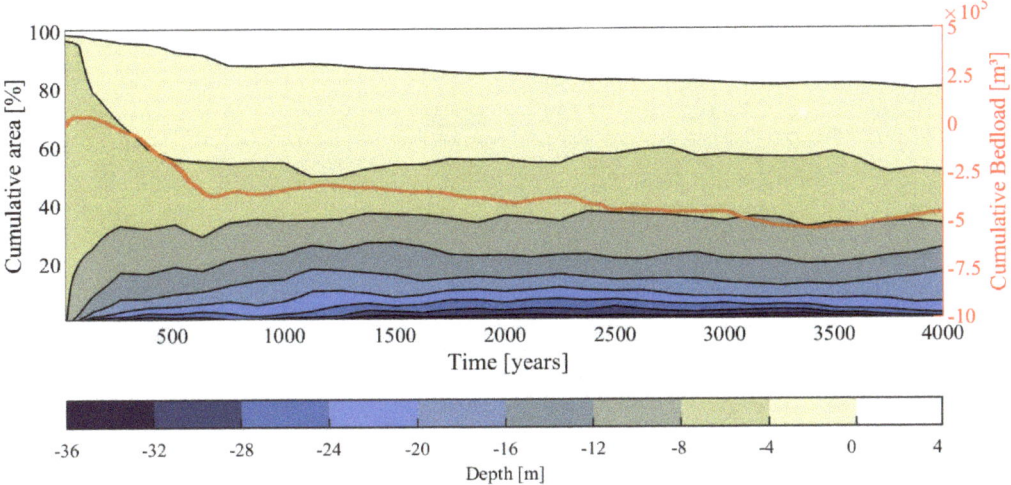

Figure 6. Development of the hypsometry over time in the area of interest (**left** y-axis) combined with the cumulative bedload transport over time (**right** y-axis). Both trajectories tend to become linear over time which is considered to prove morphodynamic equilibrium.

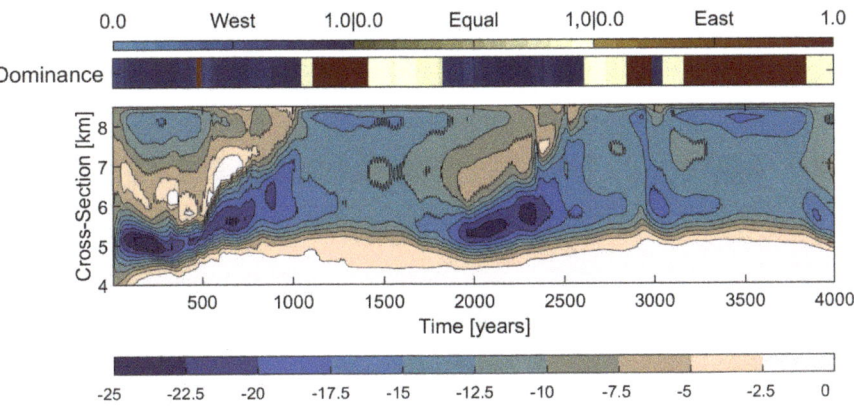

Figure 7. Depth of the investigated cross-section over time, showing the alternation of the two-channel system. The channel dominance calculated by the CASE method is displayed above, greenish colors indicating western dominance, reddish colors indicating eastern dominance and brownish indicating a balanced two-channel system, the shading within each color indicating the strength of the correlation.

As all research questions are answered positively, the influences of the predefined forcings (Section 2.4) are investigated.

3.2. Effects of Varying Tide

The effects of the tidal scenarios are presented according to the research questions and results are summarized by applying the CASE method (Figure 8). For the bathymetric development of the scenarios, see the Appendix A.

First, all three scenarios reach a morphological equilibrium and show a clear two-channel system developing (Figure 8). Comparing the two-channel systems developing in the tidal scenarios with the base case reveals similarities with respect to the general two-channel system and the formation and variation of deeper channels. However, comparing the location and dynamic alternation of the deepest channel to the base case results shows considerable variations. In a nutshell, the first two research questions are answered positively and by elaborating on the third question differences can be identified more clearly.

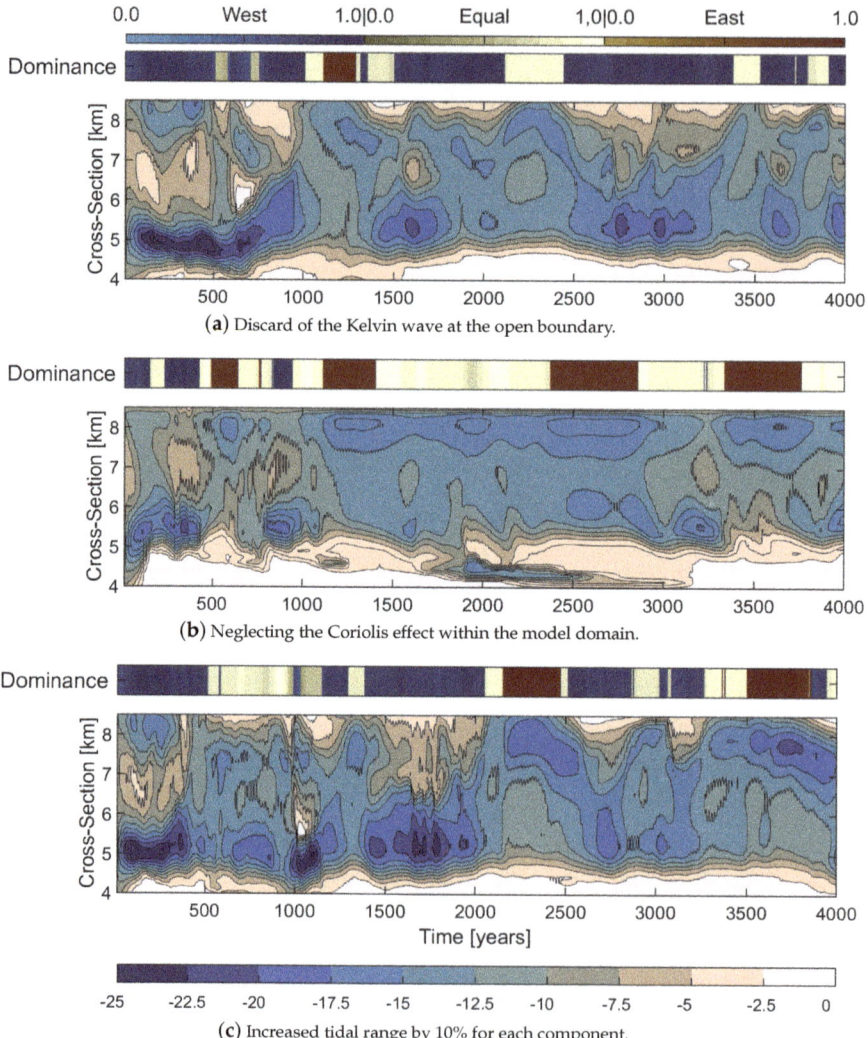

Figure 8. Two-channel system alternation for the tidal scenario simulations (description, see Figure 7).

Starting with the location of the deepest channel, the no Kelvin wave scenario shows a more distinct western channel (Figure 8a). The opposite holds true for the no Coriolis scenario (Figure 8b). Additionally, a mixed development is seen in the increased tidal range scenario (Figure 8b): Although the deeper channel can be found on the western side most of the time, the channel and domination pattern is more mixed compared to the other scenarios. Next, the dynamics of the domination pattern are found: In the no Kelvin wave scenario, an almost regular alternation is established, mainly between western and equal dominance (Figure 8a). An alternation period of 500–1000 years is shown. The absence of the Coriolis effect leads to a more stable eastern channel and less frequent alternations between eastern and equal dominance (Figure 8b). Lastly, an increased tidal forcing creates a more frequent and expansive alternation (Figure 8c). Especially between 1500–2650 years and after, a complete shift of the dominance from west to east develops.

3.3. Effects of Varying Discharge

Similar to the tidal scenarios, the river discharge scenarios both reach a morphological equilibrium and show a two-channel system (Figure 9). However, with respect to the base case, the results of the two simulation reveal significant differences. For the scenario without any discharge (Figure 9a), periodically, a two-channel system develops and disappears when only one channel is present only. This is the western channel for the majority of the simulation period. The scenario with extreme discharge (Figure 9b) reveals a two-channel system that almost unifies into one large channel for a limited period but then divides into two clear channels.

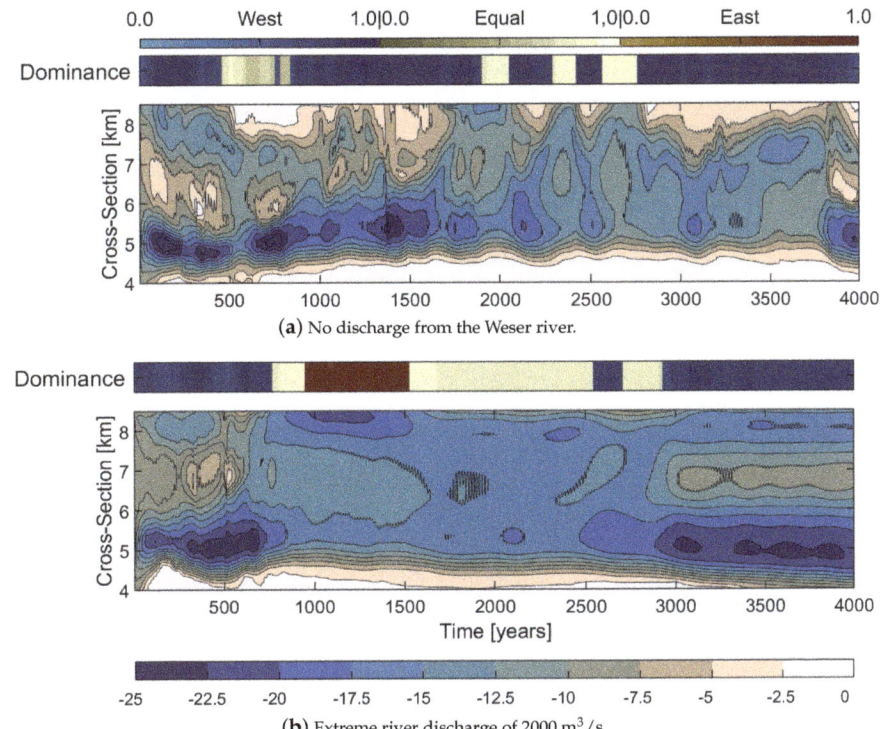

Figure 9. Alternation of the two-channel system for the river discharge scenario simulations (description, see Figure 7).

Accordingly, the alternation is relatively slow for both cases, especially for the extreme discharge scenario. Here, the CASE method indicates that there is one full alternation of channel dominance only in 4000 years. The cross-sectional plot supports this finding as described previously. In the no discharge scenario, some alternating features can be found even though the dominance does not fully alternate. Additionally, due to general orientation of the channels toward the west in combination with the established channel on the western side, a clear alternation is seen from 1750 to 3000 years. This observation is supported by the recurrent pattern in the cross-correlation revealed by the CASE method.

3.4. Synthesis

Figure 10 shows the CASE method results for all scenarios, indicating the influence of the forcing on the two-channel system. Two aspects are included in Figure 10 for each simulation: first, the individual distribution of channel dominance in the two-channel system, and second, the resulting alternation activity (counts of changes between morphological states). The alternation activity is not necessarily referred to full alternations from western to eastern dominance and back. By comparing both aspects for the scenarios with the base case, conclusions can be drawn about the increase or decrease of either channel or alternation presence.

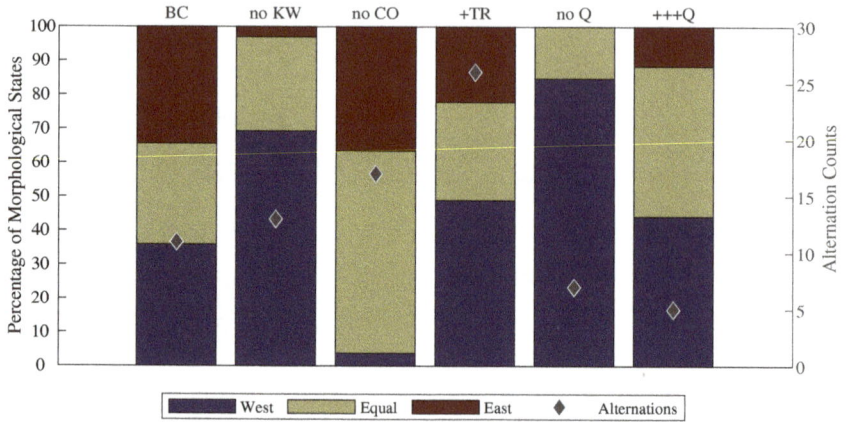

Figure 10. Comparison of the occurrence of channel dominance distribution (%) per scenario. With BC = base case, no KW = no Kelvin wave, no CO = no Coriolis effect, +TR = increased tidal range, no Q = no river discharge and +++Q = extreme river discharge. The number of alternations (changes between morphological states) is shown by the blue diamonds.

An enhanced eastern channel can be found when the influence of the Kelvin wave and the mean river discharge are included (as no Kelvin wave or no discharge show less or no percentage of eastern channel dominance). Thus, both influences have the potential to significantly increase the presence of eastern channel dominance. The opposite holds true for the effects of Coriolis (when Coriolis is actually included like it is in the base case), an increased tidal range and extreme river discharge, as indicated by the higher percentage of the green bars in Figure 10. Hence, the western channel is supported by these three effects.

The enhancement of one of the two channels correlates with a decreased alternation activity. The base case, where Coriolis and the Kelvin wave are included, has a lower alternation count compared to the simulations, where these effects are disabled. Extreme river discharge leads to even less changes in the morphological state as for the base case. Higher alternation activity is found with an increased tidal range and with mean river discharge (no river discharge compared to the mean discharge of the base case). However, the increase in alternation activity of the increased tidal range is considerably higher, compared to the mean river discharge. These findings will be discussed below.

4. Discussion

The base case simulation shows the development of a two-channel system and its morphodynamic activity over a period of 4000 years. Within a period of 650 years, a morphodynamic equilibrium is established and remains at its state from that point onward. Both aspects, the development of a two-channel system and reaching morphodynamic equilibrium, imply a successful application of the modeling approach described in Section 2.1. A comparison with nautical charts (from the time before human interventions changed the morphology of the Weser estuary) reveals that the extent and the migration area of the individual channels is plausible. However, the exact location and dimensions of the individual channels differ to some degree from the observed ones, which is presumably caused by the simplicity of the modeling approach. A key disparity is that the channels generally tend to become too deep in comparison with documented bathymetries, which is a known issue for Delft3D models as discussed by [42]. Nevertheless, the reasonable results of the base case allow the execution of the designed scenarios.

Here, the variety of developed two-channel systems offers valuable insight into the impact of several parameters on morphodynamic development. The synthesis of all scenario results in the conclusion that the development of the two-channel system is mainly caused by the relation of tides and river discharge in combination with the basin geometry. This is in alignment with the hypothesis given in Section 2.4. The relation of tides and discharge can be interpreted as the tides being the main driver and decisive for the formation of the channels. A strong indicator for this reasoning is the result of the no river discharge scenario, where a two-channel system is found based on the tidal forcing only. Due to the absence of river discharge, the western channel establishes stronger than the eastern channel as indicated by the CASE method in Figure 9a.

Thus, in order to get a two-channel system with equally deep channels, it takes a combination of tides and river discharge. The results of the increased tidal range scenario and extreme discharge verify this finding (Figure 10 and Figure A2). The results of the various scenarios reveal a trend: the more tides are dominating over discharge (+ tidal range, Figure 10), the more a western channel develops, while more discharge favors the development of an eastern channel. However, this only applies as long as Coriolis is included, causing a reflection of the incoming tidal wave to the right. This holds true for the extreme discharge scenario as well; however, it can neither be seen in Figure 10 nor in the CASE method results. The reason is that the extreme discharge scenario creates a stable two-channel system, where the eastern channel becomes dominant further offshore of the selected cross-section (see Figure A2e,f), and is thus not covered by the CASE method.

The dependence of the well-established western channel on the Coriolis effect implies that the flood flow is deflected to the western side and the ebb flow to the eastern side, causing the two-channel system with a flood channel in the west and an ebb channel in the east. The results of the scenario simulation neglecting the Coriolis effect, where the eastern channel is more pronounced, would support this reasoning. Additionally, the comparison between the no discharge scenario and the base case simulation (with average discharge) agrees with the latter observations, as the consequently larger magnitude of offshore directed flow (deflected to the eastern side by the Coriolis effect) results in a stronger eastern channel. Following this reasoning, the no discharge scenario shows that ebb flow alone is strong enough to create the eastern channel. However, the depth averaged velocities calculated in the two channels do not support the argumentation of a flood and ebb channel, as their magnitudes are almost identical ($<< +/- 10\%$). This is in alignment with the present two-channel system, which cannot be divided into a flood and an ebb channel, too.

Furthermore, the investigated aspects of the tides alone are found not to be the main driver for the development of a two-channel system as all scenario simulations develop a two-channel system (Figure 8). Figure 10 shows that the Kelvin wave supports the generation of a more eastern-dominated pattern, whereas the Coriolis effect results in an enhanced western channel. This behavior is reasonable as the incoming tides approach the east side of the Outer Weser due to the northwestern-originated Kelvin-wave-based inertia.

Although validation of the scenario simulations remains challenging due to their conceptualized character, the justification criteria applied for the base case holds true for the scenario simulations as well. All simulations reach a morphodynamic equilibrium and the developed morphology is reasonable, although channels tend to be too deep. The influence of the basin geometry is not part of this research but raises interesting research questions.

Another remarkable finding is a variety of alternation patterns (Figures 7–9) and periods (Figure 10). These depend on the domination of the tides (with respect to river discharge) and the depth of the channels. The first aspect is shown by the trend in Figure 10, where an increased tidal range increases alternation, followed by mean river discharge, which increases alternation based on the domination of tides and the more equally established two-channel system. If the tidal flow is overruled by extreme river discharge, alternation is reduced. Additionally, if one channel is more pronounced, it takes more time to alter as seen for the Kelvin wave and Coriolis effect. As fascinating as the alternation results are, a justified quantification remains challenging, almost impossible for two reasons. First, as mentioned earlier, the channel depth is overestimated in all simulations. As this is relevant for the alternation period, the resulting alternation periods are probably overestimated as well. Second, the alternation dynamics shown in Figure 10 are based on the CASE method with one cross-section analyzed, leading to a local observation. Additionally, by selecting the representative cases from the base case simulation for the CASE method, the channel and shoal patterns are simplified and therefore less accurate, despite high cross-correlation values.

In reports, alternation periods have been described varying between 20 and 120 years [4,28,30]. Compared to the time span of an alternation in Figures 7–9, these are rather short periods, whereas the simulated alternation periods are up to ten times longer. Thus, a comprehensive analysis of the causes and reasons for the alternation does not seem to be feasible with the modeling approach chosen.

To put our results into perspective, we compared them with results from similar studies of other systems. Two studies on the Western Scheldt Estuary, Netherlands [18,19] and one on the Qiangtangjiang Estuary, China [51] are considered. The comparison shows similarities, but it also reveals the importance of accounting for the specific signatures of each study site. Similarities are found in the development of a morphological equilibrium and the dependence of the locations of channel and shoals on the estuarine geometry. The studies at both systems indicate a strong influence of the basin geometry on the results of the large scale tidal channel and/or bar developments. Furthermore, Dam et al. [19] and Yu et al. [51] found that a morphological equilibrium is reached in both estuaries. Moreover, the estimated time span for reaching a morphological equilibrium has a comparable order of magnitude as the time spans determined in this study.

Partly similar results are found for the influence of river discharge on the model result. For the Qiangtangjiang Estuary [51], it was found that a channel and shoal pattern develops, even if no discharge is imposed. This is in agreement with the results shown in Section 3.3. Nevertheless, a dependence of the offshore shoal extent on the river discharge as indicated by Yu et al. [51] cannot be identified in this study. However, the average discharge in the Qiangtangjiang Estuary is an order of magnitude larger compared to the Weser Estuary and the investigation of Yu et al. [51] is more schematized (an idealized funnel shape). In the Western Scheldt Estuary [18], river discharge affects the development of the channel and shoal system in a way similar to that in our study. However, van der Wegen and Roelvink [18] found that an extreme river discharge enhances the ebb channel, unlike in this study, where there is still a two-channel system at almost the same location as for normal or no river discharge. The explanation for this difference could be the more restricted geometry of the Western Scheldt. Additionally, the deviation in ebb and flood channels is not applicable for the results in this study as discussed before.

The alternation of a more dominant channel within a two-channel system appears to be unique for the Weser Estuary and has not been detected or described in any of the previous studies. Furthermore, the influence of the Coriolis effect, the Kelvin wave and an increased tidal range has not been investigated by one of the three other studies [18,19,51].

The flat bed approach in combination with a high MorFac and simplified boundary conditions is a handy method to investigate large-scale morphodynamic features and developments with reasonable accuracy and computational effort. However, there remains some potential for optimization, which may be addressed in future research. A point that could not be improved during this research is the development of the tidal range inside the Lower Weser. While the tidal range in the area of interest meets the documented historical tidal range, the tidal range becomes too high when traveling inside the estuary compared to historical measurements. The cause for the amplified tidal range lies in the flat bed modeling approach, as there is not enough friction in the Lower Weser to damp the tidal wave during its propagation. As this is the case from the beginning, the narrow and shallow channels that are necessary to generate the needed friction cannot develop and the Lower Weser channel remains deep. An option to overcome this problem could be introducing a gradient to the initial bathymetry, but it is not possible with the same initial depth in the whole model domain. Another option mentioned in publications using the flat bed approach is the consideration of non-erodible layers [18]. As described earlier, these were applied in this study as well, but at the time, data were only available for the outer part of the model domain, and thus not available for possible model improvements in the Lower Weser.

Here, it needs to be mentioned that the analyses of the CASE method are based on one cross-section within the area of interest that has been selected as representative.

5. Conclusions

This research presents how the channel development on the Outer Weser estuary is influenced by tidal range, Coriolis effect, Kelvin wave and river discharge, based on a novel analysis of schematized long-term morphodynamic simulations. Starting with a flat bed, a morphodynamic equilibrium with a two-channel system is reached in all simulations. Differences in the developing channel and shoal patterns show that each forcing contributes more to one of the two channels than to the other. However, the two-channel system is developing as a result of the tides in combination with the basin geometry, as none of the investigated effects result in an only one-channel system, only. A classification into a flood and an ebb channel is not supported by the results. Alternation of the more dominant channel is found in the simulations, but assigning the responsible forcing remains challenging. However, it is likely that this is a result of the interaction between the tides and the basin geometry, as alternation periods are not linked to artificial time scales of the model.

Simulation results are analyzed using the correlation analysis of (cross-)section evolution (CASE) method developed in this study. It compares simulation results based on cross-section correlation and presents the morphological state over time for each simulation. The developed CASE method complements available methods for analyzing long-term channel and shoal development but should be seen as a local indicator. It might provide additional insight to further develop the CASE method to include more cross-sections. Additionally, the cases selected in the base case simulation for the correlation analysis are chosen manually and further criteria for their selection might improve the method.

Author Contributions: Conceptualization, J.G. and A.Z.; data acquisition, model setup, investigation and writing—original draft, J.G.; data acquisition, supervision and writing—editing and reviewing, A.Z., B.C.v.P. and Z.B.W. All authors have read and agreed to the published version of the manuscript.

Funding: The publication of this article was funded by the Open Access Fund of the Leibniz Universität Hannover.

Acknowledgments: This study was supported by the infrastructure of BAW. The authors want to thank for the support and comments provided by the colleagues at BAW. All figures are processed and prepared in Matlab and all color maps are taken from the scientific color maps of F. Crameri [52]. Furthermore, the authors thankfully gained ideas and supportive comments during the investigation from Sierd de Vries and feedback on the manuscript by Jan Tiede, Leon Scheiber, Christian Jordan and Zoë Vercelli.

Conflicts of Interest: The authors declare no conflict of interest.

Abbreviations

The following abbreviations are used in this manuscript:

BAW	Federal Waterways Engineering and Research Institute
DOAJ	Directory of open access journals
MDPI	Multidisciplinary Digital Publishing Institute
MORFAC	Morphological Factor
CASE	Correlation Analysis of (cross-)Section Evolution

Appendix A. Scenario Results

Appendix A.1. Tidal Scenarios

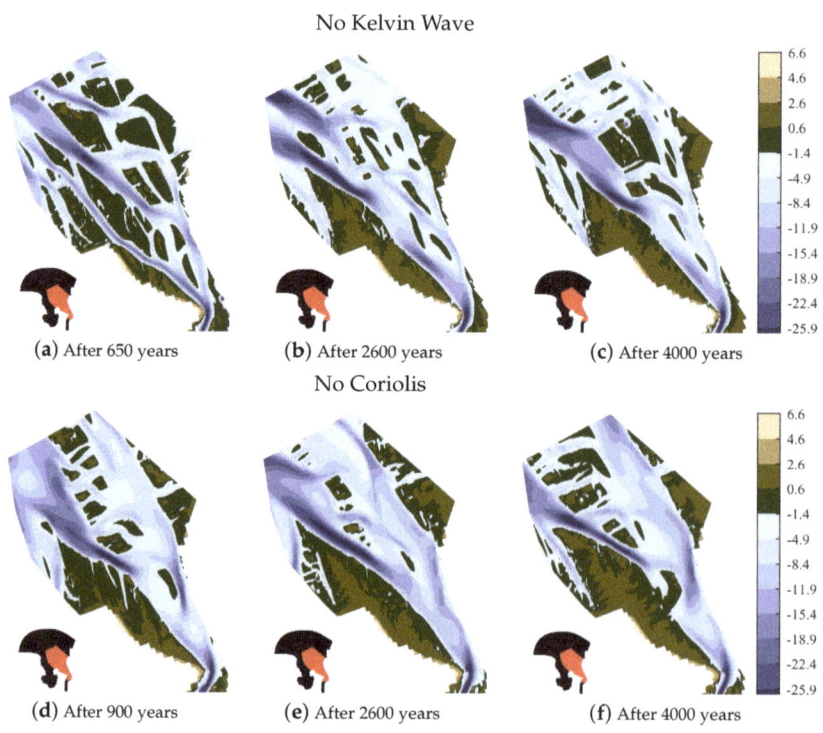

Figure A1. *Cont.*

Increased Tidal Range

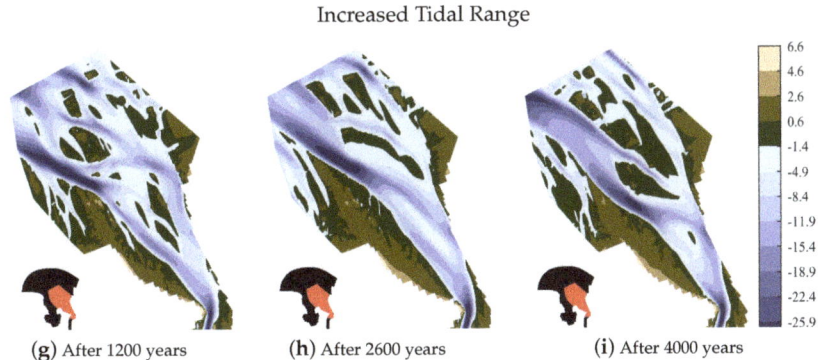

(g) After 1200 years (h) After 2600 years (i) After 4000 years

Figure A1. Results of the tidal scenario simulations at three different times in years (hydrodynamic time times the morphological factor). The first time-step is selected based on equilibrium conditions. Clear distinction between the channel (blue colors) and shoal (earth colors).

Appendix A.2. River Discharge Scenarios

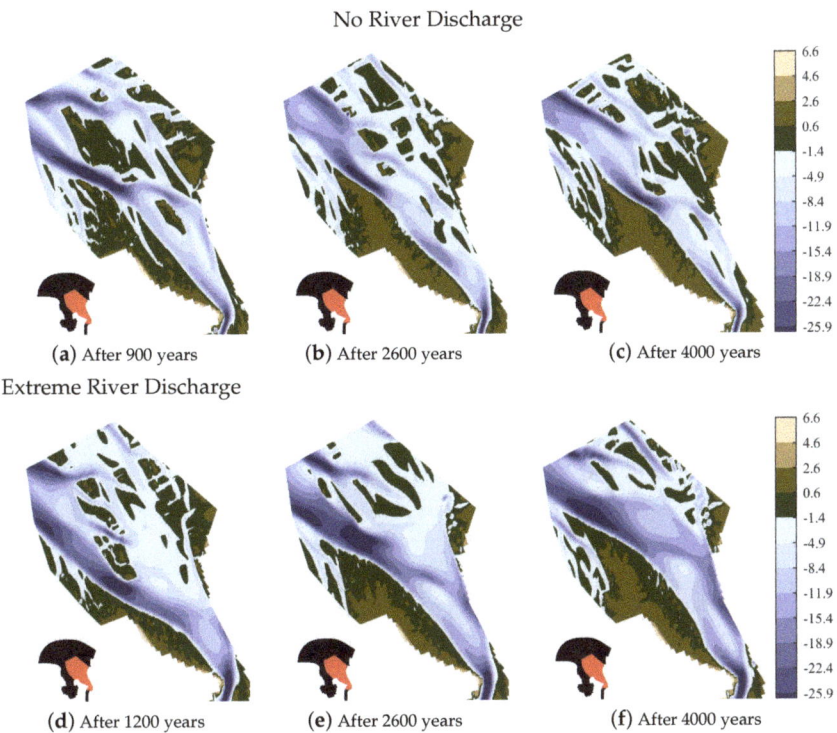

Figure A2. Results of the river discharge scenario simulations at three different times in years (hydrodynamic time multiplied with the morphological factor). The first shown time-step is selected based on equilibrium conditions. Clear distinction between the channel (blue colors) and shoal (earth colors) area.

References

1. Vorwig, W.; Wiemann, U.; Kobbe, W. Seeschifffahrt und Häfen in Norddeutschland. In *Statistische Monatshefte Niedersachsen*; 11/2014; Landesamt für Statistik Niedersachsen (LSN): Hanover, Germany, 2014.
2. Plate, L. Die Weser als Seewasserstrasse: Bilanzbericht, Bericht f. d. Küsten-Ausschuß. 1951.
3. Lange, D. The weser estuary: Heide, Holstein: Boyens. *Die Küste* **2008**, *74*, 275–287.
4. Göhren, H. Beitrag zur Morphologie der Jade-und Wesermündung. *Die Küste* **1965**, *13*, 140–146.
5. Wetzel, V. Der Ausbau des Weserfahrwassers von 1921 bis heute. In *Jahrbuch der Hafenbautechnischen Gesellschaft*; Springer: Heidelberg, Germany, 1988; Volume 42, pp. 83–105.
6. De Swart, H.E.; Zimmerman, J. Morphodynamics of Tidal Inlet Systems. *Annu. Rev. Fluid Mech.* **2009**, *41*, 203–229. [CrossRef]
7. Roelvink, J.A.; Reniers, A.J.H.M. *A Guide to Modeling Coastal Morphology*; World Scientific: Hackensack, NJ, USA; London, UK, 2012.
8. Friedrichs, C.T. Barotropic tides in channelized estuaries. In *Contemporary Issues in Estuarine Physics*; Cambridge University Press: Cambridge, UK, 2010; pp. 27–61.
9. Van Veen, J. Ebb and flood channel systems in the netherlands tidal waters 1. *J. Coast. Res.* **2005**, *216*, 1107–1120. [CrossRef]
10. Marciano, R.; Wang, Z.B.; Hibma, A.; de Vriend, H.J.; Defina, A. Modeling of channel patterns in short tidal basins. *J. Geophys. Res.* **2005**, *110*, 1155. [CrossRef]
11. Roelvink, J.A. Coastal morphodynamic evolution techniques. *Coast. Eng.* **2006**, *53*, 277–287. [CrossRef]
12. Ranasinghe, R.; Swinkels, C.; Luijendijk, A.; Roelvink, D.; Bosboom, J.; Stive, M.; Walstra, D. Morphodynamic upscaling with the MORFAC approach: Dependencies and sensitivities. *Coast. Eng.* **2011**, *58*, 806–811. [CrossRef]
13. Van Maanen, B.; Coco, G.; Bryan, K.R. Modelling the effects of tidal range and initial bathymetry on the morphological evolution of tidal embayments. *Geomorphology* **2013**, *191*, 23–34. [CrossRef]
14. Nabi, M.; de Vriend, H.J.; Mosselman, E.; Sloff, C.J.; Shimizu, Y. Detailed simulation of morphodynamics: 2. Sediment pickup, transport, and deposition. *Water Resour. Res.* **2013**, *49*, 4775–4791. [CrossRef]
15. De Vriend, H.J.; Capobianco, M.; Chesher, T.; de Swart, H.E.; Latteux, B.; Stive, M. Approaches to long-term modelling of coastal morphology: A review. *Coast. Eng.* **1993**, *21*, 225–269. [CrossRef]
16. Dastgheib, A.; Roelvink, J.A.; Wang, Z.B. Long-term process-based morphological modeling of the Marsdiep Tidal Basin. *Mar. Geol.* **2008**, *256*, 90–100. [CrossRef]
17. Zhang, W.; Schneider, R.; Harff, J. A multi-scale hybrid long-term morphodynamic model for wave-dominated coasts. *Geomorphology* **2012**, *149–150*, 49–61. [CrossRef]
18. Van der Wegen, M.; Roelvink, J.A. Reproduction of estuarine bathymetry by means of a process-based model: Western Scheldt case study, the Netherlands. *Geomorphology* **2012**, *179*, 152–167. [CrossRef]
19. Dam, G.; van der Wegen, M.; Labeur, R.J.; Roelvink, D. Modeling centuries of estuarine morphodynamics in the Western Scheldt estuary. *Geophys. Res. Lett.* **2016**, *43*, 3839–3847. [CrossRef]
20. Herrling, G.; Benninghoff, M.; Zorndt, A.; Winter, C. Drivers of channel-shoal morphodynamics at the Outer Weser estuary. In Proceedings of the 8th International Conference on Coastal Dynamics, Helsingoer, Denmark, 12–16 June 2017.
21. Hesse, R. Zur Modellierung des Transports kohäsiver Sedimente am Beispiel des Weserästuars. Ph.D. Thesis, Technische Universität Hamburg, Hamburg, Germany, 2020.
22. Lojek, O. Sensitivity Analysis of Single Storm Surges in the Jade-Weser Estuary. Ph.D. Thesis, Institutionelles Repositorium der Leibniz Universität Hannover, Hannover, Germany, 2020.
23. Kösters, F.; Winter, C. Exploring German Bight coastal morphodynamics based on modelled bed shear stress. *Geo-Mar. Lett.* **2014**, *34*, 21–36. [CrossRef]
24. Casulli, V.; Walters, R.A. An unstructured grid, three-dimensional model based on the shallow water equations. *Int. J. Numer. Methods Fluids* **2000**, *32*, 331–348. [CrossRef]
25. Luan, H.L.; Ding, P.X.; Wang, Z.B.; Ge, J.Z. Process-based morphodynamic modeling of the Yangtze Estuary at a decadal timescale: Controls on estuarine evolution and future trends. *Geomorphology* **2017**, *290*, 347–364. [CrossRef]
26. Laurer, W.; Naumann, M.; Zeiler, M. Erstellung der Karte zur Sedimentverteilung auf dem Meeresboden in der deutschen Nordsee nach der Klassifikation von FIGGE (1981). *Geopotenzial Dtsch. Nordsee Modul B Dok.* **2014**, *1*, 1–19.
27. Vos, P.C.; Knol, E. Holocene landscape reconstruction of the Wadden Sea area between Marsdiep and Weser. *Neth. J. Geosci.* **2015**, *94*, 157–183. [CrossRef]
28. Ramacher, H. Der Ausbau von Unter-und Außenweser. In *Mitteilungen des Franzius Instituts*; TU Hannover: Hanover, Germany, 1974; Volume 41.
29. BfG. *Sedimentmanagementkonzept Tideweser: Untersuchung im Auftrag der WSÄ Bremen und Bremerhaven*; BfG: Koblenz, Germany, 2014.
30. Plate, L. Forschungen als Grundlage für den Ausbau der Aussenweser. *Dtsch. Wasserwirtsch.* **1935**, *4*, 66–74.
31. Wang, Z.B.; Louters, T.; de Vriend, H.J. Morphodynamic modelling for a tidal inlet in the Wadden Sea. *Mar. Geol.* **1995**, *126*, 289–300. [CrossRef]
32. Lesser, G.R.; Roelvink, J.A.; van Kester, J.; Stelling, G.S. Development and validation of a three-dimensional morphological model. *Coast. Eng.* **2004**, *51*, 883–915. [CrossRef]
33. Deltares. *Delft3D-FLOW User Manual*; Deltares: Delft, The Netherlands, 2021.

34. Engelund, F.; Hansen, E. *A Monograph on Sediment Transport in Alluvial Streams*; Technical University of Denmark: Copenhagen K, Denmark, 1967.
35. Guo, L.; van der Wegen, M.; Roelvink, D.; Wang, Z.B.; He, Q. Long-term, process-based morphodynamic modeling of a fluvio-deltaic system, part I: The role of river discharge. *Cont. Shelf Res.* **2015**, *109*, 95–111. [CrossRef]
36. Reyns, J.; Dastgheib, A.; Ranasinghe, R.; Luijendijk, A.; Walstra, D.J.; Roelvink, D. Morphodynamic upscaling with the morfac approach in tidal conditions: The critical morfac. *Coast. Eng. Proc.* **2015**, *1*, 27. [CrossRef]
37. Bagnold, R.A. *An Approach to the Sediment Transport Problem from General Physics*; US Government Printing Office: Washington, DC, USA, 1966.
38. Ikeda, S. Lateral bed load transport on side slopes. *J. Hydraul. Div.* **1982**, *108*, 1369–1373. [CrossRef]
39. Walstra, D.; Ormondt, M.V.; Roelvink, J. *Shoreface Nourishment Scenarios: Detailed Morphodynamic Simulations with Delft3D for Various Shoreface Nourishment Designs*; Deltares: Delft, The Netherlands, 2004.
40. Van Rijn, L.C. *Principles of Sediment Transport in Rivers, Estuaries and Coastal Seas*; Aqua Publications: Amsterdam, The Netherlands, 1993.
41. Baar, A.; Albernaz, M.B.; Van Dijk, W.; Kleinhans, M. Critical dependence of morphodynamic models of fluvial and tidal systems on empirical downslope sediment transport. *Nat. Commun.* **2019**, *10*, 1–12. [CrossRef] [PubMed]
42. Lesser, G.R. *An Approach to Medium-Term Coastal Morphological Modelling*; IHE Delft Institute for Water Education: Delft, The Netherlands, 2009.
43. Dissanayake, D.; Roelvink, J.; Van der Wegen, M. Modelled channel patterns in a schematized tidal inlet. *Coast. Eng.* **2009**, *56*, 1069–1083. [CrossRef]
44. Latteux, B. Techniques for long-term morphological simulation under tidal action. *Mar. Geol.* **1995**, *126*, 129–141. [CrossRef]
45. Bernardes, M.E.; Davidson, M.A.; Dyer, K.R.; George, K.J. Towards medium-term (order of months) morphodynamic modelling of the Teign estuary, UK. *Ocean Dyn.* **2006**, *56*, 186–197. [CrossRef]
46. BAW. *Erzeugung naturähnlicher Randwerte für den seeseitigen Rand von Ästuarmodellen an der Nordsee. (BAW-Bericht A 395 502 10059)*; BAW: Hamburg, Germany, 2014.
47. Geopotenzial Deutsche Nordsee. *Die Neue Holozänbasis der Niedersächsischen Nordseeküste*; Landesamt für Bergbau, Energie und Geologie (LBEG): Hanover, Germany, 2013.
48. Boyd, R.; Dalrymple, R.; Zaitlin, B.A. Classification of clastic coastal depositional environments. *Sediment. Geol.* **1992**, *80*, 139–150. [CrossRef]
49. Brown, T. Kelvin wave reflection at an oscillating boundary with applications to the North Sea. *Cont. Shelf Res.* **1987**, *7*, 351–365. [CrossRef]
50. Hovmöller, E. The trough-and-ridge diagram. *Tellus* **1949**, *1*, 62–66. [CrossRef]
51. Yu, Q.; Wang, Y.; Gao, S.; Flemming, B. Modeling the formation of a sand bar within a large funnel-shaped, tide-dominated estuary: Qiantangjiang Estuary, China. *Mar. Geol.* **2012**, *299*, 63–76. [CrossRef]
52. Crameri, F.; Shephard, G.E.; Heron, P.J. The misuse of colour in science communication. *Nat. Commun.* **2020**, *11*, 1–10. [CrossRef] [PubMed]

Article

The Influence of Reef Topography on Storm-Driven Sand Flux

Cyprien Bosserelle [1,2], Shari L. Gallop [1,3], Ivan D. Haigh [1,4] and Charitha B. Pattiaratchi [1,*]

[1] UWA Oceans Institute, The University of Western Australia, Perth 6009, Australia; Cyprien.Bosserelle@niwa.co.nz (C.B.); shari.gallop@waikato.ac.nz (S.L.G.); idh1g11@soton.ac.uk (I.D.H.)
[2] National Institute of Water and Atmospheric Research (NIWA), 10 Kyle Street, 8011 Christchurch, Aotearoa, New Zealand
[3] School of Science and Environmental Research Institute, University of Waikato, 3110 Tauranga, Aotearoa, New Zealand
[4] Ocean and Earth Science, National Oceanography Centre, University of Southampton, European Way, Southampton SO14 3ZH, UK
* Correspondence: chari.pattiaratchi@uwa.edu.au

Abstract: Natural formations of rock and coral can support geologically controlled beaches, where the beach dynamics are significantly influenced by these structures. However, little is known about how alongshore variations in geological controls influence beach morphodynamics. Therefore, in this study we focus on the storm response of a beach (Yanchep in south Western Australia) that has strong alongshore variation in the level of geological control because of the heterogeneous calcarenite limestone reef. We used a modified version of XBeach to simulate the beach morphodynamics during a significant winter storm event. We find that the longshore variation in topography of the reef resulted in: (1) strong spatial difference in current distribution, including areas with strong currents jets; and (2) significant alongshore differences in sand flux, with larger fluxes in areas strongly geologically controlled by reefs. In particular, this resulted in enhanced beach erosion at the boundary of the reef where strong currents jet-exited the nearshore.

Keywords: XBeach; morphology; morphodynamics; reef; storm; current jets; Western Australia

1. Introduction

Sandy beach morphodynamics are the result of complex interactions between sand, meteorological and oceanographic conditions, and in many cases, geological controls. Natural formations of rock and coral can form structural constraints in the nearshore that can form longshore and cross-shore geological controls [1]. In the cross-shore direction, beaches may be underlain or fronted seaward by hard landforms such as platforms and reefs [2,3]. Despite their common occurrence [4–6], such beaches have received little attention [7], and little is known about how these hard landforms influence the spatial variability in coastal sediment transport, including connectivity of different parts of the beach alongshore, as well as erosion and accretion triggers and rates.

It is largely accepted that hard landforms such as rock and coral reefs protect beaches by dissipating wave energy through wave breaking and friction [4,8,9] and can therefore promote beach stability [10,11], such as by reducing erosion during storms by reducing cross-shore sediment transport (Vousdoukas et al. [12] and Gallop et al. [2,13]). In some cases, reefs may also reduce coastal flooding; however, there is also evidence that the risk of wave-driven flooding of coral reef coasts is increasing due to sea level rise and changes in weather patterns combined with coral reef degradation [14].

However, despite the protective capacity of reefs, studies by [2,12,13] showed that reefs may also reduce rates of beach recovery via accretion after erosive events [15], such as by being a barrier to onshore sediment transport until a sufficient sand ramp has accumulated at the seaward toe allowing sand to overtop the reef onto the beach face [16]. Thus, these studies suggest that the effect of reefs on beach dynamics is highly complex, and variable alongshore, even at a single beach. Moreover, while there has been extensive research on the cross-shore response of hydrodynamics over reefs, such as wave transformation [17–19], less attention has been paid to the overall alongshore variations in both cross-shore and longshore sediment transport [20] and the resulting beach dynamics. This is a complex task because, in addition to the cross–shore process of wave attenuation, the alongshore variability of reefs is a key factor in controlling sediment transport and beach morphodynamics drivers. These drivers include geologically controlled currents including boundary controlled rip currents that may occur along groynes and similar natural structures [21–23], and complex wave refraction and diffraction patterns [24,25], alongside their interaction with currents. Therefore, the aim of this study is to investigate how spatial variations in reef topography at Yanchep influence beach morphology by altering the cross-shore and alongshore sediment flux. To achieve this, we use a numerical model validated with field measurements to do the following: (1) investigate the relative influence of reef topographic variation on cross-shore and longshore sediment transport; and (2) undertake a sensitivity analysis on the role of reef roughness on circulation and sand fluxes. The background section describes our study area and data previously collected. The methodology section describes the model, its formulation, forcing, and validation against field data as well as the scope of the sensitivity analysis. The results show simulated flow and erosion/accretion patterns for a storm that occurred in July 2010 as well as sensitivity of currents to six model parameters. The results are then compared with similar studies in the discussion section before the conclusion.

2. Background

2.1. Study Site

Geologically controlled beaches are a common feature of the Western Australian coastline. In the Perth region, the Pleistocene Tamala Limestone outcrops on the inner continental shelf as a series of discontinuous ridges (Figure 1b). The furthest ridge outcrops 20 km offshore and forms Rottnest and Garden Islands (Figure 1b). The inshore ridge coincides with the shoreline and has highly variable alongshore topography. This creates a diverse geological framework that supports a diverse range of beaches. The reef at Yanchep (Figure 1c), located 60 km north of the city of Perth, varies alongshore in elevation, continuity and distance seaward from the beach. This makes this relatively short, 3 km stretch of coastline an ideal location to investigate how rock topography influences beach morphodynamics. The beach on the southern section (bluff beach), is perched on a sub-horizontal limestone platform (the bluff) that reaches 0.4 m above mean sea level. Heading north, the reef outcrop is further from the coast constricting a narrow lagoon. North of the lagoon, the limestone becomes patchier forming isolated submerged rock outcrops ("bommies") that cause waves to break outside of the surf zone. Further north, the reef is still present a few meters below mean sea level, intermittently buried in the sand. The northern limit of the beach is marked by a larger reef outcrop and a groyne installed in 1971 (Figure 1c). Gallop et al. [2,13] investigated the response of Yanchep to erosive events by observing the evolution of three beach profiles to strong sea breeze and storm events. Despite the profiles being only several hundred meters apart, the magnitude and timing of erosion and accretion varied greatly. However, with the spatially limited field measurements and limited measurements of the hydrodynamics, it was not possible to get a full understanding of the mechanisms of geological control that resulted in these differences.

2.2. Regional Setting

In this region, the diurnal tidal component has a maximum range of 0.60 m and the semidiurnal tide has a range of only 0.20 m [26]. There are three main wind regimes [27,28]: (1) calm winds (<5 ms^{-1}); (2) strong winds associated with the passage frontal systems in winter with wind speeds >15 ms^{-1} with wind direction changing anti-clockwise from north to west to southwest; and (3) summer sea breezes (alike to a daily storm) with wind speeds >15 ms^{-1} blowing over 2–3 days from the south. Wind data from the Rottnest

Island station over 2009–2016 indicated that the mean number of storms per year was 42 (range: 39–50) while 40% and 25% of the storms occurred during winter and summer months, respectively [27]. Similarly, the mean number of calm periods per year was 47 (range: 36–54) with the majority occurring during the autumn and winter months. Each storm event lasted between three and five days.

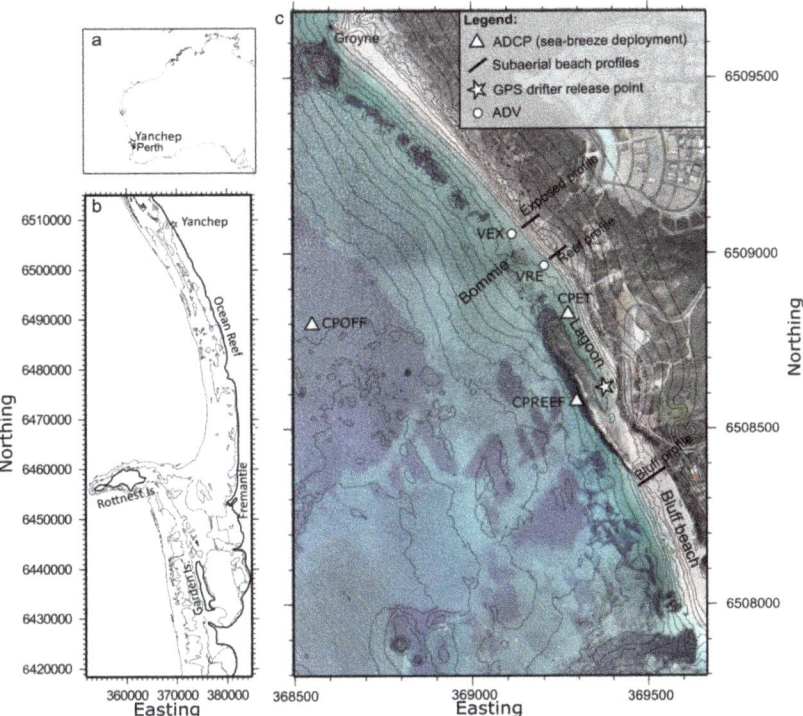

Figure 1. Location maps of the following: (**a**) the Western Australian coastline and the location of Perth; (**b**) the continental shelf near Perth, where the thick line represents the shoreline and the thin lines the 10 m and 20 m bathymetry contours; and, (**c**) digital imagery of the nearshore off Yanchep (Nearmap, 2009).where the grey lines represent the bathymetry contours with 1 m spacing and the symbols show the locations of data collection by Gallop et al. [2,11].

The offshore wave climate is dominated by swell and storms generated in the Southern Ocean. Offshore, near Rottnest Island (Figure 1b), the annual mean significant wave height is 2.14 m and exceeds 4 m 10% of the time [29]. However, most of the offshore wave energy is dissipated on the inner shelf by limestone ridges. For example, during a storm in July 2010 only 20 to 30% of the wave energy reached the shore at Yanchep [2]. Despite the protection provided by the offshore ridges, waves exceeding 1 m occur at Yanchep during winter storms and summer sea breezes [2,13].

This coast is characterized by large seasonal variation in incident wave height, and the local beaches exhibit a distinct seasonal change in morphology. In general, seasonal changes in beach morphology result in wider beaches during summer and narrower beaches during winter. This pattern is driven by the seasonal reversal in the alongshore sand transport direction [30]. In the summer, when northward sediment transport prevails due to sea breeze activity [31], beaches located south of coastal structures, headlands or rocky outcrops become wider due to the accumulation of sediment against the obstacle. These beaches will subsequently erode in winter during storms when the longshore sediment transport is toward the south [30].

2.3. Previous Field Studies at Yanchep

Hydrodynamic and morphological changes at Yanchep, during a week-long period of sea-breezes (February 2010) and a winter storm (July 2010), were measured [2,13]. During both field campaigns, wave, current and sea level measurements were made in the surf zone (Figure 1c), and subaerial beach profiles were monitored every two hours. Hydrodynamic and morphological changes at Yanchep were measured over two one-week-long periods, during strong sea breezes in summer of February 2010, and a winter storm in July 2010 [2,13]. Data collected during the sea breezes were only used for model validation, and details are provided by Gallop et al. [13]. The storm event measured was the first major storm of 2010 with two fronts crossing the coast on the 8th and 11th July. Waves were largest after the second front with significant wave height reaching 6 m offshore Rottnest Island (Figure 1b). The wind characteristics were typical of fronts crossing the coastline of Western Australia, with northerly to northwesterly winds preceding the arrival of the front then switching west to southwesterly during and after the passage of the front [27,32,33]. This cycle of wind direction occurred with each front but with stronger winds (>15 ms^{-1}) during the second front. During the storm experiment, three subaerial beach profiles were monitored: a profile north of the bluff beach where the reef reached approximately 0.4 m above mean sea level; a profile fronted by a reef at mean sea level on the south edge of the Bommie; and an exposed profile fronted seaward by an intermittently buried reef 3 m deep north of the Bommie (Figure 1c). The hydrodynamic conditions were monitored in the surf zone fronting the exposed and reef profiles, but limited data were obtained due to energetic conditions. Erosion was considerably variable alongshore and was dependent on the rock topography. Overall, the reef profile was most stable during the storm due to short periods of accretion at times of lower water level during the storm [2]. In the month following the storm, the exposed profile recovered substantially whereas the bluff profile barely changed. Gallop et al. [2] hypothesised that a scour step formed seaward of the bluff during the storm may have contributed to inhibition of recovery. They also suggested that the beach response varied with the alongshore rock topography, but due to lack of data, they could not evaluate the influence of alongshore rock topography on the sediment transport and the beach erosion and recovery.

3. Methods

In order to identify the processes dominating sand transport at Yanchep Lagoon, a numerical model was used to simulate the storm period in July 2010, which was surveyed by Gallop et al. [2]. Due to the limited hydrodynamic data collected during the storm, the model was first validated using data from the sea breeze period in February 2010, detailed in Gallop et al. [13]. Data from both the sea breeze and storm experiments were used to validate the model but the results focus on simulation of the 2010 storm. The model formulations are presented here, as well as the model set up, validation and sensitivity analysis.

3.1. Model Formulation

In order to resolve the variation in topography of the reef at Yanchep, a high spatial resolution model (~5 m) was required. However, high resolution requires a smaller time-step which typically results in slow model runs. This makes the simulation of periods more than a week long unpractical without access to supercomputers. Recent efforts in GPU computing achieved calculations that are orders of magnitude faster than using a Central Processing Unit (CPU) platform. As GPU processes are available on most desktop computers, it was chosen as a computing platform to perform the process-based morphological simulations. The model developed for this study used identical formulations to XBeach [34,35], but it was rewritten to perform the calculation on the GPU and to achieve a substantial reduction in model run times.

As in XBeach, the wave action balance equation was used to resolve the evolution of the wave energy in the nearshore. The equation is dependent on the directional distribution of the wave-action density and the frequency spectrum is represented by a single representative frequency.

The model wave dissipation includes the contribution of wave breaking using a model from Roelvink [34] and a bottom dissipation term. The bottom dissipation term is defined as:

$$D_b = \frac{2}{3\pi}\rho f_w U_{orb}^3 \qquad (1)$$

where f_w is the bottom dissipation parameter, U_{orb} is the bottom orbital velocity and ρ is the water density. In coral reef environments, suggested values for f_w range from 0.08 to 0.7 [36–39]; this wide range is due to the variable roughness in different areas of the reefs. The model used in this study was adjusted so that users can provide a separate value of the variable f_w for sandy areas and reef outcrops.

In the Shallow Water equations, roughness of the seabed was included in the bottom shear stress τ_{bx} calculated as:

$$\tau_{bx} = c_f . \rho . u_E . \sqrt{(1.16 U_{rms})^2 + V_{magE}^2} \qquad (2)$$

where, u_E is the Eulerian component of the depth average velocity; U_{rms} is the near-bed short-wave orbital velocity; V_{magE} is the magnitude of the Eulerian component of the depth average velocity; c_f is the bed friction parameter. Reefs are considered to be "rougher" than sand; therefore, the model was designed to use a separate value of c_f for the sandy area and a value for reef outcrops.

The model used in this study did not include the shoaling and breaking delay. The model also accounted for one class of sediment, defined by d_{50} and d_{90} size distribution, density and mean fall velocity, and a single sediment layer, although it included a nonerodible layer. The model was designed to assign a separate bed friction (c_f) and bottom wave dissipation factor (f_w) for the area covered with sand and areas where reefs outcrop. After each morphological time step the model checked how much sand covered each model cell. If the sand layer is less than 0.05 m deep, f_w and c_f are assigned user values for reefs. Values of c_f and f_w used in the simulations are shown on Table 1.

Table 1. Parameters used in the model for the storm simulation.

Parameter	Value	Parameter	Value
Time step (s)	0.25	Drying height (m)	0.02
Bottom friction for sand ($c_{f\,sand}$)	0.005	Bottom friction for reef ($c_{f\,reef}$)	0.01
Viscosity (m^2 s^{-1})	0.05	Roller dissipation viscosity factor (nuhfac)	0.2
Latitude (degrees)	−32	Wind drag	0.002
Breaker parameter (gamma)	0.45	Power in dissipation model (n)	8
Wave dissipation coefficient	1.0	Maximum wave to depth ratio	1.7
Breaker slope coefficient (beta)	0.15	Wave current interaction	1
Bottom wave dissipation sand ($f_{w\,sand}$)	0.01	Bottom wave dissipation reef ($f_{w\,reef}$)	0.7
D50 (mm)	0.38	D90 (mm)	0.53
Sand density (kg m^{-3})	2650	Settling velocity (ms^{-1})	0.051
porosity	0.4	Morphological factor	1.0
Suspended load calibration factor	1.5	Bedload calibration factor	1.5
Skewness factor	0.2	Asymmetry factor	0.2

3.2. Simulation Set-Up

The bathymetry grid for the model was created by combining interpolated data from a hydrographic survey, a beach survey, Light Detection and Ranging (LiDAR) data and visual interpretation of satellite imagery. The grid was aligned shore parallel (rotated 26° clockwise from the north), extending 2.6 km alongshore and 1.2 km cross-shore at 5 m resolution (Figure 2a). At the alongshore edges of the grid, the bathymetry was changed to remove gradients perpendicular to the side boundaries. In addition, in order to comply with the uniform forcing on the offshore boundary, the bathymetry was set to a constant value for the three first cells then graded linearly to the real bathymetry across 25 m. The same bathymetry was used in the sea breeze and storm simulations.

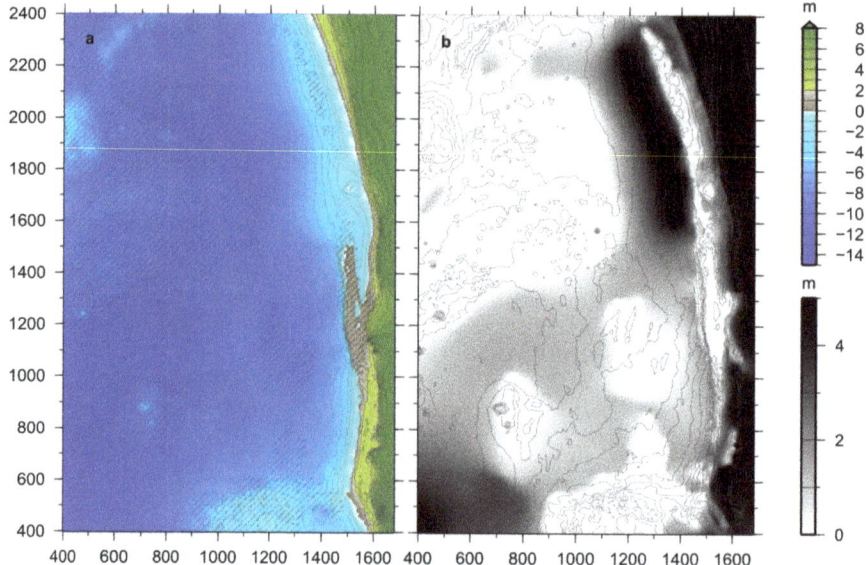

Figure 2. (**a**) Model bathymetry with line-shading showing the outcropping reefs; and (**b**) sand layer thickness.

Information on thickness of the sand layer was not directly available for Yanchep beach. Instead, sand thickness was estimated using satellite imagery available in Google Earth and field observations. The water at Yanchep is clear and one can easily distinguish between sandy areas and reef areas using satellite images. Reef areas were digitized from a satellite image from 14 July 2010 (Figure 1c). Additional images were used to differentiate between transiting wrack (sea weed) and the reef. Areas of reef were assigned a sand thickness of 0.0 m. Areas with patchy reef or close to a large reef were assigned 0.5 m of sand thickness, and the center of large sandy areas were assigned a value of 5.0 m. The digitized sand thickness values were then interpolated to a grid of identical dimension to the bathymetry grid (Figure 2b). Erosion/accretion was quantified as difference in post-storm to pre-storm topography elevation with erosion being a negative difference and accretion positive. Profile sand volume loss/gain was calculated at each model row by cumulating the erosion/accretion volume (i.e., multiplied by the cell area).

The model was forced using wave and sea level data collected by an Acoustic Doppler Current Profiler (ADCP) located offshore in 10 m water depth (CPOFF in Figure 1c). Sea level data were smoothed and subsampled to hourly values. The mean value was removed and the data corrected to chart datum. Half-hourly wind speed and direction collected by the Bureau of Meteorology at Ocean Reef (Figure 1b) was used as wind forcing. The wave spectrum from the offshore ADCP (CPOFF in Figure 1c) was used to generate the offshore wave boundary.

The storm was simulated for nine days starting on 6 July 2010. During the storm event, no hydrodynamic data were collected outside the surf zone. Therefore, sea level data from Fremantle tide gauge were used on the boundary and wind data from the ocean reef was used across the grid. Only the wave data collected near Rottnest Island were available for the storm; therefore, an intermediate model was required to simulate the evolution of the waves as they crossed the continental shelf. Simulating WAves Nearshore (SWAN) [40] was used to simulate the waves on a 10 m resolution bathymetry of the continental shelf forced with wind from ocean reef, sea level from Fremantle and the wave parameters from Rottnest Island. Spectra of wave density extracted from the SWAN model at the location of the Yanchep model boundary was used as forcing (Figure 3). Both simulations used the same bathymetry and the same parameters as specified in Table 1.

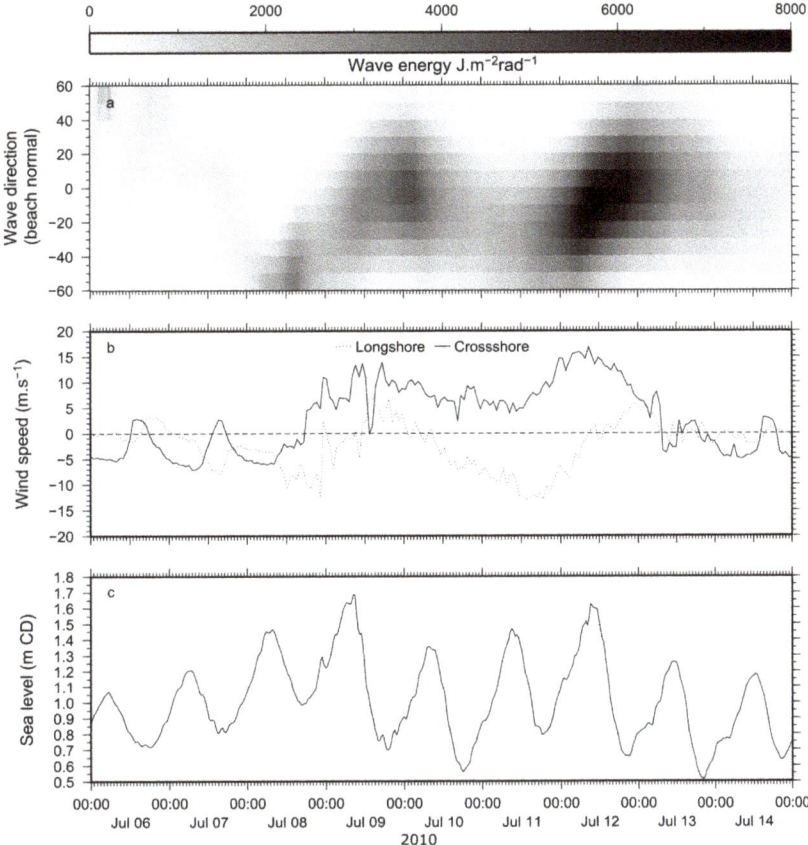

Figure 3. (a) Model forcing for the storm simulation in July 2010: (a) directional wave energy distribution; (b) alongshore and cross shore wind speed; (c) sea level relative to the model datum (c) Model bathymetry with hachures showing the outcropping reefs; and (b) sand depth.

3.3. Model Validation

Model parameters selected for the simulations are presented in Table 1. The resulting simulations were validated using data collected during the sea breeze [13] and storm campaigns [2]. The model validity was quantified using the index of agreement (skill) defined by Willmott [41] as:

$$Skill = 1 - \frac{\sum |X_{model} - X_{obs}|}{\sum (|X_{model} - \overline{X_{obs}}| + |X_{obs} - \overline{X_{obs}}|)^2} \tag{3}$$

Sea breeze simulations were compared with hydrodynamic measurements made by selected instruments in Table 2 and the morphological parameters in Table 3. Overall, the simulated depth-averaged velocities corresponded well with the measurements, particularly at CPREEF, the ADCP seaward of the lagoon reef (Figure 4). At this location, the currents are driven by wind and waves breaking on an offshore reef. The alongshore and cross-shore velocities were simulated with a skill of 0.96 and 0.86 respectively. In the lagoon, the alongshore velocity was simulated with a skill of 0.94.

Table 2. Skills for hydrodynamic parameters for the sea-breeze simulation (see Figure 1c for locations).

Location and Parameter	Skill
CPOFF, longshore velocity	0.84
CPOFF, cross-shore velocity	0.49
CPREEF, longshore velocity	0.96
CPREEF, cross-shore velocity	0.86
CPREEF, sea level	0.99
CPREEF, root mean square wave height	0.95
CPET, longshore velocity	0.90
CPET, cross-shore velocity	0.59
VRE, root mean square wave height	0.71
VEX, sea level	0.84
VEX, root mean square wave height	0.90

Table 3. Morphological skill for storm and sea breeze simulation.

Profile	Skill
Exposed (sea-breeze)	0.77
Reef (sea-breeze)	0.68
Exposed (storm)	0.59
Reef (storm)	0.85
Bluff (storm)	0.87

At the CPREEF location, simulated root mean square wave height matched measured data with a skill of 0.95. Shoreward of the area, where waves break on the reef, wave height at the south frame had a skill of 0.71. During the storm experiments, no reliable current data were collected, but root mean square wave height and sea level data were collected in the surf zone south of the Bommie (Figure 5). The skill of the simulated root mean square wave height was 0.90 and skill for the simulated depth was 0.84. Water depth measured and simulated during the storm includes the variation in water level as well as the erosion of the sandy bottom (Figure 5).

Global Positioning System (GPS) drifters (see Johnson et al. [42] for a description of the drifters) were released in the lagoon during both field experiments. The complex circulation and velocities measured by the GPS-drifters are resolved in the model simulation (Figure 6). In particular, during the July 2010 winter storm deploy, the release of the drifters corresponded to the relatively short time when the jet turned south after exiting the lagoon.

The simulated velocity along the track of the drifters corresponds to the measured velocity with skill of 0.66. The discrepancy was mostly because the drifters measured velocities near the surface whereas the simulations were depth-averaged velocities.

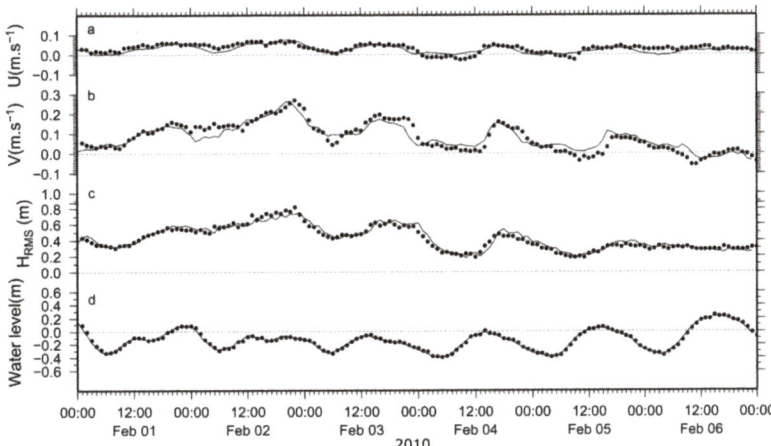

Figure 4. Simulated (line) and measured (dots) hydrodynamics parameters for the CPREEF site (See Figure 1c for locations. (**a**) cross_shore current; (**b**) alongshore current; (**c**) root mean square wave height; and (**d**) water level.

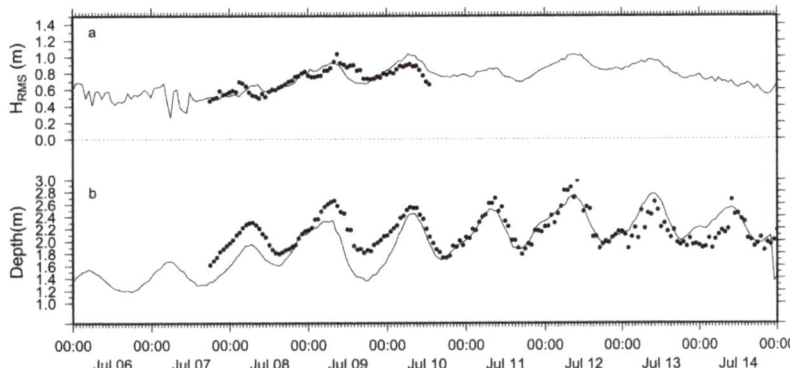

Figure 5. Root mean square wave height (**a**) and total water depth (**b**) simulated (line) and measured (dots) during the storm event at the VRE site, on the southern side of the Bommie (see Figure 1c).

During the sea breezes and the storm event, beach elevations were measured on the subaerial beach only. The measured and simulated morphology changes were compared for the mean elevation in each profile (Figure 7). General trends in the morphology were relatively well captured for the seabreeze cycle at the exposed profile and the reef profile with skills of 0.77 and 0.68 respectively (Table 3). During the storm, three subaerial beach profiles were monitored. The elevation of the beach at the reef profile and the bluff profile was simulated with skill levels of 0.85 and 0.87, respectively (Table 3). The lower part of the exposed profile eroded rapidly; hence, data were only available for the upper part of the profile. The model simulated the elevation of the upper profile with a skill level of 0.59 (Table 3).

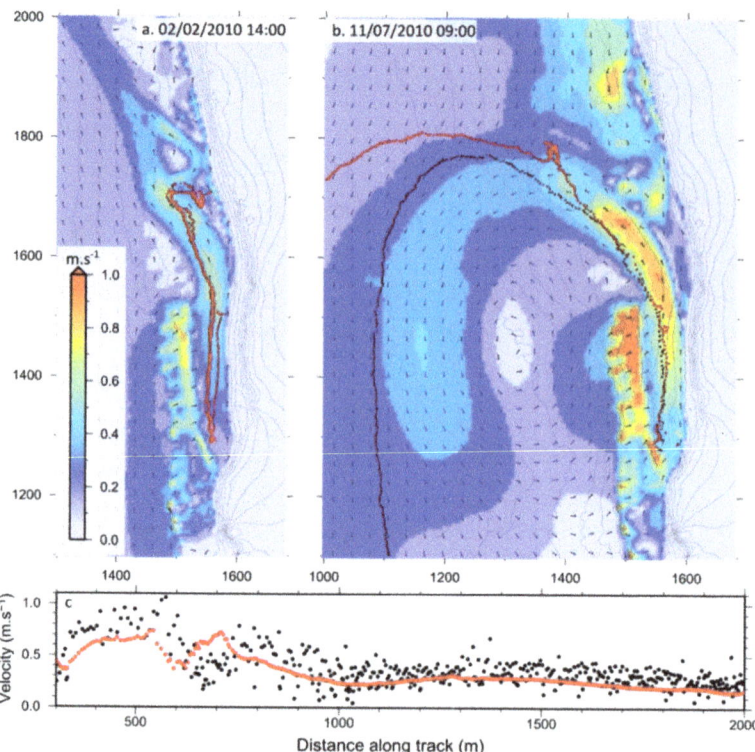

Figure 6. GPS drifter tracks (red dots) and simulated velocity (shading) and direction (vector) during (**a**) sea breeze release; and, (**b**) storm release. (**c**) Simulated velocity (red dots) and measured velocity (black dots) along the dark red drifter track in b.

3.4. Sensitivity Analysis

Understanding the sensitivity of morphodynamics to different model parameters can provide guidance on the relative importance of model parameters. Ultimately this informs where a particular model could be improved and where future research on simulation of reef hydrodynamics could be influential. In this section, we investigate the role of the roughness of the reef on the circulation by comparing the currents simulated with different values of bottom wave dissipation and bed friction. In addition to the bottom friction parameters, four other model parameters in XBeach (Table 4) were investigated: (1) roller dissipation viscosity factor ("nuhfac"); (2) breaker parameter ("gamma"); (3) power in dissipation model ("n"); and, (4) breaker slope coefficient ('beta'). Each parameter was tested across their valid range increasing the value linearly leading to a total of 55 model runs. For each value of the parameters, the model was run for two hours and the output was saved for the second hour corresponding to midnight 13 July 2010. Boundary conditions, bathymetry and other parameters remained unchanged (i.e., as in Table 1). For each parameter, the sensitivity was mapped as the standard deviation of simulated velocities for all the parameter values at every model cells. When presented in a map, a higher value of sensitivity for a parameter means that the parameter has a higher influence on the velocity at this location. Maximum and mean for each mapped sensitivity provides a measure of how much a parameter can influences the model hydrodynamics.

In addition to hydrodynamics, the sensitivity of the morphodynamics was tested with two additional model simulations: (1) a model where the roughness of the outcropping reefs is ignored (i.e., $c_{f\text{reef}} == c_{f\text{sand}}$ and $f_{w\text{reef}} == f_{w\text{sand}}$); and (2) a model where all the reef elevation is lowered by 1 m including for the buried reefs. Both cases were simulated for the duration of the storm (i.e., nine days) with all the other parameters kept as in Table 1.

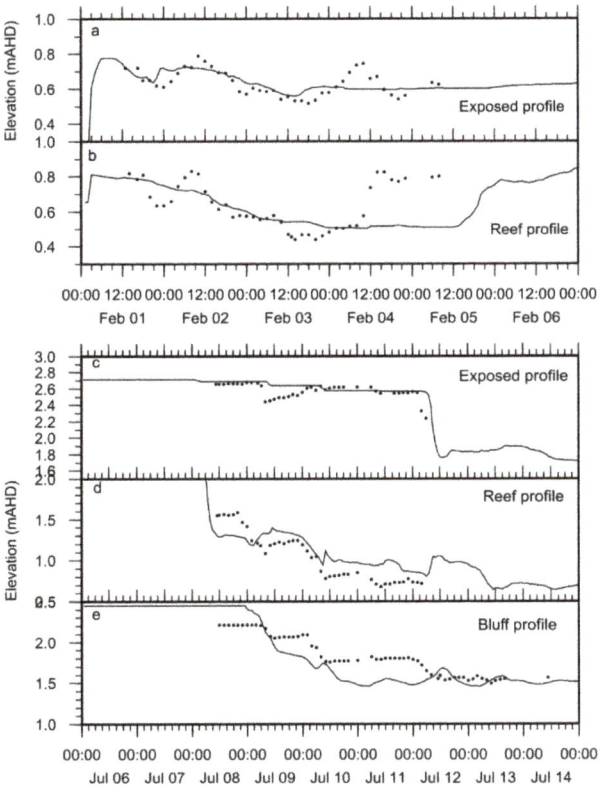

Figure 7. Time-series of changes in beach elevation measured (dots) and simulated (line) for the sea breeze (**a**,**b**) and the storm (**c**–**e**).

Table 4. Parameters and values tested in the current sensitivity analysis.

Parameter	Values
Nuhfac	0.1 0.2 0.3 0.4 0.5 0.6 0.7 0.8 0.9 1.0
n	4 5 6 7 8 9 10 11 12
Gamma	0.4 0.5 0.6 0.7 0.8 0.9
beta	0.05 0.10 0.15 0.20 0.25 0.30 0.35 0.40 0.45 0.50
$c_{f\,reef}$	0.005 0.010 0.015 0.020 0.025 0.030 0.035 0.040 0.045 0.050
$f_{w\,reef}$	0.1 0.2 0.3 0.4 0.5 0.6 0.7 0.8 0.9 1.0

4. Results

4.1. Storm Simulation

The majority of the storm erosion occurred on the section of beach fronted by reefs, rather than the more exposed area to the north (Figure 8). To the south of the bluff beach, in the lagoon and south of the groyne there was up to 4 m erosion. On the southern side of the bluff beach, 50% of the beach volume was eroded, exposing the underlying reef. In contrast, on the northern side of the bluff, only ~1 m of beach elevation was eroded.

In the lagoon, the subaerial beach eroded by 1 m whereas the submerged part of the beach eroded by 2 to 3 m. The erosion of the lagoon extended to the lagoon mouth and south of the Bommie. North of the Bommie the erosion was limited to the dry beach and the submerged beach accreted. Closer to the groyne the erosion of the dry beach was close to 3 m (Figure 9).

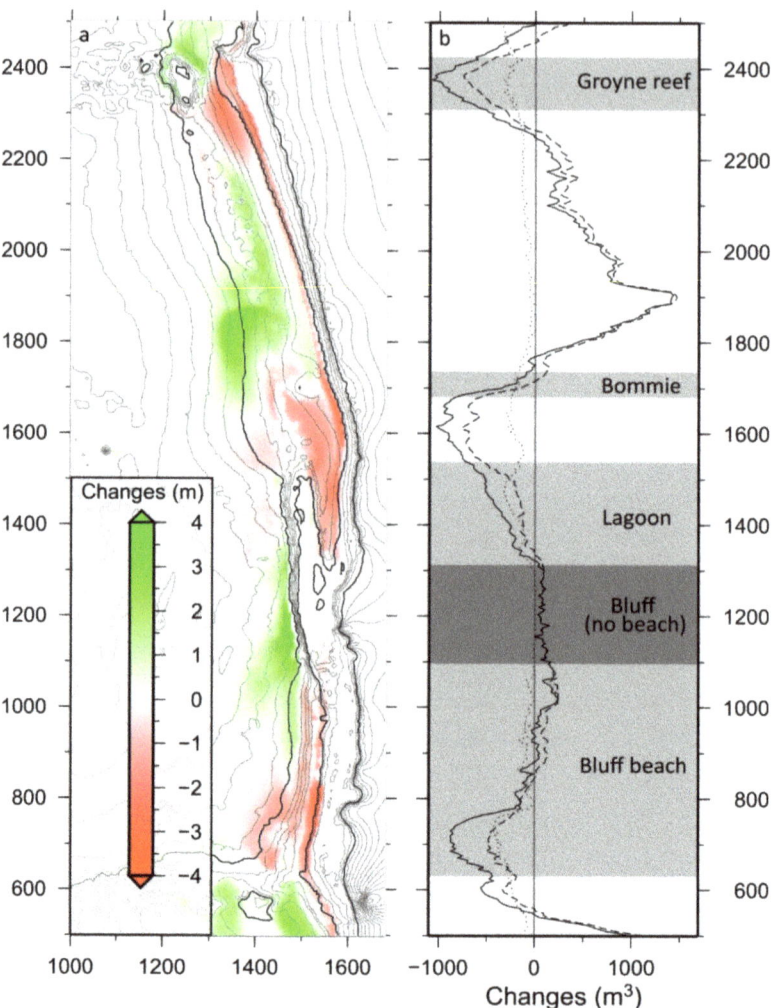

Figure 8. Simulated morphological changes after the storm: (**a**) map of the total changes in elevation overlain with the initial beach elevation contours at 1 m spacing; the thicker contours represent −5 m 0 m and +5 m; (**b**) volume eroded from the beach profiles (plain line); portion of the erosion from the subaerial beach profile (dotted line) and portion of the erosion from the submerged beach profile (dashed line). The grey shading corresponds to areas of the beach that are fronted by reefs.

Major erosion occurred at locations near submerged reefs where the geologically controlled current jets reached velocities exceeding 1 ms^{-1} (Figure 8). During the majority of the storm duration, the area between the lagoon and the groyne was influenced by the jet generated by the reef seaward of the groyne and the jet generated within the lagoon. The direction of the jets depended on the shape of the reef but also varied with the meteorological and oceanographic conditions. For example, the lagoon jets flowed northward along the shore restricted region between the reef and the beach. When these jets exited the lagoon, it flowed directly westward on the 13 July 2010 at midnight, northward toward the Bommie on 13 July 2010 at 23:00 and southward on the offshore side of the reef on the 11 July 2010 at 17:00 (Figure 9a–c, respectively). Changes in the direction of the jet to the south are consistent to alongshore wind forcing which likely to dominate outside of the surf zone.

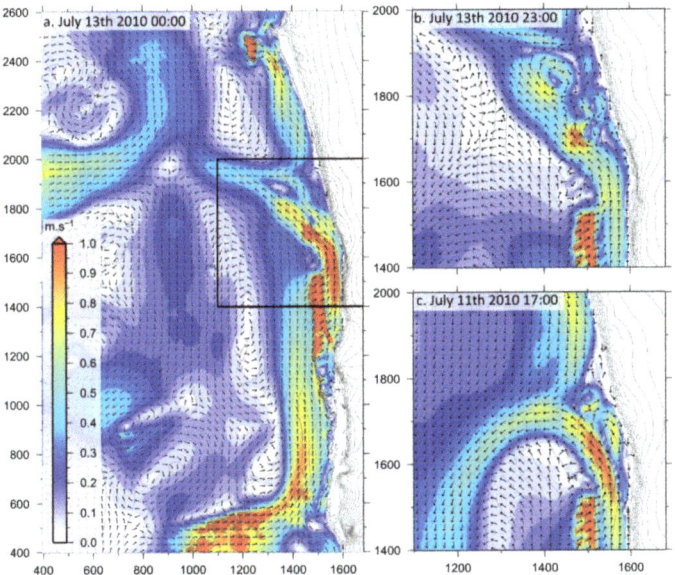

Figure 9. Simulated velocities at three different times during the storm: (**a**) at the peak of the storm with large waves and strong Westerly winds; (**b**) after the peak of the storm with southerly winds; and (**c**) during the onset of the storm with strong Northerly winds. Current speed is represented by shading and direction by vectors. The black square in (**a**) shows the area in (**b**) and (**c**).

At the location where the lagoon jet decreased in speed, along the northern edge of the Bommie, 3 m of sand was deposited. Sand also accumulated seaward of the bluff and seaward of the exposed beach during the storm (Figure 8). During the storm, the average wave height remained below 1 m except near the bluff (Figure 10b). The wave heights were a minimum within the lagoon and shoreward of the reefs. However, the wave set-up was maximum, with an average set up of 0.2 m, on the bluff grading down to 0.05 m between the lagoon entrance and the Bommie (Figure 10a). This gradient in water level between the lee of the reefs and the exposed beach was the driving force of the strong longshore jets that transported sand to the exposed beaches and offshore (Figure 10c).

4.2. Senstivity

The sensitivity of the simulated currents was tested for the six parameters listed in Table 4. The model was twice as sensitive to roughness (i.e., parameters f_w and c_f) than to all three wave breaking parameters (i.e., parameters n, gamma and beta) and three times more sensitive to roughness than to the roller dissipation viscosity factor (nuhfac) (Table 5). The mapping of the sensitivity to the roughness parameter shows that the most sensitive areas in the model were the shallow reefs and locations of strong jets. The area near the lagoon jet had a much higher sensitivity (0.3 ms^{-1}) than the average (0.05 ms^{-1}) for the whole domain. This is despite the sandy bottom where the parameters for roughness remained unchanged (Figure 11).

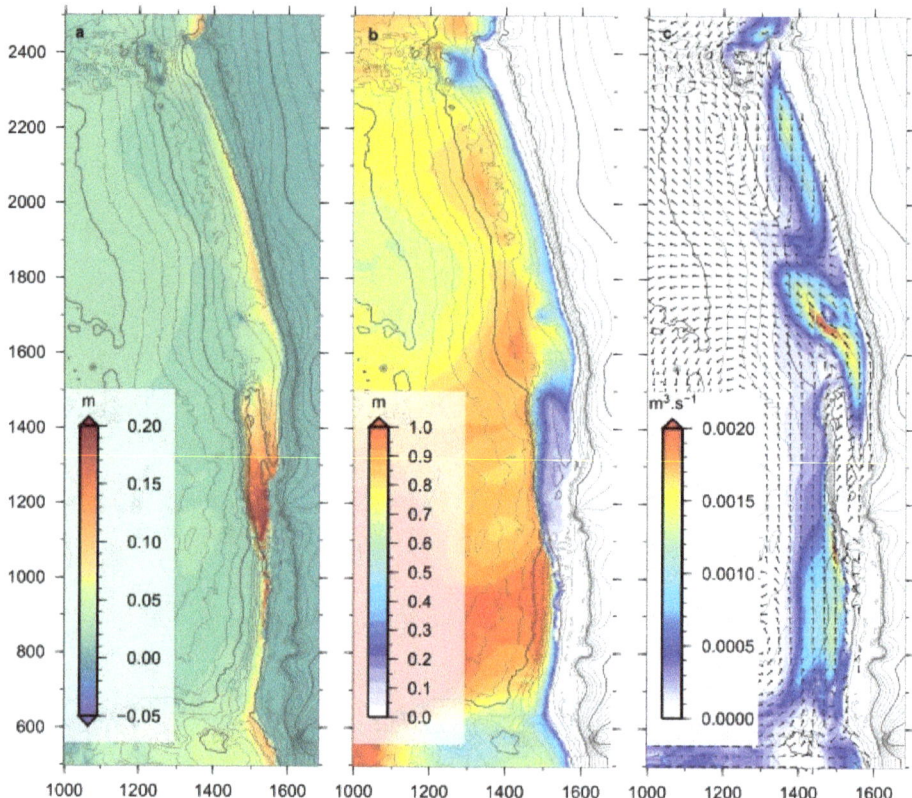

Figure 10. Storm averaged simulated: (**a**) water level; (**b**) root mean square wave height; and (**c**) sand flux.

Table 5. Sensitivity of the simulated currents to selected model parameters.

Parameter	Max. Sensitivity to Cross Shore Velocity (ms^{-1})	Max. Sensitivity to Longshore Velocity (ms^{-1})	Mean Sensitivity to Cross Shore Velocity (ms^{-1})	Mean Sensitivity to Longshore Velocity (ms^{-1})
Nuhfac	0.198	0.210	0.008	0.011
n	0.159	0.176	0.011	0.017
Gamma	0.531	0.480	0.010	0.014
beta	1.272	0.344	0.011	0.014
$c_{f\text{reef}}$	0.708	0.582	0.028	0.040
$f_{w\text{reef}}$	0.859	0.583	0.043	0.059

The role of the roughness in influencing the morphodynamics of the beach during the storm was tested using a simulation where the roughness of the reefs was ignored (i.e., $f_{w\text{reef}}==f_{w}\text{sand}$ and $c_{f\text{reef}}==c_{f\text{sand}}$). This resulted in twice the erosion of the original storm simulation near the reefs (Figure 12a). Ignoring the roughness of the reef had a larger consequence on the simulated erosion than using reef elevations lowered by 1 m. In this simulation, the erosion was quasi-identical to the simulation with the original bathymetry (Figure 12b).

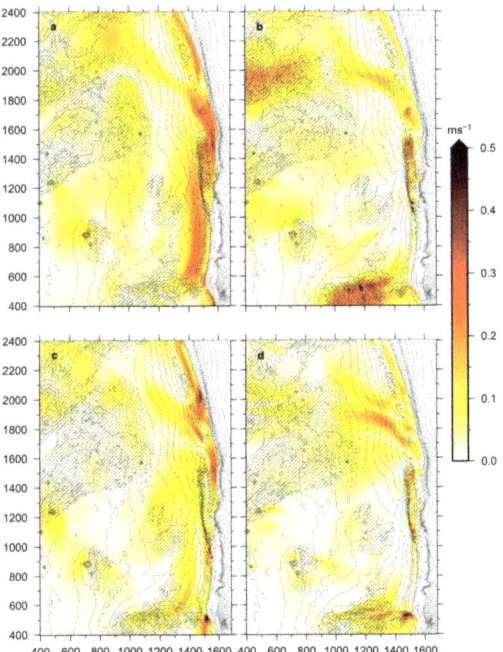

Figure 11. Sensitivity to f_w of the simulated (**a**) alongshore; and, (**b**) cross shore currents and sensitivity to c_f of the simulated (**c**) alongshore; and (**d**) cross shore currents. Hatched area indicates outcropping reefs.

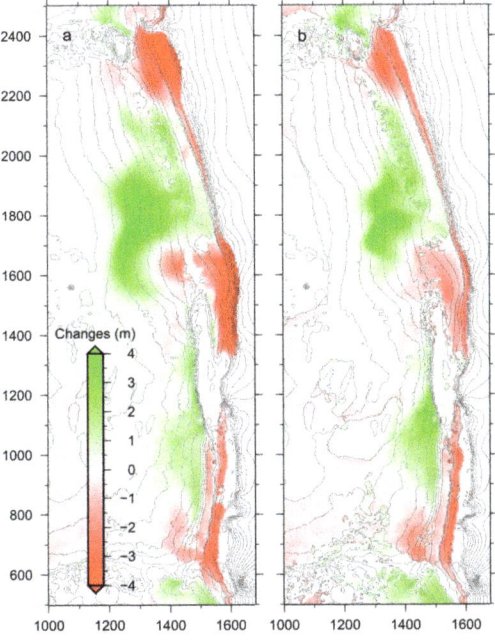

Figure 12. (**a**) Simulated morphological changes without considering an increased reef friction (both f_w and c_f); (**b**) simulated morphological changes with the reef elevation lowered by 1 m.

5. Discussion

In this study, we explored the influence of alongshore variability of reefs on sand flux during a storm using XBeach. This storm generated spatially variable nearshore current jets exceeding 1 ms^{-1}. The morphodynamic response of the beach also varied considerably alongshore. For example, the shoreline retreated by 4 m near the edge of the reef, whereas away from the reef the beachface eroded by 1 m. The contribution of the variable topography of the reef on the response of the beach is discussed below.

As expected, the subaerial beach at Yanchep eroded less in the lee of intertidal reefs, compared to exposed areas without reefs, in line with previous studies which suggested that beaches with reefs are more stable [10]. However, this study highlights that the alongshore variation in reefs alongshore resulted in significant spatial variability in currents and hence sand flux. In some areas, the intertidal reefs did prevent offshore sand flux, but this did not mean that the beach did not erode. This is because the reef created a geologically controlled current jet, which then exported sand in an alongshore direction, resulting in beach erosion in that area. The jets within the lagoon and south of the groyne were strong enough to erode deep channels on the lower beachface (Figure 8). This erosion was larger beyond the alongshore limits of the reef due to the added erosive effect of the waves and the jet turning offshore.

Therefore, in summary, at Yanchep, the alongshore variation in topography of the reef resulted in the following: (1) a reduction of the offshore sand flux; and (2) enhanced alongshore sand flux. However, at locations where the elevation of the reef sharply reduced in the alongshore direction, waves could then directly affect the beach and the alongshore flow veered offshore causing an enhanced offshore sand flux and therefore more erosion than elsewhere on the beach (Figure 8b). Circulation patterns of the flow at the edge of the reef were similar to patterns that have previously been observed during laboratory experiments and simulations on low-crested breakwaters [43–46], and they are believed to be responsible for erosion in the lee of submerged engineering structures installed too close to the shore [47]. In the case of reef beaches, this indicates that alongshore reef boundaries (such as shown in Figure 8) are likely to be beach erosion hot spots.

Erosion in the lagoon was caused by an alongshore current jet, driven by wave set-up. This jet is essentially a topographically controlled current that is forced to follow the reef contours alongshore. During the storm, the average sand flux north of the lagoon was directed northward driven by the lagoon jet (Figure 10c), which is opposite to the expected direction of sand flux with northwest waves (Figure 3). The lagoon is closed to the south so the buildup of water can only escape to the north. The current gains sufficient momentum in the process to keep flowing north even after exiting the lagoon. The occurrence of such jets around reefs also occurs in the vicinity of engineered structures [48,49] and can sometimes form circulation cells in the lee of the reef [45,50]. These jets have been linked to beach erosion in the lee of low-crested structures in the nearshore [47], but their role in beach erosion and recovery is unclear. At Yanchep, the lagoon jet was sufficiently strong to influence the nearshore hydrodynamics more than 1 km down-drift (Figure 10c). There were also other jets formed in the lee of the groyne reef (Figure 9a) and to a smaller extent near the Bommie (Figure 9c). At the Bommie, the lagoon jet was so strong that it may have prevented the formation of jets by the Bommie. At the peak of the storm, the jet from the lagoon flowing northward and the jet from the groyne reef flowing southward were converging north of the Bommie (Figure 9b). The sand carried by both jets settled at this convergence zone forming 3 m of sand accumulation (Figure 8). The extent of this sand accumulation was confirmed further by the difficult post-storm recovery of a buried (~1 m) ADCP deployed near the 7 m depth contour seaward of the Bommie. The sand fluxes during the storm were therefore controlled by the path of the jets. The lagoon jet influenced the morphological response of the beach at least as far as 700 m north of the lagoon (Figure 10c). We can therefore conclude that the classification of reef beaches cannot be solely based on the cross-shore presence and topography of hard landforms, but needs to include the presence and longshore topography of hard landforms.

Erosion in the lee of the reef was created by current jets generated from the gradient in wave set-up. This wave set-up gradient was a direct consequence of the alongshore changes in reef elevation and variation in the width of the lagoon [51]. Therefore, elevation of the reef should not be a dominant factor in controlling the strength of the jet and the resulting erosion as long as the following criteria are met: (1) elevation of the reef results in wave breaking; and (2) reef elevation is sufficiently low that waves completely overtop the reef. This was confirmed by the virtually identical erosion that occurred in the model when all the reef elevations in the model domain were lowered by 1 m (Figure 12b).

The speed and direction of the jets were not sensitive to the elevation of the reef but were more sensitive to reef roughness, represented by c_f and f_w. This is in contrast with findings from Segura [52] which found that the elevation of the reef relative to the water level is of critical importance. This may be due to a difference in the overall morphology of the reef. The reef fronting Yanchep Lagoon is more similar to a rock platform than the sloping reefs further offshore. The high sensitivity of the morphodynamics to the reef roughness reinforces findings from McCall et al. [53] on rocky shore platform and experimental work on reef system in lab experiments [54] and numerical experiments [55]. There is, however, no practical method to evaluate and map the values of c_f and f_w apart from model calibration field data. Swart [56] proposed a formulation to calculate f_w based on the size of roughness elements but mapping the roughness of reef environment is still a developing research topic [38,57,58].

Erosion in the lagoon was caused by an alongshore current jet, driven by wave set-up. This jet is essentially a topographically controlled current that is forced to follow the reef contours alongshore. During the storm, the average sand flux north of the lagoon was directed northward driven by the lagoon jet (Figure 10c), which is opposite to the expected direction of sand flux with northwest waves (Figure 3). The lagoon is closed to the south, so the buildup of water can only escape to the north. The current gains sufficient momentum in the process to keep flowing north even after exiting the lagoon. The occurrence of such jets around reefs [59] also occurs in the vicinity of engineered structures [45,49,50] and can sometimes form circulation cells in the lee of the reef [45]. These jets have been linked to beach erosion in the lee of low-crested structures in the nearshore [47,59], but their role in beach erosion and recovery is unclear. At Yanchep, the lagoon jet was sufficiently strong to influence the nearshore hydrodynamics more than 1 km down-drift (Figure 10c). There were also other jets formed in the lee of the groyne reef (Figure 9a) and to a smaller extent near the Bommie (Figure 9c). At the Bommie, the lagoon jet was so strong that it may have prevented the formation of jets by the Bommie. At the peak of the storm, the jet from the lagoon flowing northward and the jet from the groyne reef flowing southward were converging north of the Bommie (Figure 9b). The sand carried by both jets settled at this convergence zone forming 3 m of sand accumulation (Figure 8). The extent of this sand accumulation was confirmed further by the difficult post-storm recovery of a buried (~1 m) ADCP deployed near the 7 m depth contour seaward of the Bommie. The sand fluxes during the storm were therefore controlled by the path of the jets. The lagoon jet influenced the morphological response of the beach at least as far as 700 m north of the lagoon (Figure 10c). The transport of sand offshore and alongshore, far from its source, by jet is likely to drive a complex nonlinear response both in the storm erosion and recovery phase. This could help explain the complex nearshore morphodynamics patterns observed by Segura [52]. Overall, we can conclude that classification and prediction on the morphodynamics of reef beaches cannot be solely based on the cross-shore presence and topography of hard landforms, but needs to include the presence and longshore variation of topography of hard landforms.

6. Conclusions

The hydrodynamics and sand transport on beaches that consist of rock and coral reefs are significantly influenced by these structures. In this study, undertaken in southwest Australia on a beach fronted reefs, the impact of winter storm was simulated using XBeach model programmed using GPU. The model was validated using field measurements of waves, currents and morphology from the study site. The study site consisted of heterogeneous calcarenite limestone reefs that consisted of strong alongshore variation in the level of geological controls on the beach. The morphodynamic response of the beach varied considerably alongshore because of sharp variations in topography due to the reefs. This included strong spatial differences in the current distribution, including areas with strong current jets exiting the lagoon region. These current jets, measured using surface drifters, exceeding 1 ms^{-1} and contributed to alongshore sand flux. These jets also enhanced the beach erosion at the boundary of the reef and directly influenced the morphological response of the beach hundreds of meters away from the reefs.

Author Contributions: This study was undertaken as a part of PhD research by C.B. Field data collection and were performed by C.B. and S.L.G. with supervision by I.D.H. and C.B.P. Numerical simulations were performed by C.B. All authors contributed to conceptualization and methodology. C.B. was responsible for the software, C.B. and S.L.G. for data analysis, C.B.P. for resources. All authors contributed to writing, the original draft preparation was by C.B. with review and editing by S.L.G., I.D.H., C.B.P. All authors have read and agreed to the published version of the manuscript.

Funding: This research received no external funding.

Institutional Review Board Statement: Not applicable.

Informed Consent Statement: Not applicable.

Data Availability Statement: The data used in this study are available from the corresponding author.

Acknowledgments: We are grateful to the Western Australian Department of Transport for conducting the bathymetry and topography survey and for supplying the LiDAR dataset, the Bureau of Meteorology for suppling the wind data and the Port of Fremantle for providing the Fremantle tide gage data. CB was supported by a Scholarship for International Research Fees (SIRF), University International Stipend and completion Postgraduate Scholarship from The University of Western Australia.

Conflicts of Interest: The authors declare no conflict of interest.

References

1. Fellowes, T.E.; Vila-Concejo, A.; Gallop, S.L. Morphometric classification of swell-dominated embayed beaches. *Mar. Geol.* **2019**, *411*, 78–87. [CrossRef]
2. Gallop, S.L.; Bosserelle, C.; Eliot, I.; Pattiaratchi, C.B. The influence of limestone landforms on erosion and recovery of a perched beach. *Cont. Shelf Res.* **2012**, *47*, 16–27. [CrossRef]
3. Gallop, S.L.; Bosserelle, C.; Haigh, I.D.; Wadey, M.P.; Pattiaratchi, C.; Eliot, I. The impact of temperate reefs on 34 years of shoreline and vegetation line stability at Yanchep, southwestern Australia and implications for coastal setback. *Mar. Geol.* **2015**, *369*, 224–232. [CrossRef]
4. Frihy, O.E.; El Ganaini, M.; El Sayed, W.R.; Iskander, M.M. The role of fringing coral reef in beach protection of Hurghada, Gulf of Suez, Red Sea of Egypt. *Ecol. Eng.* **2004**, *22*, 17–25. [CrossRef]
5. Valvo, L.M.; Murray, A.B.; Ashton, A. How does underlying geology affect coastline change? An initial modeling investigation. *J. Geophys. Res.* **2006**, *111*, 1–18. [CrossRef]
6. Vousdoukas, M.I.; Velegrakis, F.; Plomaritis, T. Beachrock occurrence, characteristics, formation mechanisms and impacts. *Earth Sci. Rev.* **2007**, *85*, 23–46. [CrossRef]
7. Naylor, L.A.; Stephenson, W.J.; Trenhaile, A.S. Rock coast geomorphology: Recent advances and future research directions. *Geomorphology* **2009**, *114*, 3–11. [CrossRef]
8. Ferrario, F.; Beck, M.W.; Storlazzi, C.D.; Micheli, F.; Shepard, C.C.; Airoldi, L. The effectiveness of coral reefs for coastal hazard risk reduction and adaptation. *Nat. Commun.* **2014**, *5*, 3794. [CrossRef]
9. Gallop, S.L.; Young, I.R.; Ranasinghe, R.; Durrant, T.H.; Haigh, I.D. The large-scale influence of the Great Barrier Reef matrix on wave attenuation. *Coral Reefs* **2014**, *33*, 1167–1178. [CrossRef]
10. Eversole, D.; Fletcher, C. Longshore sediment transport rates on a reef-fronted beach: Field data and empirical models Kaanapali Beach, Hawaii. *J. Coast. Res.* **2003**, *19*, 649–663.
11. Muñoz-Perez, J.J.; Tejedor, L.; Medina, R. Equilibrium Beach Profile Model for Reef-Protected Beaches. *J. Coast. Res.* **1999**, *15*, 950–957.
12. Vousdoukas, M.I.; Velegrakis, F.; Karambas, T.V. Morphology and sedimentology of a microtidal beach with beachrocks: Vatera, Lesbos, NE Mediterranean. *Cont. Shelf Res.* **2009**, *29*, 1937–1947. [CrossRef]

13. Gallop, S.L.; Bosserelle, C.; Pattiaratchi, C.; Eliot, I. Rock topography causes spatial variation in the wave, current and beach response to sea breeze activity. *Mar. Geol.* **2011**, *290*, 29–40. [CrossRef]
14. Winter, G.; Storlazzi, C.; Vitousek, S.; van Dongeren, A.; McCall, R.; Hoeke, R.; Skirving, W.; Marra, J.; Reyns, J.; Aucan, J.; et al. Steps to Develop Early Warning Systems and Future Scenarios of Storm Wave-Driven Flooding Along Coral Reef-Lined Coasts. *Front. Mar. Sci.* **2020**, *7*, 199. [CrossRef]
15. Muñoz-Pérez, J.J.; Medina, R. Comparison of long-, medium- and short-term variations of beach profiles with and without submerged geological control. *Coast. Eng.* **2010**, *57*, 241–251. [CrossRef]
16. Bosserelle, C.; Haigh, I.D.; Pattiaratchi, C.; Gallop, S.L. Simulation of perched beach accretion using smoothed particle hydrodynamics. In Proceedings of the Coasts and Ports Engineers, Perth, Australia, 28–30 September 2011.
17. Young, I.R. Wave transformation over coral reefs. *J. Geophys. Res. Ocean.* **1989**, *94*, 9779–9789. [CrossRef]
18. Gourlay, M.R. Wave transformation on a coral reef. *Coast. Eng.* **1994**, *23*, 17–42. [CrossRef]
19. Yao, Y.; Huang, Z.; Monismith, S.G.; Lo, E.Y.M. 1DH Boussinesq modeling of wave transformation over fringing reefs. *Ocean Eng.* **2012**, *47*, 30–42. [CrossRef]
20. Muñoz-Perez, J.J.; Gallop, S.L.; Moreno, L.J. A comparison of beach nourishment methodology and performance at two fringing reef beaches in Waikiki (Hawaii, USA) and Cadiz (SW Spain). *J. Mar. Sci. Eng.* **2020**, *8*, 266.
21. Castelle, B.; Scott, T.; Brander, R.W.; McCarroll, R.J. Rip current types, circulation and hazard. *Earth Sci. Rev.* **2016**, *163*, 1–21. [CrossRef]
22. Horta, J.; Oliveira, S.; Moura, D.; Ferreira, Ó. Nearshore hydrodynamics at pocket beaches with contrasting wave exposure in southern Portugal. *Estuar. Coast. Shelf Sci.* **2018**, *204*, 40–55. [CrossRef]
23. Gallop, S.L.; Kennedy, D.M.; Loureiro, C.; Naylor, L.A.; Muñoz-Pérez, J.J.; Jackson, D.W.T.; Fellowes, T.E. Geologically controlled sandy beaches: Their geomorphology, morphodynamics and classification. *Sci. Total Environ.* **2020**, *731*, 139123. [CrossRef] [PubMed]
24. Loureiro, C.; Ferreira, Ó. Mechanisms and timescales of beach rotation. In *Sandy Beach: Morphodynamics*; Jackson, D.W.T., Short, A.D., Eds.; Elsevier: Amsterdam, The Netherlands, 2020.
25. Mandlier, P.; Kench, P. Analytical modelling of wave refraction and convergence on coral reef platforms: Implications for island formation and stability. *Geomorphology* **2012**, *84–92*, 159–160. [CrossRef]
26. Pattiaratchi, C.B.; Eliot, M. Sea level variability in south–west Australia: From hours to decades. In Proceedings of the 31st Conference on Coastal Engineering, ASCE, Hamburg, Germany, 31 August–5 September 2018; pp. 1186–1198.
27. Chen, M.; Pattiaratchi, C.B.; Ghadouani, A.; Hanson, C. Influence of storm events on chlorophyll distribution along the oligotrophic continental shelf off southwestern Australia. *Front. Mar. Sci.* **2020**, *7*, 287. [CrossRef]
28. Rafiq, S.; Pattiaratchi, C.; Janeković, I. Dynamics of the Land–Sea Breeze System and the Surface Current Response in South-West Australia. *J. Mar. Sci. Eng.* **2020**, *8*, 931. [CrossRef]
29. Bosserelle, C.; Pattiaratchi, C.; Haigh, I. Inter-annual variability and longer-term changes in the wave climate of Western Australia between 1970 and 2009. *Ocean Dyn.* **2012**, *62*, 63–76. [CrossRef]
30. Masselink, G.; Pattiaratchi, C.B. Seasonal changes in beach morphology along the sheltered coastline of Perth, Western Australia. *Mar. Geol.* **2001**, *172*, 243–263. [CrossRef]
31. Pattiaratchi, C.B.; Hegge, B.; Gould, J.; Eliot, I. Impact of sea-breeze activity on nearshore and foreshore processes in southwestern Australia. *Cont. Shelf Res.* **1997**, *17*, 1539–1560. [CrossRef]
32. Gentilli, J. *Australian Climate Pattern*; Nelson: Melbourne, Australia, 1972.
33. Verspecht, F.; Pattiaratchi, C.B. On the significance of wind event frequency for particulate resuspension and light attenuation in coastal waters. *Cont. Shelf Res.* **2010**, *30*, 1971–1982. [CrossRef]
34. Roelvink, D.; Reniers, A.; van Dongeren, A.; van Thiel de Vries, J.; McCall, R.; Lescinski, J. Modelling storm impacts on beaches, dunes and barrier islands. *Coast. Eng.* **2009**, *56*, 1133–1152. [CrossRef]
35. Roelvink, D.; Reniers, A.; van Dongeren, A.; van Thiel de Vries, J.; Lescinski, J.; McCall, R. XBeach model description and manual. In *Report from UNESCO-IHE Institute for Water Education*; Deltares and Delft University of Technology: Delft, The Netherlands, 2010.
36. Gerritsen, F. Wave attenuation and wave set-up on a coastal reef. *Coast. Eng. Proc.* **1981**, *1*. [CrossRef]
37. Hearn, C.J. Wave-breaking hydrodynamics within coral reef systems and the effect of changing relative sea level. *J. Geophys. Res.* **1999**, *104*, 30007. [CrossRef]
38. Péquignet, A.C.N.; Becker, J.M.; Merrifield, M.A.; Boc, S.J. The dissipation of wind wave energy across a fringing reef at Ipan, Guam. *Coral Reefs* **2011**, *30*, 71–82. [CrossRef]
39. Taebi, S.; Lowe, R.J.; Pattiaratchi, C.B.; Ivey, G.N.; Symonds, G. A numerical study of the dynamics of the wave-driven circulation within a fringing reef system. *Ocean Dyn.* **2012**, *62*, 585–602. [CrossRef]
40. Booij, N.; Ris, R.C.; Holthuijsen, L.H. A third-generation wave model for coastal regions, Part I, Model description and validation. *J. Geophys. Res.* **1999**, *104*, 7649–7666. [CrossRef]
41. Willmott, J. On the validation of models. *J. Phys. Geogr.* **1981**, *2*, 184–194. [CrossRef]
42. Johnson, D.; Pattiaratchi, C. Application, modelling and validation of surf zone drifters. *Coast. Eng.* **2004**, *51*, 455–471. [CrossRef]
43. Groenewoud, M.D.; van de Graaff, J.; Claessen, E.W.; van der Biezen, S.C. Effect of submerged breakwater on profile development. In Proceedings of the 25th International Conference on Coastal Engineering, ASCE, Orlando, FL, USA, 2–6 September 1996.

44. Van der Biezen, S.C.; Roelvink, J.A.; van de Graaff, J.; Schaap, J.; Torrini, L. 2DH Morphological Modelling of Submerged Breakwaters. In Proceedings of the 26th International Conference on Coastal Engineering, ASCE, Copenhagen, Denmark, 22–26 June 1998.
45. Ranasinghe, R.; Larson, M.; Savioli, J. Shoreline response to a single shore-parallel submerged breakwater. *Coast. Eng.* **2010**, *57*, 1006–1017. [CrossRef]
46. Villani, M.; Bosboom, J.; Zijlema, M.; Stive, M.J.F. Circulation patterns and shoreline response induced by submerged breakwaters. In Proceedings of the 33rd Conference on Coastal Engineering, ASCE, Santander, Spain, 1–6 July 2012.
47. Ranasinghe, R.; Turner, I.L. Shoreline response to submerged structures: A review. *Coast. Eng.* **2006**, *53*, 65–79. [CrossRef]
48. Dean, R.; Chen, R.; Browder, A. Full scale monitoring study of a submerged breakwater, Palm Beach, Florida, USA. *Coast. Eng.* **1997**, *29*, 291–315. [CrossRef]
49. Johnson, H.K.; Karambas, T.V.; Avgeris, I.; Zanuttigh, B.; Gonzalez-Marco, D.; Caceres, I. Modelling of waves and currents around submerged breakwaters. *Coast. Eng.* **2005**, *52*, 949–969. [CrossRef]
50. Duarte Nemes, D.; Fabián Criado-Sudau, F.; Nicolás Gallo, M. Beach Morphodynamic Response to a Submerged Reef. *Water* **2019**, *11*, 340. [CrossRef]
51. Lowe, R.J.; Hart, C.; Pattiaratchi, C.B. Morphological constraints to wave-driven circulation in coastal reef-lagoon systems: A numerical study. *J. Geophys. Res.* **2010**, *115*, C09021. [CrossRef]
52. Segura, L.E. Quantifying the Morphodynamics of Beaches to Nearshore and Offshore Rocky Reefs in Southwestern Australia. Ph.D. Thesis, The University of Western Australia, Perth, Australia, 2017. [CrossRef]
53. McCall, R.; Masselink, G.; Austin, M.; Poate TJager, T. Modelling incident-band and infragravity wave dynamics on rocky shore platforms. In Proceedings of the Coastal Dynamics, Helsingør, Denmark, 12–16 June 2017; pp. 1658–1669.
54. Buckley, M.L.; Lowe, R.J.; Hansen, J.E.; Van Dongeren, A.R. Wave Setup over a Fringing Reef with Large Bottom Roughness. *J. Phys. Oceanogr.* **2016**, *46*, 2317–2333. [CrossRef]
55. Franklin, G.; Mariño-Tapia, I.; Torres-Freyermuth, A. Effects of reef roughness on wave setup and surf zone currents. *J. Coast. Res.* **2013**. Available online: https://www.jstor.org/stable/26491086 (accessed on 13 July 2020). [CrossRef]
56. Swart, D. *Offshore Sediment Transport and Equilibrium Beach Profiles*; Technical Report 131; Delft Hydraulic Laboratory: Delft, The Netherlands, 1974.
57. Rogers, J.S.; Monismith, S.G.; Fringer, O.B.; Koweek, D.A.; Dunbar, R.B. A coupled wave-hydrodynamic model of an atoll with high friction: Mechanisms for flow, connectivity, and ecological implications. *Ocean Model.* **2017**, *110*, 66–82. [CrossRef]
58. Wandres, M.; Aucan, J.; Espejo, A.; Jackson, N.; de Ramon N'Yeurt, A.; Damlamian, H. Distant-Source Swells Cause Coastal Inundation on Fiji's Coral Coast. *Front. Mar. Sci.* **2020**, *7*. [CrossRef]
59. Herdman, L.M.M.; Hench, J.L.; Fringer, O.; Monismith, S.G. Behavior of a wave-driven buoyant surface jet on a coral reef. *J. Geophys. Res. Ocean.* **2017**, *122*, 4088–4109. [CrossRef]

Article

Considering the Effect of Land-Based Biomass on Dune Erosion Volumes in Large-Scale Numerical Modeling

Constantin Schweiger * and Holger Schuettrumpf

Institute of Hydraulic Engineering and Water Resources Management (IWW), RWTH Aachen University, Mies-van-der-Rohe-Straße 17, 52056 Aachen, Germany; schuettrumpf@iww.rwth-aachen.de
* Correspondence: schweiger@iww.rwth-aachen.de

Abstract: This paper presents and validates a novel root model which accounts for the effect of belowground biomass on dune erosion volumes in XBeach, based on a small-scale wave flume experiment that was translated to a larger scale. A 1D-XBeach model was calibrated by using control runs considering a dune without vegetation. Despite calibration, a general model–data mismatch was observed in terms of overestimated erosion volumes around the waterline. Furthermore, the prediction of overwash had to be induced by increasing the maximum nearshore wave height within the XBeach simulation. Subsequently, applying the root model resulted in a good agreement with the belowground biomass cases, and the consideration of spatially varying rooting depths further improved the results. Predictions of the root model while using locally increased friction coefficients were in line with the aboveground and belowground biomass cases. However, the effect of the root model on the erosion predictions varied among the hydrodynamic conditions, so further improvements are required. Therefore, future research should focus on quantifying the effects of land-based biomass and individual plant characteristics, such as root density, on dune erodibility at large scales, along with their influences on the temporal evolution of dune scarping and avalanching.

Keywords: XBeach; dune erosion; land-based biomass; dune vegetation; model scaling; large-scale

1. Introduction

Coastal dunes are distributed worldwide and acknowledged for their wide range of functions, including their contributions to coastal defense, ecological diversity and socio-economic services, such as recreation and tourism [1,2]. Concerning coastal protection, dunes serve as a natural barrier at the boundary between land and sea. Furthermore, they have been recommended as one example of a more sustainable, cost-effective and ecologically sound coastal protection measure than conventional hard structures [3–5]. In this regard, dune vegetation was found to have an especially beneficial effect on the resilience of dunes against storm-induced erosion [6–10]. Due to the globally observed climatically-driven increase in dune vegetation in the period between 1984 and 2017 [11] and the expected increasing frequency of sea level extremes until the end of this century [12–16], detailed knowledge about wave-driven erosion of vegetated beach-dune systems is important with respect to global climate change. Owing to its wide use in coastal management, understanding the influence of vegetation on nearshore hydrodynamic and morphodynamic processes is also essential concerning coastal numerical modeling.

The process-based XBeach model [17] has been proven to accurately predict storm-induced erosion and dune breaching [18–23]. With respect to vegetation, the model was extended to account for the damping of short waves and infragravity waves and mean flow [24,25], and the interaction between waves and vegetation [26]. From a morphodynamic perspective, the effect of vegetation is often considered by locally increasing the bed friction coefficient [22,27–29], which was improved by including a dynamic response of local bed friction coefficients in vegetated areas [30]. In addition, Bendoni et al. [31] improved the XBeach model in order to model the erosive processes of saltmarsh vegetation.

More recently, Schweiger and Schuettrumpf [32] extended XBeach's code with a literature-derived root model to account for the reducing effect of belowground (land-based) biomass on dune erosion volumes that is acknowledged in the literature [10,33,34]. The basic idea is to locally increase the critical velocity for erosion due to additional root cohesion until the cumulative erosion exceeds a user-defined constant rooting depth. Applying the root model to the small-scale wave flume experiment of Bryant et al. [34], where the presence of belowground biomass (BGB) reduced the observed dune erosion in comparison to a control dune (no vegetation), resulted in higher agreement with the BGB measurements. However, a general model–data mismatch was observed since there was no dune overwash in the simulations. Although XBeach's default parameters related to sediment transport were scaled to adapt the application to small scales, this was assumed to be one possible cause of the general model–data mismatch. The reason is that the initial calibration of the XBeach model was mainly based on large-scale dune experiments [35,36], and hence, XBeach's default parameters are optimized for large-scale applications.

Therefore, this study aimed to validate the root model based on an upscaled model setup of Bryant et al. [34]. Due to the translation to large scales, it was expected that applying XBeach's default parameters would generally lead to better model performance, especially with respect to dune overwash. Furthermore, the root model was improved to account for spatial variations of the rooting depths. Following a description of the process-based XBeach model, Section 2 focusses on the improvement of the root model (2.2) and the translation of the one-dimensional (1D) model setup to large scales (2.3). In Section 3, the model is hydrodynamically (3.1) and morphodynamically (3.2) calibrated by using the upscaled control cases of Bryant et al. [34], after which the root model is validated against the upscaled BGB cases. Furthermore, the effects of locally increased friction coefficients and their use with the root model are investigated (3.3). This is followed by discussion and conclusions in Section 4.

2. Methods

2.1. XBeach

XBeach [17] is a two-dimensional (2DH) numerical model which solves equations for flow, wave motion, sediment transport and bed evolution. While short-wave motion is obtained from a time-dependent version of the wave-action balance equation on the wave group time scale (surf beat mode), low-frequency and mean flows are calculated based on the depth-averaged shallow-water equations. These are cast into a depth-averaged generalized Lagrangian mean (GLM) formulation to account for wave-induced mass flux and subsequent return flow.

The bed friction associated with low-frequency and mean flow is considered by the bed shear stress (τ) approach according to Ruessink et al. [37]:

$$\tau_{bx}^E = c_f \rho u^E \sqrt{(1.16 u_{rms})^2 + (u_E + v_E)^2} \tag{1}$$

with ρ being the density of water, u^E and v^E the Eulerian velocities and u_{rms} the near-bed short-wave orbital velocity. The dimensional friction coefficient c_f can be determined, among others, by the Manning coefficient n:

$$c_f = \frac{gn^2}{h^{1/3}} \tag{2}$$

with g being the acceleration due to gravity and h the water depth. In order to account for spatial and temporal variations, a dynamic roughness module [30] varies the Manning roughness coefficients in vegetated areas according to:

$$n = \begin{cases} n_{sand} + (n_{veg} - n_{sand}) \cdot min\left(max\left(0, \frac{d^* + \Delta zb}{d^*}\right), 1\right), -d^* \leq \Delta zb < 0 \\ n_{sand} + (n_{veg} - n_{sand}) \cdot min\left(max\left(0, \frac{h^* + \Delta zb}{h^*}\right), 1\right), \Delta zb > 0 \end{cases} \tag{3}$$

with $n_{sand/veg}$ being the Manning coefficients associated with sand and vegetation, d^* and h^* the critical depths for erosion and deposition and $\Delta z b$ the cumulative deposition/erosion which is negative in the case of erosion.

Sediment transport is modeled with the aid of a depth-averaged advection-diffusion equation [38], where the actual sediment concentration C is calculated by the mismatch with an equilibrium sediment concentration C_{eq}. The latter can be calculated by multiple sediment transport formulations, of which one example is the Soulsby–Van Rijn equations [39,40], in which the equilibrium sediment concentration for bed and suspended load is calculated according to:

$$C_{eq,sb/ss} = \frac{A_{sb} + A_{ss}}{h} \left(\sqrt{v_{mg}^2 + 0.018 \cdot \frac{u_{rms,2}^2}{C_d}} - U_{cr} \right)^{2.4} \quad (4)$$

with A_{sb} and A_{ss} being the bed load and suspended load coefficients, v_{mg} the Eulerian velocity magnitude, $u_{rms,2}$ the adjusted near-bed short-wave orbital velocity for wave breaking induced turbulence, C_d a drag coefficient and U_{cr} the critical velocity that defines at which depth-averaged velocity sediment motion is initiated. The actual sediment concentration is used for the calculation of sediment transport rates, which in turn serve as input for the calculation of the bed-level update. Finally, an avalanching mechanism accounts for the slumping of sandy material, which exchanges sediment between two adjacent cells as long as a critical slope between these cells is exceeded. By distinguishing between wet and dry cells, the avalanching mechanism considers that wet cells are more prone to slumping.

A full description of the XBeach model can be found in Roelvink et al. [17] and in the online manual (https://xbeach.readthedocs.io/en/latest/xbeach_manual.html#id83, accessed on 6 July 2021).

2.2. Root Model

The fundamental idea of the root model is based on the effect of fibrous roots on sandy soils by increasing the resistance of the top (rooted) soil against concentrated flow erosion due to additional root cohesion [41]. Figure 1 shows the basic principle of the root model. Within the *morphevolution* module of the XBeach model, a root cohesion term increases the critical erosion velocity where belowground biomass is present until the cumulative erosion ($\Delta z b$) exceeds a user-defined rooting depth (z_{root}) (Figure 1a):

$$U_{cr} = U_{cr} + \underbrace{rcc \cdot \sqrt{\frac{1}{\rho} C_r}}_{U_{cr,root}}, \quad z_{root} \leq \Delta z b < 0 \quad (5)$$

with ρ being the density of water. The user-defined root cohesion C_r (kN/m^2) is the product of the root tensile strength t_R and the root area ratio RAR, which are both plant-specific [42]. An additional root cohesion coefficient (rcc) is used to steer the model, which can either be constant or linearly vary with the erosion depth (Figure 1b):

$$rcc = \begin{cases} rcc_0, & \text{constant mode} \\ 0 + \min\left(\max\left(\frac{z_{root}(x) + \Delta z b(t)}{z_{root}(x)}, 0\right), 1\right) \cdot rcc_0, & \text{dynamic mode} \end{cases} \quad (6)$$

with rcc_0 being the initial root cohesion coefficient which is zero in areas without belowground biomass. In comparison to its first version, the root model was extended to account for spatially varying rooting depths ($z_{root}(x)$), which are provided through an external file that has the same format as the *hardlayer* file (Figure 1c). Similarly to its application to smaller scales [32], the root cohesion term was normalized to one so that applying $rcc = 1$ corresponds to an increase of U_{cr} by $U_{cr,root} = 1$ m/s. This was done to simplify the calibration process in this study and due to the use of substitutes (coir fibers) with unknown t_R and RAR instead of natural vegetation.

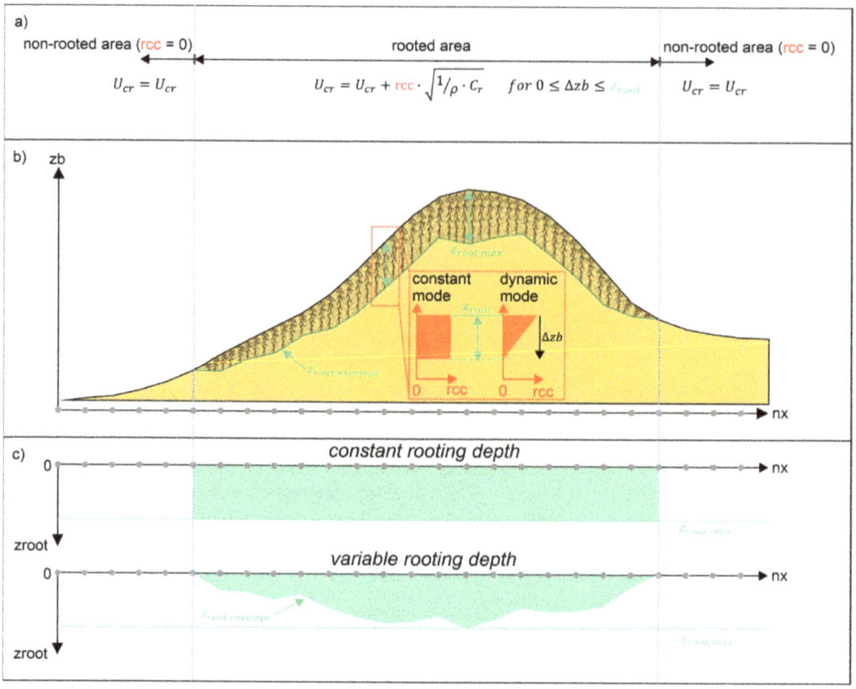

Figure 1. Extended root model: (**a**) The increase of the critical erosion velocity (U_{cr}) in vegetated areas due to additional root cohesion. (**b**) A schematic sketch showing the increase of U_{cr} simulated by the root model until the cumulated erosion (Δzb) exceeds a user-defined rooting depth (z_{root}). The root cohesion term is steered by a root calibration coefficient (rcc) which can be constant or linearly decreasing with the erosion depth (dynamic mode). (**c**) In addition to the first version [32], it is now possible to use spatially varying rooting depths.

For a detailed description of the root model, the reader is referred to Schweiger and Schuettrumpf [32].

2.3. Model Scaling

The aim of this study was to validate the root model on a larger scale problem by upscaling the small-scale model setup of Bryant et al. [34]. In general, scaling of laboratory experiments requires the correct representation of the physical processes in nature so that dimensionless numbers characterizing these processes (e.g., Froude number, Reynolds number and Irribaren number) are the same for the prototype and model [43]. The most common approach is the use of scaling laws, where the ratio between prototype and model is defined by the scale parameter $n = p_p/p_m$. Here, p_p and p_m are the parameter values in prototype and in the (laboratory) model [43]. In this regard, hydrodynamic parameters are generally scaled according to Froude [43–47]:

$$n_H = n_L = n_h = n_T^2 = n_t^2 = n_u^2 \tag{7}$$

where H is the wave height, L is the wave length, h is the water depth, T is the wave period, t is the simulation time and u is the wave orbital velocity. Concerning physical geometry, the distortion scale ratio is used [43]:

$$n_g = \frac{n_l}{n_h} \qquad (8)$$

with n_g being the distortion scale, n_l the length ratio and n_h the height ratio between prototype and model. In coastal modeling, these are usually represented by the length and the height of the beach profile being analyzed [47]. From $n_g = 1$, it follows that the physical geometry of the (beach-dune) model is undistorted. If the same applies to Froude scaling, two models will automatically have the same Irribaren number and wave steepness (H/L) [47]. With respect to sediment characteristics, however, additional dimensionless parameters need to be considered. Examples are the dimensionless fall velocity (Dean number), the Shield's number and the Reynolds number [43,47]. From these follows the scaling parameter n_{D50}, for which various scaling laws exist, as elaborated in van Rijn et al. [43]. Concerning coastal dune erosion, the following scaling relation is proposed:

$$\frac{n_l}{n_h} = (n_{D50})^{-0.5} \cdot (n_{s-1})^{-0.5} \cdot (n_h)^{0.28} \qquad (9)$$

with D_{50} being the medium sediment diameter and $(s-1)$ the relative density. In case of sand and an undistorted scale, Equation (9) reduces to $n_{D50} = n_h^{0.56}$. However, as discussed in Bayle et al. [47], sand grain size scaling always results in scaling errors: If, for instance, Froude scaling is maintained and sand is correctly scaled, then the Shield's number and the Dean number are maintained as well, whereas the grain Reynolds number is not. As a result, sand scaling is often not performed due to the permanent availability of the same type of sand and potential cohesive properties for small-scale models.

2.4. Model Setup

A good example of XBeach large-scale modeling is the application to Deltaflume test T04, which was also used for initial calibration of the XBeach model (see Roelvink et al. [17] for the details). A small dune with a height of approx. 1.65 m was located in front of a larger dune and eroded due to collision and overwash [35]. Within the scope of this study, it was therefore chosen to upscale the small-scale 1D-model used in Schweiger and Schuettrumpf [32] to match the dune dimensions of Deltaflume test T04. From the initial small-scale dune height of $h_D = 0.223$ m above still water level follows an increase in height by approximately a factor of $SF \sim 15/2 = 7.5 = n_h$. Applying an equal length ratio ($n_l = 7.5$) results in a geometrical undistorted model ($n_g = 1$).

The upscaled 1D-model with a length of approximately 475 m is shown in Figure 2. The origin of the local coordinate system equals the starting point of profile measurements ($x = 0$ m) and the initial lower water level ($zb = 0$ m), which was 225 cm above the flume floor (see Table 1). To reduce the computational cost, a fast 1D ($ny = 0$) non-equidistant grid was generated with $dx_{max} = 10$ m at the offshore boundary and a minimal grid size of $dx_{min} = 0.1$ m in the beach-dune area, which was chosen based on preliminary testing ($nx = 253$). The model setup was similar to that in Schweiger and Schuettrumpf [32]. Among others, spatially varying friction coefficients (Manning) were applied with $n = 0.03$ s/m$^{1/3}$ in the sandy section of the flume. For the concrete section, a Manning coefficient of $n = 0.01$ s/m$^{1/3}$ was used and hard structures enabled. With respect to sediment characteristics, grain size scaling would result in a medium diameter of $D_{50} = 0.46$ mm (Equation (9)). However, the initial value of $D_{50} = 0.15$ mm was maintained due to the general sediment scaling issues mentioned before (see Section 2.3).

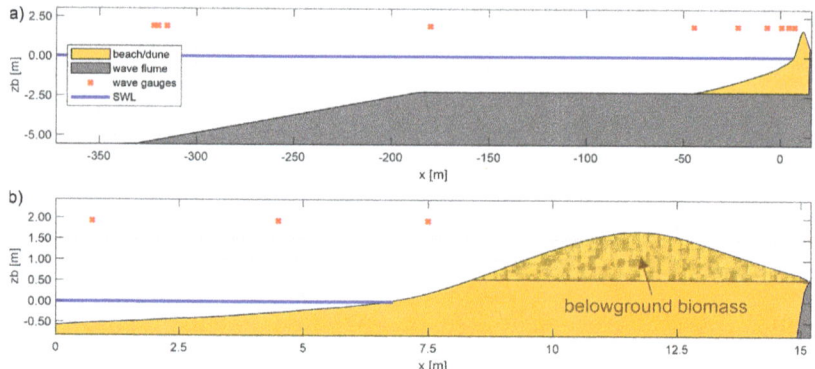

Figure 2. (a) The upscaled model setup including the beach-dune model, wave gauge stations and initial water level (S-conditions). (b) A zoom of the dune area and the section including belowground biomass, which is designated as the area above the concrete wall ($zb \geq 0.54$ m). The area between $0 < x < 16$ m corresponds to the area where profile measurements were available.

Table 1. Upscaled (hydrodynamic) boundary conditions according to Froude with still water level above the flume ground (SWL), zero-moment wave height H_{m0}, peak wave period T_p and the number and durations of wave bursts. The latter two define the applied simulation times (*tstop*).

Hydrodynamic Condition	SWL [cm]	H_{m0} [cm]	T_p [s]	Number of Wave Bursts	Duration of Wave Bursts [s]
SC1	$30 \cdot SF = 225$	$7.4 \cdot SF = 55.5$	$3.69 \cdot \sqrt{SF} = 10.11$	3	$1200 \cdot \sqrt{SF} \sim 3300$
SO	$30 \cdot SF = 225$	$12.8 \cdot SF = 96$	$3.69 \cdot \sqrt{SF} = 10.11$	3	$400 \cdot \sqrt{SF} \sim 1100$
DC	$35 \cdot SF = 262.5$	$4.3 \cdot SF = 32.3$	$3.69 \cdot \sqrt{SF} = 10.11$	3	$1200 \cdot \sqrt{SF} \sim 3300$
DO	$35 \cdot SF = 262.5$	$13.2 \cdot SF = 99$	$3.69 \cdot \sqrt{SF} = 10.11$	1	$400 \cdot \sqrt{SF} \sim 1100$

The four different hydrodynamic boundary conditions (shallow collision (SC1), shallow overwash (SO), deep collision (DC) and deep overwash (DO)) were scaled according to Froude. While the constant water levels (*tideloc* = 0) and H_{m0} wave heights were scaled by $SF = 7.5$, the peak wave period T_p and the duration of each wave burst were scaled according to $SF^{-0.5}$. The wave boundary conditions were applied as JONSWAP spectra ($\gamma = 3.3$) with *rt* (duration of each spectrum at the offshore boundary) equaling the duration of one wave burst. The resulting simulation times were *tstop* = 1,100 s for DO (only one wave burst), *tstop* = 3,300 s for SO and *tstop* = 9,900 s for the C-conditions. Similarly to the application to small-scale, the default spin-up time of wave boundary conditions was reduced from *taper* = 100 s to zero in order to prevent underestimation of the measured wave heights during the first wave burst [32]. An overview of the upscaled hydrodynamic boundary conditions is given in Table 1.

3. Results

3.1. Hydrodynamic Calibration

The model was hydrodynamically calibrated (*morphology* = 0) by comparing the upscaled measured $H_{rms,hf}$ wave heights of each wave burst with the time-averaged spatial output *Hmean* over one wave burst (*tintm* = *rt*). The XBeach default settings were applied with *gamma* = 0.5, and thus, the same settings as for the small-scale applications [32]. Varying the breaker index between $0.45 < \gamma < 0.7$ did not improve the overall results, so that a value of *gamma* = 0.5 was used for the remainder of the investigation. Figure 3 shows the comparison of $H_{rms,hf}$ wave height for conditions SC1 (a), SO (b), DC (c) and DO (d) along the wave flume for each wave burst and the scatter, the coefficients of determination (R^2) and the bias (Figure 3e) for *gamma* = 0.5.

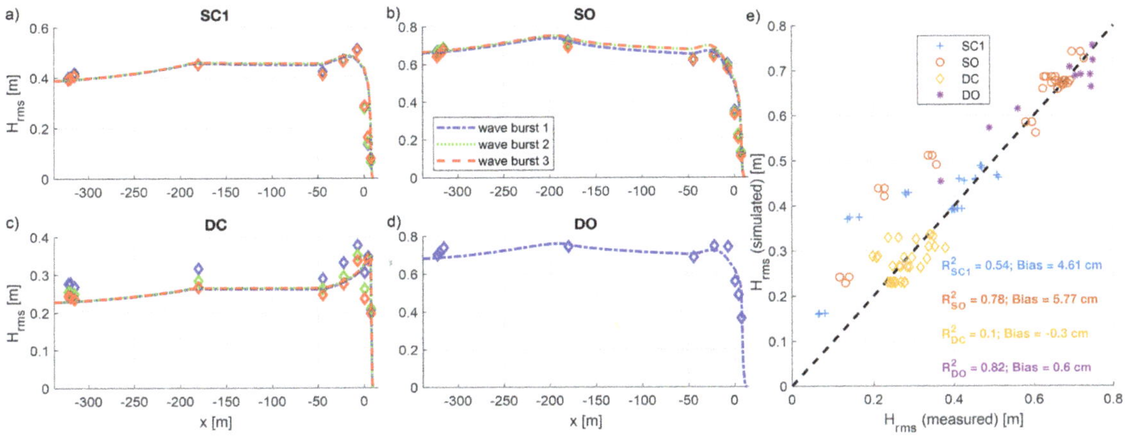

Figure 3. Comparison of computed H_{rms} wave height (*Hmean*) with measured (upscaled) $H_{rms,hf}$ wave height (diamonds) for condition SC1 (**a**), SO (**b**), DC (**c**) and DO (**d**) for each wave burst except DO (*Note*: Only one wave burst for DO as in the physical experiment). Further given are the scatter of measured (x-axis) and simulated (y-axis) $H_{rms,hf}$ wave heights including the R^2 and the Bias (**e**).

The comparison with the upscaled measured $H_{rms,hf}$ wave heights shows good overall agreement for each hydrodynamic condition, with the bias varying between −0.3 cm (DC) and 5.77 cm (SO). The most agreement with the observation was achieved for the overwash cases with R^2 = 0.78 for SO and R^2 = 0.82 for DO. With respect to nearshore wave heights, the model underestimated the maximum observed wave height, except for SO. Overall, the results are very well in line with the model's small-scale application [32], as similar statistics were derived (see Table 2), which proves that the translation to a larger scale is valid with respect to hydrodynamics.

Table 2. Comparison of wave statistics between the small-scale (adapted from [32]) and large-scale (this study) applications based on the coefficient of determination (R^2) and the bias for each hydrodynamic condition.

	SC1 R^2 | Bias	SO R^2 | Bias	DC R^2 | Bias	DO R^2 | Bias
small-scale [32]	0.58 | 0.57 cm	0.81 | 0.65 cm	0.28 | −0.12 cm	0.85 | 0.14 cm
large-scale	0.54 | 4.61 cm	0.78 | 5.77 cm	0.1 | −0.3 cm	0.82 | 0.6 cm

3.2. Morphodynamic Calibration

The morphodynamic calibration was performed based on the upscaled control cases and by reusing the boundary conditions generated during the hydrodynamic calibration (*wbctype* = reuse). Due to the similar model performance in small-scale and large-scale situations in terms of hydrodynamics, the final morphodynamic parameter settings of Schweiger and Schuettrumpf [32] were used as initial settings in this study; and the critical avalanching slopes were set to *wetslp* = 0.2 and *dryslp* = 0.7. However, the *depthscale* parameter was set to *SF* = 2 to be consistent with the upscaled model setup (1:2). As a result, the effected morphodynamic parameters were reduced to *eps* = 0.0025 m (threshold water depth above which cells are wet), *hmin* = 0.1 m (threshold water depth for Stokes drift), *hswitch* = 0.05 m (switched from wet to dry) and *dzmax* = 0.05 m/s/m (maximum bed-level change due to avalanching).

The morphodynamic calibration was performed by comparing the final dune profiles and the percentages of deviation in post-dune volume per meter (ΔV), which was calculated for both measurements and the simulation for the area above the concrete wall ($zb > 0.54$ m). Furthermore, the Brier skill score (BSS) was calculated:

$$BSS = 1 - \frac{\sum(zb_c - zb_m)^2}{\sum(zb_0 - zb_m)^2} \qquad (10)$$

with zb_c being the computed bed level, zb_m the measured bed level and zb_0 the initial bed level. The BSS defines a model skill as bad (<0), poor (0–0.3), fair (0.3–0.6), good (0.6–0.8) or excellent (0.8–1) according to the classification of van Rijn et al. [48].

Figure 4 shows the initial (dotted) and the final measured (dashed) dune profiles for each hydrodynamic condition (a–d) in combination with various simulation results (colored dash-dotted). Applying the initial settings (blue lines) led to an overprediction of the observed dune erosion for each hydrodynamic condition which was greater for the conditions targeting collision (Figure 4a,c). Similarly to the small-scale application, however, no overwash was computed for each hydrodynamic condition, which is contrary to initial expectations due to the large-scale application. Since the aim of this study was to validate the root model for large-scale and overwash in particular, we chose to induce the occurrence of overwash by additionally varying hydrodynamic parameters, although the model was already hydrodynamically calibrated.

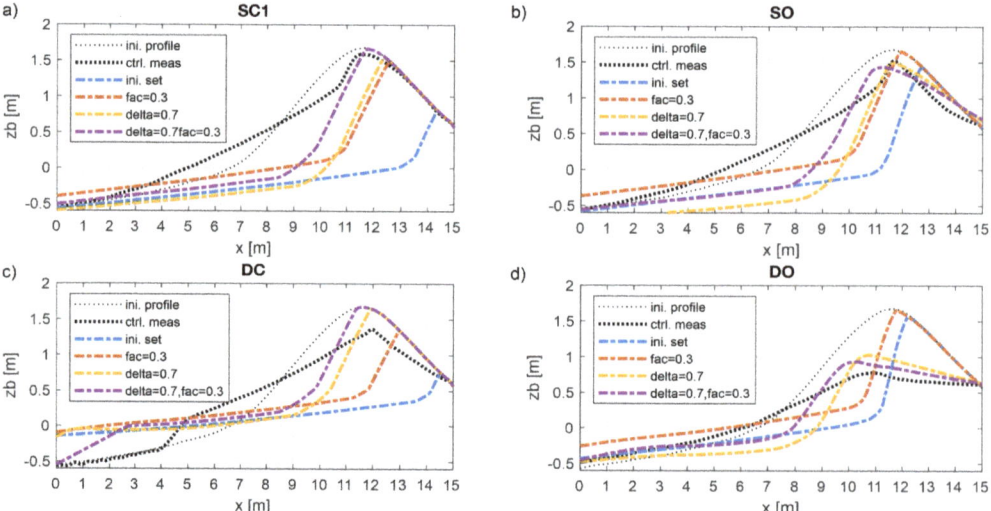

Figure 4. Morphodynamic calibration: Comparison between final measured (dashed) and simulated (dash-dotted) dune profiles for hydrodynamic conditions SC1 (**a**), SO (**b**), DC (**c**) and DO (**d**). The control cases were used as the initial input (dotted).

Therefore, various hydrodynamic parameters were additionally considered in order to induce overwash. The majority of these parameters (e.g., *alpha* (wave dissipation coefficient): 0.5–2; *gammax* (maximum ratio wave height to water depth): 2, 3; *n* (power in Roelvink dissipation model): 10, 15), and other processes (*swrunup* (short-wave runup): 1 with *facrun* = 2) had a negligible effect on the results. However, increasing the *delta* (δ) parameter resulted in the occurrence of overwash for SO and DO. This parameter, which is zero by default, defines the fraction of H_{rms} wave height that is added to the water depth h within the calculation of the maximum wave height H_{max}:

$$H_{max} = \gamma \cdot (h + \delta \cdot H_{rms}) \qquad (11)$$

where γ is the breaker index. While overwash was observed for $delta \geq 0.5$, a final value of $delta = 0.7$ was chosen due to the highest agreement with the post-observed dune crest height for SO. In addition, applying $delta = 0.7$ reduced the erosion at the dune front for all hydrodynamic conditions (Figure 4a–d, yellow). However, the downside of adjusting the $delta$ parameter is a decrease in model accuracy concerning nearshore wave heights, which is reflected by the wave statistics in Table 3. In favor of accurately modeling the relevant overwash conditions, we chose to use a value of $delta = 0.7$ in the remainder of the investigation. The reason for this was that the validation of the root model for a large-scale application was based on the comparison of the belowground with the respective control cases. Thus, deviations in terms of hydrodynamics were assumed to apply to both cases equally.

Table 3. Comparison of wave statistics when applying $delta = 0$ and $delta = 0.7$ based on the coefficient of determination (R^2) and the Bias for each hydrodynamic condition.

	SC1 R^2 | Bias	SO R^2 | Bias	DC R^2 | Bias	DO R^2 | Bias
$delta = 0$	0.54 | 4.61 cm	0.78 | 5.77 cm	0.1 | −0.3 cm	0.82 | 0.6 cm
$delta = 0.7$	0.36 | 5.76 cm	0.45 | 11.03 cm	0.14 | −0.77 cm	0.47 | 4.81 cm

In order to further decrease the erosion at the dune front, the *facua* parameter was increased to 0.3 (Figure 4, orange lines), which promotes the effect of wave skewness and asymmetry on the sediment advection velocity, and hence increases the onshore-directed sediment transport [49]. However, there was still too much erosion at the dune front for each hydrodynamic condition. Therefore, the increase to *facua* = 0.3 was combined with $delta = 0.7$, which further improved the results (Figure 4, purple). For the C-conditions, erosion at the dune front decreased and the computed dune face was in line with the observation for SC1. With respect to statistics (see Table 4), however, model skill remained low ($BSS_{SC1} < -1$, $BSS_{DC} = -0.24$), although the deviation in post-volume decreased considerably from −152% to −32.9% (SC1) and from −98% to 4.1% (DC). For the conditions targeting overwash, the computed post-dune crest heights are in good agreement with the measurements. Nevertheless, low skill was achieved for SO (BSS < −1), although the deviation in post-volume decreased from −78.9% to −4.5%. For DO, however, the final dune profile shape is very well in line with the observation, which demonstrates excellent model skill (BSS = 0.88). The deviation in post-volume (14.6%) can be attributed to the general model–data mismatch between 3 m < x < 9 m (d).

Table 4. Statistics before (ini. set.) and after (fin. set.) calibration for each hydrodynamic condition, including the BSS and the percentage deviations in post-volume between measurements and the simulation.

	SC1 ini. set. | fin. set	SO ini. set. | fin. set	DC ini. set. | fin. set	DO ini. set. | fin. set
BSS	<−1 | <−1	<−1 | <−1	<−1 | −0.24	0.15 | 0.88
ΔV [%]	−152 | −32.9	−72.9 | −4.5	−98 | 4.1	−2.6 | 14.6

3.3. Modeling Aboveground and Belowground Vegetation Cases

In order to model the effect of BGB on dune erosion volumes at large scales, the upscaled belowground cases of Bryant et al. [34] served as comparative examples, where uniformly integrated coconut husk fibers represented belowground biomass. Within the scope of this study, it was hence assumed that the influence of these fibers on the erosion resistance of the soil scales linearly with the model setup. Therefore, it was assumed that the comparison of the simulation results with the upscaled measured final dune profiles (BGB) would be valid, as would the comparison of the dune profile differences (BGB to control).

Due to the inconsistent model performance during calibration in the collision and overwash conditions, the modelling of the belowground cases was performed separately. For the C-conditions, only the constant (with respect to *rcc* value) root model was applied with a constant and a locally varying rooting depth (z_{root}). Due to the non-occurrence of overwash in the control simulations, locally increased friction coefficients were not considered. For the O-conditions, however, both the constant root model (with constant/varying z_{root}) and the friction approach were considered in the simulation. In general, the root model was applied with a maximum rooting depth of z_{root} = 1.15 m, which equals the difference between the dune crest and the height of the sloping wall. In the case of local variation, the rooting depth was defined as the difference between the initial dune profile and the height of the concrete wall (zb = 0.54 m), which was provided for each grid cell through an external file (see Figure 1).

Since locally increasing the bed friction coefficients is the common practice for the consideration of aboveground vegetation in (XBeach) modeling [22,27–29,50], the aboveground cases (AGB) of Bryant et al. [34] served as an additional source of comparison when solely using the friction approach. In the physical experiment, aboveground biomass was represented by 30.5 cm long wooden dowels which were buried half of their length deep. Finally, the combination of the root model and locally increased friction coefficients was compared to the upscaled above and belowground cases (ABGB) of Bryant et al. [34]. In this regard, it should be noted that there was no physical connection between the wooden dowels (ABG) and the husk fibers (BGB) in the physical experiment.

3.3.1. Collision Regime

Applying the root model to the belowground cases of the conditions targeting collision decreased the dune erosion at the dune front for both SC1 and DC. However, the influence of the root model remained constant for $rcc \geq 0.75$. As an example, Figure 5 shows the final dune profiles of the measurements (black), the control simulation (blue) and when applying the root model with rcc = 0.75 and a constant (orange) or a spatially varying rooting depth (yellow) for SC1 (a) and DC (b). Given as well are the dune profile differences between belowground and control for SC1 (c) and DC (d). In the case of SC1, using the root model with constant z_{root} resulted in a similar maximum decrease of Δzb_{max} = 30 cm as the measurement. However, the location of maximum decrease was shifted offshore by one meter and erosion at the dune front (8 m < x < 10 m) was too high in comparison to the upscaled measurement (c). The use of spatially varying rooting depths to decrease the influence of the root model at the dune face had only a minor effect with respect to the control. For DC, similar results can be observed. However, the model predicted a maximum decrease of Δzb_{max} = 20 cm, which is much lower than the upscaled measurement with Δzb_{max} = 40 cm (d).

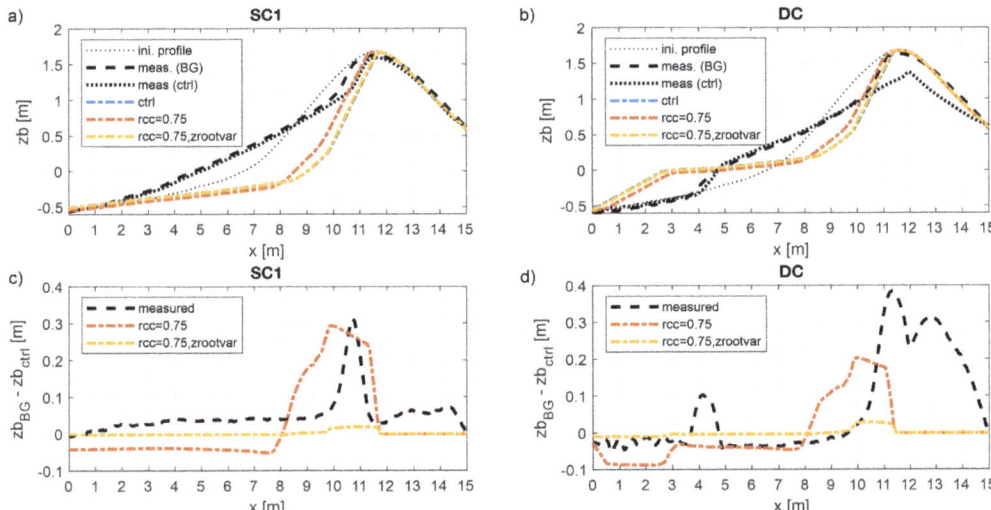

Figure 5. Modeling collision conditions with belowground biomass: Comparison of initial (thin dotted), final measured control (thick dotted) and final measured BGB (dashed) dune profiles with simulation results (dash-dotted), including the control simulation (blue) and the application of the root model with constant (orange) or varying rooting depth (yellow) for a shallow collision (**a**) and a deep collision (**b**). Profile differences (belowground to control) are shown for the measurements (dashed) and the simulations (dash-dotted) for shallow (**c**) and deep collisions (**d**). *Note*: Overlay of the blue and yellows lines in (**a**,**b**).

3.3.2. Overwash Regime

Due to the occurrence of overwash in the control simulations, the use of locally increased friction coefficients was considered in the modeling of the O-conditions. In this regard, the friction coefficients were locally increased between 0.035 s/m$^{1/3}$ and 0.08 s/m$^{1/3}$ (shrubs [28]). Figure 6 shows the simulation results, including the final dune profiles for SO (a) and DO (b) and the dune profile differences (c, d). In general, increasing the bed friction coefficients decreases the erosion on the lee side of the dune. While the measured maximum decrease in erosion (x = 11.4 m) was underestimated by 15 cm for SO when using n_{veg} = 0.08 s/m$^{1/3}$ (c, green), the maximum decrease of $\Delta z b_{max}$ = 37 cm for DO (d, green) is in good agreement with the upscaled measurement ($\Delta z b_{max}$ = 41 cm), but shifted offshore by 1.25 m.

With respect to AGB, the maximum decrease in erosion at x = 11.4 m was underestimated by approximately 5 cm when applying $n_{veg} \geq 0.06$ s/m$^{1/3}$ (green and purple). For DO, however, the effect of aboveground biomass on dune erosion volumes was overestimated for $n_{veg} \geq 0.035$ s/m$^{1/3}$.

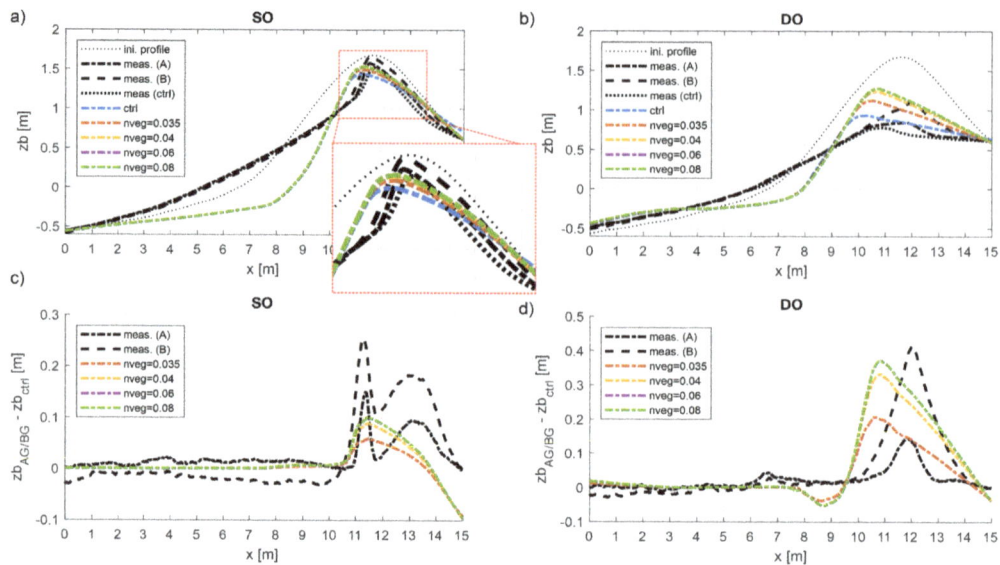

Figure 6. Modeling overwash conditions with belowground biomass: Comparison of initial (thin dotted), final measured control (thick dotted, black) and final measured BG (dashed, black) and AG (dash-dotted, black) dune profiles with simulation results (dash-dotted), including the control simulation (blue) and the application of spatially increased friction coefficients (color) for shallow overwash (**a**) and deep overwash (**b**). Profile differences (belowground to control) are shown for the measurements (dashed) and the simulations (dash-dotted) for shallow (**c**) and deep collisions (**d**). *Note*: Overlay of the purple and green lines.

Applying the root model led to results that differed with the overwash conditions and with the use of constant or spatially varying rooting depth. Figure 7 summarizes different final dune profiles (a, b) and dune profile differences (c, d) for different root model configurations compared to the upscaled measured data. For SO, using rcc values of 0.75 and 1 resulted in good agreement between the model and the measurements with respect to the maximum decrease ($x = 11.5$ m) in the presence of BGB (c). Furthermore, incorporating a spatially varying rooting depth decreased the effect of the root model on the model predicted erosion at the dune front ($x < 11$ m) in comparison to the simulations with a constant rooting depth (orange, purple). As a result, greater agreement with the measurements was achieved. For the back of the dune ($x > 12$ m), however, the predicted decrease in dune erosion was lower than the measurement. For DO, the best agreement with respect to dune profile differences between BGB and control was achieved for $rcc = 0.35$ (d). Although the location of maximum decrease was shifted by approximately 1.5 m offshore, the general profile shape was in good agreement with the observations of the front and the back of the dune. Contrary to the application to SO, the use of a spatially varying rooting depth led to only minor differences in the dune foot area (8 m $< x < 9$ m).

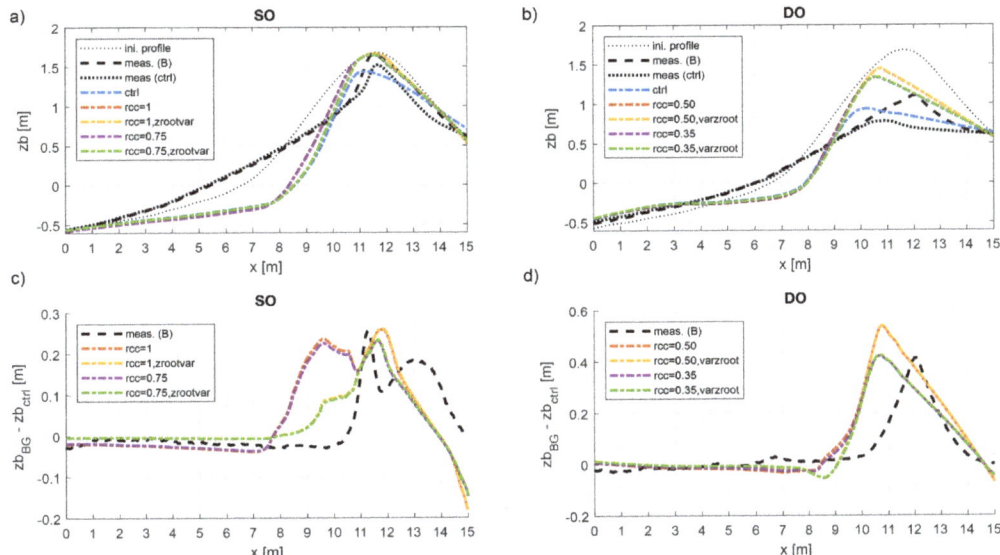

Figure 7. Modeling overwash conditions with belowground biomass: Comparison of initial (thin dotted), final measured control (thick dotted) and final measured BGB (dashed) dune profiles with simulation results (dash-dotted), including the control simulation (blue) and the application of the root model (color) for shallow overwash (**a**) and deep overwash (**b**). Profile differences (belowground to control) are shown for the measurements (dashed) and the simulations (dash-dotted) for shallow- (**c**) and deep-overwash (**d**). *Note:* Overlay of the lines of the simulations with equal *rcc* value in dune crest area.

Despite the comparison of dune profile differences, the overwash sediment volumes per meter width (V_{over}) were calculated for each simulation:

$$V_{over} = \sum \left(zb_{fin} - zb_{ini} \right) \cdot dx \text{ for } x > 15 \text{ m} \tag{12}$$

Subsequently, the percentage decrease in overwash volume in each control simulation was derived to enable a comparison to the results of the small-scale physical experiment [34]. It should be noted that the latter were obtained by collecting and weighing the overwash sediment and are hence based on total sediment mass.

The ratios between BGB and control are summarized in Table 5 for shallow-overwash and in Table 6 for deep-overwash. For shallow-overwash, the presence of ABG and BGB reduced the overwash volume by 34% (37.6 kg to 24.9 kg) and by 58% (37.6 kg to 15.9 kg) in the physical experiment, respectively. The best agreement with the BGB measurement was achieved when applying the root model with *rcc* = 0.75 with a percentage decrease of 59% (const. z_{root}) and 60% (var. z_{root}). In case of the former, this corresponds to a decrease from 0.58 m^3/m to 0.24 m^3/m. Hypothetically, the observed decrease in overwash sediment mass of (37.6−15.9) kg = 21.7 kg would be equivalent to an upscaled decrease in overwash volume of 0.04 m^3/m (the translated overwash volume follows from V_{over} = 21.7 kg/2650 kg/m^3/1.5 m · 7.5 = 0.041 m^3/m) when assuming a sediment density of 2650 kg/m^3 (XBeach default), and when using the small-scale flume width of 1.5 m and the scale factor of 7.5. Thus, the model theoretically overpredicts the decrease in overwash volume by a factor of 8.5 (= (0.58−0.24)/0.04). For AGB, the use of locally increased friction coefficients underestimates the measured percentage decrease in overwash volume by at least 5% ($n_{veg} \geq 0.06$ s/m$^{1/3}$).

Table 5. Percentage decrease in overwash compared to the control cases for shallow overwash.

Shallow-Overwash	Percentage Decrease in Overwash in Compared to Control					
Measurement * AGB/BGB	$rcc = 1$ const. z_{root}	$rcc = 1$ var. z_{root}	$rcc = 0.75$ const. z_{root}	$rcc = 0.75$ var. z_{root}	$n = 0.035 \mid 0.04 \mid 0.06 \mid 0.08$	
34%/58%	67.4%	68.8%	58.8%	60.2%	11.0%	22.8%	28.5%	28.5%	

* Please note that these values equal the percentage differences in sediment loss (kg) between belowground and control values within the scope of the original (small-scale) physical experiment (adapted from [34]).

Table 6. Percentage decrease in overwash compared to the control cases for deep overwash.

Deep-Overwash	Percentage Decrease in Overwash Compared to Control					
Measurement * AGB/BGB	$rcc = 0.5$ const. z_{root}	$rcc = 0.5$ var. z_{root}	$rcc = 0.35$ const. z_{root}	$rcc = 0.35$ var. z_{root}	$n = 0.035 \mid 0.04 \mid 0.06 \mid 0.08$	
20%/46%	67.4%	53.6%	53.7%	43.5%	20.8%	36.6%	40.5%	40.5%	

* Please note that these values equal the percentage differences in sediment loss (kg) between belowground and control values within the scope of the original (small-scale) physical experiment (adapted from [34]).

For DO, the presence of AGB decreased the total overwash sediment mass by 20% from 144.2 kg to 115.5 kg. For BGB, the total overwash sediment decreased to 78 kg (46%). As an example, the theoretical upscaling for BGB resulted in an overwash volume decrease of 0.12 m^3/m for the measurement. With respect to modeling, the greatest agreement was achieved when applying the root model with $rcc = 0.35$ and a variable rooting depth. Then, the predicted overwash volume decreased by 43% from 2.49 m^3/m to 1.41 m^3/m. The theoretical comparison between the model and the upscaled measurements found overestimation by a factor of 9 (= (2.49−1.41)/0.12). Concerning locally increased friction, using values of $n \geq 0.06$ s/m$^{1/3}$ led to a decrease in overwash volume by 41%, and hence, similar (good) agreement with the measurements.

Further analysis was conducted by evaluating the root model ($rcc = 0.35$, var. z_{root}) and using locally increased friction coefficients ($n_{veg} = 0.06$ s/m$^{1/3}$) for SO after each wave burst. Figure 8 presents the dune profiles (a–c), the cumulative erosion and the bed-level changes due to avalanching (d–f) and the maximum sediment concentration during each wave burst (g–i). After the first wave burst, erosion at the dune crest ($x = 11.5$ m) was greatest for the control simulation (blue) with a decrease of $\Delta z b_{wb1,ctrl} = -8$ cm (d). Locally increasing the bed friction (purple) reduced erosion at the dune crest to $\Delta z b_{wb1,fric} = -5$ cm. With the root model (green), erosion at the dune crest was almost prevented ($\Delta z b_{wb1,rm} < -1$ cm). As a result, the cumulative erosion on the lee side of the dune was greatest for the control simulation with a maximum bed level change of $\Delta z b_{wb1,ctrl} = -12$ cm at $x = 12$ m, which decreased to $\Delta z b_{wb1,fric} = -10$ cm (friction) or $\Delta z b_{wb1,rm} = -7$ cm (root model). The results show further that there is no contribution of avalanching for $x > 11.2$ m ($dzav = 0$). With respect to the maximum sediment concentration, only small differences can be observed between the control and the friction approach. Applying the root model reduced the maximum sediment concentration at both the front (9 m $< x <$ 11.5 m) and the back of the dune.

In the remainder of the control simulation, erosion at the dune crest and on the lee side of the dune increased to a maximum of $\Delta z b_{wb2,ctrl} = -21$ cm after the second wave burst (e) and $\Delta z b_{wb3,ctrl} = -28$ cm after the third wave burst (f). For locally increased friction and the root model, the maximum erosion decreased to $\Delta z b_{wb2,fric} = -15$ cm and $\Delta z b_{wb3,fric} = -20$ cm (friction), and to $\Delta z b_{wb2,rm} = -10$ cm and $\Delta z b_{wb3,rm} = -12$ cm (root model). In terms of maximum sediment concentrations, similar results as for the first wave burst were obtained when using locally increased friction (similar to control) and the root model (lower than control), which also applies to the non-occurrence of avalanching for $x > 11.2$ m. In summary, using the root model and thus increasing the critical velocity for erosion along the dune reduced the overall erosion, especially at the dune crest. As a result, erosion on the lee side of the dune was reduced during the second and third wave bursts without bed level changes due to avalanching, which finally resulted in lower overwash sediment volumes (see Table 5).

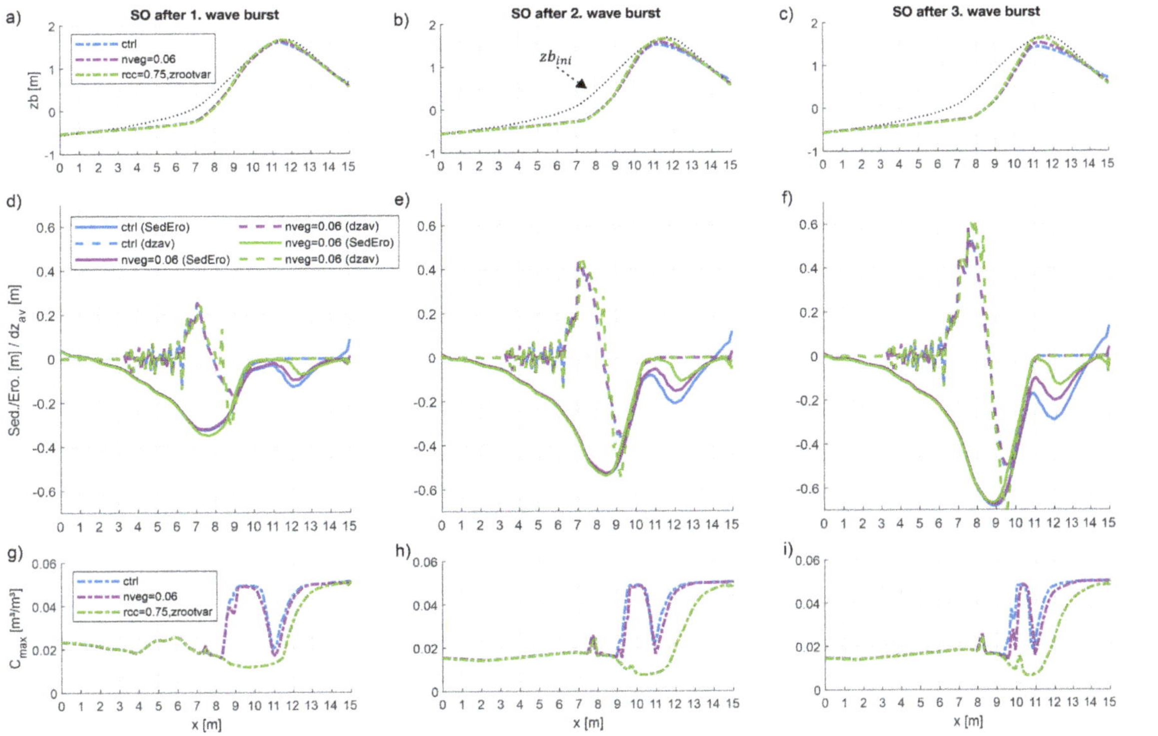

Figure 8. Time evolution of various output parameters for SO including dune profiles after the first (**a**), second (**b**) and third (**c**) wave burst, the cumulative erosion and the bed level change due to avalanching after each wave burst (**d**–**f**) and the maximum sediment concentration during each respective wave burst (**g**–**i**).

3.4. Modeling the Combination of Aboveground and Belowground Vegetation

Due to the occurrence of overwash and thus an influence of locally increased friction coefficients on the predicted erosion volumes, further simulations were conducted by using both the root model and locally increased friction coefficients. In this way, the root model was applied with varying rooting depth and with $rcc = 0.75$ for SO and $rcc = 0.35$ for DO based on the BGB modeling (see Figure 7). The results were compared to the upscaled ABGB results of Bryant et al. [34].

Figure 9 presents the final dune profiles for SO (a) and DO (b) and the dune profile differences between ABGB and the control (dash-dotted), and between the simulation and the measurements (dotted in (c) and (d)). Furthermore, the percentage decreases in sediment loss to overwash are summarized in Table 7. In general, the comparison of final dune profiles (a, b) shows that combining the two approaches decreased dune erosion volumes on the lee side of the dune compared to using the root model alone (orange). For SO, the combination of the root model with locally increased friction coefficients to $n_{veg} = 0.08$ s/m$^{1/3}$ underpredicted the upscaled measured decrease due to the presence of ABGB (c). Nevertheless, the final dune profile is in good agreement with the measurement for $x > 11.3$ m, as shown by the differences between simulation and measurement (dotted line in c). However, the observed decrease in overwash volume (86%) was underpredicted by 11%.

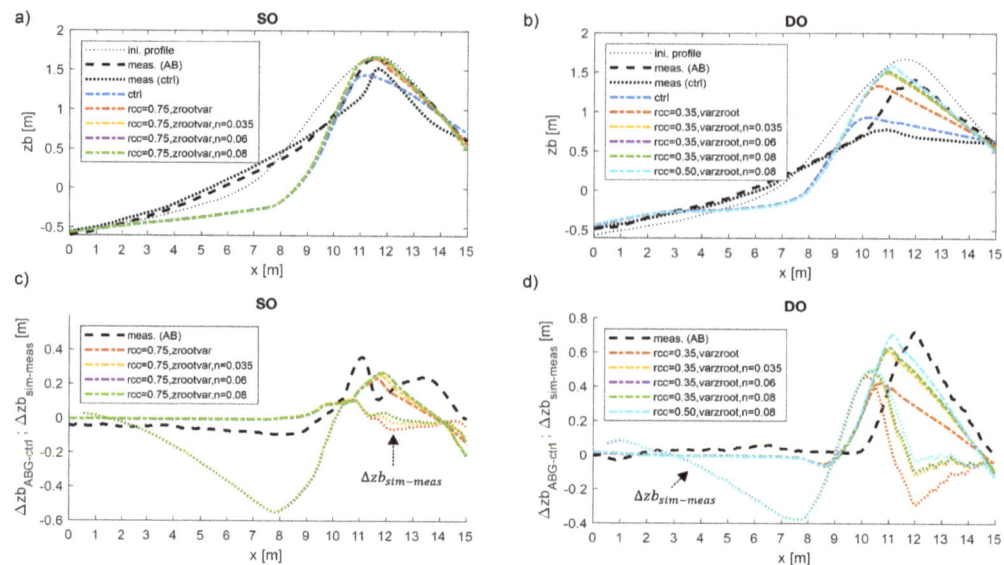

Figure 9. Modeling overwash conditions with aboveground and belowground biomass: Comparison of initial (thin dotted), final measured control (thick dotted, black) and final measured ABGB (dashed, black) dune profiles with simulation results (dash-dotted, black) for shallow-overwash (**a**) and deep-overwash (**b**). The root model was applied with a varying rooting depth (*varzroot*) and combined with locally increased friction coefficients. Further shown are the profile differences between belowground and the control for the measurements (dashed) and the simulations (dash-dotted), and the difference between simulations and measurements (dotted) for shallow (**c**) and deep-collisions (**d**). *Note*: Overlay of the green and purple lines.

Table 7. Percentage decreases in overwash compared to the control cases for shallow-overwash and deep-overwash conditions. The root model was applied with various rooting depths with $rcc = 0.75$ for SO and $rcc = 0.35$ for DO.

	Percentage Decrease in Overwash Compared to Control					
	Measurement * ABGB	Root Model	Root Model + $n_{veg} = 0.035$	Root Model + $n_{veg} = 0.06$	Root Model + $n_{veg} = 0.08$	RM ($rcc = 0.5$) + $n_{veg} = 0.08$
Shallow-Overwash	86%	60.2%	65.9%	74.7%	74.7%	-
Deep-Overwash	83%	43.5%	62.3%	64.9%	64.9%	70.4%

* Please note that these values equal the percentage deviation in sediment loss (kg) between belowground and control within the scope of the original (small-scale) physical experiment (adapted from [34]).

While for DO, the root model resulted in good agreement with the upscaled BGB measurement (see Figure 7), the local increase of friction coefficients overpredicted the effect of AGB with $n_{veg} = 0.035$ s/m$^{1/3}$ (see Figure 6). Concerning ABGB, however, combining the root model ($rcc = 0.35$) with locally increased friction coefficients underpredicted the measured decrease in dune erosion volume, even for $n_{veg} = 0.08$ s/m$^{1/3}$ (Figure 9d). Furthermore, only minor errors occurred in the simulations using both the root model and the friction approach. This also applies to the percentage decrease in sediment loss to overwash, which was 20% ($n_{veg} = 0.035$ s/m$^{1/3}$) to 18% ($n_{veg} = 0.08$ s/m$^{1/3}$) lower than observed in the physical experiment (83%). In order to increase the effect of the root model, combining $rcc = 0.5$ with a local friction value of $n_{veg} = 0.08$ s/m$^{1/3}$ resulted in good agreement with respect to dune profile differences (d) and increased the percentage decrease in overwash volume to 70.4%.

4. Discussion and Conclusions

Due to a general model–data mismatch in small-scale applications [32], this study aimed to validate the root model at larger scale based on an upscaled model setup of Bryant et al. [34]. It was expected that the overall performance and especially the predictions of overwash would improve, since XBeach's default parameters are optimized for large-scale modeling. With respect to $H_{rms,hf}$ wave heights, good agreement was achieved between the model and (upscaled) measurements for each hydrodynamic condition. Similarly to the small-scale application, dune overwash was not computed regardless of the hydrodynamic condition, which did not change when activating short-wave runup. Only the increase of the *delta* parameter, and thus, the maximum wave height in the nearshore zone, resulted in the occurrence of dune overwash for the O-conditions. From this follows that the general model–data mismatch described in Schweiger and Schuettrumpf [32] might not only result from the small-scale application, but might (also) be due to other model inaccuracies, such as an underestimation of wave runup, as discussed in previous studies [51–53].

Although adjustments to various model parameters were considered in the morphodynamic calibration, erosion volumes at the font of the dune were significantly overestimated for all conditions except DO (see Figure 4). As a result, low model skill was achieved for SC1, DC and SO (BSS < 0), whereas an excellent skill was achieved for DO (BSS = 0.88). However, the overestimated erosion at the dune face and toe is in line with the findings of van Dongeren et al. [54], who, among others, observed an overprediction of erosion around the mean waterline, possibly due to inaccuracies in the modeling of sediment motion in the swash zone (see also [53,55]). In this study, the overestimation of erosion at the dune toe could have been further reduced by further increasing the *facua* parameter, which promotes the onshore-directed sediment transport. However, this would have been followed by an increasing deviation of the dune front position between the model and measurements, which was already observed for SO when applying *facua* = 0.3 with *delta* = 0.7 (see Figure 4b). Therefore, deviations at the dune front were accepted since the main focus in this study was on the erosion at the dune crest and on the lee side of the dune due to overwash.

The effects of locally increased friction coefficients and the root model on dune erosion volumes at a large scale were validated by using the upscaled biomass cases (AGB, BGB, ABGB) of Bryant et al. [34] as a reference. Therefore, a major assumption in this study was that the effects of the wooden dowels (AGB), the husk fibers (BGB) and their combination (ABGB) on the erodibility of the sandy soil scale linearly with the translation to a large scale. From this follows that the validation of two approaches to consider land-based biomass in this study was not based on real data from a physical experiment but relied on a theoretical comparison. Nevertheless, applying the root model to the O-conditions resulted in good agreement with the upscaled BGB measurements, which was better when spatially varying rooting depths were applied. However, the best results for SO and DO were achieved with different *rcc* values. While for SO a value of *rcc* = 0.75 led to good agreement concerning dune profile differences (BGB to control), the application to DO required a reduction to *rcc* = 0.35. Although these results are based on a theoretical comparison, the effect of the root model on the model predicted erosion should be consistent and independent of the hydrodynamic conditions. Therefore, further investigations are necessary to improve the performance of the root model. Due to a lack of appropriate data concerning the interaction between belowground biomass and sandy soil, future studies should focus on quantifying the effects of land-based (belowground) biomass on the erodibility of a dune system, as suggested by Figlus et al. [33]. With respect to further validating the root model in XBeach, these studies should be conducted at a large scale and additionally consider real dune vegetation.

Using locally increased friction coefficients decreased the dune erosion volumes on the lee side of the dune. Concerning BGB modeling, using a local friction coefficient of $n_{veg} = 0.08 \text{ s/m}^{1/3}$ underestimated the decrease in erosion, which was greater for SO (see

Figure 6). Since the friction approach is the common practice for considering the effect of land-based vegetation on overwash-dominated erosion in (XBeach) modeling [22,27–29,50], the results were also compared to the AGB cases. For DO, the predicted decrease in erosion was already overestimated for n_{veg} = 0.035 s/m$^{1/3}$. For SO, however, the influence of AGB on dune erosion volumes was underestimated even when using the maximum value (n_{veg} = 0.08 s/m$^{1/3}$) that was considered in this study. Therefore, the dynamic roughness module [30], which varies the Manning roughness in vegetated areas due to burying and erosion, was not considered in this study. Since the BGB measurements were underestimated when using the friction approach (see Figure 6c,d), the greater effect of ABGB on the dune erosion volumes would presumably have led to an even greater underestimation.

Nevertheless, the combination of the root model with locally increased friction coefficients was validated with the upscaled ABGB measurements. Due to the good performance in the BGB modeling (root model with rcc = 0.35) and the overestimation observed in the AGB modeling for DO (friction approach), combining the two approaches was expected to result in good agreement with the ABGB measurements for DO. Although less erosion was predicted on the lee side of the dune in comparison to the sole use of the root model, the overall decrease due to the presence of ABGB was lower in comparison to the upscaled measurement and less sensitive to variations in local bed friction (see Figure 9d). In this regard, increasing the rcc value to 0.5 resulted in a good agreement between model and upscaled measurements. This necessary increase could be attributed to the general model setup, where the wooden dowels were buried half way. Thus, the belowground parts of the dowels could have further increased the resistance of the dune in addition to the effect of the uniformly integrated coir fibers, hence requiring a higher contribution of the root model, and hence, higher rcc values.

In summary, the application of the XBeach model to an upscaled model setup of Bryant et al. [34] showed a general model–data mismatch for all hydrodynamic conditions except for DO, which was mainly due to overestimated dune erosion volumes around the initial waterline. Nevertheless, applying the root model to the upscaled BGB cases reduced the predicted dune erosion for all hydrodynamic conditions. In this regard, incorporating spatially varying rooting depths further improved the results at the dune front, although the overall effect of the root model differed between the simulations. However, there is a lack of appropriate data to further validate and improve the root model. Although various wave flume experiments have been conducted in recent years, there is a specific need for research focusing on the effect of land-based biomass on the erodibility of dunes during collision and overwash at large scales. In particular, the separate investigation of aboveground and belowground biomass concerning wave-induced dune erosion at large scales and the individual contributions of different plant characteristics (e.g., rooting depth, plant/root density and maturity) would allow one to evaluate the specific influences of these plant-related parameters on the erosive processes. Furthermore, these studies should additionally address the effects of land-based vegetation on the temporal evolution of dune scarping, avalanching and failure.

Author Contributions: Conceptualization, C.S.; methodology, C.S.; software, C.S.; validation, C.S.; formal analysis, C.S.; investigation, C.S.; resources, H.S.; data curation, C.S.; writing—original draft preparation, C.S.; writing—review and editing, H.S.; visualization, C.S.; supervision, H.S.; project administration, H.S.; funding acquisition, H.S. Both authors have read and agreed to the published version of the manuscript.

Funding: This research was funded by the German Federal Ministry of Education and Research (BMBF) within the project PADO (grant number: 03F0760A) that was initiated in the framework of the German Coastal Engineering Research Council (KFKI).

Institutional Review Board Statement: Not applicable.

Informed Consent Statement: Not applicable.

Data Availability Statement: The data used in this study are available from the corresponding author.

Acknowledgments: The authors would like thank Mary A. Bryant and Duncan B. Bryant (U.S. Army Engineer Research and Development Center, Vicksburg, USA) for providing the data of their small-scale wave flume experiment. Furthermore, the authors want to thank the anonymous reviewers for their feedback, which helped to improve the quality of this manuscript.

Conflicts of Interest: The authors declare no conflict of interest. The funders had no role in the design of the study; in the collection, analyses or interpretation of data; in the writing of the manuscript, or in the decision to publish the result.

References

1. Martínez, M.L.; Psuty, N.P.; Lubke, R.A. A Perspective on Coastal Dunes. In *Coastal Dunes*; Caldwell, M.M., Heldmaier, G., Jackson, R.B., Lange, O.L., Mooney, H.A., Schulze, E.-D., Sommer, U., Martínez, M.L., Psuty, N.P., Eds.; Springer Berlin Heidelberg: Berlin/Heidelberg, Germany, 2008; pp. 3–10. ISBN 978-3-540-74001-8.
2. Everard, M.; Jones, L.; Watts, B. Have we neglected the societal importance of sand dunes? An ecosystem services perspective. *Aquat. Conserv. Mar. Freshw. Ecosyst.* **2010**, *20*, 476–487. [CrossRef]
3. Temmerman, S.; Meire, P.; Bouma, T.J.; Herman, P.M.J.; Ysebaert, T.; de Vriend, H.J. Ecosystem-based coastal defence in the face of global change. *Nature* **2013**, *504*, 79–83. [CrossRef] [PubMed]
4. Schoonees, T.; Gijón Mancheño, A.; Scheres, B.; Bouma, T.J.; Silva, R.; Schlurmann, T.; Schüttrumpf, H. Hard Structures for Coastal Protection, Towards Greener Designs. *Estuaries Coasts* **2019**, *42*, 1709–1729. [CrossRef]
5. Vriend, H.J.; van Koningsveld, M.; Aarninkhof, S.G.; Vries, M.B.; Baptist, M.J. Sustainable hydraulic engineering through building with nature. *J. Hydro-Environ. Res.* **2015**, *9*, 159–171. [CrossRef]
6. Barbier, E.B.; Koch, E.W.; Silliman, B.R.; Hacker, S.D.; Wolanski, E.; Primavera, J.; Granek, E.F.; Polasky, S.; Aswani, S.; Cramer, L.A.; et al. Coastal ecosystem-based management with nonlinear ecological functions and values. *Science* **2008**, *319*, 321–323. [CrossRef] [PubMed]
7. Feagin, R.A.; Lozada-Bernard, S.M.; Ravens, T.M.; Möller, I.; Yeager, K.M.; Baird, A.H. Does vegetation prevent wave erosion of salt marsh edges? *Proc. Natl. Acad. Sci. USA*. **2009**, *106*, 10109–10113. [CrossRef] [PubMed]
8. Rosati, J.D.; Stone, G.W. Geomorphologic Evolution of Barrier Islands along the Northern, U.S. Gulf of Mexico and Implications for Engineering Design in Barrier Restoration. *J. Coast. Res.* **2009**, *251*, 8–22. [CrossRef]
9. Lindell, J.; Hallin, C.; Hanson, H. Impact of dune vegetation on wave and wind erosion A case study at Ängelholm Beach, South Sweden. *VATTEN J. Water Manag. Res.* **2017**, *73*, 39–48.
10. Feagin, R.A.; Furman, M.; Salgado, K.; Martinez, M.L.; Innocenti, R.A.; Eubanks, K.; Figlus, J.; Huff, T.P.; Sigren, J.; Silva, R. The role of beach and sand dune vegetation in mediating wave run up erosion. *Estuar. Coast. Shelf Sci.* **2019**, *219*, 97–106. [CrossRef]
11. Jackson, D.W.; Costas, S.; González-Villanueva, R.; Cooper, A. A global 'greening' of coastal dunes: An integrated consequence of climate change? *Glob. Planet. Chang.* **2019**, *182*, 103026. [CrossRef]
12. Konlechner, T.M.; Kennedy, D.M.; O'Grady, J.J.; Leach, C.; Ranasinghe, R.; Carvalho, R.C.; Luijendijk, A.P.; McInnes, K.L.; Ierodiaconou, D. Mapping spatial variability in shoreline change hotspots from satellite data; a case study in southeast Australia. *Estuar. Coast. Shelf Sci.* **2020**, *246*, 107018. [CrossRef]
13. Vousdoukas, M.I.; Mentaschi, L.; Voukouvalas, E.; Verlaan, M.; Jevrejeva, S.; Jackson, L.P.; Feyen, L. Global probabilistic projections of extreme sea levels show intensification of coastal flood hazard. *Nat. Commun.* **2018**, *9*, 2360. [CrossRef]
14. Hunter, J. Estimating sea-level extremes under conditions of uncertain sea-level rise. *Clim. Chang.* **2010**, *99*, 331–350. [CrossRef]
15. Church, J.; Clark, P.; Cazenave, A.; Gregory, J.; Jevrejeva, S.; Levermann, A.; Merrifield, M.; Milne, G.; Nerem, R.; Nunn, P.; et al. Contribution of Working Group I to the Fifth Assessment Report of the Intergovernmental Panel on Climate Change. Sea Level Chang. In *Climate Change 2013: The Physical Science Basis*; IPCC: Geneva, Switzerland, 2013; pp. 1138–1191.
16. Vitousek, S.; Barnard, P.L.; Fletcher, C.H.; Frazer, N.; Erikson, L.; Storlazzi, C.D. Doubling of coastal flooding frequency within decades due to sea-level rise. *Sci. Rep.* **2017**, *7*, 1399. [CrossRef]
17. Roelvink, D.; Reniers, A.; van Dongeren, A.; van Thiel de Vries, J.; McCall, R.; Lescinski, J. Modelling storm impacts on beaches, dunes and barrier islands. *Coast. Eng.* **2009**, *56*, 1133–1152. [CrossRef]
18. Vousdoukas, M.I.; Ferreira, Ó.; Almeida, L.P.; Pacheco, A. Toward reliable storm-hazard forecasts: XBeach calibration and its potential application in an operational early-warning system. *Ocean. Dyn.* **2012**, *62*, 1001–1015. [CrossRef]
19. McCall, R.T.; van Thiel de Vries, J.; Plant, N.G.; van Dongeren, A.R.; Roelvink, J.A.; Thompson, D.M.; Reniers, A. Two-dimensional time dependent hurricane overwash and erosion modeling at Santa Rosa Island. *Coast. Eng.* **2010**, *57*, 668–683. [CrossRef]
20. Van Ormondt, M.; Nelson, T.R.; Hapke, C.J.; Roelvink, D. Morphodynamic modelling of the wilderness breach, Fire Island, New York. Part I: Model set-up and validation. *Coast. Eng.* **2020**, *157*, 103621. [CrossRef]
21. Schweiger, C.; Kaehler, C.; Koldrack, N.; Schuettrumpf, H. Spatial and temporal evaluation of storm-induced erosion modelling based on a two-dimensional field case including an artificial unvegetated research dune. *Coast. Eng.* **2020**, *161*, 103752. [CrossRef]
22. Nederhoff, C.M.; Lodder, Q.J.; Boers, M.; den Bieman, J.P.; Miller, J.K. Modelling the effects of hard structures on dune erosion and overwash. In Proceedings of the Coastal Sediments 2015, San Diego, CA, USA, 11–15 May 2015; Wang, P., Rosati, J.D., Cheng, J., Eds.; World Scientifi: Singapore, 2015. ISBN 978-981-4689-96-0.

23. Roelvink, D.; McCall, R.; Mehvar, S.; Nederhoff, K.; Dastgheib, A. Improving predictions of swash dynamics in XBeach: The role of groupiness and incident-band runup. *Coast. Eng.* **2017**, *134*, 103–123. [CrossRef]
24. Van Rooijen, A.; Van Thiel de Vries, J.; McCall, R.; van Dongeren, A.; Roelvink, D.J.; Reniers, A. Modeling of wave attenuation by vegetation with XBeach. In *Proceedings of the 36th IAHR World Congress, 28 June–3 July 2015, The Hague, The Netherlands: Deltas of the Future and What Happens Upstream*; IAHR: The Hague, The Netherlands, 2015; ISBN 9789082484601.
25. Van Rooijen, A.; Lowe, R.; Rijnsdorp, D.P.; Ghisalberti, M.; Jacobsen, N.G.; McCall, R. Wave-Driven Mean Flow Dynamics in Submerged Canopies. *J. Geophys. Res. Ocean.* **2020**, *125*, 57. [CrossRef]
26. Van Rooijen, A.A.; McCall, R.T.; van Thiel de Vries, J.S.M.; van Dongeren, A.R.; Reniers, A.J.H.M.; Roelvink, J.A. Modeling the effect of wave-vegetation interaction on wave setup. *J. Geophys. Res. Ocean.* **2016**, *121*, 4341–4359. [CrossRef]
27. De Vet, P.; McCall, R.T.; den Biemann, J.P.; Stive, M.; van Ormondt, M. Modelling dune erosion, overwash and breaching at fire island (NY) during hurricane Sandy. In *The Proceedings of the Coastal Sediments 2015*; Wang, P., Rosati, J.D., Cheng, J., Eds.; World Scientific: San Diego, CA, USA, 2015; ISBN 978-981-4689-96-0.
28. Passeri, D.L.; Long, J.W.; Plant, N.G.; Bilskie, M.V.; Hagen, S.C. The influence of bed friction variability due to land cover on storm-driven barrier island morphodynamics. *Coast. Eng.* **2018**, *132*, 82–94. [CrossRef]
29. Fernández-Montblanc, T.; Duo, E.; Ciavola, P. Dune reconstruction and revegetation as a potential measure to decrease coastal erosion and flooding under extreme storm conditions. *Ocean. Coast. Manag.* **2020**, *188*, 105075. [CrossRef]
30. Van der Lugt, M.A.; Quataert, E.; van Dongeren, A.; van Ormondt, M.; Sherwood, C.R. Morphodynamic modeling of the response of two barrier islands to Atlantic hurricane forcing. *Estuar. Coast. Shelf Sci.* **2019**, *229*, 106404. [CrossRef]
31. Bendoni, M.; Georgiou, I.Y.; Roelvink, D.; Oumeraci, H. Numerical modelling of the erosion of marsh boundaries due to wave impact. *Coast. Eng.* **2019**, *152*, 103514. [CrossRef]
32. Schweiger, C.; Schuettrumpf, H. Considering the effect of belowground biomass on dune erosion volumes in coastal numerical modelling. *Coast. Eng.* **2021**, *168*, 103927. [CrossRef]
33. Figlus, J.; Sigren, J.M.; Poesen, J.; Armitage, A. Physical Model Experiment Investigating Interactions between Different Dune Vegetation and Morphology Changes under Wave Impact. In *Proceedings of Coastal Dynamics 2017*; Paper No. 059; pp. 470–480. Available online: https://www.semanticscholar.org/paper/PHYSICAL-MODEL-EXPERIMENT-INVESTIGATING-BETWEEN-AND-Figlus-Sigren/f44bcee71e9245a0eccb921c721d46812e6e0bb3 (accessed on 30 July 2021).
34. Bryant, D.B.; Anderson, B.M.; Sharp, J.A.; Bell, G.L.; Moore, C. The response of vegetated dunes to wave attack. *Coast. Eng.* **2019**, *152*, 103506. [CrossRef]
35. Van Gent, M.; van Thiel de Vries, J.; Coeveld, E.M.; Vroeg, J.H.; van de Graaff, J. Large-scale dune erosion tests to study the influence of wave periods. *Coast. Eng.* **2008**, *55*, 1041–1051. [CrossRef]
36. Arcilla, A.S.; Roelvink, D.J.; O'Connor, B.A.; Reniers, A.; Jimenez, J.A. Delta flume'93 experiment. In *Coastal Dynamics '94: Proceedings of an International Conference on the Role of the Large-Scale Experiments in Coastal Research, Universitat Politècnica de Catalunya, Barcelona, Spain, 21–25 February 1994*; Arcilla, A.S., Stive, M.J.F., Kraus, N.C., Eds.; American Society of Civil Engineers: New York, NY, USA, 1994; pp. 488–502. ISBN 978-0-7844-0043-2.
37. Ruessink, B.G.; Miles, J.R.; Feddersen, F.; Guza, R.T.; Elgar, S. Modeling the alongshore current on barred beaches. *J. Geophys. Res.* **2001**, *106*, 22451–22463. [CrossRef]
38. Galappatti, G.; Vreugdenhil, C.B. A depth-integrated model for suspended sediment transport. *J. Hydraul. Res.* **1985**, *23*, 359–377. [CrossRef]
39. Soulsby, R. *Dynamics of Marine Sands: A Manual for Practical Applications*; Telford: London, UK, 1997; ISBN 978-0727725844.
40. Van Rijn, L.C. Sediment Transport, Part III: Bed forms and Alluvial Roughness. *J. Hydraul. Eng.* **1984**, *110*, 1733–1754. [CrossRef]
41. Vannoppen, W.; Baets, S.; Keeble, J.; Dong, Y.; Poesen, J. How do root and soil characteristics affect the erosion-reducing potential of plant species? *Ecol. Eng.* **2017**, *109*, 186–195. [CrossRef]
42. De Baets, S.; Poesen, J.; Reubens, B.; Wemans, K.; Baerdemaeker, J.; Muys, B. Root tensile strength and root distribution of typical Mediterranean plant species and their contribution to soil shear strength. *Plant Soil* **2008**, *305*, 207–226. [CrossRef]
43. Van Rijn, L.C.; Tonnon, P.K.; Sánchez-Arcilla, A.; Cáceres, I.; Grüne, J. Scaling laws for beach and dune erosion processes. *Coast. Eng.* **2011**, *58*, 623–636. [CrossRef]
44. Noda, E.K. Equilibrium Beach Profile Scale-Model Relationship. *J. Wtrwy., Harb. Coast. Engrg. Div.* **1972**, *98*, 511–528. [CrossRef]
45. Kamphuis, J.W. Scale Selection for Mobile Bed Wave Models. In Coastal Engineering 1972. In Proceedings of the 13th International Conference on Coastal Engineering, Vancouver, BC, Canada, 10–14 July 1972; American Society of Civil Engineers: New York, NY, USA, 1972; pp. 1173–1195, ISBN 9780872620490.
46. Vellinga, P. Beach and Dune Erosion during Storm Surges. Ph.D. Dissertation, Delft University of Technology, Delft, The Netherlands, 1986.
47. Bayle, P.M.; Beuzen, T.; Blenkinsopp, C.E.; Baldock, T.E.; Turner, I.L. A new approach for scaling beach profile evolution and sediment transport rates in distorted laboratory models. *Coast. Eng.* **2021**, *163*, 103794. [CrossRef]
48. Van Rijn, L.; Walstra, D.; Grasmeijer, B.; Sutherland, J.; Pan, S.; Sierra, J. The predictability of cross-shore bed evolution of sandy beaches at the time scale of storms and seasons using process-based Profile models. *Coast. Eng.* **2003**, *47*, 295–327. [CrossRef]
49. Van Thiel de Vries, J. Dune Erosion during Storm Surges. Ph.D. Thesis, Delft University of Technology, Delft, The Netherlands, 2009.

50. Harter, C.; Figlus, J. Numerical modeling of the morphodynamic response of a low-lying barrier island beach and foredune system inundated during Hurricane Ike using XBeach and CSHORE. *Coast. Eng.* **2017**, *120*, 64–74. [CrossRef]
51. Splinter, K.; Palmsten, M.; Holman, R.; Tomlinson, R. Comparison of measured and modeled run-up and resulting dune erosion during a lab experiment. *Coast. Sediments* **2011**, *3*, 782–795. [CrossRef]
52. Palmsten, M.L.; Splinter, K.D. Observations and simulations of wave runup during a laboratory dune erosion experiment. *Coast. Eng.* **2016**, *115*, 58–66. [CrossRef]
53. Berard, N.A.; Mulligan, R.P.; da Silva, A.M.F.; Dibajnia, M. Evaluation of XBeach performance for the erosion of a laboratory sand dune. *Coast. Eng.* **2017**, *125*, 70–80. [CrossRef]
54. Van Dongeren, A.; Bolle, A.; Balouin, Y.; Benavente, J. (Eds.) *Micore: Dune Erosion and Overwash Model Validation with Data from Nine European Field Sites (and Beyond)*; Coastal Dynamics: Tokyo, Japan, 2009.
55. Pender, D.; Karunarathna, H. A statistical-process based approach for modelling beach profile variability. *Coast. Eng.* **2013**, *81*, 19–29. [CrossRef]

Article

Modelling the Effect of 'Roller Dynamics' on Storm Erosion: Sylt, North Sea

Pushpa Dissanayake [1,*] and Jennifer Brown [2]

[1] Coastal Geology and Sedimentology, Institute of Geosciences, 24118 Kiel, Germany
[2] National Oceanographic Centre, Joseph Proudman Building, 6 Brownlow Street, Liverpool L3 5DA, UK; jebro@noc.ac.uk
* Correspondence: pushpa.dissanayake@ifg.uni-kiel.de

Abstract: Coastal storm erosion can lead to episodic morphological changes and hinterland flooding that requires sustainable management. An accurate estimation of storm erosion can determine the success of hazard mitigation strategies. Two morphological models, Delft3D and XBeach, were applied separately to a stormy period with "Roller" and "No Roller" wave dynamics activated, to estimate erosion of the beach and dune system on the Sylt island. This is the first numerical impact assessment of roller dynamics on coastal erosion using the two models. The choice of model had more impact on the hydrodynamic and morphological predictions than the option to include or omit roller dynamics. Agreement between measured and simulated waves was higher in Delft3D (R^2 > 0.90 and $RMSE$ < 0.15 m) than XBeach. Storm erosion in both models had the highest sensitivity to the roller parameter *Beta*. Both models predicted a similar storm erosion pattern along the coast, albeit different magnitudes. It is found that Delft3D cannot produce comparable storm erosion to XBeach, when the roller dynamics and avalanching are considered. Delft3D is less sensitive to the roller dynamics than XBeach. Including roller dynamics in Delft3D increased storm erosion up to 31% and in XBeach decreased the erosion down to 58% in the nearshore area, while the erosion in the dune area increased up to 13% in Deflt3D and up to 97% in XBeach. Both models are skilled in simulating storm impact. For the simulation of a storm period with intermittent calm periods, it is suggested that applying a time-varying parameter setting for wave dynamics and sediment transport to capture storm erosion and post-storm beach recovery processes could improve results. Such a modelling approach may ultimately increase the accuracy of estimating storm erosion to support coastal management activities (e.g., sand nourishment volume).

Keywords: roller dynamics; storm erosion; Delft3D; XBeach; SWAN; numerical modelling

Citation: Dissanayake, P.; Brown, J. Modelling the Effect of 'Roller Dynamics' on Storm Erosion: Sylt, North Sea. *J. Mar. Sci. Eng.* **2022**, *10*, 305. https://doi.org/10.3390/jmse10030305

Academic Editors: Rodger Tomlinson and Dong-Sheng Jeng

Received: 4 January 2022
Accepted: 14 February 2022
Published: 22 February 2022

Publisher's Note: MDPI stays neutral with regard to jurisdictional claims in published maps and institutional affiliations.

Copyright: © 2022 by the authors. Licensee MDPI, Basel, Switzerland. This article is an open access article distributed under the terms and conditions of the Creative Commons Attribution (CC BY) license (https://creativecommons.org/licenses/by/4.0/).

1. Introduction

Storm erosion can cause episodic morphological changes and hinterland flooding, providing a major threat to coastal regions thus requiring management [1–3]. Morphological changes during storm events may be (partially) recoverable or may lead to long-lasting coastal system modifications [4,5]. Hinterland flooding of coastal areas is responsible for some of the disasters worldwide [3]. Therefore, storm erosion can affect the socio-economic and environmental value of coastal systems, which inhabit 10% of the world's populations and important infrastructures [6,7], and diverse flora and fauna [8]. In Europe, about 16% of the population (70 million) dwells in the coastal zone, which attracts 500–1000 billion euros of investments for development activities in coastal protection, industries, tourism and urbanization (www.eurosion.org, accessed on 9 December 2021). In the Wadden Sea area, the tourist industry alone generates millions of euros annually for the local communities [8]. These activities are however directly related to the existence of coastal systems, which depend on careful management, particularly against extreme events. A comprehensive understanding of storm erosion is therefore required to provide process knowledge to identify suitable adaptation strategies that deliver sustainable yet effective coastal management.

Increased erosion during extreme events occurs due to high energy physical processes occurring across coastal areas [9,10]. In the surf zone, energetic waves break causing strong turbulence and vertical mixing that suspend more sediment. Increased spatial variation in wave induced momentum flux enhances alongshore and cross shore currents, transporting more sediment [10]. Furthermore, wave breaking can occur closer to the coast with elevated storm water levels, increasing erosion of the upper beach. After short wave breaking, long infragravity waves are released approaching beaches and dunes [11]. Impacts of the long waves are often responsible for the erosion of the upper beaches and dunes [11]. Storm erosion of beaches and dunes can be classified into four regimes [9], in a sequence of increasing erosion severity: (1) Swash (swash motion across the beach), (2) Collision (wave bores collide with the dune face), (3) Overwash (a fraction of the waves overtop dunes) and (4) Inundation (dune is breached and submerged). These main physical processes of erosion are now implemented into numerical models to simulate storm erosion [10,11].

Numerical modelling is widely used to investigate the impacts and the processes of storm erosion e.g., [2,4,10,11]. We focus here on two commonly used opensource models, Delft3D (D3D) and XBeach (XB). D3D enables simulation of the hydrodynamics (circulation and waves), sediment transport and morphological changes by currents, waves and their interactions [12]. An extension of D3D further allows simulation of the effect of short wave groups on long waves ('roller dynamics') in the nearshore and dune avalanching [13,14]. XB computes the processes of the four storm erosion regimes by the short wave averaged long wave motion [11]. Roller dynamics are one of the primary processes in XB.

D3D has been used to investigate coastal erosion in calm and storm conditions with the roller dynamics e.g., [13–15]. Hsu et al. [13,14] evaluated the model performance with the measured wave heights and longshore currents at the Duck coast, NC and at Santa Barbara, CA, USA. Both studies showed the sensitivity of the currents and wave heights to different parameter setting and improved model prediction by including the roller dynamics. Giardino et al. [15] simulated morphological changes at Egmond aan Zee, the Netherlands for different scenarios using two versions of D3D: the standard version, which was used in this study, and a modified version including a beach and dune module. The modified version caused increased alongshore currents and more realistic morphological changes. However, only standard versions are available in the public domain.

Storm erosion across coastal areas is often investigated using XB e.g., [2,16,17]. Smallegan et al. [16] simulated the impacts of Hurricane Sandy at Bay Head, NJ, USA and showed that the presence of a buried seawall increased wave attenuation and thus coastal protection. The performance of XB and CShore was assessed by simulating beach profiles at Torrey Pines and Cardiff beaches (CA, USA) for different intensity storm events [17]. Results show, both models have limited skill in reproducing storm erosion, and the upper beach profile response is predicted with a different skill to that when the entire profile is considered. Storm erosion at Formby Point, Sefton coast, UK was simulated for the established storm wave threshold (2.5 m) and a new storm classification in Dissanayake et al. [2]. The new classification is developed based on the sequencing of both water levels and wave heights. Results show that the new classification identified more storm events and caused higher erosion than the established classification providing a realistic estimation of storm erosion.

These example studies demonstrate, both D3D and XB are used to investigate storm erosion in different coastal environments and forcing conditions. However, sensitivity of storm erosion to the roller dynamics is not yet considered. Based on the implemented physical processes, these two models might have different skills in capturing storm erosion across a coastal area. In this study, we compare the performance of both models by simulating the effect of roller dynamics in storm erosion of the beach and dune system on the Sylt island.

The Sylt island is a mesotidal mixed energy environment in the North Frisian Wadden Sea, German Bight [18,19]. Measured data on water levels, waves and wind are available representing the environmental forcing at this beach and dune system. Morphological surveys are routinely carried out for management purposes by the local agency of coastal protection. However, the time span of these surveys is very coarse (~1 month to a year) and not suitable to derive storm event scale erosion at this coastal system. Simulating the morphological changes between the available surveys can provide high resolution spatiotemporal information on the storm impact. This information provides a comprehensive understanding of storm erosion to identify suitable management activities.

The main objective of this study is to investigate the effect of the roller dynamics in D3D and XB on storm erosion simulation across a coastal area, and to identify their skills against field data. The novelty of the approach is, we simulate two different morphodynamic models separately covering a major storm period between two morphological surveys, and for the first time assess the sensitivity of the storm erosion to the roller dynamics. Our hypothesis is that including roller dynamics in D3D will increase erosion in the intertidal area and the subaerial beach due to an increase in the hydrodynamics from the roller contribution. Therefore, D3D roller dynamics could provide increased dune erosion, although still lower than predicted by XB.

This study is presented as follows. Section 2 describes background and field data of the study area, and Section 3 details the methodology. The results are presented in Section 4, with a discussion of the simulated results with the previous studies in Section 5. The conclusions of the study are in Section 6, including recommendations for suitable applications of these two numerical models.

2. Study Area

2.1. Background

The Sylt island is north-south oriented (maximum width ~13 km), located in the North Frisian Wadden Sea, German Bight and connected to the mainland with a dam (Figure 1a). The western coast of Sylt (North Sea coast) is about 35 km in length and its orientation from south to north varies about 20°. The present study focused on the central coast, which encloses the stretch of the maximum curvature of coastline, and exhibits less influence from the adjacent tidal inlets on the nearshore morphology (see depth contours on Figure 1c). The nearshore morphology has generally a double-barred profile with steep slope on the beach and regular rip channels [18]. The dune system on Sylt reaches up to about 30 m in height. Beach nourishments are routinely carried out to combat storm impact on the beach and dune system [18]. The central coast tends to have high susceptibility to storm impacted erosion [19]. Sediment is characterised by medium to coarse sand [20]. The model sediment bed was established using an average sediment fraction of 300 μm.

Marine forcing continuously shapes the beach and dune system. The semi-diurnal meso-tidal range varies from 1.8 to 2.0 m during neap and spring conditions respectively (at WL in Figure 1b). The highest water level (3.55 m) occurred recently on 06 December 2013 during the storm Xavier. The significant wave height (H_s) during storm events sporadically exceeds 6 m, while the mean H_s fluctuates around 1 m (at 13 m water depth, W1 in Figure 1b). The dominant wave direction is from NW, and the waves are mainly generated from the westerly wind from SW to NW. The averaged wind speed from 2005 to 2018 was about 7 m/s, while increasing over 30 m/s during extreme storm events (at WN in Figure 1b). Data from these three observation points were used for the model simulations, and wave heights at W2 (8 m depth) were used to evaluate the model skills in predicting wave dynamics, which is the main driver for sediment transport and morphodynamics.

Three cross-shore profile locations (N, M and S in Figure 1d) are used for the analysis of hydrodynamics and morphodynamics representing north, middle and south of the model domain. On each profile, three points are further selected for the analysis. They represent nearly the lowest water level during the analysis period (1), on top of the nearshore bar (2) and seaward of the bar (3) (Table 1).

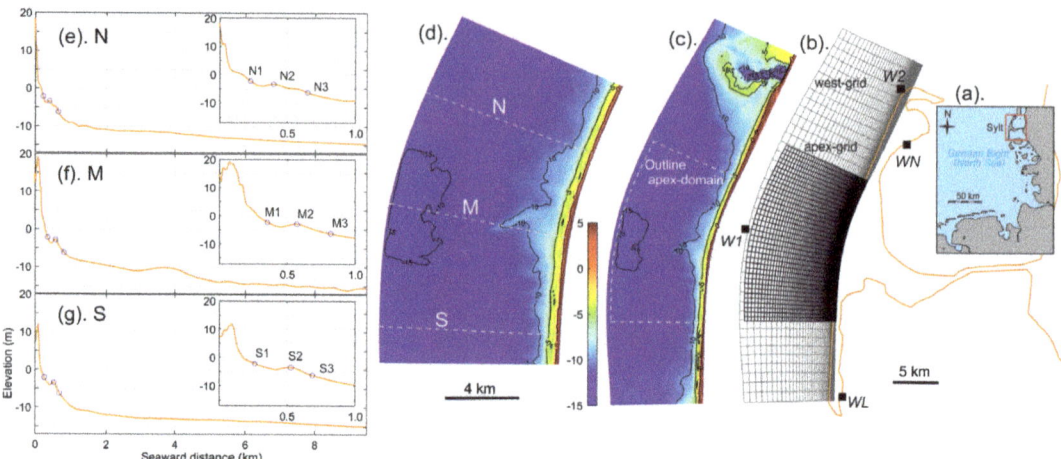

Figure 1. Location of Sylt in the German Bight, North Sea (**a**), the apex- and west-model grids (**b**), model bathymetry for the west domain with the outline of the apex domain (**c**), model bathymetry for the apex domain with the selected three cross-shore profiles (North: N, Middle: M and South: S) for the analysis (**d**), profile N (**e**), M (**f**) and S (**g**) with analysis points: close to beach (1), on top of the bar (2) and seaward of the bar (3). Zoom-out profile views of 1 km are shown for clarity.

Table 1. Characteristics of the analysis locations along the three profiles.

Location		Distance from MSL (m)	Depth (m)
North (N)	N1	58	2.1
	N2	233	3.3
	N3	481	6.2
Middle (M)	M1	67	2.1
	M2	285	2.7
	M3	531	6.1
South (S)	S1	86	2.1
	S2	356	3.4
	S3	513	6.1

2.2. Field Data

Observed water levels (at WL in Figure 1b), wave (at W1 and W2) and wind (at WN) conditions were used for the model simulations from 24 January to 26 April 2007, which covers a period between two beach and dune surveys. On 18 March 2007, a major storm event impacted the beach and dune system on Sylt (Figure 2).

Water level data at WL from the Federal Agency for Waterways and Shipping (WSV: Wasserstraßen- und Schifffahrtsverwaltung des Bundes) has a temporal resolution of 10 min. The maximum water level (3.1 m) during the analysis period occurred at spring-high water (00:45 h 19 March 2007), while the maximum tidal anomaly (TA: total water level -astronomical tide = 2.7 m) was during the rising tide after spring-low water (20:00 h 18 March 2007). Apart from the major storm event, there are other events with a TA of about 1 m (Figure 2a). The spatiotemporal astronomical tide was extracted from a calibrated German Bight model [21].

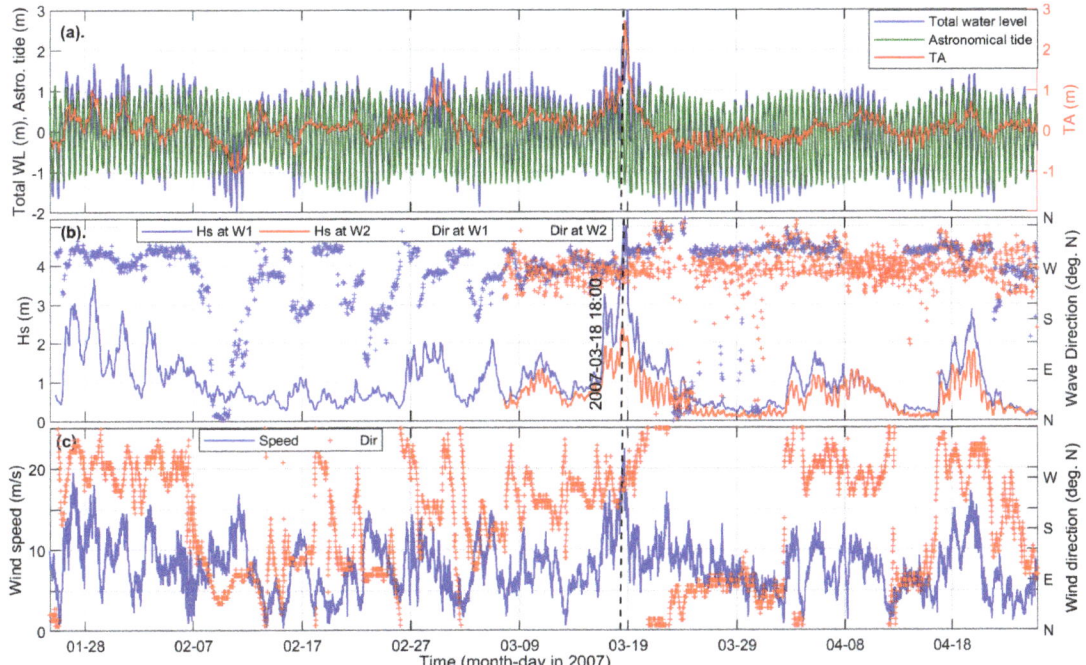

Figure 2. Field data used for the numerical simulations. Total water level (blue line), Astronomical tide (green line) and the derived tidal anomaly (TA, red line) at WL (**a**), Significant wave height (lines) and direction (+) at W1 (blue) and W2 (red) (**b**), Wind speed (blue line) and direction (red +) at WN (**c**) (see observation locations in Figure 1b). Dash-line indicates peak storm wave occurrence at 18:00 h 18 March 2007 (H_s = 5.0 m at W1 and 2.6 m at W2).

Wave observations have temporal resolutions of 1 h at W1 (from the Federal Agency for Maritime and Hydrographic, BSH: Bundesamt für Seeschifffahrt und Hydrographie) and 30 min at W2 (from the local agency for coastal protection, LKN: Landesbetrieb für Küstenschutz, Nationalpark und Meeresschutz Schleswig-Holstein). At W2, there are data only from 7 March to 26 April 2007. Wave heights at W1 and W2 show extreme events (e.g., wave heights exceeding 2 m) from the west (Figure 2b). Peak storm waves (H_s: 5.0 m at W1 and 2.6 m at W2) occurred on the rising tide after spring-low water (18:00 h 18 March 2007), when the total water level was at 1.3 m.

Wind data at WN from the German Weather Service (DWD: Deutscher Wetterdienst) has a temporal resolution of 10 min. During the major storm event, wind speed exceeded 21 m/s and approached from the SW (18:00 h 18 March 2007). In the other events (e.g., at 28 January, 27 February), the wind direction was from the NW exceeding 15 m/s (Figure 2c). It should be noted that the west coast of Sylt is exposed to wind and waves approaching from the entire S to N sector.

The model bathymetries were constructed using two sources of data, (1) Beach and dune topography from LiDAR provided by LKN and (2) Nearshore bathymetry from BSH. There are two LiDAR data sets surveyed on 25 January and 25 April 2007. These data have a spatial resolution of 1 m and extend from the dune area down to about MSL (0 m). The nearshore bathymetry represents the sea bed in 2007, and has a spatial resolution of 50 m and the highest depth reaches about −3 m. Therefore, the nearshore area from 0 to −3 m depth has no observed bathymetry information during the analysis period.

3. Methodology

A hybrid approach of numerical experiments using D3D and XB was used to investigate the impact of roller dynamics on the beach and dune erosion. Both models were initially simulated with hydrodynamics (circulation and waves) only to assess the model performance against measured wave data. Using the optimised roller parameters through a sensitivity analysis, the final model settings were applied implementing roller and no roller dynamics in both D3D and XB (see Section 3.1.4). The simulated hydrodynamics and morphodynamics were analysed to access the effect of the roller dynamics on storm erosion.

3.1. Model Setup

3.1.1. Modelling Tools

The numerical background of the two modelling tools D3D and XB is described below with their similarities and differences.

(a) Delft3D (D3D)

D3D is an open-source model that has shown skill in simulating morphodynamics in a wide range of applications e.g., [19,22]. This three-dimensional model has been developed based on a finite difference approach with an alternating direction implicit (ADI) numerical scheme [12,23]. D3D enables using different modules to simulate physical processes, e.g., hydrodynamics (FLOW), sediment transport (SED), morphology (MOR). FLOW is the primary module that interacts with all other modules. In FLOW, the unsteady nonlinear shallow water equations are solved using the ADI method to compute the hydrodynamics [24]. In this study, a depth-averaged approach (2DH) is used with the FLOW, SED and MOR modules. Wave forcing on the hydrodynamics are simulated by online-wave coupling between SWAN [25] and FLOW, in which there is a two-way communication at a user specified time interval. A 30-min interval is used to capture the tidal variation, although the temporal resolution of the wave data at W1 is 1 h. SWAN simulates the propagation of a short-wave spectrum (JONSWAP, see Equation (1)) over the model domain based on the offshore imposed wave parameters. In D3D with Roller dynamics (see 3.1.2), the short wave effect on the long wave is also computed and applied in the hydrodynamics at the scale of the wave groups. Total sediment transport under combined waves and currents is estimated using the Soulsby—Van Rijn formulations [26]. Morphodynamics are computed based on the conservation of sediment fluxes, which is multiplied by a morphological acceleration factor, *morfac* [19]. Avalanching is activated, when a critical wet slope angle is exceeded. In the grid stencil, scalar quantities are computed at the grid-cell centre, while vector quantities at grid-cell faces.

(b) XBeach (XB)

XB is an open source model, which has been originally developed to investigate hurricane impact (erosion) on beaches and dunes [11]. The skill of this model in predicting storm erosion has been shown in numerous applications e.g., [2,10,16]. XB is a 2DH morphodynamic model, which estimates the beach and dune response to time-varying storm conditions. XB estimates the main physical processes of beach and dune erosion [9] by solving coupled depth-average equations for wave propagation, flow, sediment transport and morphodynamics. The wave solver is based on the 2nd generation HISWA model [27] using the directional distribution of wave action density with a single representative frequency. This study uses the surfbeat mode, which computes the propagation of the short wave averaged envelop and accompanying long-wave motion [11]. Short waves are generated at the offshore boundary based on the JONSWAP spectrum. Similar to D3D, hydrodynamics are computed using the shallow water equations. The numerical scheme follows the method of Stelling and Duinmeijer [28], in which different depth values are used for the continuity and the momentum equation based on a velocity threshold, to improve long-wave runup and backwash on beaches. Avalanching is used to estimate dune erosion. Cross-shore transport depends on the balance of the wave skewness and asymmetry (onshore component), and the undertow (offshore component). Sediment transport is estimated using the Soulsby—Van Rijn formulations [26], and morphodynamics can be accelerated using a *morfac* as in D3D. Both D3D and XB use the same grid stencil. The main similarities and differences of both models are listed in Table 2.

Table 2. Main similarities and differences of physical processes in D3D and XB for the roller (R) and no roller (NR) applications. A detailed list of process comparison is provided in Appendix A.

Physical Process		D3D		XB	
		R	NR	R	NR
Short-wave		✓	✓	✓	✓
Long-wave from offshore		✗	✗	✓	✓
Long-wave effect from short wave breaking (roller model)		✓	✗	✓	✗
Wave computation	Directional-Domain	✓	✓	✓	✓
	Frequency-Domain	✓	✓	✗	✗
Undertow		✗	✗	✓	✓
Avalanching		✓	✓	✓	✓

3.1.2. Roller Model

The roller model simulates the effect of short wave groups on long waves, which causes the spatial variation in the radiation stresses and long waves to travel with the groups of short waves. This is an important phenomenon in dune erosion [11] and is implemented in D3D as an add-on module [29], but is a fundamental process in XB [11]. Both models do not simulate individual long waves but the forcing caused by short waves.

The roller model uses breaking wave energy from the short wave energy balance as the source to compute the propagation of the roller energy. In D3D, the mean wave direction, of which wave and roller energy are transported, and wave period are obtained from the SWAN wave computation. XB estimates wave energy propagation similar to the HISWA model [27] in the directional domain with a representative frequency. In D3D and XB models, the total radiation stresses are estimated by adding roller- and wave-induced radiation stresses to compute the wave forces, which are used in the momentum equations to estimate hydrodynamics.

The roller energy balance equation in XB is given by Equation (1). The fourth term of the left-hand side is not used in D3D.

$$\frac{\partial S_r}{\partial t} + \frac{\partial c_x S_r}{\partial x} + \frac{\partial c_y S_r}{\partial y} + \frac{\partial c_\theta S_r}{\partial \theta} = D_w - D_r \quad (1)$$

where, t: time (s), S_r: roller energy density (J/m^2/Hz), c: wave celerity (m/s), D_w: dissipation of wave energy (J/m^2), D_r: dissipation of roller energy (J/m^2), x and y: spatial and θ: directional domains.

Following Roelvink [30], the wave energy dissipation is implemented in both models based on the propagation of wave groups (Equation (2)).

$$D_w = 2\alpha f_m (1 - \exp(-(\frac{\sqrt{8E/(\rho g)}}{\gamma h})^n))E \quad (2)$$

where, α: wave dissipation coefficient (-), f_m: representative frequency (Hz), E: wave energy (J/m^2), g: acceleration of gravity (m^2/s), ρ: water density (kg/m^3), γ: breaker index (-), h: water depth (m), n: calibration coefficient (-).

The roller energy dissipation is given by,

$$D_r = 2\beta g \frac{E_r}{c} \quad (3)$$

where, β: roller slope (-), E_r: roller energy (J/m^2)

Total wave forces are estimated based on the wave- and roller-induced radiation stresses as follows,

$$F_x = -\left(\frac{\partial S_{xx,w} + \partial S_{xx,r}}{\partial x} + \frac{\partial S_{xy,w} + \partial S_{xy,r}}{\partial y}\right) \quad (4)$$

$$F_y = -\left(\frac{\partial S_{xy,w} + \partial S_{xy,r}}{\partial x} + \frac{\partial S_{yy,w} + \partial S_{yy,r}}{\partial y}\right) \quad (5)$$

where F_x and F_y: total wave force components in x and y directions (N). S_{xx}, S_{xy} and S_{yy} are radiation stresses (m/s^2), w and r indicate respectively wave and roller induce radiation stress components.

The following three roller coefficients were selected to analyse the sensitivity of beach and dune erosion, while applying the same settings for all other parameters in both models (see Appendix A).

(a) *Beta (β)*

The slope of the wave front is *Beta*, which determines the roller energy dissipation (Equation (3)). The default value is 0.1, and lower values cause delayed response resulting to pronounced inner and outer bars, and larger values result in considerable bar flattening [31]. This parameter is generally used to control the behaviour of breaker bars, which ultimately affects the beach and dune erosion. A range of values from 0.05 to 0.30 are used for D3D and XB (see Section 3.1.4).

(b) *Gamdis*

Gamdis (Gamma dissipation) is the wave breaking index, which imposes an upper limit on wave heights as a fraction of the local water depth. Therefore, this determines wave heights in the surf zone. Gamdis can be set to a constant or a depth-dependent value. The default value (0.55) is based on the wave propagation in the time scale of wave groups [30]. A depth-dependent value can be applied following Ruessink et al. [32] in D3D (−1), and other formulations (*roelvink1*, *roelvink2* and *roelvink_daly*) in XB (see Section 3.1.4). Wave dissipation is proportional to H^2 (H is wave height) in *roelvink1* and to H^3/h in *roelvink2* [30]. In *roelvink_daly* [33], two thresholds are defined for fully- and non-breaking of wave conditions.

(c) *F_lam*

F_lam indicates breaker delay, which defines a seaward weighted averaged water depth for the computation of wave energy dissipation due to wave breaking. Waves need a distance (~one wave length) to start and stop breaking, and this phenomenon is considered replacing the local water depth with a water depth weighted over a certain seaward distance from the point of interest [34]. The breaker delay, however, is less influential on the morphodynamics than the previous two parameters [35]. In D3D, there are two options, either two wave lengths offshore (−2) or no breaker delay (0: default). Applying −2, the energy dissipation due to wave breaking is computed using a weighted averaged water depth from the local water depth up to the water depth of two wave lengths offshore. In XB, no (0) and enabled (1: default) breaker delay are used to investigate the effect of breaker delay on beach and dune erosion (see Section 3.1.4).

3.1.3. Model Domains and Boundary Forcing

Two model domains, "apex" and "west", were used for the numerical experiments (Figure 1b–d). Characteristics of these domains are given in Table 3. The grid resolution of the apex domain is twice that of the west domain. The purpose of the west domain is to generate the wave parameters at the boundaries of the apex domain. This wave nesting approach is required for the D3D simulations to minimize the wave shadow-zone effect at the lateral boundaries of the apex domain (see Dissanayake and Winter [19]). In XB, waves can be simulated without this effect using the apex domain only [19]. However, to enable consistent model comparison and validation, the west domain was employed in the XB simulations as well (note. W2 is located beyond the apex domain, Figure 1b). Morphological changes in both models were simulated using the apex domain.

Table 3. Characteristics of the apex- and west-model domains (Figure 1).

Model Domain	Spatial Extent (Cross Shore × Alongshore in km)	Grid Nodes	Range of Grid Resolution (Cross Shore × Alongshore in m)
apex-grid	9.8 × 15	15,120	4–200 × 190–300
west-grid	10.2 × 38	7857	8–400 × 400–600

The model bathymetries for 25 January 2007 were prepared applying the LiDAR (25 January 2007) and the BSH bathymetry (2007) data. As mentioned in Section 2.2, there is a gap in data between 0 and −3 m depths. This stretch extends from MSL down to about N1, M1 and S1 (Table 1 and Figure 1e–g), and there are fairly linear variations along the bed profile segments before MSL, and before the trough of the first nearshore bar (N2, M2 and S2 in Figure 1e–g). Therefore, bed levels within this stretch were generated by linear interpolation across-shore at each grid point along the coast. Similarly, the model bathymetry representing 25 April 2007 was set up using the respective LiDAR and the 2007 BSH data. For the model comparison, the initial and final measured cross-shore profiles at N, M and S (see Figure 1e–g) were extracted from these two combined bathymetries, and those for the models were extracted from the final simulated beds.

Model boundaries were set up using the observed data (water level, waves and wind) and the predicted astronomic tide from a calibrated hydrodynamic model of the German Bight [21]. Spatially varying total water level (astronomical tide + TA) was applied for the offshore boundary of the domains, while the lateral boundaries were imposed with water level gradients. Such a combination generates tidal currents perpendicular to the lateral boundaries following the direction of tidal propagation [36,37]. Spatially varying total water level was prepared by combing the astronomical tide from the German Bight model (amplitudes and phases at the offshore corner points) and the derived TA at WL (Figure 1b). A spatially uniform and temporally varying offshore wave boundary was applied using parametric values at W1 to generate the JONSWAP wave spectrum [38,39]. For the lateral wave boundaries in XB, the gradient of wave energy along the wave crest was set to zero to minimize the wave shadow-zone effect. Spatially uniform and temporally varying wind fields were applied using the wind data at WN.

3.1.4. Simulations

The simulation period spans from 18:00 h 24 January to 00:00 h 26 April 2007 covering two beach and dune surveys (i.e., LiDAR data). The initial period of 6 h was used to spin-up the models so the hydrodynamics in the domain are in equilibrium with the boundary forcing. First, four hydrodynamic simulations using the west domain were run to compare the model performance, and the Roller and No Roller applications (Table 4). Then, a sensitivity analysis of the beach and dune erosion to roller parameters (*Beta*, *Gamdis* and *F_lam*, see Section 3.1.2) was carried out to identify their optimum values (i.e., 17 simulations). Using the selected values for the roller parameters, the final set of models (4) were simulated to investigate the roller effect on beach and dune erosion in D3D and XB.

Table 4. Model simulations in D3D and XB for the comparison of hydrodynamics and morphodynamics using Roller (R) and No Roller (NR) applications. Default parameters (reference scenario) are in bold-letter.

Scenario			D3D		XB		No. of Simulations
			R	NR	R	NR	
Hydrodynamics only			✓	✓	✓	✓	4
Sensitivity analysis	Beta		**0.10**		**0.15**		8
			0.05		0.05		
			0.20		0.20		
			0.30		0.30		
	Gamdis		−1		roelvink2		5
			0.55		**roelvink1**		
					roelvink_daly		
	F_lam		**0**		**1**		4
			−2		0		
Beach and dune erosion			✓	✓	✓	✓	4

3.2. Analysis

Simulated results are analysed to illustrate the model skills, and to investigate the effect of the roller dynamics on the hydrodynamics and storm erosion in D3D and XB. The models' skills in predicting wave dynamics are evaluated using wave height and wave spectral density. Measurements and simulations are compared using three statistical parameters: Correlation coefficient (R^2), root mean square error ($RMSE$) and relative change (μ). Wave height and depth averaged velocity at the time of the observed peak storm wave occurrence (18:00 h at 18 March 2007) are first qualitatively compared in both models to investigate the roller effect on the hydrodynamics. Next, water levels, wave heights, velocities and the effective bed shear stress are analysed along the three cross-shore profiles (N, M and S). The effect of roller parameters on beach and dune erosion is estimated using $RMSE$ and the mean relative change ($\bar{\mu}$) with respect to the reference (default parameter setting) scenarios. Finally, the roller dynamics on storm erosion are investigated using bed level change of the analysis points along the three profiles, and the sediment volume change within different zones (classified by depth) along the beach and dune profile.

Estimation of the wave spectral density and the effective bed shear stress in D3D and XB, and the statistical parameters used for the comparison are described below.

(a) Wave spectral density

The wave spectral density (SD) represents the distribution of wave energy as a function of frequency and its shape depends on the processes of wave growth and decay, as well as interactions between different frequency bands. The formulation for the JONSWAP [38,39] spectrum reads as,

$$SD(f) = \frac{\alpha g^2}{(2\pi)^4 f^5} exp\left[\frac{-5}{4}\left(\frac{f}{f_p}\right)^{-4}\right]\gamma^r \quad (6)$$

where, $r = exp\left[\frac{-(f-f_p)^2}{2\sigma^2 f_p^2}\right]$, $\sigma = \begin{cases} 0.07, & f < f_p \\ 0.09, & f \geq f_p \end{cases}$, α: Phillips constant (-), f: wave frequency (Hz), γ: peak enhancement factor (3.3), σ: spectral width parameter (-).

In D3D, SD was computed using the modelled H_s and peak period (T_p). XB predicts root-mean-square wave height (H_{rms}). This is first converted into H_s following a relation of the Rayleigh distribution, $H_s = \sqrt{2} \times H_{rms}$, which is however more applicable for normal wave conditions at deep water (see Goda [40]). SD is then computed using, (1) modelled H_{rms} and observed T_p at W1 and (2) converted H_s and observed T_p at W1 in XB.

(b) Effective bed shear stress

The effective bed shear stress (τ_b) represents the overall shear stress on the sea floor from both waves and currents, and their interactions, and determines local sediment transport. The depth-averaged effective bed shear stress for D3D and XB was calculated using the following formulations.

In D3D, the Soulsby [26] approach, which is based on one standard function that can be adapted for different wave–current boundary layer models, is used to estimate τ_b following the Fredsøe [41] boundary layer model.

$$\vec{\tau}_b = \frac{|\vec{\tau}_m|}{|u|}\left(\vec{u} + \vec{u}_s\right) \tag{7}$$

$$|\vec{\tau}_m| = Y\left(|\vec{\tau}_c| + |\vec{\tau}_w|\right) \tag{8}$$

$$\tau_w = \frac{1}{2}\rho f_w u_w^2 \tag{9}$$

$$\tau_c = \rho C_D u^2 \tag{10}$$

where τ_m: bed shear stress of combined waves and currents (N/m^2), u: depth-averaged velocity (m/s), u_s: depth-averaged Stokes drift, Y: a fitting function for the wave-current boundary layer [26], τ_c: bed shear stress from currents alone (N/m^2), τ_w: bed shear stress from waves alone (N/m^2), f_w: friction factor (-), u_w: wave orbital velocity (m/s), and C_D: drag coefficient (-).

In XB, τ_b is calculated based on mean currents and long waves following the approach of Ruessink et al. [42]. The x and y components of τ_b read as,

$$\tau_{bx}^E = c_f \rho u_E \sqrt{(1.16 u_{rms})^2 + (u_E + v_E)^2} \tag{11}$$

$$\tau_{by}^E = c_f \rho v_E \sqrt{(1.16 u_{rms})^2 + (u_E + v_E)^2} \tag{12}$$

where c_f: dimensionless friction coefficient (g/C^2), C: Chézy coefficient (m$^{1/2}$/s), u_E and v_E: Eulerian velocity (short-wave-averaged velocity observed at a fixed point) at x and y directions (m/s), u_{rms}: wave orbital velocity (m/s).

(c) Statistical parameters

The models' skills in predicting wave characteristics were analyzed by comparing measured and predicted parameters at W2 using three statistical parameters (Equations (13)–(15)).

The coefficient of determination (R^2) was calculated to quantify the fraction of variance in each simulation corresponding to the measurements. This is defined as the squared value of the coefficient of correlation [43]:

$$R^2 = \left[\frac{\sum_{j=1}^n (x_j - \bar{x})(y_j - \bar{y})}{\sqrt{(x_j - \bar{x})(y_j - \bar{y})}}\right]^2 \tag{13}$$

where, x values represent the parameter time series (i.e., H_s) from the measured data and y values represent the simulated values, $\bar{x}$ and $\bar{y}$ indicate the mean values, and n is the number of time steps during the analysis period.

The root mean square error (RMSE) quantifies the standard deviation of the differences between the simulations and either the measurements or the reference simulation:

$$RMSE = \sqrt{\frac{1}{n}\sum_{j=1}^{n}(x_j - y_j)^2} \qquad (14)$$

Smaller RMSEs imply better agreement between the observations and the model simulations.

The mean relative change ($\overline{\mu}$) indicates the normalised difference between the measured and simulated data.

$$\overline{\mu} = \frac{1}{n}\sum_{j=1}^{n}\mu_j \qquad (15)$$

where,

$$\mu_j = \frac{(y_j - x_j)}{x_j}$$

4. Results

4.1. Model Skill

The model skill was analysed by comparing the measured and simulated wave heights at W2 (see location in Figure 1b) and the respective wave spectral densities between D3D NR and XB R being the standard applications.

Wave height comparison is shown in Figure 3a for the measurements (W1 and W2) and the simulations (D3D: H_s, XB: H_{rms} and H_s). Measured wave heights at W2 span from 13:00 h 07 March 2007 (t_1) to 00:00 h 26 April 2007 (t_3) only. The peak storm wave height (H_s) was observed as 2.6 m at W2 (t_2: 18:00 h 18 March 2007) while it is 2.4 m in D3D and in XB, 2.4 m (H_{rms}) equal to 3.4 m (H_s). The D3D wave heights are generally higher at low wave heights and lower at high wave heights compared with the observations. The XB wave heights H_s are higher than the observations. Observed wave heights at W1 are always higher than at W2 and the model predictions. This indicates that waves decay during their propagation into the apex domain rather growing.

Wave Spectral densities were analysed at W2. The normalised spectral densities with respect to the maximum spectral density of the observed data were estimated for the waves from the observations (Figure 3b), D3D H_s (c), XB H_{rms} (d) and XB H_s (e). The highest spectral density corresponds to the peak storm wave height in all cases. Variation of spectral density from t_1 to t_3 is qualitatively in better agreement between W2 (observations) and D3D, than between W2 and XB. The results of XB H_s are higher compared with that of W2. In the analysis period, high wave heights result in high spectral densities in both model simulations (e.g., 29 January, 28 February).

Wave heights and spectral densities were quantitatively compared between the observations and the simulated results at W2 (Table 5). The highest R^2 (0.91) and the lowest RMSE (0.14 m) in D3D indicate that the simulated waves represent the measured wave heights well. In XB, these values imply low agreement between measured and simulated wave heights. Simulated spectral density in D3D is only 0.32 kJ/m²/Hz lower than the observations ($\mu = -0.03$). In contrast, it is lower (2.52 kJ/m²/Hz and $\mu = -0.27$) and higher (3.96 kJ/m²/Hz and $\mu = 0.45$) in XB using H_{rms} and H_s respectively.

The analysis of model skills showed that D3D can better capture the measured wave characteristics than XB. As mentioned in Section 3.1.1, D3D computes the propagation of wave spectrum in both directional and frequency domains, whereas XB estimates only in the directional domain using a mean frequency. This could contribute to low wave heights in XB. Overall, the simulated waves in XB H_{rms} can be treated as reasonable based on the statistical values. It should be noted that extensive calibration and validation of the hydrodynamics were not undertaken in this analysis. Therefore, the present parameter setting of these two models (see Appendix A) is used to compare the hydrodynamics with Roller and No Roller applications.

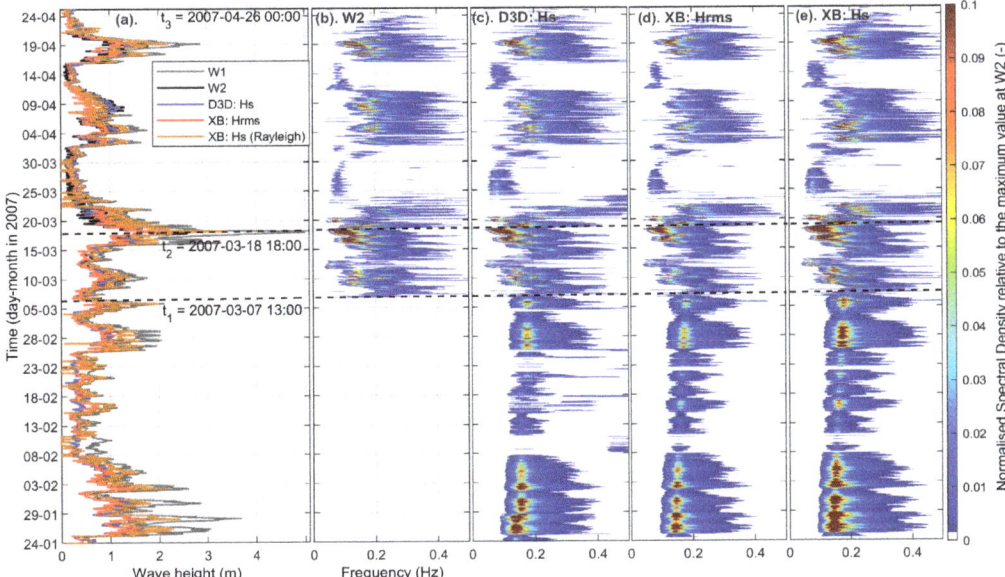

Figure 3. Comparison of the measured significant wave heights (gray at W1 and black at W2) and the simulated wave heights at W2 (blue: D3D H_s, red: XB H_{rms} and orange: XB H_s) (**a**), Normalised wave spectral density from the measured wave at W2 (**b**), and from the simulations at W2, D3D H_s (**c**), XB H_{rms} (**d**) and XB H_s (**e**). t_1 indicates the initial time, t_2 is the peak wave occurrence and t_3 is the last time point of the W2 data (see data locations in Figure 1b).

Table 5. Comparison of measured and simulated wave heights and spectral density from t_1 to t_3 at W2 (see location in Figure 1b).

Source	Wave Height		Wave Spectral Density (SD)	
	R^2 (-)	RMSE (m)	$\sum$SD (kJ/m^2/Hz)	μ (-)
Observations (H_s)	-	-	8.99	-
D3D (H_s)	0.91	0.14	8.67	−0.03
XB (H_{rms})	0.83	0.21	6.47	−0.27
XB (H_s)	0.83	0.26	12.95	0.45

4.2. Hydrodynamics

Roller effects on the hydrodynamics were analysed using the simulated water level, depth-averaged velocity, wave height and bed shear stress in both models. The first three parameters were qualitatively compared between the Roller (R) and No Roller (NR) applications at the time of the peak storm wave height (t_2: 18:00 h 18 March 2007 in Figure 3a, H_s: 2.6 m at W2). This energetic condition enables clear visualization of the discrepancies between the simulations. Average values of these parameters were then compared over the full analysis period.

Wave height and directional patterns are shown in Figure 4 for both models with R and NR simulations. For clarity, a nearshore section of the domain (water depth ~5 m) is displayed. In both applications, H_s in D3D are higher than XB H_{rms}, while the highest waves are shown by XB H_s. D3D R appears to have higher wave heights than D3D NR. However, in XB, wave heights in NR seem to be higher compared with the R. Wave direction is same between R and NR, although slightly different between the two models (~5°). Wave direction in XB is more eastwardly oriented than D3D. This could be due to the fact, SWAN uses peak wave direction and XB uses mean wave direction for the wave computation. The observed peak wave directions were provided as the input wave directions in both models.

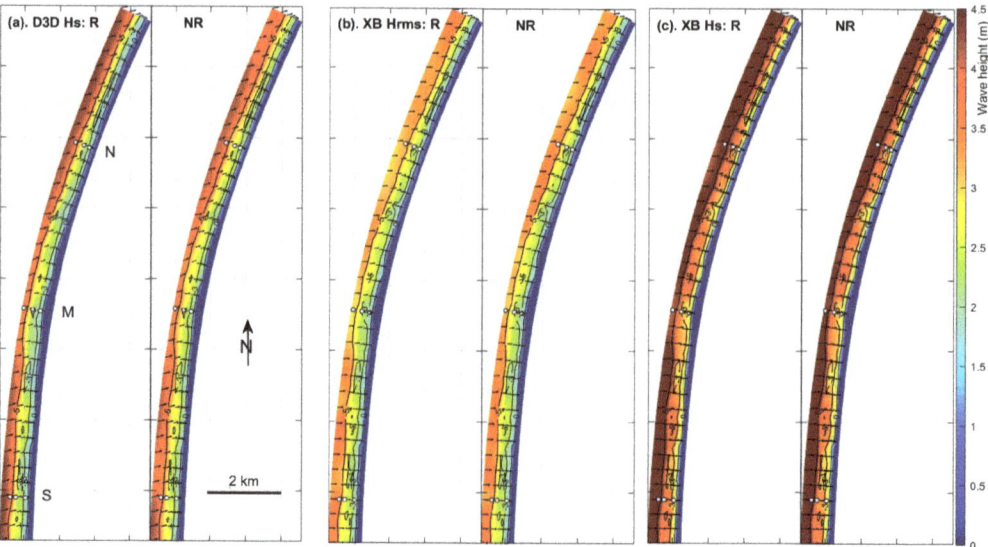

Figure 4. Comparison of simulated wave heights at the time of the peak in storm waves (t_2: 18:00 h 18 March 2007, observed H_s 2.6 m at W2) with Roller (R) and No Roller (NR) dynamics: D3D H_s (**a**), XB H_{rms} (**b**) and XB H_s (**c**). Vectors indicate direction and magnitude, and colour indicates magnitude. N, M and S are the cross-shore profile locations with the selected three points for the analysis. Depth is shown with the contour lines.

The depth-averaged velocity shows a clear wave driven alongshore current flowing along shore to the north (Figure 5). In agreement with wave heights (H_s), velocity distribution at the time of the peak in storm waves shows the highest values in XB. All applications have a similar pattern of variations along the coast but the magnitudes are different. In D3D, nonzero velocities span across the shore beyond the 5 m depth, and the roller dynamics (a) caused an increase in velocities relative to the no roller dynamics (b). The velocities are higher in XB than D3D, but they are constrained close to the coast up to 5 m depth. Similar to D3D, XB also shows higher velocities with the roller dynamics.

The cross-shore variation of water level, wave height and velocity at t_2 are shown in Figure 6 at the three profile locations (N, M and S). Water level (first row) indicates that the difference between R (solid-line) and NR (dash-line) is higher in XB (red-line) than in D3D (blue-line). This could be due to the fact that XB computes the short wave averaged long wave oscillation across the entire domain, while that in D3D depends on wave breaking. It is generally found, the roller dynamics cause high water levels in both models. Around MSL XB tends to produce higher water levels compared with D3D. Over the nearshore bar (at N2, M2 and S2) water level increases, which is more noticeable in D3D than XB.

As found in Figure 4, wave heights (second row) in D3D (blue-line) are lower than in XB H_s (magenta-line). The strong decrease in wave heights at the nearshore bar indicates wave breaking in both models. The effect of roller dynamics on wave heights depends on the profile location. In the south (S) and the north (N), the roller dynamics caused higher wave heights. However, for the middle (M) profile, higher waves are generally found with the no roller application. In D3D, there are always higher wave heights on the beach with the no roller simulation. This indicates that the roller model in D3D decreases wave heights on the beach.

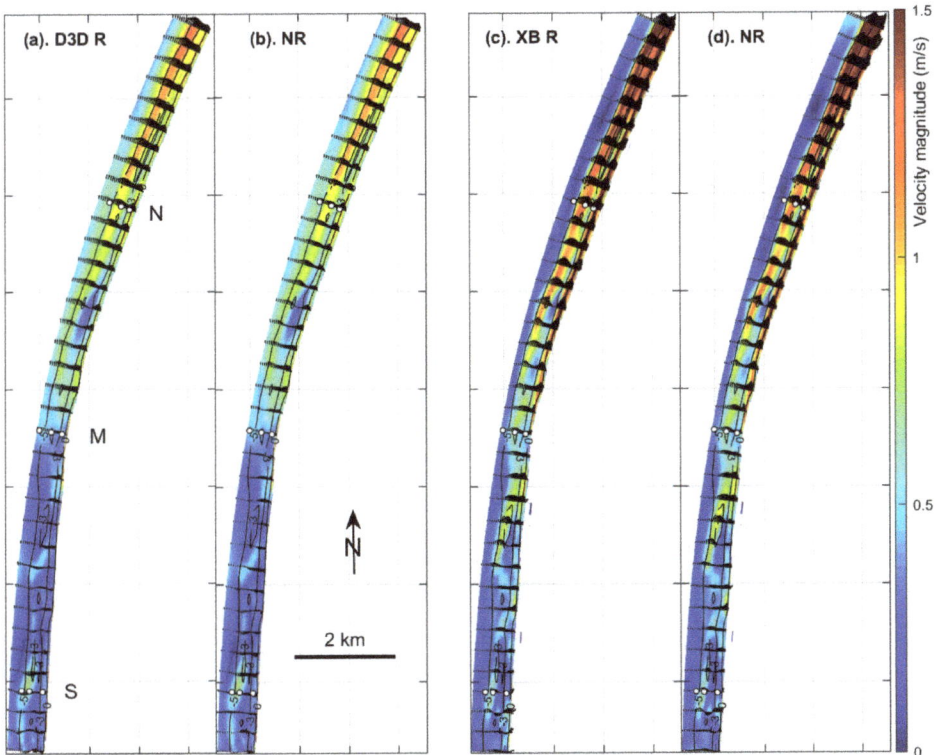

Figure 5. Comparison of depth averaged velocities at the time of the peak in storm waves (t_2: 18:00 h 18 March 2007) with Roller (R) and No Roller (NR) dynamics: D3D R (**a**), D3D NR (**b**), XB R (**c**) and XB NR (**d**). Vectors indicate direction and magnitude, and colour indicates magnitude. N, M and S are the cross-shore profile locations with the selected three points for the analysis. Depth is shown with the contour lines.

Cross-shore velocities are seaward directed (negative) in D3D for all profiles (blue-line, third row). However, they (except NR at M) are positive indicating shoreward velocities in XB (red-line). It appears that there is a difference between the cross-shore processes in the models. Alongshore velocities are northward (positive) at the N and M profiles in both models (D3D: black-line and XB: magenta-line). However, cross-shore variation and magnitudes are higher in XB than in D3D. In the south (S profile), D3D shows southward (negative) velocities, while they are northward in XB. In both models, the difference between roller and no roller dynamics varies along the cross-shore direction. Overall, the cross-shore variations of water level, wave height and velocity show that the effect of roll dynamics in each model is lower compared to the difference between the two models.

Bed shear stresses at the analysis points decrease with distance towards the sea (from 1 to 3 in Figure 7). During the analysis period (see Figure 2), it can be expected that the waves commonly break at the shallowest analysis location (~2 m depth: N1, M1 and S1) along the profiles. Therefore, a higher bed shear stresses occurred at the shallowest location than the other two points (e.g., N2, N3). However, the deeper two points of all three profiles show a strong peak in bed shear stress during the storm events because larger waves penetrate to a deeper depth causing higher bed shear stress. The difference of bed shear stresses between roller and no roller applications is more noticeable in D3D than in XB. This indicates that including roller dynamics caused increased bed shear stress in D3D. However, the effect of roller dynamics on bed shear stress is marginal in XB.

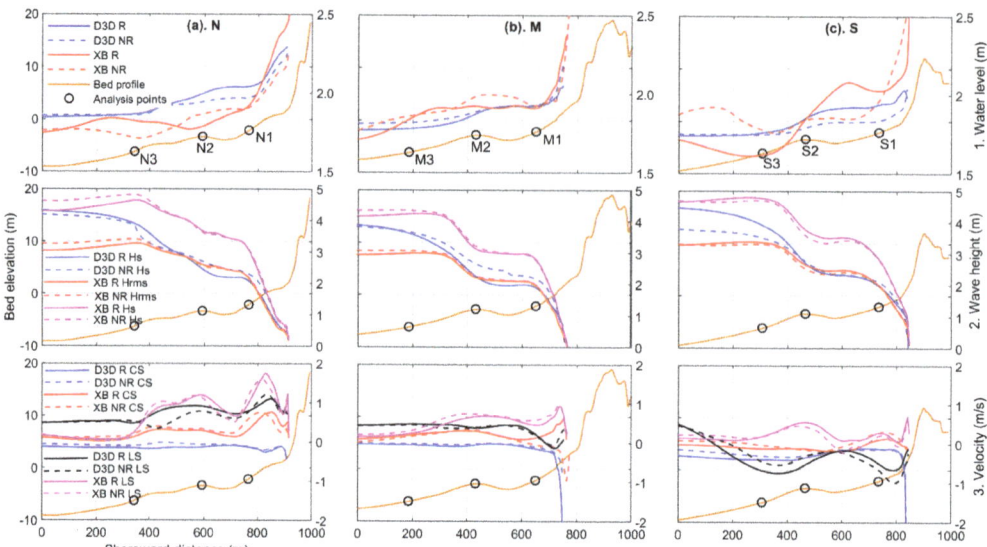

Figure 6. Comparison of hydrodynamics (rows: **1.** Water level, **2.** Wave height and **3.** Velocity) along the three cross-shore profiles (Columns: (**a**). N, (**b**). M and (**c**). S) at the time of the peak storm waves (t_2: 18:00 h 18 March 2007). Cross-shore profiles (orange lines) are shown with the analysis points (black circles). First row: Water level, D3D (blue) and XB (red). Solid lines are Roller and dash lines are No Roller results. Second row: Wave height, D3D H_s (blue), XB H_{rms} (red) and XB H_s (magenta). Third row: Velocity, D3D-Cross-shore (CS) (blue) and XB-Cross-shore (red) with shoreward positive values, D3D-alongshore (LS) (black) and XB-alongshore (magenta) with northward positive values. The second (right) y axis has a different scale than the first for a better visualization.

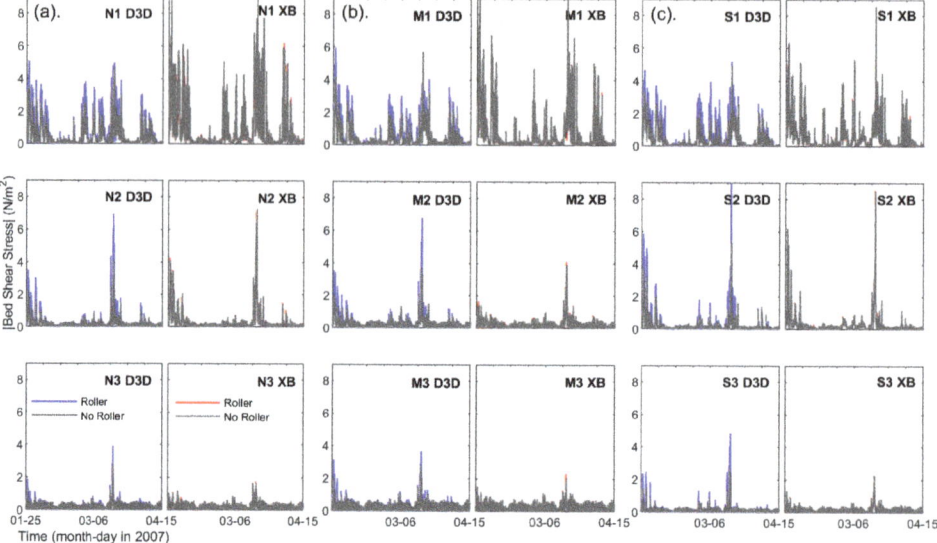

Figure 7. Comparison of temporal bed shear stress at the three analysis points (**1**, **2** and **3**: seaward) along the three cross-shore profiles, N (**a**), M (**b**) and S (**c**). First column is D3D (blue) and Second column is XB (red), results of No Roller are shown with gray lines.

The averaged wave height, velocity and bed shear stress over the simulation period are summarized in Table 6 for the analysis points along the profiles. In both models and roller applications, wave heights increase seaward, while velocity and bed shear stresses decrease. Wave breaking occurs close to the coast increasing the latter two parameters.

Table 6. Comparison of wave height, velocity and bed shear stress during the full analysis period between D3D and XB at the 3 analysis points (1, 2 and 3) along the 3 cross-shore profiles (N, M and S). R: Roller and NR: No Roller simulations. < > indicates average over the analysis period and | | indicates magnitude of vectors.

Location		<Wave Height> (m)						<|Velocity|> (m/s)				<|Bed Shear Stress|> (m/s)			
		D3D H_s		XB H_{rms}		XB H_s		D3D		XB		D3D		XB	
		R	NR	R	NR	R	NR	R	NR	R	NR	R	NR	R	NR
North (N)	N1	0.71	0.78	0.65	0.65	0.92	0.92	0.30	0.25	0.26	0.28	0.74	0.54	0.81	0.90
	N2	0.79	0.87	0.68	0.68	0.96	0.96	0.20	0.18	0.15	0.15	0.32	0.24	0.32	0.32
	N3	0.89	0.97	0.68	0.68	0.96	0.96	0.21	0.20	0.18	0.18	0.24	0.22	0.22	0.22
Middle (M)	M1	0.69	0.78	0.66	0.66	0.94	0.94	0.29	0.24	0.23	0.24	0.66	0.48	0.67	0.71
	M2	0.76	0.88	0.67	0.67	0.95	0.95	0.22	0.20	0.19	0.19	0.38	0.29	0.28	0.27
	M3	0.90	0.99	0.70	0.70	0.99	0.99	0.25	0.24	0.23	0.23	0.33	0.29	0.29	0.29
South (S)	S1	0.66	0.70	0.66	0.66	0.93	0.93	0.28	0.23	0.19	0.20	0.66	0.45	0.57	0.59
	S2	0.78	0.84	0.68	0.68	0.96	0.96	0.20	0.18	0.15	0.15	0.35	0.25	0.31	0.31
	S3	0.85	0.91	0.69	0.68	0.97	0.97	0.18	0.17	0.16	0.16	0.20	0.16	0.19	0.19

In contrast to Figures 4 and 6, the averaged wave heights (over time at the analysis points) indicate that the values in the roller application are lower than the no roller in D3D. The roller model in D3D uses wave energy from the wave breaking prediction in the SWAN computation. If waves are small (e.g., 0.5 m) and not breaking, there is no wave energy for the wave estimation in the roller model. Therefore, during calm conditions, wave heights from the roller model are zero. Thus, high wave heights become higher when the roller dynamics are considered. However, when taking the average values over the full simulation period the roller dynamics reduce the overall wave height in D3D.

Both the velocity and the bed shear stress increase with the roller dynamics in D3D. The magnitude of the estimated total wave force is higher with the roller dynamics than the no roller application because of the contribution from both wave force and roller force. This total wave force contributes to the momentum of the flow, which influences the water levels and velocities.

The effect of the roller dynamics in XB is marginal on wave height, velocity and bed shear stress. As in D3D, there is no separate module to compute the wave propagation in XB, which estimates the propagation of short wave averaged long wave motion over the entire domain. The difference of wave energy dissipation between the R and NR applications is only about 5% of the entire domain during the simulation period. Therefore, the impact of the roller dynamics is marginal in the computation of the hydrodynamic parameters in XB.

4.3. Storm Erosion

4.3.1. Sensitivity of Storm Erosion to Roller Dynamics

The sensitivity of the profile evolution during the analysis period was analysed using the three roller parameters (rows in Figure 8) for both models (columns). These profiles are from the apex domain and the locations N, M and S are shown in Figure 1d. The measured initial and final profile segments extend from the dune (~15 m) out to MSL (0 m, see Section 2.2). However, a profile segment from 10 to −10 m is shown to help visualize the storm erosion at the nearshore bar and dune relative to the overall change along the profile. Beyond these limits, there is no prominent erosion.

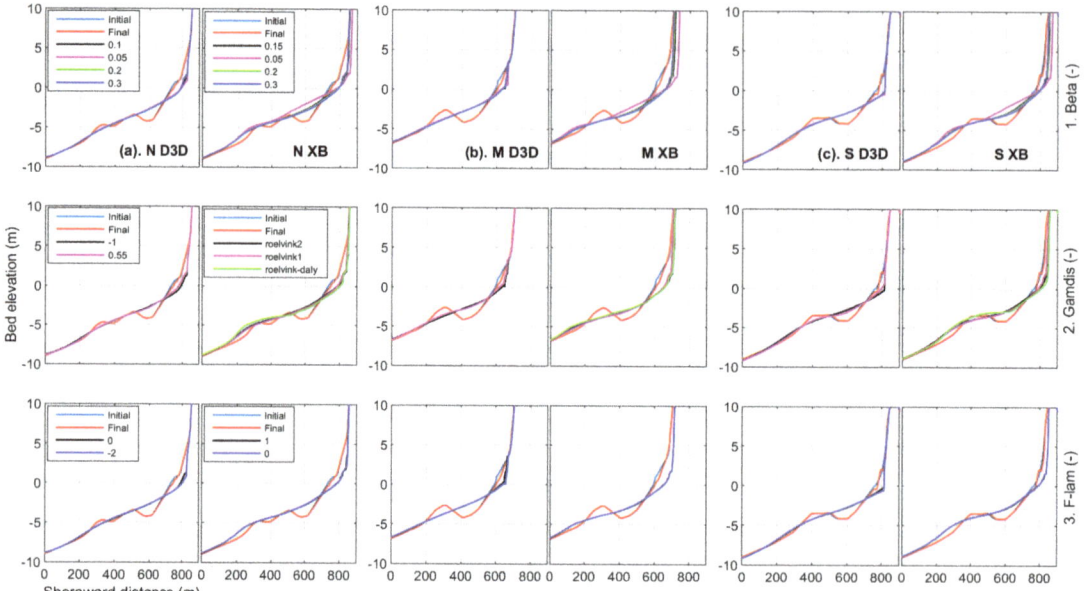

Figure 8. Sensitivity of profile evolution N ((**a**). first column: D3D and second column: XB), M (**b**) and S (**c**) for the roller parameters (rows: **1.** *Beta*, **2.** *Gamdis* and **3.** *F_lam*). Initial (light-blue) and final (red) measured profiles (first two lines) spanning the analysis period from 25 January to 26 April 2007 are shown with the simulated final profile with different parameters (colour lines). Note, linearly interpolated bed levels are used between 0 m (MSL) and −3 m depth due to the lack of measured data.

The main erosion and sedimentation patterns in both models are consistent for all parameter settings, though there are fine changes depending on their values. Erosion at the dune front is predicted to be higher than observed. In both models, the nearshore bar erodes with sedimentation in the landward trough. Strong erosion on the bar (depth ~3 m, see Table 1) can be expected given 5 m H_s (at W1 in Figure 1b) and 3.1 m water level during the peak storm wave (Figure 2). However, due to the lack of observations between 0 and −3 m, and the post-storm bathymetry, the final predicted profile cannot be validated. The predicted profiles provide a method of comparison between the simulation settings. The first row in Figure 8 shows the sensitivity of the profile evolution to the parameter *Beta* (roller slope in Equation (3)). The simulated profiles in D3D show less change compared with that of XB. The north profile (N) experienced the highest erosion in D3D. Erosion of the upper dune (above 5 m) occurred only in XB in all locations when using a *Beta* of 0.05. It is generally shown that the sensitivity of the profile evolution to *Beta* is higher in XB than in D3D. With the parameter *Gamdis* (dissipation) set to 0.55 (second row, Figure 8), D3D resulted in less evolutionary response than that of a setting of −1 [32] for all profiles. The profile evolution in XB is found to be less sensitivity to the three dissipation formulas than D3D. Evolution in both models is least sensitive to the parameter *F_lam* (breaker delay: third row, Figure 8). D3D shows an increase in bed response when applying a setting of −2. However, there is a hardly any difference between a setting of 1 (with breaker delay) and 0 (no breaker delay) in XB. These erosion and sedimentation patterns indicate that the sensitivity of the bed change under storm conditions decreases in order in response to the parameter settings of *Beta*, *Gamdis* and *F_lam*. The flattening of the beach profile in both models suggests, neither simulates recovery of a bar system during calm conditions particularly well (Note. last storm wave peak 2.9 m at W1 occurred at 21:00 h 19 April: Figure 2b).

The evolution between the observed (LiDAR) and the simulated profile from 0 to 5 m elevation was statistically compared using the root mean square error (*RMSE*: Equation (14)). D3D shows the smallest changes in the middle profile (M), while XB shows the greatest changes in this profile and the smallest changes in the southern profile (S) (Table 7). Therefore, the models have different skills in capturing the measured topography based on the along-shore location. These values agree with the profile variations in Figure 8 and further indicate that there is a low sensitivity of profile evolution for the different values of each parameter.

Table 7. Root mean square error (*RMSE*) (m) between measured and simulated profiles from 0 to 5 m elevation at dunes along N, M and S with different roller parameters.

Roller Parameter	D3D				XB			
	Value	N	M	S	Value	N	M	S
Beta	0.10	1.69	0.96	1.69	0.15	1.78	2.18	1.46
	0.05	1.83	1.14	1.79	0.05	1.97	2.35	1.55
	0.20	1.54	0.88	1.65	0.20	1.75	2.17	1.41
	0.30	1.51	0.90	1.63	0.30	1.73	2.15	1.43
Gamdis	−1	1.69	0.96	1.69	roelvink2	1.78	2.18	1.46
	0.55	1.34	0.67	1.26	roelvink1	1.66	1.92	1.24
					roelvink_daly	2.01	2.17	1.77
F_lam	0	1.69	0.96	1.69	1	1.78	2.18	1.46
	−2	1.93	1.32	1.90	0	1.77	2.20	1.44

The change in beach and dune sediment volume during the analysis period was estimated between 0 and 5 m elevations considering the initial and final bathymetries from the observations and the model predictions (Figure 9). In all cases, the net change was a loss of volume due to erosion. The lower the *Beta* the greater the erosion in both models. The best agreement with the measured data is found with 0.20 (difference ~0.02 Mm^3 in D3D and 0.06 Mm^3 in XB). Depending on the dissipation formula (*Gamdis*), the erosion volume differs in the models. In D3D, the setting of −1 [32] resulted in the highest agreement with the observations, while it is the *roelvink1* setting in XB that performs best. It should be noted that 0.55 (D3D) and *roelvink1* (XB) have the same erosion volumes, because *roelvink1* has been calibrated against a breaker index of 0.55. D3D is more sensitive to the breaker delay (*F_lam*) than XB. No breaker delay (0) provides the best agreement with the measured erosion volume. In XB, there is a marginal improvement applying the breaker delay model.

Selected roller parameters for both models are shown in Table 8.

Table 8. Selected values of the roller parameters for D3D and XB by the sensitivity analysis.

Roller Parameter	Value	
	D3D	XB
Beta	0.20	0.20
Gamdis	−1.0	roelvink1
F_lam	0.0	0.0

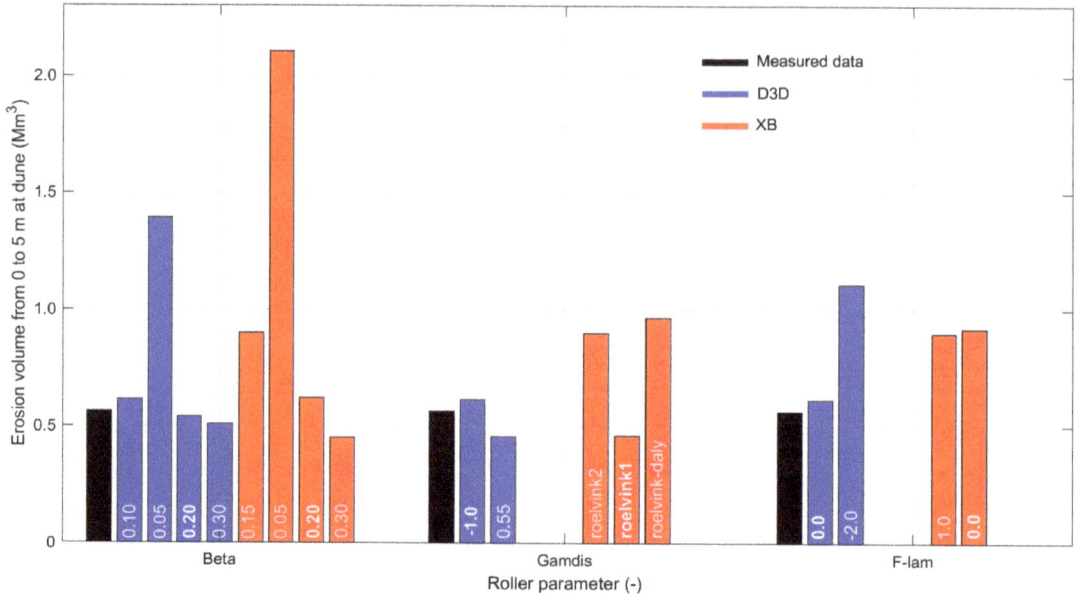

Figure 9. Sensitivity of erosion volume between 0 and 5 m elevation over the analysis period for the different values (indicated on the bars) of the roller parameters (*Beta*, *Gamdis* and *F_lam*). The estimated erosion volume from the measured data (black) are shown with the simulated results, D3D (blue) and XB (red).

4.3.2. Roller Effect on Storm Erosion

The roller effect on storm erosion was assessed by comparing the erosion and sedimentation pattern along the coast, bed evolution of the analysis points and the sediment volume change in different depth classes from 5 to −5 m elevation.

The simulated erosion and sedimentation patterns have generally common trends whereas different magnitudes in both models (Figure 10). The entire coast is impacted by the storm events approaching from the SW—NW sector (see Figure 2b). All simulations resulted in erosion around MSL (0 m), and sedimentation around −3 m depth, where there is a ridge runnel feature along the coast (see Figure 1e,f and Figure 8). The second erosion stretch occurred on the nearshore bar (see locations of the second analysis points) and the sedimentation around −5 m depth. In D3D, both erosion and sedimentation magnitudes are lower than those of XB. However, D3D R generated higher magnitudes of evolution than D3D NR. In XB, the erosion area at MSL extends towards dune providing more sediment into the nearshore area. XB R shows strong erosion particularly in the dune area, and greater sedimentation in the runnel and around −5 m depth compared to XB NR. The roller effect in XB increased the storm impact more so than in D3D.

Bed evolution of the analysis points varies depending on their cross-shore locations (Figure 11). The impact of the storm waves on the bed evolution is noticeable at all locations (e.g., at t_2). The points located close to the beach (N1, M1 and S1) show the highest impact from the roller dynamics. In D3D, the rate of bed level change increased with the roller application. However, XB R caused a lower rate of bed evolution than D3D R. This could be due to the fact that greater erosion of the dune area provides more sediment to the nearshore zone in XB than in D3D. This process of sediment supply increased in XB R compared with that of XB NR. Therefore, erosion at N1, M1 and S1 in XB R is less than in XB NR. The points on the nearshore bar experience erosion, which increases with the addition of roller dynamics in both models. Erosion due to the storm wave is greater at M2 and S2, where there is a prominent bar feature unlike at N2. The seaward points (N3, M3 and S3) show accretion. In all simulations, the bed evolution at M3 is fairly similar. At N3 and S3, XB resulted in higher accretion than D3D, and that increases with the consideration of the roller dynamics (XB R). Furthermore, the results indicate that the effect of the roller dynamics on bed evolution decreases with distance offshore from the beach into the nearshore.

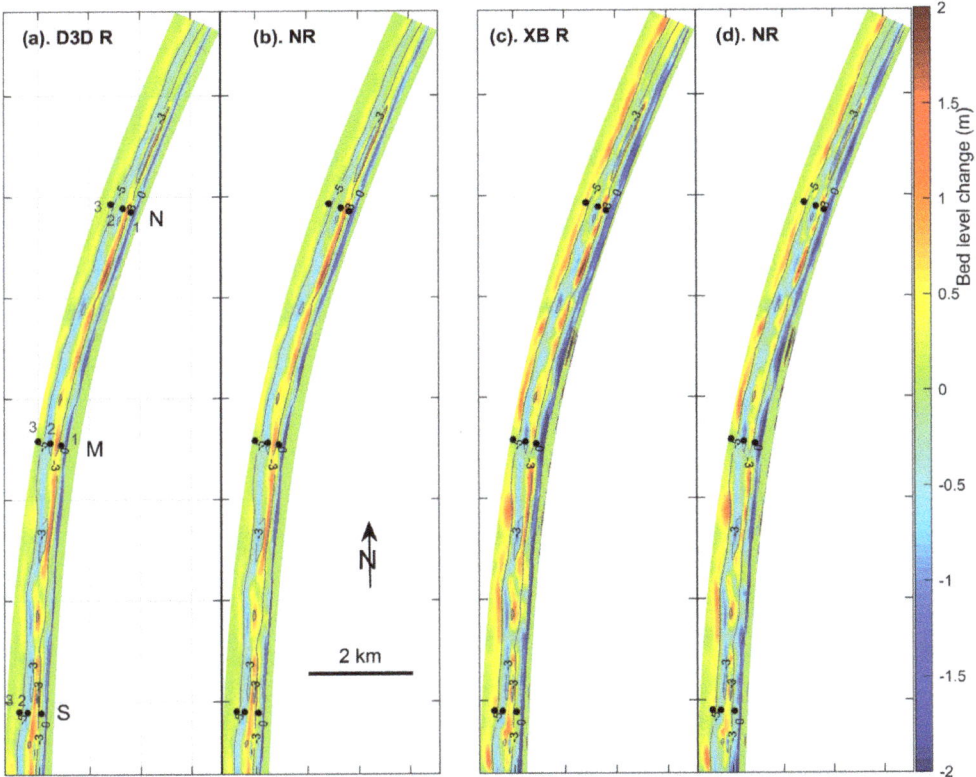

Figure 10. Simulated erosion and sedimentation patterns during the analysis period from 25 January to 26 April 2007, D3D Roller (**a**), D3D No Roller (**b**), XB Roller (**c**) and XB No Roller (**d**). N, M and S indicate the selected cross-shore profile locations, and 1, 2 and 3 are analysis points on the profiles.

Bed levels and sediment volume were analysed within the cross-shore depth range from 5 to −5 m along the entire coast of the apex domain (Figure 12). The position of the bed level for each model grid point with respect to the line of no bed change (gray-dash-line in upper row) indicates erosion (below) and accretion (above). The area below MLW (Mean Low Water) experienced bed evolution at large number of data points in all simulations (i.e., colour indicates density of data points, %). D3D (a) generally predicts accretion while it decreases from XB R to XB NR (b) (see yellow-red area with respect to the no bed change line). Between MLW and MHW (Mean High Water), erosion is predicted by all simulations. The density of data indicates that higher number of grid points experience erosion in D3D than in XB. Strongest bed evolution occurred above the DT (Dune Toe), and there are marked differences in erosion between R and NR applications, and also between the two models. In D3D, the initial bed levels above 3.5 m elevation are barely changed from the storm impacts. However, the number of erosion points increased with the roller application. Similar observation is found in XB. In particular, XB R generates greater avalanching of the upper dune front (up to ~2 m) and severe erosion at the HW (1 m) contour. It should be noted that the comparison of bed levels from the observation (initial) and the simulations (final) provides an overview of the erosion and accretion pattern. In order to find the sediment volume change, bed level change should be multiplied by the respective grid cell area, which varies in the model domain.

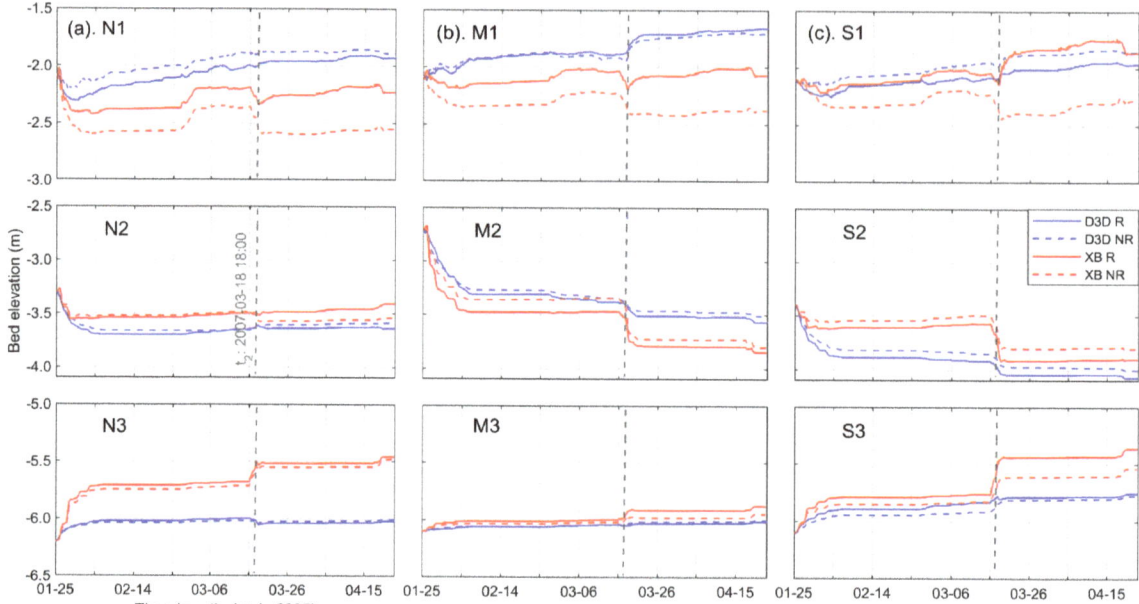

Figure 11. Bed level change (D3D: blue and XB: red) of the analysis points (1, 2 and 3) along the three cross-shore profiles (Columns: N (**a**), M (**b**) and S (**c**)). Results from the Roller (R), with solid-line, and No Roller (NR), with dash-line, are indicated. Occurrence of the peak storm wave height at t_2 is shown with gray-dash-line. Note, y-axis depth range differs based on the points' water depths.

The estimated sediment volumes within the depth classes are stacked for R (c) and NR (d) applications separately. In the R applications, the deepest depth class shows fairly similar erosion and accretion volumes in both models. This trend generally continues up to the MSL contour. From MSL to the dunes, XB shows greater erosion than D3D, and that increases as the elevation increases. It is clearly shown that D3D cannot produce the same dune erosion as in XB (see depth class: 3–5 m) when the roller dynamics and avalanching are considered. In the NR applications, the difference of erosion volume between the models generally increases in the area below MHW. In D3D NR, the erosion volume decreases from nearshore up to MSL compared with that of the R application. For the dune area (above 2 m), there is no significant difference between R and NR applications in D3D. However, XB shows that the R application results in the highest erosion. Therefore, the XB dune response estimate to storm waves is sensitive to the application of the roller dynamics, and in D3D nearshore erosion is sensitive.

The roller effect on storm erosion in each model is summarised by estimating the mean-relative-change of erosion volume with respect to the erosion in the NR application (Table 9). In D3D, the roller dynamics caused increased erosion from the nearshore up to MSL and at the dune (depth class: 3–5 m). However, the area above MSL and below 3 m experienced lower erosion than the NR application. This could be partly due to redistribution of the avalanched sediment from the upper dune area. In XB, the R application resulted in significant erosion at the dune, whereas lower erosion in the other depth classes compared with the NR application. Strong avalanching of sediment at the upper dune provides more sediment to lower depth classes causing the lower erosion. These results suggest that the roller effect in D3D increases dune erosion. Nevertheless, it is very low compared with that of XB.

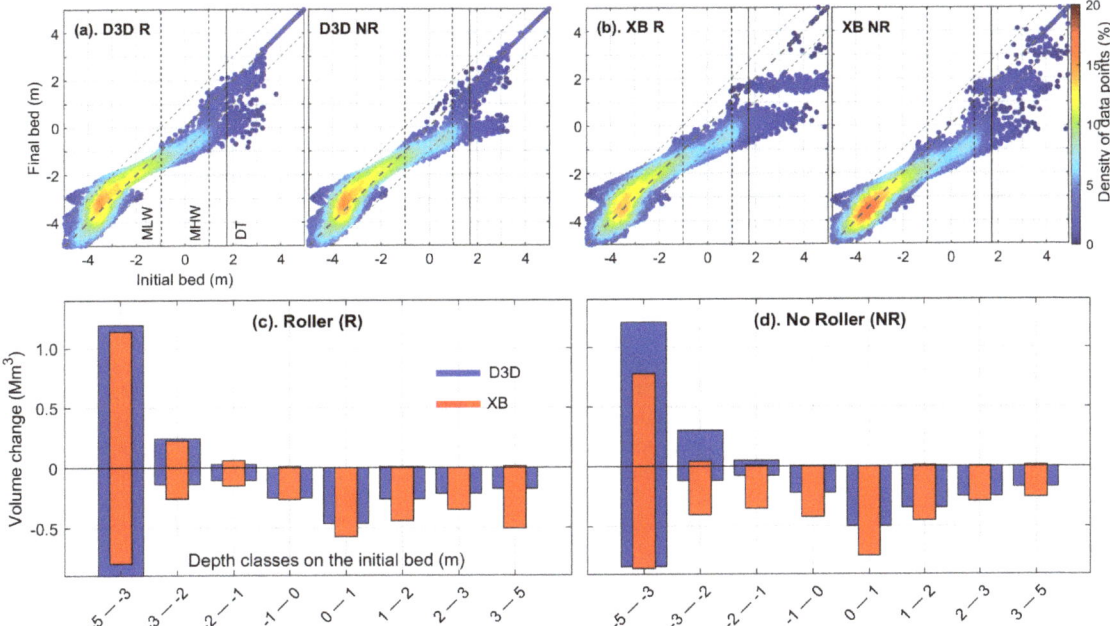

Figure 12. Simulated bed level (upper-row) and sediment volume change (lower-row) within the cross-shore stretch between 5 to −5 m elevation along the coast, D3D Roller and No Roller (**a**), XB Roller and No Roller (**b**), and volume change (erosion: negative and accretion: positive) in Roller applications (**c**) and No Roller applications (**d**) in D3D (blue) and XB (red). MLW: Mean Low Water (−1 m), MHW: Mean High Water (1 m) and DT: Dune toe level (1.8 m). Gray-dash-line: no change of bed levels and gray-thin-dash-line: 20% change of bed levels.

Table 9. Mean relative change ($\overline{\mu}$) of storm erosion with respect to the erosion in the No Roller application of each model within different depth classes.

Depth Class (m)	D3D	XB
−5 to −3	0.18	−0.06
−3 to −2	0.15	−0.36
−2 to −1	0.31	−0.58
−1 to 0	0.11	−0.38
0 to 1	−0.06	−0.22
1 to 2	−0.22	−0.02
2 to 3	−0.05	0.21
3 to 5	0.13	0.97

5. Discussion

This study investigated the effect of roller dynamics (i.e., short wave averaged long wave forcing) on nearshore hydrodynamics and storm erosion by simulating the beach and dune evolution of the Sylt island using two open source morphological models, Delft3D (D3D) and XBeach (XB). D3D computes the roller effect with an add-on module, while it is a primary process in XB. In D3D, the roller effect on hydrodynamics has been evaluated [13,14,35], whereas there has been less concern on the morphodynamics across entire coast [15,35,44]. XB is always applied with the roller effect to estimate storm erosion of a beach and dune system [2,16,17]. This raises the question, whether the D3D roller can predict comparable storm erosion as in XB. To this end, we simulated storm erosion at the beach and dune over a storm period from 25 January to 26 April 2007. Results indicated the roller dynamics impact on both the hydrodynamics and the storm erosion in the two models.

5.1. Hydrodynamics

The model skill at predicting hydrodynamics was verified by comparing measured and simulated wave characteristics at W2 (Figure 1b), which was at 8 m water depth. The maximum wave height at this location was only 2.6 m during the analysis period. Therefore, the W2 buoy captured waves prior to breaking. Hence, the verification of wave heights at this location is equally appropriate for both roller and no roller applications. For the hydrodynamic simulations, similar values were applied for the numerical parameters in both models (e.g., bed roughness, see in Appendix A). Results of D3D NR and XB R being the standard applications were used to compare with the measured wave data. Predicted waves in D3D (i.e., the SWAN computation) showed a reasonable agreement with the measured data ($R^2 = 0.91$, $RMSE = 0.14$ m and $\mu = -0.03$ in Table 5), although it does overpredict (in agreement with Boyd and Weaver [45]). The study period covered a range of wave conditions (Figure 2b). Our results indicated generally high and low waves during measured low and high waves respectively. XB showed a greater difference in wave prediction than D3D. This is expected due to the schematised approach of wave computation [10,11]. Therefore, tuning model parameters to get a high agreement with the measured waves is not plausible.

The roller effect showed different impacts on hydrodynamics in both models. In D3D, the roller application caused increased wave conditions and velocities. The roller uses wave dissipation energy by breaking as a source for the computation of the short wave effects on long wave forcing. Therefore, the roller dynamics predict high effects on long wave during the breaking of short waves and no effects during non-breaking short waves (e.g., $H_s < 0.5$ m). With the roller dynamics, the total wave force by short waves and short wave averaged effect on long waves, which contributes to the momentum computation, increases (see Equations (4) and (5)). This results in increased water levels and velocities in the nearshore area. Hsu et al. [13,14] also showed that an increase of nearshore hydrodynamics occurred by including the roller model. Alongshore wave heights and velocities in XB indicated that the difference between the R and NR applications is marginal. XB computes the long wave oscillation across the entire domain and that appears to dominate over the roller effect in the nearshore area. Difference in wave computation is mainly based on the schematised approach in XB [10,11] compared to D3D [25]. These results indicated that the roller effect on hydrodynamics is higher in D3D than in XB.

5.2. Sensitivity of Roller Parameters

Suitable values for the roller parameters (*Beta*, *Gamdis* and *F_lam*) were selected through a sensitivity analysis, while applying the same values for other parameters (see Appendix A). For example, the bottom friction in the wave energy dissipation was set to zero in both models. Bottom friction is not important for wave energy dissipation in the surf zone because the main process is wave breaking [46].

Beta determines the rate of wave energy transfer between the roller and the underlying water. The beach profile evolution showed that low values cause higher erosion above MSL, and the sensitivity is higher in XB than D3D (Figure 8). These results were further evident within the erosion volume (Figure 9). All applications resulted in strong flattening of the nearshore bar, on which strong wave breaking can be expected (e.g., at peak storm wave, Figure 6). Brière and Walstra [31] and Walstra et al. [35] showed that bar flattening increases significantly for higher values (>0.1). Therefore, higher roller energy dissipation causes strong bar flattening, but lower impact to the beach and dune area as found with the present results. *Beta* has a considerable impact on the cross-shore evolution. It can be used to tune the roller model as shown by Giardino et al. [46]. A value of 0.2 provided comparable erosion volume in both models compared to the measured data.

Gamdis controls the wave energy dissipation by breaking in the surf zone. D3D predicted less profile erosion with the constant value (0.55) than the depth varying values [32]. In XB, the three breaker formulas (i.e., suitable for the here on used surf-beat version [30,33]) applied showed greater erosion along the profiles than D3D. Both the constant value setting in D3D and the use of *roelvink1* [30] in XB had the same erosion volumes because the D3D constant value has been estimated based on the Roelvink [30] wave propagation model, which describes variations on the time-scale of wave groups. Walstra et al. [35] compared the bed evolution in D3D between a series of constant values and the depth varying expression of Ruessink et al. [32]. Large constant values resulted in low wave breaking on the bar leading to a pronounce bar, as in the depth varying expression. In Figure 9, the erosion volume of the depth varying expression (i.e., −1) showed a good agreement with the data, better than the constant application.

F_lam imposes a delay distance for the actual start and stop of wave breaking [34]. The profile evolution showed a low sensitivity compared to the previous parameters in both models. However, D3D predicted a greater erosion volume with the breaker delay than without, while there is no considerable difference in XB between the two applications. Walstra [45] showed that the breaker delay generally improves the wave prediction during swell conditions whereas it leads to an overprediction during wind sea conditions. Our analysis is based on a storm period, and the effect of breaker delay overpredicts wave heights leading to a greater erosion volume. Analysis of the cross-shore profile after one year, Walstra et al. [35] showed that there is a marginal impact of breaker delay on the profile evolution. Furthermore, Roelvink et al. [34] found, exclusion of breaker delay does not lead to an improved bar response. The XB results agree with these investigations. *F_lam* is not suitable to use as a tuning parameter for the roller model, particularly in analysing storm erosion. Therefore, we carried out simulations without applying the breaker delay in both models.

5.3. Roller Effect on Storm Erosion

Storm erosion over the analysis period showed different roller impacts in both models. All simulations produced cross-shore variations in erosion (above MSL and on the nearshore bar) and sedimentation (nearshore runnel and seaward of the bar). These patterns in D3D are less prominent than in XB.

In D3D, there is no considerable difference in the erosion and sedimentation pattern between the R and NR applications. However, the erosion volumes within the depth classes indicated that the roller application caused higher erosion below MSL than the no roller application. As discussed earlier, the nearshore hydrodynamics increase with the roller dynamics [13,14,35]. Therefore, increased sediment transport in the roller application can be expected, causing relatively large erosion. Above MSL, the no roller application generally produced greater erosion compared with the roller application. This suggests that the no roller application has more wave energy approaching the upper beach, while dissipation of wave energy in the nearshore area is strong in the roller application. Therefore, applying roller dynamics in D3D increases storm erosion in the nearshore and decreases storm erosion in the upper beach area.

In contrast to D3D, the erosion and sedimentation pattern in XB showed significant difference between the two applications. In the nearshore area, the roller application produced more sedimentation than the no roller application. In the upper beach area (up to the dunes), the roller application resulted in strong erosion compared with the no roller application (e.g., at the dunes: 3–5 m elevation, ~100%: Table 9). Strong erosion, particularly at the dunes, occurred due to the impact of the estimated long wave oscillation causing avalanching of the dune front [2,4]. The eroded sediment is removed to the nearshore area by the undertow resulting in progressive erosion of the upper beach area and sedimentation in the nearshore area [10,11]. Therefore, the roller model has an important role in computing storm erosion in XB.

Different model physics in D3D and XB contributed to the difference in storm erosion predictions although both models apply the roller dynamics. Besides the roller dynamics, XB computes long wave oscillations across the entire domain. Furthermore, the undertow facilitates progressive erosion [11]. These processes are not estimated in D3D [12]. On contrary to XB, the computation of avalanching in D3D seems to be limited to the inundated area. As hypothesised, the hydrodynamics in D3D increased with the roller dynamics leading to increase erosion below MSL, and at the upper dune (3–5 m) although very low compared with XB. However, the area above MSL and below 3 m showed lower erosion than the no roller application.

5.4. Model Applications

In general, both models can be applied to investigate storm erosion. Besides short-term storm scale applications, D3D is used in long-term decadal scales to investigate climate change impacts and morphodynamic evolution of coastal systems [37,47,48]. Application of the roller dynamics in D3D increased the nearshore hydrodynamics. Previous studies with the roller effect have shown better prediction of nearshore currents and waves [13,14], and bar morphodynamics [15,35,45]. Therefore, D3D R is thought to be suitable to investigate nearshore dynamics. D3D NR (the standard application) predicted greater storm erosion in the upper beach area, albeit rather small. XB R (standard application) estimated morphological changes along the entire cross-shore profile [2,16,17]. Both models predicted strong bar flattening, and no bar recovery after storm impact. Therefore, different (time varying) parameter settings for wave dynamics and sediment transport are required for long period simulation depending on the conditions (calm and stormy). Such a modelling approach could be used to understand the beach response between bathymetry surveys, which are generally separated by periods of at least a few months.

6. Conclusions

The effect of roller dynamics on storm erosion on the beach and dune system of the Sylt island was investigated using Delft3D and XBeach. Simulated wave heights in Delft3D No Roller (standard application) produced a reasonable agreement with the measured data. Wave heights of XB Roller (standard application) had a considerable difference with the observations. Including the roller dynamics in Delft3D caused increased hydrodynamics in the nearshore area, while turning these processes off in XBeach had marginal impact. Suitable roller parameters for both models were selected by a sensitivity analysis comparing simulated and measured erosion volumes. In Delft3D, the nearshore morphodynamics increased applying the roller dynamics. However, there was no increase in the upper beach erosion. In contrast, XBeach predicted storm erosion across the entire cross-shore profile, and showed the impact of including the roller dynamics.

Our results conclude, both models are generally able to produce storm erosion depending on the cross-shore area of interest. However, an alternative (time-varying) calibration parameters for wave dynamics and sediment transport are required to simulate calm and storm conditions in both models for coastal systems with intertidal bars to capture the intermittent beach recovery processes. Using the models to understand the evolution processes over different months could support the planning of storm erosion mitigation measures (e.g., sand nourishment volume), thus increasing the effectiveness of the selected coastal management strategy.

Author Contributions: Conceptualization and methodology, P.D. and J.B.; software, formal analysis, validation, investigation, resources, data curation, writing—original draft preparation, P.D.; writing—review and editing, P.D. and J.B.; visualization, supervision, project administration, funding acquisition, P.D. All authors have read and agreed to the published version of the manuscript.

Funding: This research was funded by German Research Foundation (DFG), grant number DI 2139/2-1 and the APC was funded by the same grant.

Institutional Review Board Statement: Not applicable.

Informed Consent Statement: Not applicable.

Data Availability Statement: Not applicable.

Acknowledgments: This study is part of the MoDECS (Modification of Dune Erosion by adjacent Coastal Systems) project funded by German Research Foundation (DFG) under the grant number DI 2139/2-1. Authors greatly acknowledge Christian Winter for providing access to the field data. The Federal Agency for Waterways and Shipping (WSV), the Federal Institute of Hydrology (BfG), the Federal Agency for Maritime and Hydrographic (BSH), the local agency for coastal protection (LKN) and German Weather Service (DWD) are greatly acknowledged for providing field and environmental forcing data.

Conflicts of Interest: The authors declare no conflict of interest.

Appendix A

Table A1. Comparison of processes and applied model parameters in Delft3D and XBeach.

	Process	Delft3D	XBeach
Hydrodynamics	Wave model	Stationary (SWAN), Non-Stationary (Roller)	Non-Stationary (Surfbeat)
	Wave from model nesting	✓	✗
	Short-wave at boundary	✓	✓
	Long-wave at boundary	✗	✓
	Short-wave spectrum	Jonswap	Jonswap
	Lateral wave boundary	✗	*wavecrest*
	Wave computation	Direction/frequency	Direction domain only
	Wave breaking index	0.73 (SWAN), −1 (Roller)	*roelvink1*
	Lateral flow boundary	*Neumann*	*Neumann*
	Wave current interaction	✓	✓
	Bed friction—flow	C = 55 m$^{1/2}$/s	55 m$^{1/2}$/s
	Bed friction—wave: SWAN	0.067 m^2/s^{-3}	✗
	Bed friction—wave: Roller (f_w)	0	0
	Roller dissipation coefficient (α_{rol})	1	1
	Time step	6 s	CFL = 0.7
	Communication with wave	30 min	in-build
	Min. depth for Undertow ($hmin$)	✗	0.2 m
	Horizontal eddy viscosity	0.1 m^2/s	0.1 m^2/s
	Horizontal eddy diffusivity	1.0 m^2/s	1.0 m^2/s
Sediment transport	Bed Sediment	Single fraction (300 µm)	Single fraction (300 µm)
	Sediment layer	5 m	5 m
	Transport formula	Soulsby-Van Rijn	Soulsby-Van Rijn
	Bed slope	$\alpha_{bs}=1, \alpha_{bn}=1.5$	*roelvink_total*
	Effect of wave Asymmetry	$f_{susw}=1, f_{bedw}=1$	$f_{As}=0.1$
	Effect of wave Skewness	✗	$f_{Sk}=0.1$

Table A1. *Cont.*

	Process	Delft3D	XBeach
	Morphological acceleration	*morfac* = 1	*morfac* = 1
	morfac option	×	1
Morphological changes	Avalanching	wetslope = 0.3	wetslope = 0.3, dryslope = 1
	Avalanching time	1 day	×
	Dry Cell erosion (*ThetSD*)	1	-

References

1. Harley, M.D.; Ciavola, P. Managing local coastal inundation risk using real-time forecasts and artificial dune placements. *Coast. Eng.* **2013**, *77*, 77–90. [CrossRef]
2. Dissanayake, P.; Brown, J.; Sibbertsen, P.; Winter, C. Using a two-step framework for the investigation of storm impacted beach and dune erosion. *Coast. Eng.* **2021**, *168*, 103939. [CrossRef]
3. Kron, W. Coasts: The high-risk areas of the world. *Nat. Hazards* **2013**, *66*, 1363–1382. [CrossRef]
4. Dissanayake, P.; Brown, J.; Wisse, P.; Karunarathna, H. Effect of storm clustering on beach and dune evolution. *Mar. Geol.* **2015**, *370*, 63–75. [CrossRef]
5. Huang, S.Y.; Yen, J.Y.; Wu, B.L.; Shih, N.W. Field observations of sediment transport across the rocky coast of east Taiwan: Impacts of extreme waves on the coastal morphology by Typhoon Soudelor. *Mar. Geol.* **2020**, *421*, 106088. [CrossRef]
6. McGranahan, G.; Balk, D.; Anderson, B. The rising tide: Assessing the risks of climate change and human settlements in low elevation coastal zones. *Environ. Urban* **2007**, *19*, 17–37. [CrossRef]
7. Neumann, B.; Vafeidis, A.T.; Zimmermann, J.; Nicholls, R.J. Future coastal population growth and exposure to sea-level rise and coastal flooding—A global assessment. *PLoS ONE* **2015**, *10*, e0131375. [CrossRef]
8. De Jong, F.; Bakker, J.F.; van Berkel, C.J.M.; Dankers, N.M.J.A.; Dahl, K.; Gätje, C.; Marencic, H.; Potel, P. *Wadden Sea Quality Status Report, 1999*; Wadden Sea Ecosystem No. 9; Common Wadden Sea Secretariat, Trilateral Monitoring and Assessment Group, Quality Status Report Group: Wilhelmshaven, Germany, 1999.
9. Sallenger, A. Storm impact scale for barrier islands. *J. Coast. Res.* **2000**, *16*, 890–895.
10. Roelvink, D.; McCall, R.; Mehvar, S.; Nederhoff, K. Improving predictions of swash dynamics in XBeach: The role of groupiness and incident-band runup. *Coast. Eng.* **2018**, *134*, 103–123. [CrossRef]
11. Roelvink, D.; Reniers, A.; van Dongeren, A.; van Thiel de Vries, J.; McCall, R.; Lescinski, J. Modelling storm impacts on beaches, dunes and barrier islands. *Coast. Eng.* **2009**, *56*, 1133–1152. [CrossRef]
12. Lesser, G.; Roelvink, J.A.; van Kester, J.A.T.M.; Stelling, G.S. Development and validation of a three-dimensional morphological model. *Coast. Eng.* **2004**, *51*, 883–915. [CrossRef]
13. Hsu, Y.L.; Dykes, J.D.; Allard, R.A. *Evaluation of Delft3D Performance in Nearshore Flows*; MS 39529-5004, NRL/MR/7320-06-8984; Naval Research Laboratory: Stennis Space Center, Hancock, MI, USA, 2006.
14. Hsu, Y.L.; Dykes, J.D.; Allard, R.A. *Validation Test Report for Delft3D*; MS 39529-5004, NRL/MR/7320-08-9079; Naval Research Laboratory: Stennis Space Center, Hancock, MI, USA, 2008.
15. Giardino, A.; Van der Werf, J.; Van Ormondt, M. *Simulating Coastal Morphodynamics with Delft3D: Case Study Egmond aan Zee, Deltares Delft Hydraulics*; 1200635-005; Deltares: Delft, The Netherlands, 2010.
16. Smallegan, S.M.; Irish, J.L.; Van Dongeren, A.R.; Den Bieman, J.P. Morphological response of a sandy barrier island with a buried seawall during Hurricane Sandy. *Coast. Eng.* **2016**, *110*, 102–110. [CrossRef]
17. Kalligeris, N.; Smit, P.B.; Ludka, B.C.; Guza, R.T.; Gallien, T.W. Calibration and assessment of process-based numerical models for beach profile evolution in southern California. *Coast. Eng.* **2020**, *158*, 103650. [CrossRef]
18. Blossier, B.; Bryan, K.R.; Daly, C.J.; Winter, C. Spatial and temporal scales of shoreline morphodynamics derived from video camera observations for the island of Sylt, German Wadden Sea. *Geo Mar. Lett.* **2017**, *37*, 111–123. [CrossRef]
19. Dissanayake, P.; Winter, C. Modelling the coastline orientation on storm erosion at the Sylt island, North Sea. In Proceedings of the Virtual Conference of Coastal Engineering, Sydney, Australia, 6–9 October 2020; Volume 36, p. 20.
20. Ahrendt, K. Expected effect of climate change of Sylt island: Results from a multidisciplinary German project. *Clim. Res.* **2001**, *18*, 141–146. [CrossRef]
21. Chu, K.; Winter, C.; Hebbeln, D.; Schulz, M. Improvement of morphodynamic modelling of tidal channel migration by nudging. *Coast. Eng.* **2013**, *77*, 1–13. [CrossRef]
22. Van Ormondt, M.; Nelson, T.R.; Hapke, C.J.; Roelvink, D. Morphodynamic modelling of the wilderness breach, Fire Island, New York. Part I: Model set-up and validation. *Coast. Eng.* **2020**, *157*, 103621. [CrossRef]
23. Stelling, G.S. On the construction of computational methods for shallow water flow problem. In *Rijkswaterstaat Communications*; Governing Printing Office: Hague, The Netherlands, 1984; Volume 35.
24. Stelling, G.S.; Lendertse, J.J. Approximation of Convective Processes by Cyclic ACI methods. In Proceedings of the 2nd ASCE Conference on Estuarine and Coastal Modelling, Tampa, FL, USA, 13–15 November 1991.

25. Booij, N.; Ris, R.C.; Holthuijsen, L.H. A third-generation wave model for coastal regions, Part I, Model description and validation. *J. Geophys. Res.* **1999**, *104*, 7649–7666. [CrossRef]
26. Soulsby, R. Dynamics of marine sands, A manual for practical applications. *Oceanogr. Lit. Rev.* **1997**, *9*, 947.
27. Holthuijsen, L.H.; Booij, N.; Herbers, T.H.C. A prediction model for stationary short-crested waves in shallow water with ambient currents. *Coast. Eng.* **1989**, *13*, 23–54. [CrossRef]
28. Stelling, G.S.; Duinmeijer, S.P.A. A staggered conservative scheme for every Froude number in rapidly varied shallow water flows. *Int. J. Numer. Methods Fluids* **2003**, *43*, 1329–1354. [CrossRef]
29. Ruggiero, P.; Walstra, D.J.R.; Gelfenbaum, G.; van Ormondt, M. Seasonal-scale nearshore morphological evolution: Field observations and numerical modeling. *Coast. Eng.* **2009**, *56*, 1153–1172. [CrossRef]
30. Roelvink, J.A. Dissipation in random wave groups incident on a beach. *Coast. Eng.* **1993**, *19*, 127–150. [CrossRef]
31. Brière, C.; Walstra, D.J.R. *Modelling of Bar Dynamics*; Report Z4099; WLlDelft Hydraulics: Delft, The Netherlands, 2006.
32. Ruessink, B.G.; Walstra, D.J.R.; Southgate, H.N. Calibration and verification of a parametric wave model on barred beaches. *Coast. Eng.* **2003**, *48*, 139–149. [CrossRef]
33. Daly, C.; Roelvink, J.A.; Van Dongeren, A.R.; Van Thiel de Vries, J.S.M.; McCall, R.T. Short wave breaking effects on low frequency waves. In Proceedings of the 32th International Conference on Coastal Engineering, Shanghai, China, 30 June–5 July 2010; pp. 1–13.
34. Roelvink, J.A.; Meijer, T.J.G.P.; Houwman, K.; Bakker, R.; Spanhoff, R. Field validation and application of a coastal profile model. In Proceedings of the Coastal Dynamics Conference, Gdansk, Poland, 4–8 September 1995; pp. 818–828.
35. Walstra, D.J.R.; Van Ormondt, M.; Roelvink, J.A. *Shoreface Nourishment Scenarios*; WL|Delft Hydraulics Report Z3748.21; Deltares: Delft, The Netherlands, 2004.
36. Dissanayake, D.M.P.K. *Modelling Morphological Response of Large Tidal Inlet Systems to Sea Level Rise*; Taylor & Francis Group, CRC Press/Balkema: Leiden, The Netherlands, 2011; ISBN 978-0-415-62100-7.
37. Dissanayake, P.; Yates, M.L.; Suanez, S.; Floc'h, F.; Krämer, K. Climate Change impacts on coastal wave dynamics at Vougot Beach, France. *J. Mar. Sci. Eng.* **2021**, *9*, 1009. [CrossRef]
38. Donelan, M.A.; Hamilton, H.; Hui, W.H. Directional spectra of wind-generated waves. *Philos. Trans. R. Soc. Lond. A* **1985**, *315*, 509–562.
39. Hasselmann, K.; Barnett, T.P.; Bouws, F.; Carlson, H.; Cartwright, D.E.; Enke, K.; Ewing, J.A.; Gienapp, H.; Hasselmann, D.E.; Krusemann, P.; et al. *Measurements of Windwave Growth and Swell Decay during the Joint North Sea Wave Project (JONSWAP)*; Deutches Hydrographisches Institut, A8: Hamburg, Germany, 1973; pp. 1–95.
40. Goda, Y. *Random Seas and Design of Maritime Structures, Advanced series on Ocean Engineering 33*, 3rd ed.; World Scientific: Jokohama, Japan, 2010.
41. Fredsøe, J. Turbulent boundary layer in wave-current interaction. *J. Hydraul. Eng.* **1984**, *110*, 1103–1120. [CrossRef]
42. Ruessink, B.G.; Miles, J.R.; Feddersen, F.; Guza, R.T.; Elgar, S. Modeling the alongshore current on barred beaches. *J. Geophys. Res.* **2001**, *106*, 451–463. [CrossRef]
43. Krause, P.; Boyle, D.P.; Bäse, F. Comparison of different efficiency criteria for hydrological model assessment. *Adv. Geosci.* **2005**, *5*, 89–97. [CrossRef]
44. Walstra, D.J.R. *Unibest-TC User Guide*. Report Z2897; WLlDelft Hydraulics: Delft, The Netherlands, 2000.
45. Boyd, S.C.; Weaver, R.J. Replacing a third-generation wave model with a fetch based parametric solver in coastal estuaries. *Estuar. Coast. Shelf Sci.* **2021**, *251*, 107192. [CrossRef]
46. Giardino, A.; Brière, C.; Van der Werf, J. *Morphological Modelling of Bar Dynamics with Delft3D, the Quest for Optimal Parameter Settings*; 1202345-000; Deltare: Delft, The Netherlands, 2011.
47. Dissanayake, D.M.P.K.; Ranasinghe, R.; Roelvink, J.A. The morphological response of large tidal inlet/basin systems to relative sea level rise. *Climate Change* **2012**, *113*, 253–276. [CrossRef]
48. Elmilady, H.; Van der Wegen, M.; Roelvink, D.; Van der Spek, A. Morphodynamic Evolution of a Fringing Sandy Shoal: From Tidal Levees to Sea Level Rise. *JGR Earth Surface* **2020**, *125*, e2019JF005397. [CrossRef]

MDPI
St. Alban-Anlage 66
4052 Basel
Switzerland
Tel. +41 61 683 77 34
Fax +41 61 302 89 18
www.mdpi.com

Journal of Marine Science and Engineering Editorial Office
E-mail: jmse@mdpi.com
www.mdpi.com/journal/jmse

www.ingramcontent.com/pod-product-compliance
Lightning Source LLC
LaVergne TN
LVHW070444100526
838202LV00014B/1661